Derek Hudson

Poor Boy

Travels The World

Hast thou then still the old unquiet breast

Which never deadens into rest,

Nor ever feels the fiery glow

That whirls the spirit from itself away,

But fluctuates to and fro,

Never by passion quite possessed,

And never quite benumb'd by the world's sway?

And I, I know not if to pray

Still to be what I am, or yield and be

Like all the other men I see.

Mathew Arnold, 1882-1888.

A Summer Night

Contents

Chapter 1

Earliest Faraway Dreams

The first I became aware of my wandering adddiction comes from a time around the age of twelve, when my old man presented me with a full-sized racing bike that he'd picked up off some builder at work. The significance of this second hand gift would be overlooked in most people's lives, but I recognize it now for the stirring effect it had upon me, not only in extending my worldly boundaries, but in releasing something inside which, throughout my earlier life, had always seemed to be there. On the instant of receiving this wonderful machine, perhaps even on the same day, I took it to the furthest limits that a trailing wind would take me, and came back much the wiser, but near dead with exhaustion. Exploring the quiet country lanes and dangerous highways of the North West, I searched out new and ever more distant places. Occasionally I rode with friends from home, but mostly I progressed in a manner that all real travellers will recognize; compulsively and alone. The relevance of this period is that it seems to mark the point at which I first became drawn to the furthest horizon. But it doesn't quite capture the moment at which I became bound to a life of constant travel and from where exactly this trend took a hold. Things would need to go a lot deeper and further back than that.

1

Following on about three years from these solitary experiences I became friends with a boy at school who, through influence of an older brother, steered me soon towards the novel business of hitch hiking. Here was an activity then at the height of its popularity where, through urgent necessity or on a youthful whim, you could take to the road at any time and travel somewhere for free, provided you had the patience to stick with it. Our first serious try out was to a game involving our local football team, neglecting to tell our parents that the fixture was actually away at Coventry, about ninety miles south. The one significant change I noticed from this moment onwards was that, while most of the kids back at school would talk about whatever relevant game they had witnessed over the weekend, we would talk largely about the trip.

Towards the end of that particular year I left school and began work as an apprentice printer at a large factory in Macclesfield. It had the kind of whittled appearance that might now provide interest at some sanitised industrial museum, but was no place in which to spend half your waking life and I absolutely hated it. I got paid off after a year and a half for absenteeism, which saved me serving six years at a trade I may never have used beyond that time, and in which I would have spent not a solitary thankful moment.

The one shining light through these drear days was the escape provided by a two week annual shut down in August, during which time, with no holiday plans made, I simply took to

2

the road one day and, carrying little more than a sleeping bag and a fortnights' pay, ended up in Cornwall. It was the summer of 1968, the mere mention of which now brings forth all kinds of flowery, Beat Generation images, though it never seemed especially significant to us at the time, apart from the fact we were young and growing up fast. The most powerful image of that period I now possess is not of how greatly the world was changing then, but of how much it has changed ever since.

The roads were fairly light of traffic, even though the motorways ran nothing like the distances they soon would, and provided you'd picked the right spot, there always seemed room for a ride to pull in. Along the way, on long journeys, you would unfailingly meet other hitch-hikers, ageing drifters and week-end hippies, some on a mission, others lost, but all of them fired with a strong sense of optimism, for hitching was an optimistic business. This early journey, my first independently far from home, would have seemed like a huge deal at the time, though much of its memory has been lost under layers of repetition, but one thing I do now recall is of travelling the narrow A30 beyond Exeter, feeling as though I was the real deal out here at the age of 15 and encountering a bold young lad called Dai Davies from Cwmbran, also travelling alone, who was actually a year younger than me, at just 14.

When finally I did escape the evil printworks it was spring of the following year, when the culture of the time was still very strong on the idea that you could make a future in life by simply growing long hair and becoming a layabout. I got a job for a while as a trainee plumber, which may have been a handy skill to have going forward, but the toothless bloke I was working with kind of spoiled it for me by explaining how underground frozen pipes could be unblocked by lying yourself down next to the open manhole and ice-picking away at "all the jam rags and the shit." I slung my hook a little early after this and moved on.

As Springtime turned to Summer I revived the earlier trend of spontaneous journeys to further destinations. I visited a different part of Cornwall with a friend from home and stayed a while in Torquay at a squatted property with some lawless anarchists who had been involved in an eviction riot in London, which had featured on national T.V. We eventually got kicked out of the squatt because someone had tried to cut through a lead pipe with a view to weighing it in, and a permanent jet of water was in danger of bringing the ceiling down. Through the rest of that year and into the next I made an increasing number of small trips to places all over the UK, usually on a surge of impulse and always with the least of financial preparation. On many summer weekends I would hitch to North Wales with a young companion, who is now an old friend. We stayed in the places where we could meet loads of girls of our own age, though I'm not sure how we would have presented ourselves, with our sleeping bags and our rough clothes. Despite our chosen poverty, we always had the surest feeling we would somehow get by. We

4

lived on unsliced loaves stuffed with chips, slept in church entrances and could always starve or shiver for a day or two, until we got back home.

Our style of hitch hiking involved an arrangement I would have liked to continue throughout my travelling life, but which unfortunately never surfaced again. There was always going to be an issue with two young blokes thumbing together, so we would separate and agree to meet later on, at our final destination. If we had knowledge of the place we were going to we would pick a familiar spot, otherwise it would be the local railway station, where it was ok to hang around. This easy-going plan allowed us to each do our own trip, while also having company, which I later part-recreated by travelling with people for a while and then diverging through course. It was the nearest thing I could find to the kind of ideal I needed; plenty of personal encounters, a full head of steam and also my own free space.

The power of local culture had always a more pronounced feel about it in those days, with strong dialects and archaic sayings commonly heard. I can be sure it's not just a pining of my own towards nostalgia, but when I travel across rural Southern England these days I sense a strong drift in speech towards the Thames estuary and the choice of phrase is commonly TV show American. The weight of population movement and collective media have no doubt had their effects, which seem right now quite irreversible, but on early trips into

Cornwall almost everyone I met sounded like a stage pirate, whereas on recent visits they sounded like nothing distinctive at all.

By this time, after what would have been a couple of years of part-time travel, I was beginning to develop a soulful attachment, not only to this wandering life, but to the actual road itself, its core essence and the perceived romance of its history. I read the travel poems of Mathew Arnold and W.H. Davies and held them both high on a pedestal. I worshipped Stephenson more as a Pacific traveller than the writer of adventure novels. I held fast to a fanciful notion that open roads led to some kind of freedom, conjured up Canned Heat playing travel songs on a loop, while somewhere in the background, here came the sun. It all seems a bit comic now, because when you mention open roads these days the only image you can muster is of someone cutting the ceremonial ribbon on a new relief road, but back then a clear highway was a common feature. If a swiftly vanishing one.

In terms of preparation for the wider world that would have been about it for my early travels in the UK, were it not for an ill set of circumstances which befell me during the opening year of the Seventies. I suppose I was lucky in the initial sense that when I fell off a railway bridge at Christmas and landed on the stone paving thirty feet below whilst out on a beer drinking tour of Manchester, I survived with just a badly broken arm and some observable injuries that kept me in hospital beyond the

6

New Year celebrations. It was an injury that I thought might keep me out of trouble, but unfortunately the opposite was true. While playing football that spring in a park kickabout I was clean through on goal when someone tripped me from behind and I suffered severe ligament damage to my right knee. It was also noted, when I went for the x-ray that I had an undiagnosed busted knee cap, suffered sometime before and I was put into plaster. When I'd recovered sufficiently from these injuries to have the castings removed I made one of the biggest mistakes of my entire life. I didn't set about getting myself fit straight away. I didn't really know how to go about it, with home training not being a big thing at the time, but I surely could have done something and this has always been a major regret.

During the time I was off sick I slipped too easily into the dole wallah syndrome and began to enjoy a carefree, if rather narrow existence. I had a couple of lads staying at my house who were in a similar predicament and through having done little in the daytime, we were able to prowl the streets at night when most well behaved people were asleep in bed. It was only a matter of time before we got nicked for some misdemeanour and I was summoned to court for the following November. One month before this was due, by which time I was back at work, I was called in for a cartilage operation on the knee injury and I attended Knutsford Quarter Sessions with my right leg still in a large splint. I was hoping for a bit of leniency in light of my recent infirmities, but there was no such luck to be had and, having spent the previous Crimbo and New Year in hospital, I now spent this one banged up eating porridge and sausage meat. I came out in January with just one thing of value, a heightened appreciation of liberty which has since never left me.

The relevance of this to my future life is fairly significant, particularly in that, with my footballing days over, I was never again quite one of the lads and it seemed as though a gradual progression were taking place, pushing and pulling me out onto the road. The die was cast way back it seemed, but it is only now, with time to dwell on these things, that I am able to realize just how far back it actually was. Riding an old Raleigh push bike around the country lanes of Cheshire and hitching to a few footy away grounds wouldn't set someone off on the kind of life I led, unless there was something buried there already deep down and had I sensed this much earlier, it would have saved me a lot of time in trying all the least suited ways of existence, which seemed to be most of the ones I could see around me.

From what I remember of my early childhood it was not the happiest of times. One mustn't bleat about an upbringing that was free from major handicap and where I was fed and clothed in fair comparison to my local peers, but all the happy times I had as a kid, without exception, were experienced far away from the family home. There were miles of open country then, beyond our edge of town location and while we rummaged in quarries and rivers, we experienced the joys of unrestricted play and a truer understanding than people would grant us of the meaning of

8

freedom. My ways could have been set from that period onwards, but even then I feel there was something in place with its wheels in turn, ready to hit the ground.

When I was very small, at what age I don't know, I was put into a small box-bedroom at the front of our house, which would represent my own private space during the years of my growing up. The view through my window, which I could just about reach, was one of plain council houses, fringed by a row of tall pylons, from the close regions of which would pass the sporadic excitement of steam goods trains. Nothing much held the distance but a row of far hills, usually captured in haze. Very occasionally, mainly in spring, or even in the sharpest days of winter, the right angle of light would shine upon these hills, the town haze would fall away and a magical patchwork landscape would appear along the Cheshire-Derbyshire border. Here was the view I preferred by a mile, more inspiring from my distant room than it likely would have been right up there and the true focus of my earliest faraway dreams. By sheer coincidence, the room I set aside for my own child looks out onto a hillside ridge, greener and closer this time, with an ancient country townscape clustered in between. I laid this out quite without thinking, as it merely suits the arrangement of our house, but there might now be some possibility that, without persuasion from any other quarter and minus the discontent that fires most bouts of ambition, a similar course to our own may follow. And so, may it be.

Chapter 2

The Europe - Morocco Year

My first time ever outside the UK was in May 1971 when I hitch-hiked to Dover with fifty quid in my pocket and took a boat to Ostend. I was eighteen at the time and travelling alone. My aim was strongly driven, but rather light on the details of planning; I simply wanted to go everywhere all at once, and right now if possible. In a little over a month I travelled through eleven countries from Norway down to Yugoslavia, claiming very few of the usual tourist merits, but absorbing bucket loads. Sometimes for sure, it was slightly boring, fishing for rides for hours on end, but at others I was very lucky indeed and these are the moments that draw you back for more.

My first night in Europe was spent in Amsterdam, to where I'd hitched in a single late afternoon. I had no pre-set arrangements at that moment, unlike the seasoned traveller of later years, and I bedded down in the shadows of a quiet parkland, near an old canal, beside the grass-sweet smell of a gardener's shed. Having departed the Dover Cliffs that morning and enjoyed the experience of linguistic demands through Belgium, my head was reeling with the events of the day. Resting there in a haze of forced sleep, I heard soon a soft voice above me, first in Dutch, then in English and looked out to see a friendly grey-haired fellow of around 50, which seemed then a grand old age. Fearing I was being moved on, I told him I wished

10

only to pass the night there and depart the next morning; whereupon he immediately invited me to stay on the black silhouetted barge that lay tied close by.

It is common now to refuse invitations from strangers due to the accepted dangers, but these must have been far more trusting times because, as a young adult, I never felt any such apprehension and I was in like a shot. If things ever did go pear shaped I figured I could always battle my way at least as far as the door and even at this early stage I came to realise that, had I turned down every on the road invitation I'd received, I would have steered a course around most of the best people I'd ever met.

Canal barges you see in most countries these days are a middle-class weekend thing whose standard of upkeep matches the poshness of the areas in which they are moored, but here was a right old throwback, coated in tar with rope marks across the rails and hobnail tracks along its deck. The interior was stacked with items in the manner of a backyard shed and it looked permanently well lived in. I never appreciated it fully at the time beyond a free place to kip, but its atmosphere has grown on me ever since and so the value of my luck in finding it. For where could you see this now; an old family workboat, with proprietor on board, parked up in the middle of a European capital?

How closely central it was I was soon to discover, as the owner's ten year old son Johnny directed me next morning the short distance to the main railway station, where I was able to

11

change a couple of quid into guilders. Bright as a button was the son. He spoke English with barely a trace of accent, which is quite common in Holland, but still shouldn't be taken for granted, especially in someone as young as ten. He'd been named Johnny in honour of the British and US soldiers who had freed Holland from 5 years of Nazism, which warmed your heart to know that those sacrificial efforts were fully appreciated in some, if not all parts of the world. As I made this trip through much of Western Europe I came to see first-hand how highly regarded British people still were, at what was merely 20-odd years after that huge conflagration. It was no cinematic myth that the generation of that time had acquitted itself bravely and behaved, in large part, with fitting dignity. That was before package holiday mobs, boozy stag weekends and football-type hooliganism came along to take the shine off our image somewhat.

For a couple of days further I remained in Amsterdam, held by its placid atmosphere relative to its large size and then, fearing perhaps that if I stayed longer I may be forced to start spending a bit of real money, I moved on. I hitched easily through North Friesian towns and on into Western Germany, where some people who'd given me a lift also gave me a free place to stay in Hamburg. The Hamburg of that time was rather bland and recently rebuilt, but the people were friendly enough, even though the Dutch still didn't like them.

I wandered on through Denmark and Sweden in freak lucky weather, taking ferry-boats between islands where there are now interconnecting bridges and only turned around when I got to Oslo. This narrow blaze through Western Scandinavia was just a try out for a later intended journey up into Lapland, which never quite came to fruition, the discouraging factors being the high cost of living and the generally cold weather which would force you to spend heavily on nutrition and warmth.

Many years after this journey, whilst in post-Soviet Estonia, I discovered by chance that there was a ferry service running the relatively short distance across to Helsinki and, never having been in Finland, I bought a ticket for the following day. Recalling that Helsinki was once regarded as the most expensive capital in the world I booked ahead at the cheapest digs in town and stocked up on two days of groceries from a Tallinn supermarket. When travelling in Scandinavia this seems to be the answer: get your stall set out early and take sandwiches.

My way back down through Sweden and into Central Europe seems remarkable in hindsight for a series of warm personal encounters rather than all the other strong images that would hit me along the way. At the small town of Halmstad some young people on a beach holiday kindly allowed me to share their giant tent rather than sleep outside, while at the Danish port of Helsingor a young man I'd met along the road invited me to stay at his parent's house beside the ferry harbour at which his father worked. Shortly afterwards, from somewhere in North

Germany, a fellow allowed me to sleep in the caravan he was delivering down to Heidelberg, which was the fifth time I'd been offered free accommodation in just under two weeks. If one thing amazes me now about this time in comparison to today it is what a trusting and far more honest world it must have been.

I liked Germany during this period and have liked it just as much ever since. The great developments that have emanated from Germanic lands over the last couple hundred years have resulted almost entirely from intelligent hard work. It is however, just those first fifty years of the 20th century which cast a dark pall over all their other achievements. Germans almost never discuss the finer details of war with foreigners, as it marks a very low period in their history, while some Brits are quite free with their comments, as it marks what might be the last real high point in theirs. Occasionally however, with a bit of trustful familiarity or a few extra drinks, the constraints do fall off, and the outcome is usually something dark and/or humorous. Like the later time when our Berlin landlord came home after a boozy day and coming over all pally, asked me where I was from? On being told that I was from somewhere close to Manchester, he turned suddenly misty eyed and sentimental.

"Ah, Manchester", he said, "Yes I remember Manchester; I used to fly over it in the war!"

Another time, in foreign lands, I met a young German fellow of the hippy persuasion, whose father pointed a withering finger towards his unkempt appearance and said,

14

"You wouldn't have long hair like that if Hitler was alive today."

Which might have meant he had something to be thankful for?

Still, that's enough about old wars. I don't believe that anyone, particularly of my generation, can pass first time through Germany without reflecting upon that terrible period, but after the country grows on you these old images fade and you move on. As I said to a German traveller some many years ago, it is the German people themselves who should keep a reminder of this period, and the rest of us should just drop it.

Through the Alpine lands of Switzerland and Austria I came to Yugoslavia, a country then in the semi totalitarian grip of Marshall Tito, where everything looked dowdy and forty years backward; though some of the coastal resorts were attractive in their time-frozen sort of way. In the North Adriatic bays of Croatia there were tiny picturesque villages that commonly looked out onto a sea of glass. In viewing photographs now of the concrete march throughout these areas I wonder about the fate of such lovely places. For where is it now in Mediterranean Europe, the once quiet haven that hasn't sold its soul?

It was around this region where I met with one of the most enthusiastic visitor promo efforts I've ever encountered when a very large man in a tiny car, who was driving me towards Rijeka, suddenly pulled up at some locally heralded show caves and, with a strong jab of the finger, insisted that I 'GO IN

THERE.' I was reluctant to part with an entrance fee due to my skinflint budget and the fact of never having heard of the place, but I could feel his eyes burning on my back as I loitered at the turnstile and so I took the plunge and there, at Postojna, witnessed a magical underground world, the likes of which I've never seen bettered anywhere. If you wanted people to see the proudest features of your country then this is what you did. You dragged them off the street and bundled them in head first.

I made my way beyond Yugoslavia by entering the Italian city of Trieste, a place that had been pushed around between various states as though it were a sacrificial chess piece and which even had a treaty named after it which decided how this part of Europe would look. From here I hitched on to Mestre, a slightly drab town of tall, cement-rendered tenement blocks that provided the ideal foil for the kind of place I was about to visit next. An overly dull district always comes in handy when you are about to visit one of the wonders of the civilized world and here was the perfect mix as, within a few moments of my arriving at Mestre's seafront pier, I was sailing past salmon pink palaces along Venice's Grand Canal, on my way to the Piazza Di San Marco. It is hard to recreate the sense of joy and wonder I felt at actually finding myself here, but an American bloke with whom I'd teamed up temporarily along the way summed it up fairly suitably as he hung on the outside of the main passenger cabin, (now banned) and yelled out in his loud, un-self-conscious voice,

"Wow! This place blows my mind!

A cliché' of the day perhaps, but really you couldn't say much else.

At San Marco we followed the trend of half a billion former visitors, as we stood and gawped at the greeters in silken bright medieval robes who milled around the doors of the ancient basilica, while across the square a tail coated orchestra played overtures by Verdi and Rossini to seated alfresco diners. I felt then that if I only had an extra tenner and that was the cost of sitting there to drink a thimbleful of acrid coffee, it would have been cheap at the price.

Away from the main hub during this period you could wander through side passages, over hump bridged canals and pinch a bit of the place to yourself, though I fear this has lately become a procession. Yet I suppose even now there are times when you can narrow your gaze and, blotting out the motor vaporettos and the bizarre modern clothes, you can imagine yourself in the midst of a scene by Canaletto. The most reassuring feeling one gets from this is that, despite all the scare and disaster stories, this place will remain in something like its present state for longer than it has existed. It will be protected with a zeal greater than that reserved for any other inhabited site, because people love it, not as they love a fleeting beauty or a sporting success, but really love it. There are many places you will meet over the years of which you had very high hopes which fall flat, and others, of which you had almost no hope at all, that will take your breath away. Venice for me was a combination of both these things in the sense that, if I had a high regard before my visit, it was greater still forever after.

Soon it was time to depart, as I'd measured my resources in a way that was later to become common, by gauging how much I'd need to support myself on the journey home and then over extending by a couple of days. It led to a desperation that would be hard for us to take now, but when we were this young we always wished we'd wrung it out a bit further. For the rest of this journey there was not much I could absorb after Venice and soon I was home, changed little as a person perhaps, but greatly in my sense of awareness. My eyes had been opened to the most distant of possibilities.

Back in my own place I was at first a little tired after my recent excursions, then re-energised and eventually bursting with impatience to move on to somewhere new. In need of quick finance I took a job at a local sweet factory, where it was easy to get a start because people found it just as easy to leave. A common refrain among many of the workers was of how they had all their own teeth when first starting there, before the mint imperials had taken their toll. Intending to knuckle down through the winter and save a bit of real dough, I made it into the fourth week when, one sunny September lunch-time, rather than go back indoors to face the afternoon shift, I wandered out beyond the main gate and just carried on walking. Within 15 minutes I was at the town library, where I took down an old leather bound

18

volume of the Encyclopaedia Britannica. I read about the Greek Islands, a region then becoming popular though not quite yet over touristic; but on skimming over the climate section I noted that the autumn weather was prone to be stormy and so I put the book back on the shelf. I took down another volume, this time encompassing the letter M, and read a brief entry on Morocco, which described a land of colourful culture where the sun shone warm into December. I returned the book to its former place and then went home. The following morning I attended work early, filled with a buzz of enthusiasm not previously seen by my colleagues and while out on the quiet floor, before all the steam of the sweet boiling began, I could see the foreman making an angry bee-line towards me, intending no doubt to bollock me for my earlier disappearance act. I cut his stride short with some careful words I'd been practicing all the way to work,

"Is it possible I can have my cards and week-in-hands' pay by Friday, as I'm going to Morocco on Saturday?"

The foreman was a decent enough chap, chosen no doubt for his integrity and didn't deserve this mild humbling by a youth, but the picture of him standing there with his mouth locked open in halted speech and a once wagging finger frozen in mid air, was one of my most prized memories of the time. It was such a liberating way to leave a dull job that I wondered if I'd ever feel so alive again.

*

When Saturday came there was a touch of fear in the air as I'd told all and sundry about the trip and even arranged for a couple of mates to drop me at the Knutsford roundabout in the back of their grey mini van. I may have now wished that I could quietly back out but the potential accusations of cowardice were, not for the last time, what propelled me forwards and I was on my way. Had I been more informed of the difficulties ahead I may have been discouraged even more, as hitching through France was an absolute bitch and Spain wasn't much better, with the further off-put that General Franco was in power, which turned it into some kind of Fascist's paradise; but there are many countries that I have visited since then that weren't as warmly welcoming as Northern Europe in the hippie early seventies and you just came to accept these things and make the most of whatever else was there.

The first that I began to feel truly absorbed in this new trip was around the time it began to get warmer, in the red dusty lands of South Western Spain. The undeniably grand cities of Cordoba and Seville had a history largely unknown to me then , but it was this region, that of Andalucía, that had largely populated the early settlements of South America and whose ports greatly profited from the incoming trade. It was a story with which I'd become far more familiar later on. While heading by I was encouraged to stay at a place called El Puerto de Santa Maria, a simple Spanish town, where I lodged cheaply at a very

20

old hotel with chess-board floors and wooden beams that were coated in mariner's tar. My window veranda overlooked what once would have been a quiet main street and the view was no grander than a typically provincial Spain. Lately I discover that the town has become highly valued by those Spaniards who are keen to hang on to those period set districts that have not been over-modernised. Much in the same way as in our own country, where a town has been once by-passed by economic development, only to benefit greatly from such a state later on.

It was shortly after leaving this place, while somewhere on the road beyond Cadiz, that I met with the first really memorable encounter that I'd had with a fellow hitch-hiker, one indeed that I should remember for the rest of my life. It would have been towards evening, on a narrow highway between grey scrubland, that I fell into company with a young Japanese fellow who was headed for the south coast of Spain. It was only just becoming common then to see Japanese travellers abroad, usually in large groups and rare yet to find a more intrepid type travelling alone. Still more exceptional it was to find one hitching a ride, especially someone such as this, who was born stone deaf.

Somewhere within his many pockets he carried a small notebook in which he would scribble conversational sentences in a rather neat and well structured English and, in the couple of rides that we hitched together, he would present a few words to the driver, which was doubly impressive, as they were written in

21

a tidy looking Spanish. I was impressed then with his skill in learning, his fine handwriting in a foreign script and his polite amiability, but what I have come to be far more respectful of over time is his great courage in overcoming whatever disadvantages beset him, and in getting out there regardless. There are people with every opportunity laid before them who avail themselves of not one, but here was a man determined to live life on his terms. I have both encountered and heard of several similar cases over the years, a Danish man I met in Afghanistan who had Tourettes, a man I heard of in the Canary Isles who was hitch hiking in a wheel chair, an Englishman from Brum who ran out of money in India, but still made it home overland running on empty (more of him later) and I have come to realise, in recalling these, just who my real travelling heroes are. It's not the people who make contrived journeys with their parent's money, or cross the Polar icecaps with a quarter million in sponsorship, but the people who have fought their own battles from the outset and I salute each one of them.

The small port of Algeciras sits on the western rim of its own bay, overlooked by the Rock of Gibraltar. Though hardly related socially, its proximity is so close that in the early parts of a sunny day, a shadow from the Rock may fall full-lengthways across the town. Being little more than swimming distance apart you would have thought it a simple task to stroll around the bay and take a look into Gib, if only to observe its strange out-of-time atmosphere and add another territory to your growing list.

22

But the opportunity was sadly unavailable. In the late 1960's, under Franco's direction, the government of Spain had closed the border to break Algeciras' economic lean towards the British territory and perhaps intimidate its 20,000 residents into adopting Spanish rule. One of the plainest ironies in life is that if you pummel and browbeat people into accepting your view they will automatically adopt the opposing one and thus was the likely inevitable union set back by about a century. The only permissible way to negotiate this seemingly short distance was to take the ferry the 21 miles across to Tangiers and make a return journey in. But I had little interest in such palaver for what would have been only a tick-box effort and so I took my own route into North Africa, on a subsidised ferry to the tiny enclave of Ceuta, one of the last outposts of Spain's once mighty empire and their very own Gibraltar.

As I came closer to entering Morocco I became filled with a deep sense of trepidation. For not only was this a total leap into the dark, in the most culturally different country you could find in proximity to Europe, the customs regime of the time had imposed a new regulation that would strike fear into the heart of every young hippie. If you appeared to be a little untidy around the collar, they made you have a haircut! This mad rule, in force for a couple of years, was concocted for something like the reason that foreign hippies were corrupting local youths by indulging themselves of the free availability of Moroccan hashish. The strangest thing in all of it was that, once you'd had your locks trimmed to something like that of a customs officer, it was deemed you had been purged entirely of any partiality toward soft drug and the idea again would never enter your head. People now may scoff at this seemingly trivial matter, but at the time the length or otherwise of your hair might cast you into a completely different social tribe, whom you may mutually despise and whose colloquial language you may not even speak. It was something that could make you faint with anxiety should a barber go a bit military on your locks, or trim an inch too much off your sideburns. My own tribal statement hadn't been near a pair of scissors in nearly a year and I was beginning to feel quite settled in the way I looked. For this reason it was that I crept nervously up to the little customs window with my collar around both ears and most of my hair tucked under my shirt, while turning rigidly as though wearing a neck brace. As I departed free down the opposite side along the goat-strewn road into Bab Sebta, I exhaled deeply and on rounding the first bend, pushed a clenched fist under my nose, while letting out a loud celebratory Yessss! For not only had I made my aim in reaching Morocco, I had done so with all my hair intact.

The short journey from Spain into Morocco during these days provided the sharpest contrast between any two countries bordering Europe and the difference between the calm streets of Ceuta and the bustling alleys of Tetouan was like travelling from a genteel retirement area into a hustler's alley trap. For anyone planning a journey to some of the more disquieting street districts of the world this would be the ideal preparation as, once you had passed through here or the neighbouring Tangiers, you could deal with almost anything. If such was the attention you received on a normal day then I shudder to think what kind of propositions you would have received during the night, (of which I was fortunately too skint to enquire), but from what I gather, the list of activities included some that were decidedly rum. The cheap wooden hotel that I stayed in was frequented by people who stayed in such a place for weeks on end, never going anywhere else and the hooded-eye looks that passed between them suggested that each thought the other were up to no good. I escaped beyond the sleeping hours and by the following nightfall had made it to what remained of the old border post between Spanish Tetouan and French Morocco, where I slept on a station ramp that had once housed the customs kiosk. As I looked at the stars and began to drift I imagined that I was resting upon some scene of ancient history, as would much later become the case; though not on this occasion alas, as the Spaniards had only been gone 15 years.

During what remained of my brief journey from here I followed a two lane country highway that ran through towns with the names of market days until I reached the medina walled and too often by-passed city of Rabat. Someone dropped me by the sandstone entrance to the souk, beyond which the sound of cars and trucks faded into a muted, scented world, where the rustling sound of loose fitting women's clothing could easily be heard and brown-hooded men mimicked the scene of a medieval play. There was not the desperate pestering I'd experienced further north, as many visiting people had taken their medina experiences up at Tetouan or Tangiers and were now headed for more celebrated destinations further on. The scene was one of everyday Moroccan market life and all the more appreciated for that. A town called Mohammedia on our western flank shone from a distance more brilliantly than it ever would close up. More recently built but in the classical style, its domes and crenels fluttered in reflection like giant white birds on the slow river that passed.

And then at last we were in Casablanca, a name synonymous with old cinematic romance, but where the enchantment for me began to fade. I hadn't prepared myself for the eventuality that the town, though celebrated in popular culture, was a plain, relatively new place put there by the French as a colonial administrative centre. It was perhaps appropriate that my enthusiasm should here be checked, as it kept me from blazing ahead into ever more impoverished circumstances. I'd not made the inroads to Morocco that I'd hoped for and regretted a few minor overspends along the way that may otherwise have taken me further. Within a couple of years I would be back in this region to do things far more justice, but for now it was time to take one last longing look at the southern map and head for home. It is practicalities that govern these things in the end and

26

the one relative to my own journey was that, I'd only left home with twenty five quid.

Throughout most of its history Tangiers must have been a town of some fairly rough comings and goings and in such a place, where the transiting hordes passed daily, those who made their living from this changeable trade knew damn well you'd be soon gone, to be replaced by others and not much time was wasted on the personal niceties. Away from the mad aggressive hustlers the bulk of population were likely quite civil in their daily business, but the aim of the former was a forthright one, to bug and question you, to dog your every step on the slightest encouragement and to steer you along the way into every trinket shop of their choosing. Thus were you accosted every time you ventured outdoors, until you scurried inside for cover, or as in my case, the ferry port for a boat back to Spain. It hadn't dawned on me just then that the routes I'd been taking recently and those for a year or two to come, were just a narrow channel along which 90% of travellers would pass. For as long as anyone did this they would be subject to similar attentions to the ones here described.

Many years beyond this time, in the latter days of my travelling life, I arrived in Calcutta at the end of a long bicycle ride from Bombay. Upon reaching the area known for cheap traveller hotels I was almost instantly besieged by tenacious touts and fighting fit beggars who would follow me in relays a hundred yards at a time, Having the advantage of sturdy wheels I was able to leap into the saddle and pedal like mad to just a block or two distant, where people would wish merely to get on with their own business and leave yours alone. I never had the time to find out, but perhaps Tangiers was largely the same.

Travelling over on the boat felt like a culture shock in reverse, where the dusty rambling town was replaced by a highly varnished neatness and deck officers in white South Pacific uniforms. For the first few days of heading north it was some relief to be away from such a place, where you didn't know what next would leap out in front of you, but after a while of waiting for rides in quiet lonely spots or wandering through towns ignored or positively shunned, I began to miss the intensity of recent times. Which is when I started to realise that travel destinations like Morocco were really rather my sort of thing.

At this end of journey time, when most of your travelling ambitions had been realised, it came to be apparent that, rather than dwelling upon your own achievements, you tended to be more receptive to the tales of others. A vague suggestion or a line thrown away here could grow into an idea so solid that you may have laid out your next ambitious plan even before the present one had reached its conclusion. It was a feature I would meet commonly along the way and probably a large part of what kept me hooked on this way of life. In the corner of the ferry-boat station at Ostend, to where the lifts had taken me despite my having aimed for Calais, there was a small waiting room with dark-stain wooden seating which, though unprepossessing, served as a transit point for young travellers heading to and from Europe. It was easy to fall into conversation with people of a similar mind to yourself and before you had left, you could often have talked yourself half way round the world. Here I joined easy company with an English fellow a little older than myself and while we exchanged the glories of our two thousand mile journeys we were interrupted by someone nearby who brought to our attention the presence of a calm young man who was seated cross-legged in the corner. Long hair centre parted, perhaps six years older than ourselves, looking tired but contented, this was a fellow said to be from Birmingham, whose dusty appearance and well worn luggage was something which we all then, for some reason, aspired to.

"You see him there?" he said, "He's just travelled all the way back from India with no money. It took him about a month."

Were I to hear such a statement about someone now I would likely say what a freeloading bastard, but right then I was in complete awe of him, There was a minority line of thought we had in those days where great merit was to be had by expanding your resources over the most adventurous distance, rather than blasting it in a fortnight at a Costa resort and much better still if you could weave into it a life experience you'd likely never forget. From that moment onwards I was totally nailed on to my next escapade, a long and eventful journey to the East.

Chapter 3

East

Back in the place from where I began, in contrast to the maelstrom of sights I'd recently witnessed, it seemed that not a thing had changed at all. In my vain efforts to explain these past events I was beginning to hit barriers with people I'd known for years and though this bothered me not greatly, I came soon to realise that had I tried to carry the mood of my experiences into what was then my normal home life, I'd have been flogging a dead horse. I had not the least desire to fall into my earlier settled ways and couldn't have done so had I tried. All I required was a job starting soon and a programme of hard saving that would put me back on the road for early Spring. For surely then I would be heading away to the Indian Subcontinent and beyond that all was secondary.

I found a job within days at some museum piece factory that was run on line shaft belts, that drove the paddles of huge wooden blending vats. The electric power source was the only sign the place had been modernised, as it originally ran on steam. I'd been hearing since forever how hard it was to come by a job and of people being unemployed for years on end but I always found that, when you really needed work, you simply went out and got it. I once footslogged my way round the industrial areas of Stockport calling for work at 26 different premises in a day. At the last place I visited they were just wrapping up to go home and told me to come in for a trial run in the morning. I kept that job and pissed off somewhere else after a few months of saving up. This was not that occasion however and the lucky start here was at only about my fifth attempt.

During my brief stay at this place the country was plunged into what most would have considered to be a national crisis, which fortunately, however, was not an ill wind for everyone. This was the miners' strike of 1972, which was related to a stoppage in the power industry, where one union or another came out in sympathy with their fellow brethren. It was not as famous as the Scargill strike of '74 which brought down the Heath government, but was disruptive enough to cause electrical black-outs and force the introduction of a three day working week. Throughout this long test of wills a few enterprising firms took it as a positive and turned production on full blast during the hours when electrical supply was guaranteed. This led to a boost in trade at some companies, as they picked up work from others who couldn't cope with the inconvenience and, in the place I was fortunate to find myself, it turned out to be an earnings bonanza. Pre-dawn early starts, split shifts, working nights and fourteen hour Sundays. Long, long hours at higher overtime rates. God bless Vic Feather and his Bolshie mates said I, as within three months I had saved the prodigious fortune of a hundred quid and I was on my way again.

During this period there existed a strange, almost spiritual fascination with India which seems now difficult to

31

fathom. It could have been that after the years of military conflict in the West, India was seen as some kind of peaceful Utopia where everyone lived harmoniously under the same sun; which would be a huge laugh to anyone who actually knew the place. But perhaps a further reason, for those not focused entirely on the end result, was that the business of travelling there by affordable means from Europe entailed what was then, and probably still is now, the greatest overland journey on earth.

Due to political changes that have taken place in recent years, it is now possible to travel into Central Asia by all manner of routes, taking you across countries once obliterated from the map, but during this period, owing to the barriers presented by Soviet territory and the peace that then existed in the lands to the south of it, the way to the East was compressed into a narrow channel that ran through Turkey, Iran and then either Afghanistan or Baluchistan. If you crossed Europe at the beginning and finished with the long descent beyond the Khyber, it would represent the most kaleidoscopic mixture of world history and culture that it were possible to encompass over any similar distance.

The point at which you become fully engaged in any new journey is precisely the moment you venture beyond the comfort zone of familiarity and this for me was around the provinces of Southern Yugoslavia. Here there were surprising echoes of my recent trip to Morocco, as the departed Ottoman Empire had left behind its prominent images of dome and

32

minaret, with the novel appearance of the odd red fez. I realised then that I was catching first real sight of the approaching East.

Across the border into Greece however we were cast back into something like our own culture, albeit with an Eastern Orthodox slant. There were things here I appreciated tremendously over the course of time, but for now it was all about the affordability of basic items. Nothing gladdens the heart of a traveller more than when prices drop by half and this was to be a steady progression all the way out to India and Nepal. Sometimes it saddens me to see great changes in a place when I return, but I thank my luck for having seen Greece when the traditional life was still very much in evidence. All along the coast from Salonika to Alexandropoulos the common scene was of low rise white villages surrounded by olive groves and tiny fishing boats tied to old harbour walls. Somewhere along a narrow street there would be a cafe, where old boys would sit in the shade and strain sludgy coffee through their enormous moustaches, while out by the urban limits women in black linen would compete to see how many sticks of brushwood could be loaded onto a single donkey. In the tiniest village there would always be a shop, often with no signboard, but of which everyone knew, where you could buy soft goats cheese, odd shaped tomatoes and pita bread which, along with some wine or cheap retsina, you would carry to a nearby pebbly beach upon which, rested at last, you felt as though you'd arrived in paradise and were enjoying a feast. I mention this now not with any

33

feeling of maudlin sentimentality, but merely because it was and now no longer is. Oh, I know that standards of living have risen with modernity and work is far less manually tiring, but much, very much has been lost in all of this.

In recent times I made a short trip to Cyprus where, in company of my wife, I hired a car and set off in escape from the tourist compounds. Already well into my fifties, it was the first package holiday I'd ever been on, though I regret to say, not quite the last. From the busy resort of Paphos we set off up into the hinterland in search of this old Greek way of life and in one week found virtually nothing. By the welcome sign to a couple of villages were some rusting wine presses, placed in memory to those who once operated them, a woman led a donkey through thorn bushes along a village edge and high up somewhere, the goats had been left to fend for themselves. Beyond that were stacked rows of identikit houses to which people rarely seemed to arrive or leave. As for those who formerly dwelt in these regions, you had to look far down the valleys to the ever spreading resorts, into which they had all thrown their lot. People talk of disappearing worlds as though it were just red painted faces and bows and arrows up in a jungle far away, but it's much closer to home than you really think.

While some countries change at a rapid rate others move more slowly, not by any purely economic force, but because they make a point of holding to old ways, and one such as this was Turkey. Here was a mixture of several powerful

34

elements, attractive and bothersome in varying degrees, but the most striking of these were not in the much visited places such as Istanbul or the Marmaris coast, but in the wilder areas over in the central and eastern parts of the country, into what some would regard as the real Turkey. Although this was a fairly easy region through which to hitch rides it was one that would fill you with constant unease, as you never knew what to expect from one moment to the next. Great warmth and fierce hostility could be found here in equal measures and added to this was the unpredictability of a road littered with the wrecks of those who never made it. Over a period of four years I hitched through Turkey six times, from various directions, and had some kind of trouble every single time.

I guess I should have clocked the signs early on when crossing the border from Greece, as a number of vehicles coming back the other way had mesh grille across their windows and over their headlamps. I merely thought there'd been a motorsport rally taking place nearby and these were either modified production camper vans, or just a few fans getting in on the spirit of things. I hadn't yet become aware of the roadside rock throwing epidemic. Along the edge of most towns and villages, where a scrub wasteland generally began, you seemed never able to travel far without encountering a huddle of people gathered by the roadside. You hardly could tell who it was until you drew close, as it could be farmers waiting to haul their bundles onto a bus into some market town, or families awaiting the return of relatives. But more commonly it would be young teenagers entrusted with a flock of brown sheep or goats. I don't know how the business began, or why it was specifically here, perhaps it came from a slower age where horses could be halted or pedestrians accosted, but what had developed was a kind of violent begging, not for the purpose of survival, but just as a youthful pastime, for the gain of a few cigarettes and loose change. The routine was for a small force of one or two to stand closely by the roadside to the point where they were leaning over into it, while making a smoking sign with two fingers of one hand and holding a fist sized stone in the other. If it became clear the driver was not about to halt and hand over some kind of gift then, Wham! The missile was launched to full effect. Whether it was only foreigners who were targeted in this way I can't be certain, but I never heard once of it happening to Turks and the end result could be often catastrophic. To locals however it seemed no serious matter at all. Save where their own interests became later to be affected by it.

I once heard of a Dutchman driving his car alone into Eastern Turkey who'd had his windscreen blown out in this manner, near blinding him in the process. Being fit, he chased the assailants into a nearby settlement and cornered them near their home. Expecting some kind of help or sympathy to arrive he was absolutely flabbergasted to find himself near lynched by the village residents and even the local cops took similar issue against him. Some years later I heard from an old truck driver who was on the Persian Gulf run that this business had been clamped down upon through some heavy sentences being handed out, but not before a long and well publicised number of incidents had occurred stretching way beyond a decade; which were largely ignored by the authorities until they became a threat to local trade. The safest position to be in all this, believe it or not, was right out on the roadside. Here you could see the situation about to develop and stock up on good ammo well in advance and once the first rock was thrown it would be returned in larger form and with far greater intent. As soon as people realised you were well up for it they usually scarpered quick. You couldn't take a chance on kids who were sometimes nearly the age of men and as for the local cops, who would bother?

Another matter of great concern on this first journey through Turkey, one of a more disquieting nature, was some of the attention I received from the normally hyper masculine truck drivers. Despite some people's sensitivity in these matters, I feel it would be highly irresponsible not to record that, while hitching from Eastern Turkey into Central Iran I received no less than 7 lifts consecutively from people of an aggressive homosexual nature. Under the general laws of Islam such activities are regarded as haram and even open boy-girl relationships are largely frowned upon. Ironic it is though that, while public representation of sexual matters is largely subdued in these kind of countries, it's repressed obsession among the public was constantly obvious. The most disturbing aspect of the whole

37

situation was that those whose preferences veered in this direction usually weren't too polite in making their intentions known and, in place of the usual hints and fruity suggestions we might have encountered elsewhere, was often just a crude grab for the inner thigh or some rough hand signal which might, if misinterpreted, lead you into something highly unbargained for. It was certainly not welcome.

As it suited my necessity, I tried to hold a fine line between polite refusal and simmering menace, while hurrying the conversation toward some innocuous item of passing scenery and thus did I work to keep the lift together until I could leap out some miles down the road into comparative safety. Only once did I really lose my cool and ended up being dumped out at the highest point of a snow filled pass, only to be given another lift shortly afterwards from someone else of ironically the same persuasion. Which dragged us again through the whole discomforting process. When I made my first trip through these rough lands I was a wide eyed 19 year old, with fine health and a trusting fresh face. Within a couple of years I would make similar tracks through this region in a rather more weatherworn condition and receive nothing like the same kind of attention. Which seemed to suggest a remedy to these kind of unwanted approaches. If you wish to avoid the notice of predatory homosexuals, then grow old and look rough. It's worked just fine for me.

The roads of Eastern Turkey then consisted largely of compacted shale with gradients often so steep that trucks were forced to weave in zigzag fashion in order to reach the top. A few forgiving miles of smooth tarmac brought you to the town of Dogubayazit, from where you were shortly over the border and onto what seemed like a different page of history.

*

With the benefit of hindsight you may have identified the road to Iran from nearly as far back as Munich, as the convoys of brand new Mercedes truck units seemed to have no returning equivalent. Trailer loads of kitchen white goods and high quality furniture continued their journeys through the Balkans and, while other road transport melted away, they never seemed to stop. At the heart of Turkey a column of these vehicles would melt away south to the gradually developing Gulf States, but most would plough ahead on a three week return trip to a land with more money than they knew how to spend. For the wealthy Emirates of today, read Iran before the Ayatollahs came to power; one of the richest per capita countries in the non Europeanised world, at the very height of its prosperity.

In a land progressing so fast, there could be seen some striking contrasts, as traditional dress would mingle with designer clothing, swish BMWs would weave their way between donkey carts and medieval architecture would reflect on the gold-mirrored glass of office towers. In travelling east it was as though you'd suddenly lost your bearings and tripped back west in error. If there was resentment among some in the disparity of wealth, it was welcomed by most as being better than equal austerity and donkey carts all round.

The final judgement on any revolution will never be a fair one, as it will largely reflect the views of those who either strongly opposed or supported it in the first place, but between all the arguments and re-writes of history will run one common truth in that, rarely to almost never do these events bring about an economic miracle. From the exact moment that fundamentalism took a hold, Iran's financial boom was at an end. Whether this was a result of people being given responsibility on the sole strength of their religious beliefs, or through the external pressure of embargoes will forever be open to debate, but there would be no return to those affluent days, not in the near future, nor perhaps ever.

From as far away as we are now and the crap we hear on the news, it is hard to tell how much has really changed here and what has not, as travellers tales relate that the locals are still pretty much as they were - willing to be sociable, sometimes very friendly and as always, part of an east-west never quite meeting world; but the image that the country represents abroad has changed out of all recognition. In the downtown area of Teheran, which had been widely thoroughfared during the early days of the oil boom, the streets were named after victorious leaders of the recently ended Second World War. There was a Churchill Boulevard, a Roosevelt Avenue and roads named after George Marshall and G.S. Patton. Among travellers, the most famous street was the one that contained all the cheap hotels. It was called General Eisenhower. I haven't passed this way in a long time, nor have I enquired of those who recently have, but I bet they're not called that now.

Either of the main east roads out of Teheran, be it the shorter mountain route or the more southerly desert diversion, will bring you eventually to Mashhad, a city that grew from a small oasis into a grand metropolis largely on the strength of its appeal to pilgrims. From a vast distance away it was plain to see that here was a place of some significance, as its most prominent feature, the gigantic blue domed Goharshad Mosque, towered over the dry surrounding landscape. As with many such towns reliant on fleeting business its traders were geared towards any new passing custom and the waves of Western hippies were treated pretty much as the pilgrims of past generations, with an eye for their wallets and the least of ceremony. It was however, not a place you could brush off easily, as all travellers on from here were required to halt for at least one day to obtain a visa for Afghanistan. Though I found the delay frustrating and the stay, at times, a bit like running the gauntlet, it was not without its lucky surprises, as the visa section provided me with not only legal entry but also a lift over the border to Herat from some camper van travellers I'd met in the queue.

41

*

From here on there became, for a while, less of a randomness about my travels, as I discovered that the standard public transport fares were so low as to make hitching barely worthwhile. Added to that was the extra danger involved in wandering alone beyond the urban limits, as the two million Kuchi nomads who roamed the desert considered it fair game to pick off isolated foreigners and have them for breakfast. The bus from Herat to Kandahar was only a pound for an eleven hour journey, repeated similarly each time from there onto Kabul and Peshawar, Which brought you from the borders of Iran to the Indian subcontinent for three quid. You hardly needed to weigh it up.

Within the confines of the town there was plenty enough to not only hold you spellbound, but to test your consciousness of the surrounds and lead you to wonder how the hell you got there. And that was without the effects of the herbal smoke that seemed to waft continually from every hotel window. The contrast here between one side of the border and the other was greater than anything I'd ever witnessed and certainly more profound than anything in the world today. From Mashhad to Herat was a half day drive, but in that short distance it was almost like you'd travelled back from a developing oil state into the time of Christ. I thought I'd had the ultimate in this

42

experience when travelling from Spain to Morocco, but this was about a thousand years back.

When approaching from the desert plain the first image you caught of old Herat was that of a dry rocky outcrop topped with the crumbling remains of a mud fort which, in the latter stages of day, might glow red with the late sun behind you. Constructed of such frangible materials, it had been rebuilt many times with raw earth from around where it stood and had been used in 330BC by Alexander the Great. Shortly after my own arrival I would attempt an impulsive ascent to find, not the expected haven of peace that generally inhabits these places, but a crowd of squatters huddled against each interior wall with their clothes-lines staked out like territorial markers. Following a few silent stares I beat a hasty retreat from ten year old kids armed with rocks.

The people who brought me from Mashhad had dropped me outside a double-storey row of earth-brick buildings that had a wooden walkway running before them and a line of posts for hitching up donkeys. Having little wish to wander further I checked into the place which lay right before me, which was the New Bezhad Hotel. You can become immune to the sights and conditions of a place very quickly, but on initial entry its mud daubed interior walls seemed to breathe a porous odour of animal sweat, as though it had been part of something still alive. The nightly fee of ten pence (20 Afghanis) bought me entry into a shared room, where the single naked light bulb hung

43

low and was powered so weakly that you could make out the filament glowing like an orange zigzag inside it. I found my bed and, once accustomed to the gloom, made my acquaintance with the rooms three other occupants; some heavily zapped out Danes a little older than myself, who were some further way down a road for which it was too scary for me then to look.

One of them, an intense looking fellow with a jutting bearded jaw and exploding pillow hairstyle, was slumped on a bed with his back against the wall, glaring hard into an imaginary distance. His friends drew my attention pointedly towards him and chuckled in conspiratorial fashion. He was obviously gone about as far as it were possible to go while still being conscious and put me in mind of a song by Three Dog Night, or one of those Sunday scandal sheets that asked if this were Heaven or Hell? Welcome to Afghanistan at the height of the hippie invasion, whatever you made of it.

A feature that stayed with me for long afterwards from this time in Herat was the existence of whole families of beggars congregating along the boardwalk and around the market place. The usual practice was for the parents to hide in the background while their youngest children tugged on sleeves in the street. It was a routine I was becoming familiar with in the regions just outside Europe and could never decide who was genuine and who opportunistic. The begging styles I've seen around the world usually had some little act to go with them, like brazen cheek or overstated helplessness, but there was an intense level of seriousness in the appeal here, the like of which I have never seen since. It would be long afterwards that I discovered the true cause of this situation and the national crisis that had brought it about.

During the first couple of years of the 1970s a severe drought had swept this already arid region, which resulted in not just the predictable crop shortages and higher prices, but a withering of the scrub vegetation which separates the desert from arable land. It was the loss of this generally unregarded strip that caused the worst of the disaster, as the Kuchi nomads who roamed this area and had once been wealthy in the ownership of livestock, were forced to slaughter and feed on their starving animals until, falling through the various stages of hardship, they had reached this level of destitution. It now explained the crowded state of the old fort and why the elders sat so proud and stoical before their now neighbours and possibly recent enemies.

I once caused some rumpus by handing out a 2½ p coin here (5 Afghani) to a single beggar, which created such a bee-swarm among those nearby that I had to be grateful to a local shopkeeper, not only for rescuing me, but for an extremely sound piece of advice. He told me that, when handing out money you should never give so much in one go, but break it down into more distributable shares and with this in mind, he changed me a ten Afghani note into a giant pile of centime-like coins, some with the embossing worn off and one simply a ⅜″ brass washer. I then went into the street to cause an even bigger commotion by

45

dispersing this amount into a clawing, snatching sea of hands, which brought me one other early lesson here. If you wish to give money to desperate strangers, then do it quickly and move on. Never look back.

Before I left this place for the first but not final time, I was engaged in conversation with an American fellow about ten years my senior, who had travelled out this way in the late 1960s. I would have been standing at a door on the upper wall of our hotel that opened inwards to reveal a wooden banister rail across its jamb, which presented what passed for a veranda out here, and I would have been gazing in amazement over the Biblical, mud-walled town. The fellow paused briefly by my shoulder to see what had caught my interest and I must have explained how blown away I was by this atmospheric scene and how great in contrast it was to what I had recently witnessed. His reply was of a type I would be hearing for many years to come.

'You should have been here five years ago man. There were hardly any of these hand painted trucks then and the evening light came mainly from oil lamps. When country people came into town they would arrive in a posse on donkey-back and tie up their mounts at the market hitching posts. They would fill the cafes, trade their goods then ride out again in a fading cloud of dust. Everyone knew who they were from the direction in which they arrived and you could see them coming and going from nearly a mile away.'

The golden age of travel is always about ten or twenty years before you yourself hit the trail. A time recent enough for you to feel familiar with, but just too far away to touch. This might be why I am far more attentive to traveller tales from the 1950s and 60s than I am to ones of my own day. Among those who know me well I have frequently been posed the question of which was the best country I've ever visited and the answer is always subject to this long kind of time factor. A once paradise island might have turned to rat's once the developers moved in, or conversely, Flanders may be fine and dandy in the present day, but wouldn't have been so swell in 1915. But if I had to nail down a definitive list of the most amazing destinations during my time there, then Afghanistan in 1972 wouldn't be far off the top of it.

The long desert bus ride to Kandahar, with its crowded space and thin-padded seats, would have been a tough ordeal in most circumstances, but for someone new to these kind of things it was a pure piece of magic. Almost everything I'd heard of such trips would have been there in some kind of measure, such as tethered goats and live chickens in shopping bags, plus a few I hadn't heard of, like burkahs, huge luggage bundles, sacks of agricultural produce and the high grinding rev of an engine pulling treble its recommended weight.

The memories of such journeys all blend into one after a while, but I'm sure there must have been men on the roof, who ascended in greater numbers than they ever seemed to come

47

down and somewhere along the way a farmer would climb
aboard with a pile of rice sacks that weighed half a lorry load
and should you be so naive as to allow them to be shoved under
your feet, you would suffer the extra discomfort of having to
continue the rest of the journey with your knees crammed an inch
below your chin. Whether you were fascinated by your new
surroundings or not, it would still be a long old day, taking you
from dark early morning into well after nightfall.

Following the near spiritual atmosphere of our arrival at
Herat our entrance into Kandahar would never produce anything
like the same impact. In place of the yellow desert that blushed
in the late sun was a region composed of cement-like dust, which
continued its greyness into the buildings that rose from it. Any
prominent hill or castle was lacking, but if you climbed to an
open flat rooftop, which always seemed to be easily accessible
here, you could take in a quiet, timeless view of mud domes and
turrets that would lead your thoughts into a haze of timelessness.
The most remarkable thing about this scene in hindsight was not
just its handmade symmetry, but the complete absence of any
public advertising, neon or otherwise. It may have been a highly
urbanised area, but from up here the sight was one of
unblemished purity.

In town I checked in at the Peace Hotel, a name very
indicative of the times, and must have known about it from some
way back, as was generally the case. The desk staff were out
front waiting for us as the bus pulled in. From this abode I

48

explored on foot with neither manual nor map and only a directional sense to return me to base. It was harder work that we probably would now wish, but it helped with our fitness and took us beyond the pages of any guide book. Among the foreigners already here much of the conversation centred around the odd business that was soon to be taking place on the main square, namely the public hangings. At a date prior to my arrival a double murder had been committed in one of the cheap pensions, where two French people had been killed by three Afghanis, one of whom was a mullah. The motive had been robbery and all deeds had apparently since been confessed to. Such were the limits of my funds and visa that I was forced to move on before further developments and by the time of my return three months later, fate and justice had already taken their course. For the sake of my curiosity this may have been a disappointment, but at the same time was something of a relief, as those foreigners who did attend were forced down to the front of the crowd and, not perhaps being of the strongest mind during these spaced out days, I'm not sure how I would have handled it.

If later times were ought to go by, where I witnessed cockfights and bullring spectacles, the most revealing part of the whole show would have been in the reaction of the crowd rather than the poor, or deserving victim. If you've never seen the varied public reactions to an act of slaughter then there's a part of human nature which, for you, has forever remained hidden. And it's not always nice.

49

Kabul, when at last we arrived, seemed located in an entirely different country to what we had so far seen. Spread high on a plain surrounded by near distant summits, it had an atmosphere unique to itself, which seemed to care nought for whether people took it or left it. It felt in some ways like a more ancient version of Eastern Turkey with its cold mountain landscapes and wild looking locals, but whereas in Turkey the toughness was largely a case of bluster and bravado, here you felt that it probably wasn't. Lately, an area had spread itself by the edge of town into wide streets, where the embassies and large houses stood, but the bulk of population lived in the most tightly cramped areas, such as the river banks and nearby hillsides, where the breeze-block houses rose so steeply that they appeared to sit on the roofs of those below them. It was likely the ground here was cheap to buy, if ever it got paid for at all and even though pleasing to the landscape, you could sense close up the harshness of living here and the struggle. In late spring weather, with snow still on the peaks, the people wore car-tyre sandals with no socks and by the way they bore the chill, you felt that self-pity, or the same for others, was here in fairly short supply. I could have realised then, if not sooner, that this would not be a good place in which to upset someone.

The Shah Foladi Hotel was a large cement-rendered building with few merits other than the availability of its cheap rooms. From its tall front windows you could look out along the confined banks of the Kabul River that snaked generally in a thin

50

black trickle between wide pebbly shores. In late Spring, with the high snows melted, it would run in a torrent to sweep away the waste packaging and raw sewage that had built up on its channel edges. Which made you wonder about its purity by the time it reached the Indus, not to mention its flow out into the sea.

On a bare strip of land out the hotel front, on every day but Fridays, there would be a two-row market of wooden stalls which, in times of inclement weather, would continue upon a sea of blackened mud. With acclimatisation to the pace of life here it could be quite a tranquil place to wander, provided you were willing to endure the occasional shock to the system. It could occur mostly when you were wrapped in a cocoon of indulgent haze that you could be wandering along and a raucous cry would erupt from somewhere close by, as though ordering a battle charge. Turning around, you might see something like a small runaway hill moving towards you, which on closer look would turn out to be a broad handcart, piled to the sky with hessian sacks. Running on tyres so bald they looked like inner tubes, the vehicle would be balanced upon a single axle from the rear of some long deceased motor, while at the front would be two thick shafts and a crossbar, not for the purpose of securing some tamed beast, but for putting to work a couple of gasping heaving men. The passageways between the stalls could be uneven and slippery and the precariousness presented by a single pair of wheels meant that momentum once gained must be continued. Hence the warning shouts, which could have meant 'shift or be

51

squashed.' In more dramatic moments the wheels may have caught on loose boulders in the road, laid there to combat the sinkage and, while poorly shod haulier's feet slid on wet ground, idle shoppers or even passing hippies might lean their shoulders to the task. Though in the case of the hippies, it wouldn't have made a great deal of difference.

The only time I was genuinely worried in Kabul was when I got dragged away to an innocent seeming and rather fancy eating place, in company of some Dane I'd met at the hotel. Though I noted the fellow's talkativeness at the outset I could not have foreseen how things would progress as, during the 20 minute walk over there, he became wound into an excitable state and, not that I'm the over sensitive type, ever more repetitively rude. On entering the restaurant things initially went well, as the place was wonderfully atmospheric with colourfully woven wall drapes and fine Afghan carpets. We were seated upon camel saddlebags padded with cotton and felt like we were lording it among the Sheiks of Araby. As the initial wonder subsided however I couldn't help noticing that something was brewing beneath the brow of my companion, which before long would erupt into a series of violent outbursts directed towards everyone present, the abruptness of which threw everyone into a state of shock. It must only have been the unexpected nature of such a thing that saved our day, as even the meaner looking punters seemed completely nonplussed and had we been in our normal kind of cheap haunt, among the market porters or the visiting nomads, you sensed something really might have gone amiss.

During these times I, along with a lot of others, had never heard of Tourette's Syndrome, a condition that recurs in the manner of epilepsy and will more likely reappear during periods of stress or tiredness, particularly when brought on by long overland journeys into strange lands. Our fellow here would have been well aware of it though, through many a painful encounter and had learned, in his way, to fly with it. It hadn't dampened his desire to seek the kind of life that others had and with this in consideration, his journey was far more a statement of courage and adventure than any of our own. I have met many people over the years who struggled in circumstances temporary or, in this man's case permanent and among those who were afforded the lowest share of merit, were to be found some of life's true battlers and those most worthy of respect. I'm not sure where this fellow would have fitted on any list of travelling heroes, as he could be rather taxing company but, like the deaf Japanese bloke hitching through Spain and the wheelchair-bound man in the Canaries, he deserved nine points out of ten simply for being there.

The most keenly anticipated feature of my departure from Kabul was the forthcoming journey through the Khyber Pass and the long descent into Continental India, yet it was a passage through the lesser renowned Kabul Gorge that provided the most scenic drama of the day, if such a thing could ever be achieved through a bus window. Here, beside a churning white river, the road ducked between steep gully walls and rocky overhangs through a landscape redolent with the air of many a past struggle. It could be a harsh route at any time of year but especially in the depths of winter, as a retreating British company discovered in January 1842, when they were wiped out to the last sole survivor, in a deadly ambush. Even now it appeared the most inhospitable spot on all these roads through Central Asia.

*

Beyond the border post, which then was little busier than a rural bus stop, the Khyber itself began, not in the form of sudden twists and climbs, but over a graded 33 mile stretch of loose ashen slate, between tribal lands with leaders beholden to no one. Somewhere along the way we were halted by woollen-hatted tribesmen who climbed aboard to exact a fee of 20 Afghanis or one rupee from everyone present. Some regarded this as highway robbery, but a price such as this to buy safe passage through the Khyber seemed like the bargain of the century to me, especially when set beside the alternatives.

Continuing on from here to Peshawar provided no great excitement, but in looking back I find one strong memory of something in which I wished I had become a lot more involved. This was a glimpse of one of the more challenging and interesting ways to travel through the Pass, not on a bicycle or on foot, but in one of the large bulbous fronted, 'sixties Russian taxis that plied this route and which always seemed to carry about a dozen people in a car for six. There would be four in the back, two beside the driver up front, possibly two on the roof, some on the bonnet and, in a reverse opening boot, a couple more with their backs to the trailing dust. If any came through with less than half this compliment you would consider it a returning empty.

Once you overcame the suffocating humidity and attuned yourself to the huge increase in tiny road vehicles, the feature that most urgently caught your attention in Pakistan was that, whenever you engaged in an activity that included opening your wallet, the price you were asked to pay seemed to have been picked out of a tract of thin air somewhere. This wasn't just in the realm of market barter, but on public busses, at rail booking offices, in cafes and at roadside tea stalls, and by watching what others paid for the same thing you had to beat hard to get the price down to something only marginally above what it really should have been. Were I to face such a situation nowadays I would simply pay the extra to save hassle and then dust my heels forever, but during these days I was on a mission to stretch meagre amounts to the furthest limits and many a purchase would turn into the haggle of life and death. It was a bit like the transit mentality I'd witnessed elsewhere, only far more extreme. One further notable thing to come out of this was that,

55

among travellers passing through, there developed a level of paranoia about overcharging, when the deal in fact may have been perfectly straight. The general consensus however leaned so heavily in the opposite direction that it would be impossible to ignore it, and dishonestly misleading not to mention it.

I remember a local newspaper report around this time of an open meeting with then Prime Minister Zulfikhar Ali Bhutto where an audience was invited to discuss why overland travellers spent three months in India but only two days in Pakistan. Among the attendees were a number of foreigners who aired their complaints freely over price hiking on grounds of nationality, ill treatment of foreign women and disrespect towards non local beliefs. This response was said to have left Bhutto completely stunned, which may have been a feigned surprise, but if not, it made you wonder whether political leaders really did get out as much as other people do.

Despite the difficulties endured by through travellers here there was something to marvel at in what, for us, was yet another different world; the geographical beginnings of Old India. In the busy streets where traffic never seemed to jam but slowly swirl, policemen on point duty would direct double decker busses between screaming tuk tuks and horse drawn tongas, wooden barrows and steaming foodstalls narrowed every crowded pathway, while shop entrances had their hessian wrapped deliveries dumped in piles right across the thoroughfare. It created a scene that will probably never be repeated, where ancient and modern had neither fully departed, nor quite won the day.

Following a noisy bus ride to Rawalpindi, a tidily polished steam train brought me to Lahore and much into the front line of what ills had befallen Pakistan in recent times. The war over Bangladeshi independence had ended only 4 months previously and, had you not known of Pakistan's resounding defeat by Indo-Bangla forces, you would have suspected something of the sort by the atmosphere on the streets. The sight on beggars row of discharged servicemen with lately acquired disabilities, the downcast faces of a nation in retreat and, following the yet uncorroborated reports that Pakistan soldiers had committed upto 400,000 rapes against young Bangladeshi women and girls, some as young as eight, there was a sense of resentment that the world had not judged them well. Dark days indeed.

Had these traumatic events not taken place and their unexpected reverberations failed to overtake us, I would have been through Pakistan in the customary couple of days, but one of the fall outs from this situation was that the land border between Pakistan and India was still closed and I was forced to delay a few days to find alternative means. Whenever obstacles like this exist it is not usually long before an enterprising solution arises and it was left to Afghan Airlines, acting in the role of a neutral party, to provide the means with a short hop flight from Lahore to Amritsar, the travelling distance of a

couple of local motorway turn offs. The one-way price was
fourteen quid, which provoked the odd swoon and a clutching of
the chest, but it was worth the outlay for the extra few moments
of excitement. The degree of climb here was so sharp and brief
that we barely had time to see a cloud before the steep descent
back to earth. Knowing that the highest risk part of flying was in
take off and landing, it was the only time on the whole trip that I
was truly scared.

*

When you picture your main arrival point at some
longed for destination, the image you conjure would hardly be
that of a small country airstrip, surrounded by open grazing, that
led to a low adobe painted building, but if there was one cause
for optimism it was that, things could only get better from here.
On the hot two-lane road that skirted the runway a small cluster
of us travellers flagged an ancient bus that had a barely visible
sign wedged with a conductor's bag against its inner windscreen.
It said Amritsar. Once aboard we were lost in a huddled crowd
which blocked any view of windows, let alone what lay beyond
them and we guessed our whereabouts into town, at which point
we disembarked into a falling rain of luggage at some all purpose
place which served as a shopping centre, street-market, hotel
area and conveniently for now, a bus station. On wrestling our
way beyond the melee we were accosted, not too aggressively,

by people offering all the best in cheap accommodation, yet we paid no heed to these, as our course was already set on a place of far greater attraction to us, as it was almost free. This was the Guru Ramdas Hostel, a stay over for pilgrims to the centre of world Sikhism, the famous Golden Temple.

The most common fallacy concerning India during this time, as earlier noted, was that it was a land of peace, tolerance and harmony, but were you to be parachuted into this complex to soak up its vibe, then quickly airlifted out again, you would, had you visited no other part of the country, have departed not only with this view intact, but quite probably enhanced. To all Sikhs the city of Amritsar represents the home of their most significant religious site, their Holiest of Holies and all followers of the faith are required to make at least one visit to here within their lifetime. When Sikhism was centred mainly in the Punjab this was a fairly easy task, but now they come from all corners of the largely English speaking world. For foreign overlanders, mostly of the budget version like ourselves, a room had been set aside containing neither beds nor furniture, which was available for a small donation and, as a consequence, it was rammed full every night.

Over the next few years I would encounter a number of these temple grounds, providing free accommodation and sometimes a communal meal, not just in India but in Indian communities in East-Central Africa and though it suited our budgetary methods of the time, you couldn't escape the gnawing feeling you were being a burden upon your hosts, while deep down inside, they felt the same. I realise however that those who devised these customs were playing surely for the longer game, in the hope that those who would clutch at such offerings, the desperate needy, or young opportunists like ourselves, would carry on with a positive image of Sikhism throughout the rest of their lives, which has pretty much been the case.

A visit to the temple itself was a momentous occasion far more appealing in its general vibe than in any specific detail. The layout was simply a shallow pool within a white walled courtyard, with a causeway leading out to a golden shrine. But the effect of this in bright sunlight, or especially in the evening, with the various images reflecting from the water, along with the devotional atmosphere that constantly prevailed, was more overpowering than anything with which I could compare it. I guess the effects of contrast may have made a difference for me here, as I'd begun the morning in a hectic Lahore, ridden a bucking flight across the border and endured a jam packed bus ride into town, which made it hard to believe we were still in the same day. But as we eddied around among the slow moving worshippers I began to have one of my spiritual moments among a crowd whose beliefs I knew very little of. Swept by momentum to the inner Darbar Sahib shrine I found a narrow staircase and ascended to a balcony where I could sit, among a few others, behind a tiny balustrade fence and listen to a live performance below, of a small group playing harmonium, tabla and sitar.

Bright flowers were presented at an altar and joss smoke swirled up, mingling with their strong scent. After long enough sitting on a hard floor I rose and retreated to my shared hostel room, pie-eyed and staggering like a drunk in the night.

Beyond a certain point all rail journeys in modern countries are pretty much the same, you board a train going hopefully in the right direction, find a soft place to park your carcass, observe briefly all fellow passengers for sources of private amusement along the way and then peer out the window to catch a few passing images, which may have actually been of some interest had they been viewed in something like real time. Rarely in our own world do you recall a travelling day where you learned a lifetime lesson, or witnessed things that would either repel you or touch your heart. The widely variable nature of Subcontinent transport could produce these kind of encounters in bucket loads at either end of the scale, especially if you had chosen to make your way via the parallel universe of Indian Railways. Everyone who has ever travelled out this way will have their own favourite Indian Railways story, visitors and, one suspects, Indians alike. My favourite is of a time when a corpse got on the train, but before then, in chronological order, is the tale of how I became inducted into the ways of Indian rail travel.

The regular non-express service between Amritsar and Old Delhi had a grand sounding name like the North Western Mail or something similar, which was a fine disguise for a sluggish stop-start that called at every sorting office along the way. It was uncommonly large for a passenger train, possibly twenty carriages in length and was pulled along by a huge old steam engine. As the empty wagons rolled into the platform, I was at first impressed by their fine livery, but as things trailed further from the engine their condition blanched out, until at last we reached our own humble level at the rear, where dim-lit compartments were viewed through whole-frame open windows and the doors seemed never to have been closed. A large number 3 painted alongside inspired a new sense of novelty in me, as I'd never been in third class before.

A hard lesson learnt is a best remembered one and I well recall my naive belief that the open door at either carriage end represented a means of boarding the train in a proper manner. My self-satisfaction at having been one of the first few to enter turned to disbelief however, as I found not only all seats occupied but the floor space beginning to fill up beneath a wave of baggage and bundles. What had occurred it seemed was that, while we were politely playing the game by struggling six abreast to pass through a single door, the more able bodied had dived in through the open window and hogged all the space. The memory of this setback may have well faded had it not been for the excruciating ten hour night journey that followed, which was passed among an all-standing crowd wedged in so tightly that you could likely have raised both feet off the ground and sunk hardly an inch.

Rarely do such lessons go to waste however and the next time such a situation arose, (I think it was from Delhi to Agra a week later), I made sure I was ready as the empty train reversed in and, just as it slowed to a manageable pace, I was first in through the window with rucksack in tow and by the time the wild mob had fought its way through, I was ensconced in my comfy seat on the opposite side, back to the engine and away from the incoming flies. In those few active moments I had achieved what so many had sought to gain by this soulful journey to the East. I had become wise.

After such a journey by rail and whatever day had preceded it, my urgent need then was for a quiet space in which to lie down, but what I got instead was a buffeting reception that marked my full on entry into this strange new environment. In the 20 yard distance between the station foyer and the street outside I had to battle my way through a kind of human obstacle course created by hotel touts, street money changers, taxi drivers, cycle rickshaw operators and Olympic fit beggars, all competing for your perceived wealth, as though your rough clothing were merely the disguise of some eccentric millionaire. Having negotiated all these at minimal loss I was then accosted by a man leaping from a shop doorway wearing a huge live snake around his neck, who offered it to me for God knows what purpose. In later times I could appreciate these characters for whatever services they provided and would learn how to treat them with courtesy, even when refusing their frantic offers, but for now I

63

was interested in none of their dealings, as I was headed for an encounter to which I'd looked forward for some while. It would be not quite a case of getting on down with the kids, as I was barely more than a kid myself, but bedding down with some real on the road people, who for some reason I then strongly admired. I would be sleeping outside in New Delhi's Hanuman Park, with a bunch of Western hippies.

The earliest occasions when I slept outside were quite fun, as I was largely among friends and the people we met around us were usually warm and affable, with a sharing togetherness that we all felt at the time. It is clear now that our mood evolved from notions of fancy barely beyond our own childhood, and as we all had safe homes to return to, we were probably just playing at it. Those who wholly spend their lives on the road, while surviving each day as it comes, do not present, I'm afraid to say, a very attractive picture.

Within moments of arriving in this run down park you could see there would be no coming together of beautiful people. A bare worn patch amid occasionally tufted grass led us to a broadly spread tree, beneath which a few slouched foreigners had thrown their flimsy belongings. As I lay down my own and looked around for response, I was met by a wall of stony faces, with a strange dissecting suspicion in their eyes. Talk was stilted from the moment I arrived and when I did manage to briefly engage a neighbour, the first meaningful question I was asked was if I did any junk? On answering in the negative I was met with a sneering look of contempt, as though I were a breed of some freak alien tribe. I must have been a bit green not to have sensed it from a mile off. For here, in contrast to the generally positive types I'd been meeting along the way, was a bunch of people who'd travelled all this distance only to finish up in their own dead end.

Notably present was one young lad of sixteen, who'd worked some scam on his father's credit card and booked a flight from the US to Kathmandu. He had drifted down here to eke out the last of his old man's dollars, before it was time to hand himself in and face the music. I gave little thought then to the worry of his parents, or of the people back home scanning every pond and household dumpster. I merely felt a wave of envy in wishing I'd hit the trail a bit earlier myself. His adventure reminded me of Kipling's Kim, who had travelled the Grand Indian Trunk Road in the days of wandering troubadours and bullock carts. But that was only a storybook with a contrived ending and he wasn't camped out with a bunch of deadbeats in Needle Park.

Located not far from this hopeless scene and within walking distance of the old Connaught Place, there stood a partitioned cloth emporium trading under the name of Mohan Singh. In a far corner of the warren interior could be found a number of cubby-hole cafes where, for around 2p, you could nourish yourself on rice and dhal, or something very similar. Across the park island that formed many people's memory of

65

New Delhi there stood a corner shop behind a classical Luytens frontage, where you might purchase, in the early morning, pints of milk sold in returnable glass bottles. At both of these locations and down on the rail station forecourt, I saw Western hippies of the type I'd met in Hanuman Park, begging in downright brazen fashion from foreigners and Indians alike, and that's what did it for me. In a land where people might be driven into cities by famine in the countryside, or where sudden disability may lead to a life on the street, to see these unworthy cretins, having made their own mess, now seeking to beg bread out of the mouths of the more deserving, was just shameful beyond belief. I was out of here.

When setting the course of any long journey, one of the hardest tasks is often in choosing which places to take in and which to leave out. I have by-passed many a great location over the years, thinking there would always be an opportunity to call back, but much of my life has passed, only for those occasions yet to arrive. Florence, Rome and New York are notable in this respect, where I was virtually in the suburban traffic in some cases, but thank God the list does not include Agra and the wonderful Taj Mahal. Although due to an aversion with over visited tourist places I had at the time, it very nearly did.

We all think we know the Taj Mahal from a distance, the view through the petalled arch, the long reflecting pool leading to the raised platform and the rest is there, easy to see. But step a way closer and you may become lost in a trail of discovery that, had you the time to dwell, may fascinate you forever. Walking across a hot marble forecourt on bare feet is a passage that will not be forgotten by many people and likewise the relief when reaching the cool dark interior, but once there, things begin with a puzzle. What is here? Why is the place so empty? The walls, seemingly plain, begin to reveal a thin floral pattern once your eyes have accustomed to the shade. Sweeping vines that seem to have neither source nor end support brightly coloured birds that turn their faces as if specifically towards the doorway light. The door frames, in marble white, have been carved into a bas relief of hanging fruit and, as you look towards the wall closer and again, you realise that the scheme is not one of surface colouring, but a highly skilled inlay of stone parquetry. Outside in the blazing heat, perhaps on a patch of shaded ground, you notice that this creeping floral pattern has spread its way, not just up the walls but right over the domes and into places where most will never see. Which is when you begin to realise just what devotional architecture really means. Departing at the sandstone petal entrance with one long look back, you felt that you'd been taken in ambush by a place you figured you already knew.

Had you boarded a train at the mid-way point of any long journey you could abandon hope of obtaining a standard seat on any Indian rail route of this time and furthermore, should you be low on the instinct of fighting for your ground, then you could dump the idea of boarding any kind of major transport at

67

all. There many times we travelled in the most sardined of circumstances or sat on the roof and saw others cling perilously to the sides, but one journey in particular stands out, not merely because of the crowded conditions, but because of a strange and silent group who later arrived onboard.

I recall taking this train as part of a cross country journey where, every time I joined on to a new connection I was faced with a row of crammed full carriages, from which few departed and many wished to board. Through each wall of people I had somehow to wedge, then open a path and, on this occasion, being well beyond shyness, I had managed to find my way into an old style carriage passageway and onto a spot no larger than my two juxtaposing shoes. Thus did we continue, on another long journey into the night.

As this train was another of the all-stops variety we would pull up at halts along the way at which there didn't seem to be a station at all and it was at such a one as these, with people milling around on the track below our window, that we were joined by a small band of people who had been attended to the station it seemed, by some kind of flaming, torch lit procession. While they climbed onboard I saw, in what pools of light that followed, that they were in possession of a long package, in the form of a bamboo stretcher bound with a kind of gold reflective wrap. As they bustled along I noted that an uncommon degree of respect was afforded to this party and people made way, not just for the members themselves, but for the strange bundle, which was pushed along, end-on fashion and left to rest, just below the left foot I had politely raised in order to allow them to move on. In this upstanding crush where it was impossible to see much beyond heads and shoulders, it was hard to tell if anything of real value lay within the golden wrap and I was just on the point of lowering my foot to make light contact with it when I was sternly warned by someone nearby that under no circumstances should I do this. It contained, they said, the body of someone's dear old grandmother, who was now on her way to Benares to be consumed in a funeral pyre with her ashes to be later cast upon the Holy Ganges. Leaning at 20° to the wall, with one foot cocked in midair, a single big toe steadying my weight, tired already and fearing that one false slip could cause an outrage, I realised once again that it was going to be a long old night.

The Northern plains around the border town of Raxaul displayed all the typical features one would associate with rural India and may have displayed, to any new arrivee, an accurate picture of what to expect of the landscape ahead. Stubbly fields of harvested rice, parcelled up with ridges of dry mud, were nibbled at and fertilised by free roaming cattle. Motorbikes bounced along the sun-warped edge of roads while, over at the suddenly busy rail terminus, you were greeted, upon arrival, by the familiar station air of cooked spice, steaming tea and that tasty metallic smell of thick black engine oil baking dry upon the hot rail tracks. Coming down here from the hills it may have fit exactly your expectations of a typical Indian country setting. But

69

we were headed the far way up, into the Nepali highlands, which was about as inapposite to here as it were possible to get without leaving the continent altogether.

*

Beyond the customs post in the early morning an old bus lay in wait until such time as enough passengers would arrive to make its trip viable. But parked close by, a tall sided truck honked its horn in opportunistic fashion, inviting people to switch allegiance for a much earlier start. And so we clambered up top, a young farming couple, a local rice trader, a returning Ghurkha and one person of presently undecided cultural background, myself. As we climbed testily away on the road to Kathmandu I found a place on the cab roof, where tarp sheets had been folded into a shallow frame and sat to enjoy what would be a 360° view of the most staggeringly beautiful landscape I can ever recall. Through tropical valleys over wooded hills and terraced slopes of electrifying green, we exhausted ourselves with wonder and excitement, eager to miss nothing.

My memories of Nepal would initially be fond ones, but from mid life onwards they would be tinged forever with a deep regret. It was ok to congratulate yourself on travelling thus far on meagre resources, a feat which means little to me now, and whatever else I would have done may not have been a better way of spending my youth, but I always think about how much more

I could have done. Although born within sight of the hills, it wasn't until in my late twenties that I began my long affair with upland country, during which time I had travelled to the Alps, the Himalayas and the Andes without even raising a step in the right direction. To anyone with a love of the outdoors these regions would read like a fantasy wish list and to turn up these chances through pure inertia seems now like a criminal waste. If there was but one grain of compensation in this it was that, beyond a certain time I would use these overlooked opportunities as a driving force, to never let such moments slip by again. For the meantime however I merely followed the general trend of the day by pursuing a dope fuelled lifestyle, which progressed from a passing habit into a strain of character, which became harder to shake off.

The images of lethargy were all around us here and nowhere more so than in the market place, where stood a small shop, devoid of shelf goods or window display and possessing nothing within its interior beyond an old wooden desk, bearing a set of brass scales. This was the Ganesh Hash Hish and Ganja Stores, which was trading openly and even had its own pictorial calendar. Within a block of this place, just off the Dhurbar Square, I sat upon the wooden floor of a pagoda temple, while a hot chillum was passed around between Canadian hippies, a young Sadhu and eventually to myself who all, in historic re-writing of the time, smoked but never inhaled. I recall listless freaks sloping around in cheesecloth shirts with tiny burn holes

71

scattered across their chests and wondered if there was some new fashion here that I was missing out on; until sometime later when I came to recognise that my own shirt was beginning to disintegrate with all the hot hemp seeds popping out onto it.

There is some fondness in looking back to this, as you would look upon an innocence that could not last, but it seemed like a small amount of high for a whole lot of waste in terms of whatever else you could have done. There are all kinds of substances around for artificial euphoria these days, some leading to desperation and others that are quite manageable, but the best form of exhilaration that I ever managed from life was upon fighting myself back to fitness again, where I felt I could deal with near anything thrown at me. Still, as everyone knows, even that doesn't come cheap.

Modern developments of age old cities leave you with a barrel of mixed feelings. Kathmandu would be a small country town when I visited it, surrounded by green fields, and rice terraced almost into the suburbs. Some of the side roads were bare earth, filled in with river cobbles for when the mud had been deep and the market floor was made of broken bricks. Urban progress is a fine thing if managed correctly, but it can also bring its downside. I have seen recent online videos of cities in this region, where a swarms of 90cc motorbikes roared away from traffic lights as though it were a Grand Prix starting grid and imported second hand cars belched out fumes unhindered, and I rather wished then that I'd looked away. Lives here have been changed irrevocably and the culture of the street will never be the same.

One group to feel the full weight of this would be the many street beggars who used to congregate around the central temple district and who were the most placid bunch of such people you could meet in any town. Those of us who spent time on the street got to know some of these reasonably well and discovered they had fallen into low circumstances largely through a mixture of psychological illness and learning difficulties, for which there was neither much local care, nor understanding. In the way of this region many of them had been declared outcast by their families, due to variations of poverty, superstition and public embarrassment. Abandoned street kids were also a constant presence. Lively, cheeky little buggers they were, largely illiterate but bright as a button and savvy way beyond their years. Towards evening and without the chance of a crap all day, they would retreat to the shadows beneath the overhanging eaves. Which reminded you to step carefully when walking home after dark.

On journeys lasting many months it comes as a welcome respite to remain for a while in one place, but too long spent there can leave you wondering whatever else you may have missed. I'd way overstayed in Kathmandu by renting a room at a pound a month, which gave me time to catch a few books I'd been meaning to read and though the local monkeys were an entertainment, as they tried to nick stuff through the windows,

73

the conditions were sparse and the lazy days left me debilitated. Stoned out escapism seemed the easiest flow to go with in this hippie Shangri La and for a while we went with it, but then, as the homeward route beckoned, we were jolted awake by a sudden reminder that there was another world outside of the one we had comfily settled into. This was the day when a large swish tourist bus, maybe the first of its kind to reach here, turned up on the approaches to Dhurbar Square.

Gleaming like a streamlined train it began to disgorge its cargo of beige clothed, Panama hat wearing Europeans and, as the roadside crowded up, a very odd kind of exchange began to take place. They peered at us, we peered back at them and it was like one of those times when the first explorers had entered the heart of a new continent somewhere, which made it hard to tell who were the onlookers and who the spectacle. I'm sure there would be tons of visitors to Kathmandu these days, as it is now a major destination, but this was only five years after the country opened its borders, following more than a century of seclusion and those who came here at this time still saw themselves as something intrepid. For such a cold visit to occur into this midst was like having your parents come in to break up your house party by sitting down on the sofa and putting a soap opera on TV. I recall the words of someone nearby who was crouched upon a roadside kerb, as the more wasted freaks were prone to do. It was a tone I would be hearing all down the years, as some new scene started up and then began to fade.

74

"Ah, it's finished man. It's aaall finished!"

Once the wind has gone from your sails there is nothing left for it but to follow the tide home. As with many of my trips around this time, having left with but the bare essentials, I had taken even that to the limit and must now put the travel blinkers on in order to get back before real starvation set in. Despite my haste however there was still opportunity for an encounter or two that would live in the memory, the most significant of which to me was a meeting I had in Peshawar, at the eastern foot of the Khyber, in the midst of the most gigantic of electrical storms.

On the rear balcony of the Rainbow Guest House I stood and watched as cascade of purple lightning lit the jagged peaks of the outerlying Himalayas. Seated already there, on a chair taken from the room, was an English fellow marginally older than myself and for a while we remained in silence, in awe of this show of natural power. Eventually we spoke, first of the rainless spectacle and then of our journeys, and where we would go next. Both of us agreed we would travel again when opportunity arose, with the only question being, to where? We hoped for new journeys partly similar to the one we were on, Where you could immerse yourself in an interesting culture, in places that were cheap, with an ambience warm and welcoming, but at an earlier stage of being mass touristed, which does affect the social climate considerably. The Andean regions of South America were muted, with their colourful, haunting traditions amid a dramatic backdrop, but travel costs were high due to standard only fares being available.

The seated fellow had a relative who'd recently returned from an area which might interest us, where the encroachment of tourism had so far been low level and people were not yet greatly changed by its presence. This was the region centred around Kenya and its East African neighbours, which was then most peaceful and, from the tales arriving, seemed to have no bad edge to it. And so, in the way that was becoming common to these things, a new journey was born, even before the present one was ended.

Chapter4

Arab World

If the postscript to a long trip had any kind of pattern it was that three days of homecoming euphoria would be followed by a two week trough of depression, leading to a stoical state where you figured that here is where you were and rather than rage against the unavoidable, you might as well just get on with it. It may be that I would have the outlet of another interesting journey to look forward to, but for the foreseeable future it would take longer to save up the dough than it took to do the trip. The simple adventures where you could hitch from the bottom of the lane with a few quid in your pocket were all now played out for me and any future travels would come at a much higher cost, not only in money, but what it took from the rest of your life.

Soon at home I managed to find a job in commercial decorating with some people I already knew. I heard it said that everyone will, at one point, end up with some kind of brush in their hand and it was a step into a trade that served me very well during the time I needed it. The changing outdoor scenery was something I came to appreciate, and the fitness it developed was certainly an upward lift. In fact, with a few different turns of event, I could have settled my future right there, driving a little painter's van, with my name emblazoned along the side.

There were a few unbargained for features arising in my hometown life during this period, largely due to the great contrast between the romance of travel and returning to a rather bare existence. Before I wandered abroad I was always straight in with girls, full of the local banter, even though I cared not much for strong attachments, while thankfully neither did they. By now, and particularly after the India trip, there seemed to be a durable veil that had formed between myself and the whole culture of my past, its vernacular, its core interests and the habits to which I could not return. While realising this, I was just learning to live with it and was on the verge of forming some deep new bonds, which, to my present disappointment, never actually came to much. Though the mixed fortunes of this time brought me as much pain as it would to most young people, I must now see this as some kind of blessing, as, with so much of travelling left in me, it may have led otherwise to a chained future of nagging regret, while directing thoughts of frustration to some clearly blameless individual.

My mind then was set upon adventures that some around me thought were rather scary, or even a little reckless, but which to me were the only kind of activity I felt really comfortable with. The things I really feared all centred around enclosure and being smothered by a life that presented me with little of further interest. Other people's fear of the great beyond was, to me, just a walk across the street and a life sustaining one to boot.Thus it was that, by the following Spring, with barely sufficient funds, the vaguest of plans and a belief that all journeys were pure miracles of deliverance, I pitched myself out of the prison home and breathed free again. With the birds singing and the sun shining, the pull of gravity was stronger than anything known to humanity as I set off again, along familiar departing roads, convinced beyond doubt that I would thumb rides overland, through wars and disputed territories, all the way to Kenya.

In order to vary my trek across Europe I made my way this time along the Adriatic coast of Yugoslavia, through what are now the territories of four different countries. Here, if you ignored the rank state of the economy, was a gorgeous region, unspoilt by over development, on whose behalf you can only feel concern as the major developers move in. I was astounded by the largely ignored city of Dubrovnik in its medieval defensive huddle and even more so by the Montenegrin town of Kotor on a calm day, reflecting in the mirror of its perfectly sheltered bay. It seemed surreal to be having your breath taken away by a town of which you'd previously never heard. In the early nineties I recall seeing news coverage of these lovely coastal towns being under naval bombardment during one of the more demoralising phases of a civil war and was appalled, not only by the human carnage, but the act of wanton cultural destruction. But here we were, less than thirty years beyond WWII, when much of classical Europe

79

had gone to ruin and considering this, you became suddenly aware not only of the wasting of life, but the loss of much else that had existed there.

*

Descending the Taurus Mountains toward the broad Turkish strip that fringes Northern Syria you felt as though you'd already entered another country, as the mood became more placid and marked by patience. An anomaly of the collapsed Ottoman Empire had left a large number of people on what was, for them, the wrong side of the border, and a common sight here was the thawb Arabian robe and the keffiyeh headdress. Though this spectacle would presently reassure me, it was still with some trepidation then that I stepped into a whole new region, of which I had very little knowledge and no returning traveller information. Yet I needed worry not as, until my later arrival into the Kingdom of Jordan, the friendliest country I had been in so far without a doubt would be Syria.

The people here seemed commonly motivated to offer you a warm welcome and hitching a ride was so easy you could often find you'd scored a lift even before you'd stuck your thumb out. If you didn't achieve success with one of the first three passing vehicles then you were having a real bad day. Cultural strains and ancient history touched everything you saw in this part of the world, making it hard to keep your mind on the present, which may explain why Arabian deserts have often been the haunt of romantic dreamers. At Damascus I stayed at a cheap rundown place with parquet tiled floors and glazed ceramic walls that awaited its re-evaluation as something to be highly prized, but checked out soon to sleep beneath a clear sky of shooting stars, in surrounds with which I enjoyed a far greater bond.

Aleppo was the most celebrated of the towns I briefly visited, due to it being regarded the oldest inhabited city in the world, though due to its rambling over development it was hard to find much that reflected its true ancient past. It was the smaller city of Homs that rather caught my eye here, with its quiet broad streets and gentle pace of life. In addition to its chilled, friendly atmosphere, there was something in its architecture which rather struck a chord. Thanks to developments during the long Ottoman Turkish period, the civic buildings reminded me of how the British Victorians had shared this polychromatic brick style in the frontages to many of their cottage hospitals, rail stations and notably in public swimming baths. In a country such as this, with the distance short and the travelling easy, the time in passing was all too brief and believing that opportunities for return would always arise, it was soon over the border and into another country of which I knew not much, nor expected a great deal.

*

At the weight end of a manually operated barrier that marked our exit from Southern Syria there stood a blue wooden sentry box which formed an outpost to the nearby customs hall. From within its shadows as I approached, there stepped a neatly dressed officer who held out a hand towards me, not as a threat or deterrent to my passing, but in the form of a warm greeting.

"Welcome," he said. "Welcome to the Jordan."

It seemed unfair on Syria to be friendliest country for only a few days, but Jordan was going through one of those springtime peaceful periods just then, between the storms which had, and later would surround it. I can't see quite such a cordial atmosphere having survived the huge changes that have taken place there since, which have transformed parts of the country from a region recently evolved out of nomadism into a largely landlocked version of the UAE, but this sparse area then, though lacking any strong element of the spectacular, was truly one of the most laid back, easy going places to be.

On the quiet desert road into the country I paused for a while in the highly preserved Roman ruins beside Jerash and had an entire amphitheatre to myself, with not a vendor nor a visitor the whole time I was there. On a later journey I would sleep here between the colonnades of a forum, being completely undisturbed from arrival until departure. For the present though I was headed to Amman, a not over engaging city at this time, but a place which has since been commercially developed almost out of recognition.

An abridged history of Amman upto this period would depict a settlement founded in Old Testament times, which was expanded by the Greeks into a more ordered metropolis called Philadelphia; one of several places from that period to bear such a name. Through the lifespan of several empires, Nabatean, Roman, Byzantine and the occurrence of two major earthquakes, it fell into a near ruined state until, in the late 19th century, the ruling Turks developed the Haj railway to run from Damascus to the holy cities of Mecca and Medina. It was due largely to this pilgrim trade that the present city began to re-establish itself and much of the urban layout of my time was dated to this period. The place I then knew was one of coral mound hills spread with near identical pale block houses that ran away to the edge of barren desert. The layout looked far less than a century old, but having been built around in a more recent development, this is now known ironically as the Old Town.

When the troubles were raging throughout Lebanon in the mid 1970s many people were debating over where the bulk of major trade would move to from a ruined Beirut and likely destinations were put forward from Cairo to the Gulf. But all the while the quiet money was on this unheralded location, where existed a calm stability that businesses actually prefer. And thus has Amman grown, from the situation in Lebanon and similar fall outs elsewhere.

In this new looking place, which was soon to become an old town, I found accommodation in the unexpected quarter of a

83

youth hostel, which was something I then thought only existed among our damp green hills. It was the start of an affinity that would continue through adult life with a marvellous association that continues providing affordable quarters in the finest of locations. The great thing about traveller hostels on international routes is that they are frequented largely by people on their own grand adventures and if some of those are going your way, or better still, returning from areas you intend to visit, then they are just the sort of people you need to be among. I recall someone on the road telling me that occasionally on your travels you will encounter a person who will be very important for you at that time and this was the first instance among several where that statement bore true.

Hans was a confident, outgoing fellow from Eindhoven who was on his way out to India but had dipped down into this Levantine region to rekindle happy memories of the previous year, when he had toured the area with his girlfriend. During that time he had put himself on good terms with a family of Bedouins who dwelt in and around the Nabatean ruins of Petra and was on his way down there to search them out. On sensing my great enthusiasm for such an adventure he kindly invited me along, which required not a seconds' thought to accept. On earlier travels through Central Asia I had seen wandering desert tribes from a distance, but was discouraged from drawing near due to a sense of unease at their fierce reputation. Here however were not the wild multitude of Afghan Kuchis competing over meagre yields, but a far more placid type, happy it seemed to disarm their neighbours with hospitality rather than harry them to ground. Our only task now was to search them out among a billion grains of sand which, in the nomadic world, is a lot simpler than many people think.

Hitching separately in this land of easy travelling, we arrived within minutes of one another at the corrugated village of Wadi Musa, from where we followed a tumbled ravine of boulders, the largest of which was said to be that struck by Moses in search of water. We however were headed towards an object of a far more definitive substance, but one nevertheless with its own degree of mystery. Were you to write down the prerequisites for the perfect historic site in an Arabian desert you may begin with some miraculously well preserved ruins, throw in an atmospheric natural enclosure and view the whole in surrounds of near undisturbed peace. Having found such a rare place your sole impulse then would be to dwell there enchanted, and this we surely did.

Of the many layers of interest regarding this site, notwithstanding the scenic one, the area which most caught my imagination was that regarding how, after centuries of habitation and such a wealth of development by its various occupiers, it was suddenly abandoned in the 4th Century AD. The reason for its demise has been speculated upon in all manner of ways, from plague to wars and divine justice, but the one that seems to fit most plausibly to records of the time relates to a major earthquake which struck this region around the date of its abandonment, causing not so much structural damage to the carved rock dwellings, but crucially a shifting of the existing water table. In their prime the Nabateans had been not only merchant traders, but engineers in ground water extraction, and the channelling or transportation of such over vast areas. When the main source became lost it halted not only this profitable activity, but made the place hardly sustainable as a settlement. Over the fourteen centuries following its abandonment however, until its wider rediscovery in 1812, the site remained known to one group of people, who would roam here among the hawks and lizards, to feed their goats upon the seasonal scrub . These were the ones who saw themselves as the inheritors of Petra, possibly even the true Nabateans and the people we were going to see right now. It was the local Bedouins.

In the solitary local store, cut neat and square into a sandstone cliff, the proprietor was unaware of where we would find the acquaintances of Hans. The family for whom we searched were headed by a fellow called Mohammed Mohammed, which is a distinctive enough name, but the problem was that, in this small vicinity there were at least two Mohammed Mohammeds, plus a host of others who might answer the shout to this most common of names. Adding further confusion to the search was the fact that, beyond the few people in the nearby village and the local shopkeeper himself, no one around here seemed to live anywhere in particular, at least not what you would call a domiciled address. Eventually though, by way of elimination, we were able to settle upon what we figured to be the right camp area and were directed towards a white chalky outcrop, standing as would a coral mound amid this calcified bed of sand.

As we strode uphill towards this feature we began to notice that part of its interior had been hollowed out into some sort of cavern, the bowels of which had been blackened by years of cooking fires. A square carved opening provided some form of window space at the front which led to a rising plume of smoke stain, as though the fumes had always followed the same draught. Beyond the wandering goats the first thing you became aware of was the shy inquisitiveness of the children, tall to the front, small at the rear, probing cautiously closer, though not bold enough to step forth outright. Far within the rocky shadows a couple of women in black robes engaged themselves in some urgent household task, while out front in the bright sun, there sat a contented cross-legged fellow in his early forties, shirt and trousered in a modern workday fashion, wearing the red check Bedu keffiyeh and the broadest of smiles. The news of our advance had quickly preceded us, as Mohammed Mohammed was already out front with his welcome.

What I found most heartwarming of all at this stage was the affection that was bestowed upon Hans, not just by Mohammed himself, but by his family and the cluster of others who were camped nearby. Hugs were exchanged, women waved

87

and smiled, while the kids became less reticent, observing closely our strange luggage and road weary clothes. A neighbour was called across who spoke good English and we were invited to rest, not on the bare sand as others would, but upon a large soft mattress which had been brought out for our own use. As the gathering began to expand and the dark night swept over us, a brushwood fire was lit, while there we sat, slightly higher raised than the rest, like a couple of Nabobs come to oversee the workings. Which was a flattering state indeed for two young blokes who, just a week or so earlier, had fairly hoboed it from the far side of Europe.

Although we had bought food at the village store there was never much chance we'd be allowed to open it in present company, as there had already been some large meal preparation underway since before our arrival and so, while our nostrils swooned towards the rich smell of stewing mutton, the long conversations and the questions began. The subjects levelled at us regarded not our late journeys across Europe, with which we were still much consumed, nor our recent impressions of Syria and Jordan, but rather how many brothers and sisters we had, whether we had children and why, into our early twenties, neither of us were married. It was a mundane procedure that would commonly accompany us from here on, but seeing the pride and togetherness that existed within families here, you could sense it was the one thing that mattered most to them.

Mohammed Mohammed had two wives, one young and another slightly old, both of whom seemed to get on surprisingly well, at least in public. Perhaps a bond can develop between people in triangular relationships, especially if you can talk about the third one while they're not there? Along with a part time job in town he was supported in his way of life by the raising of animals, notably goats, and a ragged kind of brown sheep. While some may have considered his existence one of mere subsistence he seemed entirely proud of where he was and what he had made of the world around him. Particularly his firm hold on freedom, the power to offer a rare type of hospitality and a sense that all he could see within the present horizon was somehow his.

When the food was finally ready it emerged from the cave at the head of a ceremonial procession, borne along in a vessel the size of a baby's bath; whilst behind there followed a plate of pita breads piled so high as to near obscure the face of the carrier. As the spread was laid out before us it made a fine display of mounded yellow rice, seasoned and steaming with a heavy pour of goats stew and there we sat, in groups of six at a time, eating our fill, using bread for cutlery, in a dish so deep that the bottom never came into sight.

Many are those who measure the worth of things purely in commodity terms and nothing else, as though the sum of a good time was something you could save up and withdraw from a bank, but only a few can value a moment above any amount of material loss or gain and such a clan, you felt, were the family of

Mohammed Mohammed. Especially when the clapping, the singing and the dancing began. In a row before us, with tallest members at the centre and smallest hanging on the outsides, stood the boys of the family, with arms linked, about six of them together. Commencing in time with an Arabian song, they began to dance in stepping fashion in a form normally associated with the Greeks, although it could just as well have been Egyptian or even Nabatean. The remaining audience, still seated on the ground, began to clap their hands in time with each step and, while they did so, the fire lit a bright side to their faces as kicked up sand threw sparks into the dark. The most popular of the songs was one called Reedaha Reedaha Kefima Reedaha, which was reprised on several occasions and which, being a rather poetic love song, suggested there had been a wedding here recently. Though fairly unpolished in delivery the singing seemed well practiced and had a quality that could not be replicated outside of this open desert culture. Lacking instruments but well timed, it came across as a guttural kind of folk music, straight from the soul.

At last, as the craving for festivity had exhausted itself, the party began to break up. Neighbours who had wandered in from places we couldn't even see during daylight, now drifted off to find them in the dark. The hosting family retreated to their coral cave and we were left alone by the foot printed dance area and the ash greying fire. The large soft mattress had been respectfully left outside for our own use and as we lay there back

90

to back, re-living snippets of the day as though each were a journey in itself, I stared at the star blazing heavens in order to surface from the present and lull myself into a manageable slumber. With my mind still racing on a fuel of songs and dancing sparks, I found my lids to be loaded on springs that knew only the setting of wide awake and I eventually must have gone to sleep in a state of hypnosis, with my eyes fully open.

The following day, in need of rest, we remained in Petra to take in what we could of the ruins. While seated around the steps of the Treasury or by the tumbled stones of the Roman Theatre, we played our little game of looking down upon the few tourist groups who were shepherded by. Glued to their guides and with cameras for eyes, they had been gone in a minute and on to some other snap-shot souvenir. We felt cooler and superior to them in every way, never thinking of course that any of these people could have been as enamoured with this place as we were then, that they could have been equally or better informed of their surroundings and may have been bound by the responsibilities of a busy life that would consume us all one day. They might have been the smug bourgeois tourists with their tidy travel arrangements and the buffet laid on, but we were the smugger still budget travellers on two bucks a day and our share of the reward was far greater than theirs.

Later on in that final day we came upon the grand sight of a flat sided Bedouin tent that had been erected on the sand somewhere by the craggy entrance to the ruins and were waved inside to drink sludgy coffee from a set of Ottoman brass cups. Thinking this to be a continuation of the warm reception we had so far received, we were taken aback to be charged a sum that was several times the norm, which reminded us in timely fashion that this was still an area of tourist potential, if presently a rather under populated one and not all Bedouins were so well disposed towards foreign visitors. Despite this however it was a fascinating opportunity to sample closely the material of the tent, which looked and smelled as though it had been combed that day off the back of a goat and woven right there. In fact the roaming livestock seemed to have a strong affinity for its lanolin smell, as they may have done to their departed elders.

At early sun up the following day the moment had arrived for us to move on. You couldn't remain a guest if you tarried too long and the moment now was just about right. It was emotional for us to leave this place, as it remains now to think of it so many years later. The hospitality was pure and though the interest devoted to our lives was perhaps only an act of politeness, the real interest we showed towards them was received in the warmest fashion.

To meet Hans, the architect of this whole episode, was one of those great moments of travelling good fortune, but to engage closely with the Bedouins of Petra and the family of Mohammed Mohammed, to enter their camp, dip at their bowl and share their song and dance in the fire lit desert night, was an honour indeed.

From Petra to the north east arm of the Red Sea was no great distance and it must have taken us longer to walk the boulder strewn track to the main highway than it did to hitch on down to the port of Aquaba. Our main aim upon arrival tended towards soothing our aching bones in the warm blue waters after a long spell on the road and beyond that there was little in our thoughts. I hadn't read The Seven Pillars of Wisdom at this time and Hans was not greatly interested in this one Arab revolt in which the British at least did achieve some form of credit, be it largely in the name of T.E. Lawrence. But all the old traces were there, from the hideout at Wadi Rum through the oft harried rail line, to the fortified coastal shore with the gun emplacements all facing the wrong way. We weren't on a war history trail at present, but had we been so we may have thought more then of Lawrence's companions, a hardy bunch who, rather than face the towns' strong south defences head on, had approached it by stealth across a star lit desert, slept rough and risen before dawn, to charge in like lions as they overran it from the north. It was the local Bedouins.

In common with many Middle East places that had figured large in history, Aquaba was a town of no substantial size and had little on the surface that would suggest any long continuous occupation. Unless you could identify certain clearances and foundations, the most conspicuous features seemed to have been constructed within the present century, prominent among which were a tourist class hotel at the head of

93

the gulf (empty due to international tensions) and a couple of cheap lodging houses. None of these were of much interest to us as we were headed to a place presently better known around these parts than the exploits of Lawrence of Arabia. This was Ibrahim's Tea Shop, a plywood shed built under a large car-port, basically, which had enough floor space for plenty of tables and chairs and fronted onto a coral beach that was faintly lapped by a tepid sea. The establishment sold very little beyond very hot and slightly cold drinks, but its popularity lay in part to its provision of free sleeping space on the cafe floor, a reliable place to leave your gear and largely to the warm human qualities of its proprietor and the welcoming atmosphere he provided.

Like Mohammed Mohammed, Ibrahim was another of those fellows who drew in company from all corners for the sheer joy of it, regardless of whether there was any profit to be had. His good natured tone and engaging demeanour was regarded well by many over the years, as testified by the blaze of chalked messages written in many a different script across the inner walls of his fire trap brew cabin. The few extra fils he made from the sale of each glass of tea could not have been the spark for his lively endeavour, as it traded at a mere few pence in profit, but the genuine joy he displayed when told that his name had been mentioned in countries a world away revealed the one true pleasure of his present life, which was to share his time among as much human company as possible and to escape the woes of his past.

During the early years of his upbringing Ibrahim had been a resident of Jaffa, a then mainly Arab city on the Med coast. Written versions of its late history vary according to which course of events or acts of God you are willing to follow, but what is undeniably true is that, in the last few days before the first partition of Palestine in 1948, the majority population, including a young teenage Ibrahim, were driven from their family homes under military bombardment. By treaties drawn up at the UN, Jaffa was to have been part of a Palestinian state, but by a geographical curse, had found itself in one of those enclaves surrounded by largely impassable territory. It was a circumstance later successfully endured with great stoicism and outside support by West Berlin and Russian Kaliningrad, but there was no such help for Jaffa. As the dust settled and what was believed to be stability came into being, a delegation of former city elders who had now become refugees in Lebanon, submitted an appeal to the US to redress their grievances. The appeal ended with a prophetic warning that, *"unless the refugees are effectively resettled in their own homes, the peace sought for this part of the world will never reign, even though it may appear on the surface that the trouble has subsided."* And so it all began.

The fall-out from this conflict has now spread worldwide, with forces geared solely towards perpetuating or solving the strife, while religious views, as ever, have become adapted to suit the times. As for Ibrahim, over whose head these battles were being fought, it was interesting to note that he was neither heavily politicized nor fundamentally religious. He had no desire for revolution, nor did he harbour a wish to invade other people's lands. He merely wanted to go home, to a place that was his.

This narrow beach of sharp coral on the Red Sea shore, though happy to experience and luxuriously soothing after our earlier exertions, represented alas something of a dead end for both of us. Hans had dallied over his departure to India in a spate of indecision, which I now realise was based upon self reassurance. He told me that nearly everyone he'd met who had been out East had come back either weird or wasted and I wasn't sure how or whether I'd changed his mind on this, but soon enough our interesting short while had come to a close and he'd be on his way.

My own proposed route lay straight ahead, towards a region I could almost touch beyond this slender sea channel, but I'd realised already that there was really no way through, either across the disputed Sinai, or along the continuing southern road that led into Saudi. In the optimistic way that many travellers have I had hoped that something would just turn up, which, to be fair, it most often did; though it was not to be this time and I prepared myself for one of the only two options available. The first was indeed a trip into Saudi, not via road but a hop on flight to Jeddah and a three day visa, allowing you to fly straight out to Ethiopia, but the cost was prohibitive to the point where arrival would have signalled the time for instant return, which would have made it a fairly inconsequential few days out. By chance however a late deal had sprung up on Jordanian Airways where, provided you were under 26, (I was 20), you could fly to Cairo for just over 20 quid. From there you would ride down to Aswan in the rough conditions of lower class Egyptian Railways (an experience in itself), then take a listing Nile ferry for two days, followed by a rail journey, far harsher and twice as notorious as the first, down to Khartoum. There could be another stumbling block down the track, which I was beginning to become aware of, but apart from it being the only way to add further value to our journey, it came to seem more appealing the longer it was considered, not only for the points of great interest along the way, but for the expected physical challenge of it, which turned out to be quite right on both counts.

Up to this point I had been very little involved in the luxury world of air travel and can only hope that my naiveté did at least provide come degree of comic charm. Apart from my hop across the Indo-Pak border in recent times the only other time I'd flown was on a school trip to the Isle of Man when I was ten. All we got there in the way of refreshment was a barley sugar sweet to take our mind off things. When the flight attendants came around with their trolleys I actually asked if the food was free, before thrusting out my hungry hands in receipt. Which did bring the odd condescending look, but saved me the possible later scenario where, having wolfed down the mulch in record time, I would have waved the bare tray over my head to ask if there was any more?

I'd said my farewell to Hans on a patch of arid land before the Amman youth hostel, which was fitting in a way, as the background to where he stood was one of desert rocks before a budding date palm which, along with his easy standing appearance, is pretty much how I remember him. He was headed now through Iraq to Kuwait and from there by forty dollar boat to Bombay. As we turned away with no look back I wondered if, upon returning home, he would fall into that dissipated airy fairy state that he so disapproved of in others and, seeing what I knew of him, I rather doubted it.

*

My view of the Arab World at that moment seemed to me a fairly rounded one, where I felt at ease with most aspects of life and felt I'd taken in a very large part of what there was to absorb. But this, as I would very soon discover, was more than a million miles from the truth. From a long way off it may appear that the desert lands of the Middle East are pretty much of sameness. A few thousand miles of sparsely populated terrain, a language that would vary little across the whole expanse, with a religious culture that was suited towards a slow fateful existence. Just thirty seconds in downtown Cairo, among the cluttered walkways and madcap traffic system, would disabuse you of this innocent notion entirely and forever.

When placed comparatively beside Syria and Jordan, Egypt appears a spacious country with plenty of room in which to disperse its many inhabitants. What most people overlook however is that, as a populated nation, it consists of little more than a long river, an adjacent two-lane road and an up-down railway track, all three of which run in parallel progression from the northern delta down to the Aswan Dam. There are a few towns dotted by the irrigated new plots, plus some resorts along Sinai and the Med, but other than the transit dock towns of the Suez Canal that's about it. Eighty- odd million people living along a narrow route in one of the most densely populated areas of the world. Imagine the whole of Spain compressed into a thin ribbon running between Santander and Malaga with double the population and half the natural wealth and there you'd roughly have it.

The levels of crowding in urban Cairo could match anything throughout the world and the creaking infrastructure was typified not just by the hazard strewn pavements, but by the various modes of public transport which would weave their way through the streets with such a mass of people clinging onto them that it was hard to tell what lay beneath. Such events would present the image of a large Rugby scrum gliding along the road, with an occasional swinging figure conducting fares among the precarious hangers on. Following close upon my India trip of the

99

previous year these scenes were met with a warm sense of recognition rather than dismay, but set sharp against the recent serene atmosphere of Jordan it left you scrambling to adjust your senses and led you to wish you had eyes in every place you needed them.

A further aspect of Cairo life that impressed upon you was not just the widespread level of poverty, but the extraordinarily high number of beggars crouching in doorways and at street corners. It was something I came to think of as fundamental to the area, but was a condition, I later learned, that had been greatly exacerbated by events recent to that time. The most telling long term effect of the 1967 Six Day War upon Egypt was that, owing to the part occupation of the Sinai and the scuttling of large ships within its seaways, the Suez Canal had remained closed for a following period of eight years. The running gears of a nation's economy remain often invisible when all is working smoothly, but the moment they begin to fail the whole world knows about it. Open begging is not a condition that sits easy with the people of this region, but it was as common here as in any other part of the world I'd been so far and when you saw the downcast faces of the participants, or their rheumy eyes peeping in shame through swathes of turban, you could tell that, away from the odd tourist location, their efforts were in no way opportunistic.

Coincidental to my writing this, I have recently returned to Cairo on work business and have noted the effect that thirty years of open trade has had upon the place. With the canal now cleared and back in Egyptian hands, the supporting infrastructure has been vastly improved. Not all are in profitable employment, but people seem to make a better living and there is little open trace of the destitution of former times. It remains nevertheless a part of the Old Middle East, where the images of maintenance and manufacturing are more in evidence than conspicuous consumption and when departing your accommodation, you are more likely to stumble over the scattered tools of a vulcanising shop than you are a perfumed gold souk. As for the general traffic alas, we can only look back to happier times, before it trebled in volume and speeded up.

The one essential obligation for first time visitors to Cairo, I suppose, is to make the short trip to the outer desert suburb of Ghiza, to take a look at the Pyramids and the Sphinx. These iconic features you may think would form a central part of most people's memory of the country, or even the Middle East as a whole, but the view I generally gathered from those who had been there was that, the levels of harassment visitors were forced to endure completely blocked out any fair recollection of the celebrated items themselves. Holding your ground amongst a hustling mob is all a part of the traveller's passage rites and, with hindsight, a thing to be looked upon with some pride. But in a place such as this, with so many engaging matters with which to interest yourself, it gave you barely a moment to rest, let alone think. From the instant of your first entry into the ticketed

101

compound you were descended upon by an army of people whose cries drowned one another out to the point where you could only guess their business by the type of wares they waved in front of you.

"Mistah! Mistah!" they would shout from fifty yards distant and would be shouting the same were you fifty yards passed beyond. The solitary hope of being permitted some peace lay in the arrival of each new tourist coach, at the point of which the whole ensemble would decamp in its general direction and the most relieving sight I can recall of the whole day was in watching these hordes swarm off thither, while stumbling over jalabiyas and flailing their encumbered arms in the air.

Among the beleaguered sea of foreign faces there was one I recognised as a fellow guest at the Nile-side youth hostel, at which we both stayed. This was a young Englishman from heaven remembers where, who was as nonplussed by the whole situation as I was and we soon agreed to mount an escape to some comparatively calmer spot. In the cool upper burial chamber of the Great Pyramid of Khufu, via an upward sloping tunnel that may no longer be open to the public, we sat upon a bare stone floor and admired with wonder the millimetre precise jointing of the huge building blocks on each wall, made all the more intriguing by their irregular size and perfectly planar form. In the midst of the room lay an old stone sarcophagus, rough hewn and busted now wide open in some early act of research or crime of antiquity. While seated in this manner we were able to

102

indulge once more in the self righteous pastime of observing the scurrying tourists, who would take their photos, wander toward the bare stone walls and perhaps comment about there being 'nothing here.' Later, chilled and content at having made our own connection with this hugely significant site, we faced the bright blinking sunlight of a normal Pyramid day, where once again all hell broke loose.

The one part of Cairo where you could dwell upon Pharaonic matters unmolested was round at the National Museum of Egyptology, though even here the abiding image you took away was not one merely inspired by the artefacts on display, but by the prevailing set-up. It would be unfair to say that the keepers of the building had held their stock of treasures in low esteem, but so large was the volume of exhibits in relation to the room afforded their display that the overloaded cabinets and stone-littered floor resembled more a builders scrap yard than a high profile museum. Upstairs in a long gallery there existed some semblance of order, where the more celebrated items were held behind rope fencing or, in some instances, under lock and key. These were the granite features of historic rulers, tomb guarding statues of the dog-headed Anubis and housed within glass casing of a flimsy looking nature, some personal items of Tutankhamen, including a spindly full sized chariot and his unmistakable golden death mask, looking very chic Art Deco, even to this day.

Throughout the dusty lower halls however, fine items of Bronze Age carving, which would have been prized highly in most other parts of the world, lay scattered in random fashion, propped against walls or protruding into passageways in a manner that must have occasioned many a stubbed toe. It was even stated by some that stone artefacts had been used for doorstops, but though while there I could have done with a fresh draught of air, I never saw such a thing in practice. My feeling at the time was one of slight shock that these items should be treated so off-handedly, as though, having recently been dug up, they were being allowed a slow re-burial. But having heard recently of the modern revamp of Cairo Museum, I am left with a slight sense of loss at the demise of the old toe-stub version, as though a distinct kind of personality had vanished with it.

For the trip back over town to my river-side digs I jumped on a crowded bus and clung to the stair rail with my face into the streaming breeze. It was a minor leap into freedom which brought soon its sense of underachieving regret, as I really wished, on reaching my stop, that I'd hung from the outer window bars instead, along with all the rest of the Rugby scrum.

Possibly discouraged by what I'd seen of the local busses so far, I chose to continue my journey south by train and found in this a further resemblance to my earlier travels in Asia. At the outset of my first rail journey, which took us roughly half way down the country, the carriages seemed packed enough already, with every space taken, but as we progressed I began to recall from elsewhere what fully packed really meant. It was fortunately not a gigantic haul however and the thinly padded seats, along with the littered floor of corn wraps and roasted nut shells, though admittedly untidy, had an easy going feel to it, with a strong nostalgic air of somewhere you'd passed through before. I can't recall exactly whether third class still existed in Egypt during this time, but the quality of the cheap seats was roughly what I'd earlier experienced, though unlike India where people seemed placidly resigned to such conditions, here they were very far from it and bickered territorially the whole way. The seemingly argumentative atmosphere may have been exacerbated by the guttural local dialect, which made it sound as though violently aggressive exchanges were taking place. I had heard it said that the most finely spoken Arabic is to be found somewhere among the valleys of Lebanon, while at the opposite end of the scale the coarsest and most slang ridden is largely associated with Egypt. Which might, if one were being kind, explain the force of banter taking place here? Unless of course they really were just threatening one another.

The one saving grace of this rough riding situation in the lower class was that there would always be plenty of natural ventilation, sometimes in the form of doors wedged-ajar and more often than not, large open windows running along the whole side of the carriage. The most notable extra benefit of this, apart from a scenic one, was that whenever the train pulled up at a major halt, the opening would act as a giant serving-hatch for local vendors of cooked maize, iced drinks-in-a-bag and some strange local delicacies, for which you would search high and low into the future and never find again. If there was just one thing among all the pains and pleasures of travel that you wished you could take home and preserve for your own daily use, then this surely would have been it.

The long time that it took me to become more deeply interested in the story of Ancient Egypt was perhaps not a bad thing because, as fascinating as the subject could sometimes be, by the time you reached Luxor you were faced with a host of opportunities for getting completely bombed out with the stuff. Following the obvious attraction of the town centre ruins of what had been the ancient city of Thebes, were the uniquely preserved burial tombs at the Valleys of Kings and Queens plus, at not much greater distance, the temple remains at Karnak which, if not having drained you enough of finance and energy, could be followed by a visit to the isolated statues of Abu Simbel on your way out.

By the end of my arrival day in Luxor I had already spent a couple of late hours wandering the preserved remains around which the modern city is carefully situated and was beginning to feel punch drunk with the whole business, therefore it was with some effort that I prised myself up early the next morning for one last shot at this monolithic subject. I had hired a squeaky old bicycle and was now on my way, by empty road and quiet ferry, to the Valley of the Kings, forcing myself along on one of those classic journeys where you wished you didn't have to do all of this, but then feeling forever afterwards that you wouldn't have missed it for the world.

On first engaging with the tombs of Upper Egypt, the one thing that fascinates people above all else, whether they be professors on the subject or people who just happen to be passing and feel they must call in, is the amazingly well preserved condition, not only of the few sacred items remaining, but of the highly decorated chamber walls themselves. Having been sheltered from UV light and wind blown debris since the days of their creation and sealed since then in a humidity near to zero, the tombs, with their network of connecting vaults, are embellished with narrational images embossed, engraved and painted in such colourful brightness as to appear the work of no more than a generation earlier. Whatever level of interest the viewer follows, the overriding reaction must be the sheer astonishment of how well these roughly 3,000 year old relics have survived.

At a safe viewing distance from this processional tour area, in one of those quiet places that always seem to exist when crowds are focused elsewhere, there lay another revelation in connection with this great historic tale of ancient Egypt. Not quite such a vivid one it's true, but a site feature of which I would, at the time, liked to have been far more aware. It was one of those stand-aside spots that I would normally seek for myself but which, on this one occasion, under the constant gaze of

107

guides and guards, I was perhaps a little reluctant to approach. It was sometime after I'd left this place for good that I encountered a young fellow who had indeed wandered over to the quarter of which I mention and had come away, not only with a broader picture of the site, but also a quite striking reminder of this valley of the dead.

The young traveller, an American student, had toured the scene in the company of a local guide and having by now become dazed by the wallpaper effect of hieroglyphics and perhaps muddled in his memory of which Ramases belonged to whichever page of history, had asked his chaperone if there were a more peaceful way of witnessing the area, with perhaps a short wander outside the wadi and re-entry from some other point. The guide felt he knew exactly what the fellow was getting at and drew him away soon to a location above the rocks, which provided not only a quiet vantage point, but also an interestingly wider view of how the necropolis had evolved beyond its purely royal reserve. In a tract of desert devoid of any real pathways, our man was brought to a scrap of broken land that he thought initially to have been a rubbish tip, but which on closer view turned out to be a place where people had been digging stuff out of the ground, rather than throwing it in.

I am sure that the following practice would since have been clamped down upon, especially in close proximity to such a nationally important site, but it seemed as though some kind of clandestine treasure hunt had been taking place, evidenced largely by the type of lesser valued items cast aside, namely a scattering of mummified human bones. In a perfect piece of theatrical timing, the gentleman was about to whip one out now in fact, with a triumphant "da-da!" A forearm it was, or possibly a very thin leg, wrapped in tarry bandages and with yellowing joints projecting from either end.

Myself and those present were completely awestruck and speculated wildly as to which millennium BC it could have belonged, not realising of course that embalming in Egypt continued well into the Middle Ages, by which time it had seeped down from the nobility into use by the artisan middle classes. Such news would never have dampened the fervour of our tomb raider however, who was already off on a trip of royal incarnations and Pharaonic curses. I did wonder though if this latter possibility had encouraged him to go for something as distinctly unscary as a forearm, or whether in fact the sculls had already gone.

Until the completion in 1971 of its landmark hydro dam, there was not a great deal, either in ancient or modern times, to attract much acclaim to the small town of Aswan and even beyond this development period the project never received anything like its true share of recognition, at least not in the eyes of the Western media. Aside from the major disruption caused by its initial construction phase, the Aswan Dam has brought little other than benefit to the whole of Southern Egypt, providing a greater control over irrigation, better flood protection and more affordable energy for a region which, until then, had been haunted by frequent tragedies and locked into a cycle of poverty. Its denial of due credit, however, even up to the present day, may be traced to two significant factors in the country's modern formation, the first being that the dam was constructed largely with aid and technical assistance from the Soviet Union during the time of much strategic East-West tension and secondly, a major share of the Egyptian finance that went into the project was acquired through a recently new source of income which had resulted from an event remembered with great discomfort in the West. This was the nationalisation of the Suez Canal in 1956, by the government of Jebel Abdel Nasser.

It was evident at the time and is still noticeable today, that more praise was heaped upon the archaeological rescue taking place on the river shores at Abu Simbel than to the important works here, but this nearby tandem scheme was being aided by the more user-friendly UNESCO and not by our sworn rivals in world domination. People will celebrate the best of their own nations' history, with their failings largely airbrushed over, but though the names of Khrushchev, Nasser and Sadat have been sidelined from our own memory of the past, they still stand here as the key figures in an emerging Arab world.

On the high level side of a great concrete wall facing upstream towards Central East Africa, there lay a small wooden jetty, abreast of which were two oddly-matched craft, one tall the other short, lashed tightly and leaning onto one another as if in need of support. The taller vessel looked more like a tram than a boat, with rounded rails at front and back, covered with sheet metal panelling, while the smaller one was tuggish in appearance due to its wide lower decks and heavy protective prow. Though departure was not due for at least a couple of hours the spaces were already beginning to fill and I enquired from someone nearby which of these two I should board for the journey down to Wadi Halfa. I was surprised to learn that not one but both were leaving at exactly the same time and, for the one ticket I had already purchased, I could take my pick of whichever deck space I chose. In the way therefore that we usually did, I headed for the most roomy and sun-shaded spot I could find, before rolling out the old sleeping bag. During the long delays of loading up we dozed awhile upon the ship's deck and, by the time of departure, it seemed as though we'd done a hard day's journey already. But once the ties had been loosened and we idled into open water these early impressions were cast aside, as the next day and a half turned out to be, if not quite a self made adventure, then one of the strangest experiences it were possible to have while travelling afloat.

The most common instinct to follow when setting out across open water is to gaze into the distance in search of new scenery. It was therefore with great surprise, once out into mid stream, that I turned suddenly toward shore to discover that the small tug-like vessel beside which we had earlier been berthed was leaned onto us still, in a kind of listing fashion and there was

111

imminent fear over which would capsize the other first. Sensing a strange lack of concern over this among either crew or passengers, I looked for signs as to why it should be considered here as normal and noted, upon some investigation, that the two vessels were in fact permanently fixed onto one another by a series of plates and rods, which formed them into a rather lopsided catamaran and thus did we flounder around for a while, until the raucous engines turned to full throttle.

Immediately on the point of acceleration my attention was drawn towards an incongruous looking shed which had been placed upon an assembled platform between the two boat ends and, to accompany the mechanical roar, there now came a rather odd threshing noise from the water below, which sounded at first like the wheel of a paddle steamer, or even a busted stern letting the tide in, but which turned out to be the propellers of two separate engines, disturbing the surface by pitching too high in the water. The ceaseless racket and uncertain stability left us wondering how we would ever achieve rest while we remained on board but somehow, through the musicality of the noise and the numbness of fatigue, we managed to become oblivious to the whole thing, as we sailed on in such a fashion down into the Sudan.

As a pure journey this two day, 300km sail along the dammed up lake section of the River Nile was no great scenic event. Being the only passenger boat to ply the calm waters our craft took a straight line mid channel, which left the banks either side at such a distance as to make them appear coastlines of a foreign shore and the desert in passing appeared quite featureless. Images of a much rarer kind could be found in the evening however when, under just the right blend of stars and moonlight, the folded landscape of dry hills would suddenly burst into three-dimensional form, at which time you may climb above the pilot's wheel house to imagine, now that your ears had already become engine deaf, that you were gliding alone through your own tract of the universe.

Quirky old modes of transport such as this are often looked back upon with fondness and bring memories of jaunty, carefree times. There would be no such sentiments aroused here however as, sometime in the 1980's the decrepit combination of already worn out vessels somehow broke apart in mid water and did what it had threatened to do for years, as both halves keeled onto one another. The disaster took 550 lives, which might have been nearly everyone on board and was marked in our own news by a tiny inner paragraph in the Guardian newspaper. I was shocked at such a great loss of life, until I remembered that the steerage course was often a mile from each shore and, during the time I spent upon its decks, I never once saw a life jacket. Which is a reminder, statistically, of the greatest danger that all travellers face, namely the kind of everyday traffic accidents that occur during travel itself.

For all the talk and expectation of it along the way, Wadi Halfa was a nothing kind of place that existed for no other

113

reason than to provide a docking stage for the Nile boat, which connected at this point with the train to Khartoum. The town had first been established by the military forces of Herbert Lord Kitchener, as part of a British scheme to link Cairo to the Cape, but its original siting had since been flooded beneath the waters of Lake Nasser at the creation of the Aswan Dam and so now here it stood, a few miles from where it had first been established. A more recent development, built to replace an already recent one.

A picture of everyday life here would be a difficult thing to establish for most travellers, as the town really only had one day a week in which to justify itself. This was when the two modes of arriving transport would disgorge their loads of human cargo, a thousand people would by-pass along the bare main street and while the dust settled once again, the traders would be left behind, to either count their profits or consume the leftovers. What happened during the remaining 85% of the week was hardly worth a guess, as there was no knowledge of anyone having stayed long enough to find out. Uninspiring as the place was, it had nevertheless a name that bore real significance among a certain type of traveller to the region, not only because of its situation at the lower end of a rather characteristic boat-ride, but because it formed the head of one of the most memorable, if probably not the greatest rail journeys on earth.

The single track railway that runs six hundred miles from here down to Khartoum provides a hard enough trip as a one-off experience and a ripe excuse to bluff ,or boast, about how powerful is your own endurance. But to travel along, in even its lowest class of comfort, bears not a trace of comparison to how difficult were the lives of the men who actually built it. The course of the line was engineered and laid by a small corps of regular British soldiers, aided in part by a troop of early released prisoners from whom, as in many such overseas work postings, the least palatable of news would be held back until the moment of their arrival. The men would be working, job to finish, through this searing Nubian Desert while being exposed sporadically to hostile enemy fire. The danger of such times had thankfully now passed, though the landscape surroundings had remained near identical and conditions inside the carriages may have even considerably deteriorated.

The locos in these later days would be diesel not steam and the rolling stock a more recent update commandeered from the Germans when they relinquished their East African colonies, but these carriages had been running through here almost continually since 1919 without much of rest or renovation and still retained their original mustard coloured coating. As with services in other developing regions, the quality of coach standard declined sharply with distance from the engine, but unlike in India for example, where the upper class sections gleamed in fresh livery, the front carriages here contained merely fewer people and perhaps a half-padded seat, while the ones at the rear were jammed full in conditions of enforced

115

comradeship. Feeling it was going to be a hard journey whatever the degree of comfort, I had set my mind towards travelling in third, but upon drawing near I'd heard of another option and therefore, as a challenge rather than an economic necessity, how could I possibly resist travelling in fourth class?

I was wondering how there could possibly be a lower standard than third, but as the train eventually began to roll, it was pointed out to me that the track sleepers could actually be seen through large gaps that had been worn in the wooden floorboards. This at first was viewed with amusement but, as we gathered pace, the desert drifts that had been storm-blown across the rails were drawn vortex fashion into the cabin, which soon came to resemble the working interior of a blast shed and the further back in the train you were situated (we were last), the more extreme was the effect. The local plan for combating this was to wrap whatever protection you could around nose and mouth and after a bustle of rooting in luggage for towels and tee-shirts, everyone surfaced looking like a Wild West bandits. Whereupon all aboard, Arabs, Europeans and Sub-Saharan Africans alike, began gradually to turn the colour of orange sand.

Some relief from these conditions could be obtained by climbing the footholds beside the end doorway to access the carriage roof, which was a refresher for those afflicted by the clamminess, but a mortal danger for anyone about to fall asleep. Despite the privations inside however, a strange camaraderie of suffering soon built up among the never to meet again strangers,

116

which was the brief moment when challenge turned to pleasantry, but beyond this it was basically a stick-with-it situation of two nights and a day bolt upright on a bench with your skin and even your breathing channels being scoured with silica abrasive. Following on from our couple of days in noisy deck-class, it was a change that didn't equate to much of a rest. The most remarkable feature of this situation, on looking back, was not only our own stamina in bearing up to things, but the resilience of the local people, including mothers, babies and frail elderly men, who were able to take much more of the vexation without the least of complaint and it left me wishing, in a sense, that I really had come up the hard way. Eventually at last we reached our southern destination, in a state of such complete fatigue that it felt as though the blood red streaks of dawn were some hallucinatory kind of vision and the whole arrival experience was happening outside of our own presence. Had there not been a vacant youth hostel within yards of the station, we could have walked straight into a deep state of sleep.

Khartoum, during these days, was a quiet, slow sort of place, of which I have no recall of ever seeing a backed up queue of traffic. It was far more impoverished than the recently departed Middle East, but friendlier still and had a strong tendency towards material hospitality, should you ever wish to draw upon it. Out in the public street complete strangers who had engaged you in conversation, would invite you to the nearest sandwich stall, in order to further your acquaintance. It was an

117

offer that, with a true conscience, you could never take up, but it set the tone for an incredible ambience, where you felt just for one moment that you could trust the whole world. Traveller accounts of a later day may bring back tales of similar such encounters, but the general type of news from here is one that would provoke only despair and I wonder, if ever again, you could find anything like the same country, or indeed the same world. The modern version of Khartoum, to which I so far have never returned, would appear to be a city largely shaped by its recent turbulent history. Either as a victim of outside influences, or as a power too eager to make its own mark in the region, it has been involved in a civil war, an enforced famine and the internal migrations that such upheavals usually engender. A population once fairly stable has been swelled by mass numbers fleeing the greater conflicts elsewhere, most notably in Chad, Uganda, Ethiopia and the more recently ravaged Darfur region. For a troubled land unblessed by any great natural resources, you fear at times for its cohesion, but while instability continues in varying degrees, I become mindful of the fact that the capital itself was only founded in times as recent at 1821, as an outpost of Egyptian military interest and those civilians who came here then, to form its early population, must have been driven by some force or urge to depart their previous homes and attracted to a place that, presumably, was better than the ones they'd left behind.

118

From here on, I had intended to continue by road down to Ethiopia and from there directly to Kenya, by which stage I may have retained funds for a month of easy travel before making my customary bolt for home. As it was, the events of the wider world had overtaken us, which was slightly unfortunate for my own aims, but infinitely more so for those whose lives would soon be torn apart. A period of murmuring unrest had recently begun in the North Ethiopian province of Eritrea, which was then barely known, but would later become renowned as a war and famine disaster zone that eventually spawned an independent country. Road blockades were intermittent and attacks on public vehicles becoming ever more common, which would lead soon enough to the common side effects of civil war and the harrowing scenes we would all later witness on TV.

Our own light misfortune in regard to these circumstances was that the national through road was deemed soon to be part of a no-go zone and all those wishing to enter Ethiopia from the north were forced to take a short flight-hop from the Sudanese town of Kassala to Asmera, which was under the control of Addis Ababa. I had made a recent flight from Amman to Cairo, where the airline seemed to be going out of its way to attract my custom but here, with demand greatly outstripping supply, there would be no more budget deals. It was a situation I'd seen rising from afar, but which, in the usual manner, I'd optimistically wished aside. People beset with such obstacles do sometimes manage to wriggle a way through and if

119

you hung around long enough you might find a way to either fluke it, or even wait for new routes to open up, as they later did from here to Uganda, or through Kenya's northern desert. But for now, it was by this means, or no means at all, and I was forced to shelve my plans of travel on into East Africa until such time as I could realise them in a better fashion, perhaps with a little less spontaneity, but certainly with a greater degree of financial security.

I don't recall any great mood of despondency as I turned away northwards, only a comforting sense that I'd done what I could with my resources of the time. My recent travels through Syria and Jordan had provided moments to treasure and the final stretch from Cairo to Khartoum was beyond compare when set beside the alternative of three days in Jeddah. When mountaineers return from an unconquered peak, they console themselves with the thought that the mountain will always be there and perhaps these were my present feelings. In the meantime I was already listing my reasons for an early return home, but as it turned out this unpredictable meandering trip was far from burned out.

*

On the way back up into the Old Middle East, I eased the rail hardships either by padding the seat with my sleeping bag, or riding on carriage roofs a lot more and at least I knew which queues to dart into first. At Cairo once more, the relics did re-engage me for a while, but if there was one regret, it was that I never got to swing on the outside of a public bus. With the time of year being barely into September, I was looking to continue my travels into some new region, as there was much within reachable distance that I wished to see. I figured that a spell of work in the Autumn fields might raise some funds and perhaps do me good into the bargain, which is how it came about, through the usual chance meetings and a recommendation of someone's hometown, that I ended up heading for a place just north of Lyon and a long association with the European wine harvest.

Within the fortnight or so that it would take me to hitch-hike there, plus whatever time remained before the fruit gathering began, there was just a glimmer of opportunity to take a short diversion into a country which, during that period, had always been reported on most favourably and while allotting only a small amount of time to my passing, I believed I'd always have the chance to make a more thorough visit later on. It seems barely credible nowadays but there was a considerable passage of time, perhaps from the end of WW2 until the mid 1970's, when the small state of Lebanon enjoyed a healthy reputation not only in regard to its fine inland scenery, but for a liberal, cosmopolitan atmosphere that led it to be compared with the Paris of the 1920's. This however was before the social balance

121

was upset by the migrations resulting from upheavals elsewhere and its capital Beirut became a by-word for urban mayhem. Had I foreseen any of this I may have dwelt a while longer, but you can never predict how alarmingly an area may change and the chance forever be gone.

There is much sorrow to be felt when reflecting upon the decline of Lebanon, as a culture and as an economic force in the region, but for me the saddest aspect of all relates to the way its resident majority were badly let down. When the minorities of the former Yugoslavia found themselves being persecuted in the early 1990's, Western military forces rushed to help them, but in the case of Lebanon the logistics proved simply too difficult to overcome and those against whom the numerical tide had turned were merely cast adrift to fend for themselves. George Orwell described tragedy as when people were nobler than the forces which destroyed them, which was a line that could have been written for Lebanon forty years in advance.

With the Vietnam war about to slip from the news the most pressing issue of this day was the nuclear stand-off between East and West, with its constant threat of thermic doom, yet in the course of everyday life most of us hadn't realised just how relatively peaceful the world then actually was. With Eritrea descending into its blockaded misery, Yom Kippur only a few weeks away, Lebanon perhaps a year from the sparks of combustion and the first signs of Yugoslavia's painful break-up

122

beginning to show, it seemed as though I were leaving a trail of wars in my departing wake.

*

Hitch-hiking across Europe was a grind of a task, filled with hours of tedium and frustration, that could nevertheless be suddenly set alight by the type of chance event you never would have encountered in any other way. You could learn more about the mood of a country through ten minutes as a vehicle passenger than you could in a decade of train riding, as people thought out loud to give their opinions freely. It was an impromptu situation fashioned by the idea that that, in all likelihood, neither side would ever see the other again. It was also an opportunity, whenever you did get a ride, to meet some of the most courteous and helpful people in the world, who would steer you towards fascinating galleries along the way, or drop you in engaging towns of which you may never have previously heard. I must have hitch-hiked twenty times across Europe, over a ten year period and on each occasion I did so, there would be at least one stand-out event or a meeting with someone whose words would leave a lasting impression. Which meeting matched with whichever journey or year was hard to tell after a while, as they all tended to blend into one, but on this occasion I do remember that we were soon along the beautiful length of the Austro-Swiss Alps and descending toward the trellised hills of Burgundy.

To this eastern mid-French region it was that I had been led and which, despite the local bias in its recommendation, turned out to be one of the best places I could possibly have found. Of all the areas in which large vineyards existed across the southern half of France, the small riverside town of Macon was the one where most followers of *le vendanges* would prefer to work. With its late seasonal start and the absence of student labour, the employers were forced to go that extra yard in order to attract temporary workers who may have been reluctant to turn out in the damp mists of early morning, not to mention the odd lash of autumn rain. Sleeping accommodation and general conditions were said to be among the best for this type of work, but the highest praise was usually reserved for the local farmhouse cooking which, around these parts, was a great source of pride. On the farm where we worked, about sixteen of us permanently on site, the farmer's wife would begin preparing dinner as we filed from the breakfast table and the whole leisured-lunch social side of things made it seem more like a traditional party occasion rather than a service of labour.

October memories in Europe often have a warm glow about them, regardless of the subject to which they relate and here not least, as the vine leaves glowed like burning ivy from the moment their fruit was picked and the trellises became morning dressed in spider-webs of diamond dew. In the local villages, whenever we happened to pass, the air was filled with that wine soaked odour of upturned vats which, rather like the

124

effect of strong tobacco, created a scent far richer than its full flavour could ever match. All these sweet recollections however must be a subconscious gloss to hide the most overpowering sensation of the time, which centred upon physical weariness, the wish for just one good night's sleep and the constant pain that filled your lower back, which would only reach manageable proportions around the moment the last grape was picked.

By the time this moment was reached, after less than three weeks of toil, we had become physically nourished, marginally fitter and were richer in pocket to the point where we were now well funded to make another reasonable trip. This time it would be back over a corner of the Alps, down the length of Italy and across on a boat from Sicily to Tunis. From there I would hitch along the Atlas coast of Algeria, make some amends for my earlier underperformed journey to Morocco and then return via Spain and France, before winter caught me out. It was a quick turnaround that still felt part of an interesting journey and one that gave me a valuable lesson about raising travel funds through seasonal jobs. Regardless of the daily rate, it was always preferable to find one that provided free food and accommodation. In which case, during the whole time you were there you would save every penny you made.

*

In Italy I found much of great interest, though had little time to dally, as I was eager to feel the sun on my back after weeks in the Northern damp. Among the tight steep slopes between Torino and the coast it was still a deciduous autumn and the russet colours were more overpowering than any I'd ever seen. The small town of Bobbio caught my eye in passing and would now be a resident escape from the grime of Genoa. I was neither kitted nor inclined to explore its wooded trails, but merely blazed on, believing I could return at any time. I saw Florence merely as a collection of signs on the autopista and likewise Rome, where I passed close enough to enter the ring road, yet in both cases and after half a life, my first visit still awaits.

Napoli was a much harder place to steer away from, with the main southern highway running right through the city streets. From the hillside approach its view was one of the picture postcard type, with terracotta rooftops spread like a fan around a blue bay. Close at hand however, along its urban pavements or the climbing road that exited its far side, it would throw up images of a far more characterful nature, that stuck longer in the memory than any distant scenery. The black cobbles of its down-town thoroughfares seemed to hiss with the oil from a million leaking sumps and the two-lane national highway that ran out either side appeared always on the point of rippling away in molten tar waves. It may have been that the bin-men were on strike at the time of my visit, as many of the street

126

corners were piled with bagged-up rubbish and the turret-shaped billboards that spread across much of the town seemed always to be in a state of tatters, as if ripped by passersby who were rival to their content. The notices themselves, whenever legible, spoke of much going on, in a place with a lot to say for itself. In these former times, when Vespa scooters were allowed to rip along the alleyways and car horns played counterpoint to one another, the life of the street was filled with a distinct buzz of activity, that grew fonder in the memory the further you drew away from it. Which was probably the best place to be, all things considered.

By the departing southern roadside in the broadest of daylight there was conducted a type of trade I had never seen before in such a strangely open form, nor can I remember having witnessed it on anything like the same scale ever since. Your attention was drawn initially toward this by the presence of a number of large fires that were lit at the roadside. Contained in punctured fifty gallon drums, they resembled the kind of brazier heating beside which night-watchmen would sit in an age gone by. Camped around these however were not the aforementioned fogey types guarding work premises, but a varied assortment of youngish ladies, often plump, usually tightly clothed in the upper body region and wearing skirts that were further from the knee than they were from the waist. In their rear-heated, semi-clad state at the side of the road, they would wave to the drivers of passing vehicles, sometimes indifferently but at others with wild enthusiasm, particularly at those, (often truck drivers), whom they appeared to recognise.

There was a suggestion that they would frequently get picked up in vehicles and then be dropped off, either in the same or a very similar place, but much later I was informed that right there among the corkwood trees, would be some kind of clearing where a mattress was laid upon the ground. Around this may, or may not, have been some form of sheltering screen within which a form of commercial activity would be taking place. It sounded like a grimy old business, whatever it happened to be.

Despite the clear signs of a district in dire need of regeneration, I never once met a person from around here who was not one hundred per cent proud of their own place of origin, as though its every setback were a badge of merit and every slighting arrow a layer of strength to its armour. Whenever locals uttered the name of their home-town they would always pronounce it with about five letter a's in the middle like *Naaaaapoli*, which was commonly accompanied by two fingers and a thumb raised together, as if to emphasis just how terrific it was. There are a number of places around the world and in particular back home, where I have recognised this trait in which people believed that, despite the shortcomings of a certain town, its hearty life-spirit, the highlights of its history and most of all, the sturdy souls of its inhabitants, were the greatest there could be on God's earth. And if they're happy with that, then I'm more than happy for them.

The way on from Napoli led you into the province of Calabria, from the south-west tip of which you may be toe-poked onto the island of Sicily, or cross-channel ferried as the case then was. Here was a part of the world notable for many things, but famous, alas, for only one of them. On the edge of Palermo's quiet harbour district I was tempted for just one drink, into a characterful old bar which, from the street outside, could be viewed as a wide pair of shutter doors leading to a long counter, behind which stood an up-ended row of huge barrels painted predominantly green. The floor of the place was red-tiled like an old warehouse and visibly empty, apart from a cluster of three men drinking closely together near where the bar-tender stood. As there were neither chairs nor table I parked myself close to this group and ordered a beer. But on being informed that there was only local wine on sale, I settled for a large glass of this, which turned out to be well kept, cheap and surprisingly decent. Unaccustomed as I then was to this form of drinking I guzzled the dry red contents in about two swigs, as though it were a half-pint of ale, and swiftly ordered more.

Mid way through the rather slower draining of this second glass, I became overtaken by a feeling of cheerful warmth and fell into discourse with the three Sicilians, at least one of whom was far further on with the wine tasting than I. The tipsy fellow in question had worked a while in Belgium and spoke a bit of French which, matching the standard of my own poor attempts, allowed us to pigeon on in a drinkers' kind of language,

129

where not a great deal made sense and nothing was memorable beyond the last sentence. Babbling along in this way and being not in a dissimilar state seemed, for a while, to make us firm friends and as the glasses were emptied, it came somehow about that, on departing the bar, we had all joined together for a drinking tour of the town. I have always been a sucker for such random invites, which have often transpired into the best and most unexpected adventures I possibly could have had, but on this one occasion it was an offer I might better have refused, to use a local phrase.

When setting off for a night on the town, the soundest advice you could possibly take would be to leave all motorised personal transport at home and, should this suggestion be ignored, then the next best advice to follow would be to not hand the keys to someone who had never properly driven before but, having seen other people do it and being filled with the dander of drink, figured it must be easy. From the moment we left the raised shelf of the parking place I knew we were in trouble. The spare piece of land from which we had started was situated on the ground floor of a row of demolished buildings, possibly of an industrial nature, the surface of which was still about five brick courses higher than the level of the road. Instead of taking the one exit that had been made obvious by the trace of many car tracks, our man at the wheel now decided it would be better to drive at speed straight off the front, in the manner of some popular action shot of the time which, rather than coming to

130

resemble the scene he evidently had in mind, left us speared motionless onto the road like a builders plank.

A normal course in these circumstances might have been to have gotten out to assess the situation from a better viewpoint and move on from there, but our driver had more determined ideas and with a mighty clog on the accelerator, we edged scraping along until the coarse sound of metal on tarmac was replaced by a weightless fall to earth. The circumstance of our bowed heads being touched against the ceiling, followed by a juvenile bounce upon the furniture, was a source of some amusement for us all, until we realised that the man in charge of events probably couldn't even drive when sober, as he looked in frequent curiosity at the pedals and confused the indicators with the dried up windscreen wipers like some madcap comedy conjurer. As we careered on in this fashion toward the crowded town, it wouldn't be long before the inevitable happened.

Being unfamiliar with the right of way rules on Italian roundabouts, I couldn't really pick a winner in a dispute over priority, but if you were to drive straight onto the thing without once applying the brakes and T-bone someone at high speed, then I'm sure that really wouldn't be in the code. The static nature of most other traffic here on an early Saturday evening was something that saved us from far greater misfortune, yet this was not the ending of our night of trouble, only the beginning.

In parts of the world where people like a good argument, a trend I have noted over the years (and one which is

131

becoming more frequently widespread), is where someone who is completely and utterly in the wrong, will make a hugely over-emphatic show of being affronted by such accusations and so it was here that our driver, unaccepting of any degree of blame, simply leapt out of the vehicle and threw himself, arms outstretched, at the other fellow involved in the accident, grasping him tightly by the throat, whilst uttering what seemed the most whorish of abuse. At this we, to a man, jumped in accordingly, either to break things up or provide reinforcements, I can't remember which, and it all got a bit confusing for a while with the adrenaline and the fresh drink. I may have been on the verge of battling for whichever side would have me, until one of our company, a tall silent fellow with slick Teddy-Boy hair style and football-lace scar down the side of one cheek, saw the situation way ahead and reaching into the back of what had been our car, dragged out my luggage before thrusting it one-handed into my chest. I was saved by a man with a much better head for these things than I had.

I examine my memories of this fracas now and figure it wasn't much that I hadn't seen in a score of places before. Of drink taking over from common sense and someone starting a scrap hoping that others would finish it for him. The tall fellow with the facial scar may have told a lively tale had you prised it out of him with electrical cables, as for the rest, the drunken troublemaker and the hanger-on, who was so far in the background that I can barely picture him, were just a couple of average minor yobs that you'd meet on any big town Saturday night out, who perhaps, just for now, wanted to be seen as major characters. As much as I would like to bask in the reflected notoriety of an early evening out with the worst of company, I don't think I really met the Sicilian Mafia, or if I did it was a very low level, odd job version of them. I did however enjoy the honour of spending a night among the local Gypsies.

Around the old fishing harbour of Palermo, where small-mesh sardine nets hung over trawler sides and men rowed single-oared, silently on the lookout for purple octopus, I was waiting for sundown in the hope that the shadows would be long enough to hide my nightime whereabouts. This was some diversion from my normal routine, where I would scour the urban limits for cover and space enough to lay out a sleeping bag, but I needed to be back in town early the following day in order to book on the ferry across to Tunis and so here I remained, with some hazy notion of rolling under a flap of tarpaulin or an upturned rowing boat, like some idealised illustration I may have seen in the Boys Own paper.

On the sheltered stretch of water, two competing pairs of octopus chasers would peer into a calm pool that had been created by them through cutting both ends off a five gallon drum and, with long poles, fitted each with a plate of spikes, they would haul in, at regular intervals, a wriggling victim in a high state of unsettling discomfort. On the second occasion this happened, within twenty or so minutes, I had to back-track a few seconds to take in what the man had actually done and realised that he had dislodged it forcefully from the bed of nails and bitten it right between the eyeballs, before chucking it among a heap on the rowing-boat floor. To some it may have been an everyday scene in the search for food and profit, but for me it brought a queasy feeling through a sudden recent empathy with pain, which made me glad now that I hadn't taken on that fight.

Towards early dusk, with most people departed from this workday part of town, I loitered a while on the harbour wall, trying to look as inconspicuous as I could and soon became aware of someone nearby doing fairly the same which, with both of us just seemingly hanging, is how I fell into easy company with a poor, yet friendly fellow, of about ten years older than myself. Upon our first greeting, he made an enquiring gesture as regards my purpose there and, in that descriptive way that we always employ to save us the effort of finding new words, I pointed to my sleeping bag and made a vague sweep towards the encroaching darkness. At this, he bid me follow, as if knowing of a better place to sleep, and soon we came to a spot much nearer the road than I would have wished, yet more secluded that expected, where a low slung tent, pitched wide and held down with concrete blocks, lay hidden among the working area of an operational quay.

On closer viewing, the shelter appeared to be pieced together from odd scraps of cloth which, being largely black in colour, made it resemble the homes of Bedouins, though a more

134

practical touch was added with an overlay of ex-builders polythene sheeting. Through the open folds of this could be seen a large comfortable mattress, scattered around with blankets, unfolded clothes and a surprising number of the other cosy items that one may find in a settled home. The fellow had a wife, a not unhandsome woman of roughly his own age, who wore black robes embroidered along their outer hems and with her head bound rather classically in a similar material. She held a very new child, warm and happy, attached to the breast. Both parents were aglow in their fresh parenthood and smiled together easily. After welcoming my entry to their tent, they invited me soon to eat.

From somewhere of safe-keeping, beneath a pile of family rubble, a blackened pan was produced, of a size that may have cooked for all-comers at a local restaurant and this was now placed, rather incongruously, upon a ceramic charcoal hob. Everything that was ever cooked, it seemed, would be thrown into this pan and tonight it would be fluté pasta, stirred with a large full tube of tomato puree. It seemed a bit light on the requirements of full sustenance now I think of it and perhaps it was a feature of the time to value food more for its actual quantity that its nutritional value, but my own equal share was wolfed down with some gusto, hardly touching the sides. When sleep time arrived, which was not long after dark, I was allowed a small line of space between the mattress edge and the weighted

135

flap of the tent, where I safely slept, not so much as a passing guest, but as a briefly adopted member of the family.

On the surface of it, this street-living scene of what we would call homelessness may appear to be a cause for pity, yet there was no trace of such a thing here, either from me or the couple themselves. Had they been inducted for a while into a settled way of life you felt they would have returned soon to this form of itinerant vagrancy with a sense of relief and would even have passed the trend willingly to their young child. There was something quite brave about their defiant existence, romantic even, in the way they stuck it together whatever the situation and their hospitality, in the circumstances, was extremely moving. Many of us have pined, at some time or another, for a life that really was as free as a bird. Where you woke up each morning and trusted the day for what it would bring. Now here were two people, with another to follow in their footsteps, who would do just that, not through any thoughtful decision or contrived way of fashion, but just effortlessly and with some pride in their identity. Which made it, in the context of this moment, seem all rather wonderful. The trouble with dreams however is that they always have a rub with reality and one wonders what became of people like this when tired old age set in? The truth is though, it rarely ever did.

*

For someone who'd done the little bit of travelling that I had by now, Tunis was not a city to take your breath away. There were hints somewhere of an ancient Arab settlement among the modern walls, but none of it would match the winding ginnels of Aleppo and Rabat, or the soon to be visited Fez. The greater urban part had been built by the colonial French and with lightning speed at that. There was nothing much to keep me here and besides, I'd had it with cars and crowds all the way down from the Saône to Sicily. The call now was from somewhere along a tree-lined empty road, that would lead me to a quiet beach, adjoining a place that existed for no other reasons than to haul in a few fish and beyond that, mind its own business. Somewhere like Tabarka, in fact, on the North Tunisian coast heading out towards Algeria.

The topography of this small seaside town may have changed much out of recognition, as the only recent images I have seen of it include a large terraced hotel in the place of what was earlier a deserted and rather attractive crag. But then, and particularly at what would have been its close-season, it appeared as it had been for many years before, just a fairly attractive part of a sunshine coast. No one yet holidayed here from distant parts and the plywood chalet camp on the curve of the bay stood boarded up at year's end. The pine-strewn sands were unswept of natural debris, but the sea was still warm and the wide expansive view was all yours.

137

I had arranged to meet someone here whom I had met on the boat over from Palermo to Tunis. A young English fellow who had worked as a goatherd in Southern Italy, a task as mundane probably as grape-picking, but which sounded proportionately more romantic the further you got away from it. We'd hitch-hiked separately, for the sake of good speed, but with things here being as easy as in much of the rest of the Arab World, we made it rapidly, at roughly the same time. Having constant companionship was not quite the bonus it may have appeared for those who chose to journey alone, as our day could have been packed out with varying local company from morning till night, but it gave us the assurance to dump our gear on the beach while each of us took turns for a grand luxurious swim. After the backache memories of Burgundy, the brief cold of the Alps and a long slog through a thousand Italian kilometres it felt, while swimming, as though we were dissolving like dye into a background of fluid scenery.

Our short stay here was fairly uneventful and would have barely stuck in the memory were it not for one incident, that was tiny enough at the time but which, over the course, would grow in significance to epitomise one of the prevailing moods of the time. It was after we had found our way into the holiday camp itself as temporary squatters, that we began to make ourselves at home in this place. The first door that I had tried turned out to be unlocked, which was a stroke of good luck, as none of the others were, and so we became snuggled upon a soft

138

bed each which, though bereft of any blankets, was a good level of comfort above that which we normally endured.

On one of these nights while reclining on our beds, with the sun having recently set, we put the world to rights with our conversation, as our faces darkly glowed with what warm light remained from a candle stub we'd found in a bedside drawer and whose flame was now waning to a faint blue dot in a pool of clear wax. As the wick swooned over in its final throes, I probed at it with a splinter of plywood veneer, in order to restore it to its earlier upright position, at which point my companion became suddenly rigid with interest and shouted,

"Don't touch it!'

We both watched silently with an intent purpose, as the flames changed from yellow back to blue and the wick curled its tail like some perishing insect. Soon I was drawn into the scene myself, with its flickering radiance against the now impenetrable dark and the primeval mood aroused by the sliver of fire. There are some people however, who are never content with the role of mere spectator and will just not refrain from their own habit of meddling and so it was that the craving urge overcame me and the moody atmosphere was suddenly altered. I blew it out.

"Oh, you've ruined it now man!" he cried in a loud and wounded tone.

I was taken aback by the power of reaction. Had I committed the ultimate sin for which there could be no pardon? Was this delicate scene not safe in my own rough hands? Perhaps I should feel a sense of shame at having fallen short of the accepted standards? I was no longer fit, it seemed, to be classed as a mid-Seventies hippie. This fellow, whose name and small town it would be unfair to recall, never spoke a word to me again. He went to sleep in afflicted silence, woke up early and departed in a huff before I had opened my eyes.

I am reminded, whenever I think of this, of a sketch in the mid Eighties TV programme The Young Ones, where a long-haired drippy character stares in fixation at the diminishing spot on a recently switched off TV set. To break up his indulgent mood, some hyper active yob arrives to rip the plug from its socket and Drippy complains of the other's behaviour in predictable phrases of the time. Such wallowing moments might bring a smile of nostalgia from those whose lives passed through this period, but all things being considered, thank God for Johnny Rotten and his mates is all I can say.

The following day, not wishing to be too hot on the heels of my departed room-mate, I remained at Tabarka and continued in what was now a little routine. Before final departure however, there was one other event I recall that, though fairly minor, would grow in significance through the course of time and which began on the simple occasion of my taking lunch, at rest upon the sands. Scoffing my daily spends-worth of sardines, bread and whatever would go with it, I heard all of a sudden, a loud commotion very close by and turned to see a jalabiya clad Arab gentleman, giving vent to some fury, while standing completely alone. At first sight I thought it was just some strange personal rant, until I realised that the point of his ire was directed specifically at myself. I couldn't imagine how I had managed to upset someone merely by sitting quietly in one place but then, among the babble of largely unfamiliar phrases, I caught hold of the word Ramadan and realised my great error. Although it was not quite forbidden here to consume food or drink during the daylight hours at this religious time, it was considered very poor form to do so before the eyes of someone who was making the fast. My apologies were profuse and, as the fellow departed to regain his composure, I gathered up my belongings to scurry away, holding fish-tin level in hand as I went.

Around the curve of the long beach I made my way to where the tall crag formed a shelter for the small bay and behind this, over fallen boulders, to the real beginnings of open Mediterranean sea. I had thought here to find a place of solitude and was initially disappointed to discover the area far more crowded than the town's edge from which I had recently departed. But on closer approach it appeared as though something rather merry was going on, as eating, drinking and smoking cigarettes seemed to be the prime activity. With a half eaten tin of sardines held out before me it was hard to disguise my own intentions and I may have expected, from a distance, to receive another harsh rebuke, but I was made to feel most royally at home.

"Welcome," they said, "Yes. Welcome to our place".

141

It seemed I had walked into a veritable den of Ramadan dodgers.

The individuals present, about a dozen of them in number, were all of around my own age and at a period in their lives when flouting the laws of their parents may have brought them great pleasure. I commented unavoidably on the sensitive timing of their own refreshment and they answered in joyously defiant tones.

"We hate the Ramadan," said one.

"Religion is all bullshit," cried another and as many of the rest nodded in joyous agreement, some toasted the air with pita bread and fish, while others blew smoke rings in expressions of triumph.

The only troublesome feeling I have with the memory of this incident is that, in the days when ecology was merely an obscure branch of science, there did seem to be a lot of debris left around by these people and perhaps the visitors of earlier days, but the general taste for tinned sardines, I noted, was a shared affinity, as was their passion for personal freedom. Religious values are something to be respected in all parts of the world, but so are the views of those who prefer to go peacefully, yet determinedly, along their own way. Up the rebels! As some might say.

*

The most shocking thing to appear in the media among all the bad news items towards which you've been insensitised, is when catastrophic changes take place in somewhere that you had once known and loved. I would witness these things develop from Yugoslavia to Lebanon, Syria to the Sudan and later on through Rwanda, Burundi and Zimbabwe. But the cruellest contrast I can recall was the one which affected Algeria between the Seventies and the Nineties. During the two short spells that I stayed here in the early to mid 70's, Algeria was a whole world away from what it would later become. An optimistic country then, seemingly carefree and at peace with itself, it was one of the most agreeably welcoming and friendly places you could ever wish to find. Hitching a ride was little more difficult than flagging down a cab and complete strangers would hail you from across the street with cries of, "Bonjour!" They assisted with great patience as you worked on your French (unlike *the* French) and were more than overjoyed when you took some interest in their own language of Arabic.

Among the many pleasing engagements I enjoyed on a few brief passages through here, the one I recall with most fondness was an encounter I met with while walking my way along the main street of the narrow-strip town of Mascara. Accustomed as I was by now to unusual welcomes, I rather took it in my stride when accosted by a busy old gentleman who, filled with some spirit of enthusiasm, guided me toward the entrance of his small house and bade me enter. With hardly much of a choice in the matter, I followed through a low front doorway, to a room larger than expected, into which had been moved a single line of tables that had been laid as one, as if for some special banquet. Seated already were a local Algerian fellow and a young Frenchman, dragged randomly off the street in similar fashion to myself, while spread before them was the kind of party feast you dreamt of when you'd just spent a week living outdoors on tinned sardines. It was as though my own arrival was the signal to begin and so, on the very moment of my taking the last spare seat, the old man clapped his hands and cried, "*Manger, manger*", at which we set about the food, politely to begin with and then with great gusto.

I never did discover the whole reason behind this unusual occasion as my French wasn't quite up to the task at that time and I can only surmise that the old man had received some good news, which I suspected was in regard to a son or some other young relative. If this was a local custom, then it was a nice way of sharing your happiness with whoever happened to just come by. The oddest thing about this small event though was not so much the out-of-the-blue welcome or the tidy dinner itself, but the way of its abrupt end where, at the very moment we put down our knives and forks, we were shooed straight out into the street, as the old fellow scurried off in search of fresh guests.

In re-considering this one experience, I can picture now the many other occasions where people were kind to me along the way here, not only in the courteous provision of lifts, but in the offer sometimes of free travel refreshments in the form of fresh grapes and honey melons from the roadside plantations they were supposed to be guarding. I can feel, even to this day, the warmth of goodwill that we took from these events which, as it always seems to do, leaves us very well disposed, not only towards the people of that time but to the whole country itself, despite what became of it in the years thereafter.

Whatever the primary reasons behind the Algerian Civil War, and historical reasons range from religious duty to the preservation of democratic freedoms, it was marked by a viciousness rarely seen elsewhere, as people were bombed, butchered and beheaded in acts of rage and self righteousness to the cost of upto 150,000 lives. While feeling dismay at the scale of violence, much of it against innocents, we may wonder how these things came suddenly about, but perhaps in the wider context of things, there was nothing remotely sudden about it. Just 12 years before my arrival here the final battle had been won in one of the bitterest wars of independence the world has known and way back beyond the passing conflict of WW2, another fierce struggle had spread through the forty years it took the French to subdue the country in the first place. In light of these sporadic past events it may have been quite natural for the locals to feel upbeat about life in that present time, as you have to treasure these moments of peace and prosperity whenever you can.

*

The stark disorientation I first felt when entering
Morocco from Spanish Ceuta was something quite absent here in
this quiet corner of the Atlas shelf, partly because there was no
great dissimilarity between cultures and landscape either side of
the border, but also due to the lack of any large medina Town
that could compare to the bombshell experience of Tetouan.
Plain walled, flat-roof villages along the way surrounded by
cactus fencing, seemed hardly worth a diversion from the by-
passing road, were it not for the use of a communal water tap and
the alimentation stores. This unremarkable tone continued
beyond a hundred miles of thin grazing land until, as if to rescue
us from the eternally ordinary, we arrived at the ancient,
unforgettable and largely changeless city of Fez.

Whenever you spoke to people who'd travelled a while
in Morocco, their second or third favourite place was usually the
old-town part of Fez which made it, in my opinion, above all the
rest, as it provided a great level of interest without all the
attendant tourist-tout hassles. The ancient quarter here, within its
crenulated walls, had the reassuring feel of having maintained its
preservation through prolonged local use, rather than a wish to
attract visitors from afar and the kind of trade that continued
beneath its dim lit archways was about as country market as you
could get.

Through the warren of narrow alleys, scented with spices and old fashioned soap, there was a world more intensely real than anything you'd escaped from outside: a place where common traffic noise was replaced by the rustle of loose clothing, the flap of sandals upon a concave-worn floor and the nearby, undisturbed wail of Arabian tea-shop music. The tall adobe surround that parted the new town from old, represented a barrier never to be eroded and gave you the heartening feeling that most of this would still be here long after you'd departed. Somewhere among this maze, in the days before global web sites or even decent travel guides, I managed to find a cheap room, from which I was able to immerse myself in the hourly changing atmosphere of this place, not only during its busy trading hours, but under the closing lights of evening and in the open-up early morning.

At alleyway level, by the foot of my stairs, there was an open-fronted cafe, tiled in a fashion that had survived through lack of finance for its redecoration, but which would soon be appreciated in perpetuity. The food was the usual doled out couscous and the pale tea filled with mint leaves, while the over-worn wooden furniture gave it the feel of a well used, workaday place. In the small space of a cosy corner table, looking as though he would barely ever move, a bearded young fellow sold kief in squares that would fit into a matchbox. He told me he would listen to the wailing Koranic prayers that were sung on radio to accompany each setting sun, not because he was deeply

147

religious, but for their lyricism and the beautiful tone of their delivery. I took his example, along with his wares and was swept away in a smoking, musical atmosphere of something recognisably deep, the relevance of which I had not much of a clue.

Some travelling days later, through hills of pale greenery, I came to another ancient town surrounded by high walls. I had arrived here in the company of a young-ish couple I'd met along the way. Two Croatians in a tiny car which they were hoping to fill with leather goods they would sell at the pop festivals of Europe. They invited me along to their scouting mission of the Kasbah stalls in order, I think, to give them some strength in numbers. In tiny stores where the hanging wares seemed to take up more room than the remaining vacant space, they haggled hard in a way that gave little of benefit to the trader and, while news of their approach spread ahead of us, the tension began to build. By the far edge of the market, where trade would be thin, the vendors were doubly anxious to make a sale, but the prices they were offered for quantities in bulk would freeze their hearts. One young stall-man, whom I remember well, was loud in bonhomie greetings, but secretly must have seethed with the whole fed-up business. As we paused by his entrance, he called up from a painted leather stool,

" Mister, Mister. Yes, come into my shop!"
And then, as we drifted on by, he bawled behind us,

"Fuck you! Fuck you then! You're rubbish!"

148

We were genuinely taken aback, having never before encountered a market atmosphere as fierce as this, though not much of the type would shock us ever after. For here we were, in the home of aggressive trading. A street-level barter between confrontational hustlers and grasping foreigners out for the big bargain which, once you'd run its gauntlet, would leave you never so intimidated again in any marketplace of the world. It was the induction ritual of our entrance to Marrakesh.

In a place such as this you had to treat each separate moment on its own merits, as it could be all things to all people and quite often was if you weren't too careful. From the winding hill road down to its desert-edge, it was plain to see what had developed here, as the town had perched itself in the ideal spot for the exchange of goods between nomadic hauliers and the farmers of the slopes. Traditions had grown, not only in the local world of commerce, but in the area of public entertainment, as singers, jugglers, dancers and snake charmers would descend upon the marketplace to draw in the crowds and perhaps loosen their purse strings. Dispersed between these colourful turns would be the occasional seated figure of an old gentleman, using no prop beyond a basic wooden chair and surrounded by a large crowd who were hanging on his every word. I wondered what could be the attraction here when set beside the lively alternatives and it wasn't until much later on and further away that I discovered this to involve the narration of amusing and rather dirty stories. Had I known this at the time I may have

149

stuck around for a while to be amused by people's reactions to the smutty innuendo.

It's hard to tell when Marrakesh first became a place that was visited by people as part of a fashionable trend. Perhaps it began in the mid 1960's when flower power pop idols would come here wearing broad hats and dark glasses, aiming to blend out indiscreetly. Or a generation earlier, when Churchill would stand on a rooftop in his pith helmet to paint watercolour scenes of views half a mile away. But whenever it was and for those who shortly followed, it would always feel like a moment too late.

At one time, this final outpost between the Atlas foothills and the Western Sahara would have represented not only a realm completely different to our own, but the gateway to another far less frequented region which seemed, to those of the period, to be the very edge of the known world. Signs of this could be intimated among the musical drums and snake-charming pipes of the main public square, where business went on in the same old haggling fashion, yet in the truest sense you couldn't avoid the thought that the core of this town, its main reason to exist, was no longer quite as an Arab souk nor even a real public market. The material necessities of people's daily lives, whether locally sourced or brought from afar, were all now on sale at larger and more travel-convenient outlets, while that which remained on display here was merely a few useful house-furnishings, among so many hanging trinkets.

150

One couldn't be too unkind towards a place of such visual vibrancy and of the people I met who'd ventured this far, none would utter a word of real regret, but it was hard to overlook the unfortunate atmosphere, the underlying tension that existed between visitors and local traders, which strayed, at times, beyond hostility and on into pure contempt. To partly mitigate this, you could cite the issues of high cost overheads against the competitive scramble for profits and all the local rivalries that develop when a town becomes heavily dependent on one industry, such as tourism. With too many feeding at the same source, there would always be some who succeeded less well than others, which brought on all the visible features created by anger and desperation.

The old Souk of Marrakesh, with its broad forecourt of entertainments, was a sight to behold in the passing of an instant, but a place to dwell it certainly was not. Whether the busking street-acts were really any good, I don't think anyone had much of a clue, as you were hassled out of your wits whenever you paused to observe them. Money-tins would do the lightning rounds in both clock and anti-clockwise directions, yet only seemed to stop at your position, even had you deposited thrice already. And so you followed the practice of so many before, which would be continued by countless others afterwards. You simply paid your token respects, made a snapshot in your memory and moved on.

151

Away south-west from Marrakesh, through the twisting folds of the rather prosaically named Tiz n Test Mountains, you eventually descended towards the white shimmering city of Agadir. Here was a place that looked terrific from a distance, but rather dull close up, as it had been near totally destroyed by a 1960 earthquake and re-constructed in plain cement, two kilometres away from its original siting. A few miles to the north of here, beyond any visible range of the town, there lay a clean wide beach which would have been completely clear of any development, were it not for the wood-framed and wicker building which stood at its southern end. In the tarmac parking space around this, camper vans would roll up, people disembark from buses or hitched rides and most would stay for a few days to camp among the dunes, or simply sleep on the beach.

The initial attraction of this place was the Atlantic surf, which rolled in high at certain times of the year but, as in many another such fashionable spot, the surfing equipment remained largely unridden and the main draw was simply the scene itself, where everyone just lay around largely stoned and chained to the cafe; which is what the wicker shed had become. The purpose here, for most of us, was to appreciate our escape from the mad swirl of busy Moroccan towns and complain of the difficulties encountered therein, whilst feeling rather glad at the time that we'd all endured them. The great advantage of there being just one establishment on an otherwise deserted beach was that the hub it created formed almost all of eating, drinking and social

152

activity and it was here, within the sand-blown lattice walls, or on the sunset facing beach outside, that impromptu acoustic music sessions would start up between previous strangers, intense conversations take place about swathes of the world where people had already been, or ones where many others would wish to visit.

Around the northern headland, at the now rather more developed village of Taggazoute, there was a tiny alimentation store, from where we could bring most of the items that we needed that were not sold in the beach cafe and, with the absence of most of the things we didn't need, it made it one of those ideal haunts favoured by hippies, or perhaps earlier beatniks that, once the wider world becomes aware of, are swiftly blown away by the interests of commercial tourism. As you tried to pan things out slowly in such a laid-back spot, the time would pass deceptively quickly, but while juggling thoughts between measuring our remaining funds against how long it would take us to arrive home penniless, there was much opportunity still to laze, to swim, to pore wishfully over maps and listen, within range of earshot, to the travel tales of whoever passed on by.

One of these to whom I spoke directly was a young Englishman, similar in age to myself, who planted an idea in my mind which, in the course of time, I rather wished he hadn't. The story he told involved an older brother who, in recent times, had found himself at the West African port of Dacca and quite without searching, had fallen into the casual company of an

153

Atlantic sea captain. Whatever level of earnings the Skipper enjoyed, there was always room for welcome top-up and in addition to cargo haulage, the fellow was willing to run a sideline of accommodating passengers, even though the ship had no licence to do so. Under these chancy circumstances it was then that our friend's brother was most fortunately able to embark on a trip across the shortest stretch of southern ocean to Recife in Brazil, for the extremely attractive fare of thirty pounds sterling. The length of time the brother had remained in Brazil and however he got back I was never able to find out, as I'd stopped listening by then; for I was already locked on to this great prospect of affordable travel to a new region, presently considered way beyond our range.

Among travellers of my own level of experience, the talk at that time was much about finding new areas to roam which, unlike the trails through Europe, North Africa and India, had not been heavily altered by a traveller influx. East Africa was an area much discussed, but so was South America and only less so because the cartel-style air fares made it so much unaffordable. Now here was an answer that not only got you there for the cost of a weeks' pay, but which could near replicate the casual terms of the last great travelling age, where you could roll down to your nearest seaport, sign onto a ships manifest and either work or steer-passage your way to the other side of the world. I must have left as a different person to the one who walked into that Taggazoute beach cafe, as all I could think from

154

then on, up through the rest of Morocco and an increasingly blustery Europe, was of my next travel departure when I would re-create this one in a million chance event.

Chapter 5

Adrift

During the next recess from this roving lifestyle things ran into a fallow period for me and though it may be uplifting to recall struggles that were finally overcome, none of it was very amusing at the time. I'd figured on dropping straight back into decorating on my return, with a place at the job I'd left. But of course things move on in your absence and, not quite having the experience to blag my way in with a recognised firm, I was faced once more with the tiresome business of long, mind-numbing hours of factory labouring. By the following summer, when I'd saved nearly what I thought was enough dough, I set off impatiently for the West African coast, en route I thought, for Brazil.

Mid August was certainly not the time for hitching across the Algerian Sahara and, had I prevailed in doing so, the Recife boat would probably never have materialised anyway. But undeterred, I made enquiries further up at Casablanca, Cadiz and

Lisbon for passenger-carrying cargo boats, clearly without success. Had I made good contact at any of these points I may have congratulated myself on my persistence, but as it was, it became clear that I was chasing a lost cause.

What I should have done then was to backtrack to Algiers and take one of the weekly busses running beyond the harshest part of desert to Tamanrasset; contenting myself with a few months among the lightly travelled countries of West Africa. When easy finances became later available, the presence of civil strife in Sierra Leone, Liberia and Nigeria, plus a rapid rise in fatal robberies throughout, had made this a far different proposition and the opportunity was gone.

With the date now running into late September, I thought it far too early in the year to be running for home and so continued to wander. I crossed Southern Europe on my way out to the Middle East in hope of reviving the East Africa trip, but the port of Aquaba was dying for lack of trade and so I moved on, not for home, but further East. I don't know how I saw myself at this time, but it seems I was trying to be like those idle rich who just follow whatever season suits them. But I was doing it on a shoestring and it wasn't really a period well spent, either in terms of interest or of adventure. What I actually should have been doing
was facing up to a few looming situations in my life, such as health, fitness and useful qualifications, but all this would eventually turn up later, which was far better than never.

On my return from these escapades I felt failure on several levels, but there was never any thought of simply giving up and moving onto something else. One of the main difficulties of bearing an obsession is that when things don't quite work out, you've still got the obsession and I couldn't let myself rest until I'd overcome a couple of outstanding set-backs. I began with the usual round of applications for jobs I knew I'd hate, but then decided that, if I was to work, I might as well combine it with the one thing that aroused most of my interest, which was clearly travelling to foreign parts. I went to Holland and sifted tulip bulbs in long dark sheds, between week-end bike rides out to Haarlem or the Rijksmuseum at Amsterdam. In the middle of Crete I picked oranges in scented valleys and then grapes once more in the glorious French Autumn. The money I earned went largely to keep me alive and when reaching Corsica too late for its citrus harvest, I counted my low returns and headed back home.

Quite soon I was out again, in the company of a friend, roaming from the Rhineland to Berlin and then further on alone. I searched in all kind of destinations. One week I could be in Spain or Portugal, the next I would be half way to Greece. To those not closely involved, it could have seemed a brave and defiant way to live your life, but in reality it was a ragged existence, tending to despair. Somehow, during the course of these leaner times, I had turned into a drifter. I had become adrift.

And then, as things were getting darker by the day, they suddenly began to pick up.

Down at my local job centre, one strange day in May, I came across an item which so perfectly fitted my own purposes that it felt like one of those personal column newspaper ads in a spy novel, where an innocuous entry was really a secretly coded message meant for only one person in the whole world. It related to a vacancy in a food-packing factory at Etten Leur, in Holland, where food and accommodation would be provided free of charge. The wage on offer was marginally higher than what I'd been used to and a further bonus was that, for a non-Dutch resident, the first few months of pay would be tax-free. Skills and previous experience were not required, as it only involved rummaging through a few Spring vegetables that had been recently harvested and they wanted people over there straightaway. It so perfectly suited my present needs that I was amazed it was still available and was further astonished that the desk clerk was so keen to offload the opportunity in my direction. Had I made the ideal wish for something to elevate my circumstances, then this surely would have been it. It suddenly felt as though I were someone in a holiday poster, with the wind of good fortune billowing me along .

Pretty soon, after hastily-packed bags and a few hitched rides, I was over in Holland and things went well. I worked a few months while saving nearly all of what I earned and, as things tend to do when on a roll, I moved on smoothly from one

158

useful engagement to another. The job around the peas and pickles was followed by another spell in the tulip-bulb sheds and then, with hardly a break, a final few weeks among the French vineyards; until, by early October, having spent barely a loose centime of my earnings, I was stacked with enough dough and packed to go.

Among the myriad of road events that had occurred over the previous months there was one that would not have been remembered were it not for a tiny scrap of paper that I carried for long afterwards, in order to remind me of it. I had been in the company of another friend from home when we hitched a short ride around the Southwest German town of Freiburg am Briesgau. A group of young people in an already crowded VW Kombi, had barely time to make conversation during the brief time we were together, but in the few moments available, we were able to inform them we presently searched for work and when having succeeded, would save up determinedly for a long trip to South America.

This certainly drew their attention, as some of those onboard also had a similar plan and they were able to tell me about a local radio advert they had heard recently of a ticket agency offering very cheap flights to that region, from an office in nearby Mulhouse. In the days before newspaper cheap ads and online booking deals, such non-cartel arrangements were extremely rare and I can hardly imagine having heard of this situation in any other way than through this random short lift. In the few moments before we were tipped out again at the next but one turn off, there was just enough time to scramble for a pen and piece of paper to write down the address and, through several attempts at trying to lose the thing, here we now were, at the front entrance of l'Agencie le Point, at No 4, Rue des Orphelins. The street of the orphans.

The classical building in which the agency was situated looked like it had once been a school or possibly even the orphanage itself. There was a wooden parquet look about its interior, emphasised by the musty smell of old timber. But the feature I most remember was that a huge hall of a room was occupied by just one large desk shoved into a plug-hole corner, at which sat a solitary young Frenchwoman, peering over a small grey computer. There was no queue around me, nor would one form during the time I was there, which suggested that travel to these destinations by such untried means was yet to quite catch on.

On making my enquiry as to prices v destinations, I was handed a single A5 leaflet containing the relevant information and the return ticket prices were truly astonishing. I had always noted that wherever budget air-fares were advertised, the actual purchase price could go up by around 30% from that stated in the original promo material, but these truly were the real deal and about half the standard rates of the time. It was hard to see how any company could show a profit on such prices, unless their operations had been stripped to the bare bones, which was of course exactly what was happening. For slowly but surely, accompanied by scepticism and with a few dodgy scenarios to be encountered along the way, the age of budget air travel was dawning upon us.

What should have been my euphoria here was then tempered by some doubts as, having conducted the entire business in French, I had left a few details rather up in the air. But greedy for time as ever, I had jumped straight in with an on the spot choice and upon departing the premises, found myself a wad of cash the lighter, but in possession of a two-way, non refundable ticket from Zurich to Lima, Peru. I forget what I'd paid, as the prices are not really relevant to today's rates but, with what I'd saved on flights, I had left in my possession enough money to just about do a basic six months trip of mildly roughing it. By the time I walked away from this place, I must have run through all the emotions from jubilation and relief, to the deepest dread at what I had signed up to, but as the days went by there was an overriding regret that, through lacking the best of foresight, I had not planned things quite as well as I might.

In my naiveté I had expected to turn up, buy a ticket and then head for the airport, as had earlier been the case, but due to the lazy schedule of this new kind of service, I was obliged to wait a further six weeks before the next departure slot. In the lull between autumn harvest and the run up to Christmas, the availability of casual jobs would be fairly thin and in light of this, with the weather already closing in, I took the easy option of a hop back across the channel to rest myself before the next winter's efforts. In doing this however, I broke with a sequence of which I might have been justifiably proud. How much better it would have been if, with a more carefully planned schedule, I had been able to say that I left home with twenty quid, worked around Europe, travelled six months through South America and still came back with a tenner?

Chapter 6

South America

There were many times throughout my travelling life where I have said, just this one more trip and I'm done, but if there's one escapade that I'm glad I hung on for and wouldn't have missed for anything, then it's this one. I speak of this journey more than any other when people ask of my travelling days and it stays strong in the memory, not because it was more enjoyable than the others, but because it was far more eventful and had a huge element of what the others largely did not have. The fear factor.

The most prominent news stories to reach us from South America during the period when I was planning this trip centred largely around the widespread disappearances of people in Chile and Argentina, leading to so far unsubstantiated rumours of state sanctioned genocide. Added to this was the long running issue of urban street robbery and armed banditry on remote country roads. I discovered, in the course of time, that the politically related matters would only become a problem if you made a positive step to involve yourself, and the crime hot spots were almost exclusively in Colombia and parts of the Brazilian coast. Had I been really aware of what lay ahead on this long and varied trip I may have been less concerned with the only news deemed relevant on our far side of the world and more worried

163

about the hazards of everyday life here, for God knew there were certainly enough of them.

When finally I arrived in Lima, in what would be a Southern Hemisphere Spring, I found myself in a greater state of disorientation than I had experienced for quite some time. Accustomed as I was to having my senses assaulted by noise and gesticulation whenever I travelled beyond the Europeanised world, I found here a region much harder to fathom, where people walked past you at shoulder height with rarely a sideways glance and public business was conducted in near silence.

The city was a crowded, yet muffled sort of place, covered almost continually by a grey blanket of cloud, created by some strange collision of northern and southern sea currents. Below this the traffic would hiss slowly along on an oil spilled, half molten road that ran toward the classical buildings of a Latin colonial centre. Through the outward suburbs, from which I had ridden in a battered bus, the wall graffiti screamed for *Revolucion* and denounced someone as *un Assessino*, which promised a lively political climate. But these were largely the night time dawbings of a raging impotence, as consensual politics had been locked in cold storage by a continent-wide trend of military crackdowns.

The cheap hotel I'd earmarked before my arrival turned out to be one of those faded grandeur sort of places with a brass plaque at the door, a sweeping staircase and huge upper floor space which had been partitioned now into a warren of tiny rooms. Before attempting to deal with the town at length I lay down here on a steel-framed bed, grasped at my whereabouts, quickly abandoned the task and then slept for what could have been a day.

To get your eye in at a newly visited city may take a while, even were you keen on the idea, but in Lima right now I had not the least intention. I was more than eager and even a little anxious to confront my fears of this fresh open road, upon which I had imagined so many perils; to test my luck alone and see if anyone could understand the barest word of the Spanish I'd been teaching myself. During the day or so I spent around town however, stretching myself after an exacting flight, preceded by what had been already a strenuous hitch to Zurich, I was able to mark my time with a gentle bit of acclimatisation.

The cathedral of Lima was a large plain-walled structure that housed various wooden figures in glass processional cases and a string of poor paintings faded to obscurity beneath decades of lamp smoke. It would've been largely indistinguishable from colonial churches across the Spanish world were it not for its one distinct feature, which happened to be a withered corpse lying within a dusty display case suspended six feet up on a facing wall to the main entrance. The remains were said to be those of the 16th Century Conquistador Francisco Pizarro, a man remembered for his great personal crimes and undeniable acts of colonial heroism. His presence here, in this weird form of sanctity, was most strange,

165

for in appearing to laud him as the founder of this city they may, in his shrivelled state and grinning hollow skull, have actually set him up in a kind of freak show pillory. I did read, some years later, that this exhibit had been entombed elsewhere, due largely to doubts over its authenticity. Although it more fittingly could have been removed as a mark of respect to Peru's majority indigenous population, who had Pizarro to thank for precious little and to blame for nearly everything.

Away from this slightly spooky feature I came to a different kind of cultural experience, in the form of an open air food stall site which had been set up on a small traffic island outside the Riña de Gallos, the ring of fighting cocks. Here, among the steamy Primus light and tables that migrated wherever customers went, was the one striking feature that seemed to symbolise where you were in the same way as a gondola would in Venice. This was the three-wheeler bicycle that thought it was a restaurant. What you had here was a really sturdy custom made rig, pedal driven at the rear and steered by a wide bar connected to the two front wheels. The front section, which in some countries may have been equipped with a wide rickshaw seat, was fitted with a broad dining table, bracketed at the side with bench seating and various struts for cooking paraphernalia. Occasionally, there would be a large umbrella or some roofed sheeting which gave a hint of permanence, yet the whole thing, when folded and ridden away, would resemble the compactability of a pocket army knife. Beyond the sheer novelty,

166

it became not only a useful convenience, but something of a social occasion and I would often rue its absence in the more formal regions to the south. Feeling that springy tyre sensation as you sat down with the tabletop momentarily sloping towards you made you feel as though you were stepping over into a right cosy atmosphere, where people had no choice but to acknowledge your presence. As time went on however, I did encounter a few drawbacks to be aware of. One was in the storage of food and how long it appeared to have been there and the other was the caution required when cocking your leg over the plank seating while taking your place at the table, during which you may catch your toe-end on the wheel-treads. Which could have rolled into something on the way there. And it could have been anything.

The approaching task of hitting the road from Lima had turned into some huge big deal by the time it finally came around, but though the fear of the unknown is near always greater than the visible, I had to smile on my way back up because, despite the presence of many dangers throughout South America, this, at the time, was far from being one of them. For a capital that spread itself large and wide, the pace of things here had seemed measured at the very most, but that was all to change once you reached that ever confusing district of a developing city, where the street clutter of urban life met the roar of departing traffic. At this type of conflux, the greatest hazard came not from street crime, political riots or any of the other reported issues that were said to prevail here, but from a source

167

too common to seem newsworthy. The plain risk of getting run over.

In my eagerness to depart into the wide yonder I had taken a bus to the most southerly suburb on the map, not realising that, due to the sprawl of unlicensed developments, the real edge of town may actually be a few miles further on. Once arrived at this chosen spot I was confronted with a situation where the vehicles I wanted to hitch rides in were ploughing at speed along the outer lanes, while close to my dusty verge there came a slow procession of horse-drawn carts, stalls on furniture castors, scooters up the wrong side of the road and morning versions of those distinctive culinary establishments, the three-wheeler bike restaurants. Before too long however, in this eddy of everyday Lima life, I manage to pull over the lift that would cast all earlier worries aside and set me on my way. Riding on the back of an empty sand tipper, my arms spread wide above the cab roof and screaming silent like a rushing bird, I raced into the wind and to the point of no return.

It was with a new sense of calm that I dropped back to earth at some quiet rancho turn-off about thirty miles down the road and by the end of this first day, on a run of beginner's luck, I had made it to Ica, around two hundred miles further on. With darkness having already fallen, I passed over the traipsing task of a searching out digs and laid my gear in the doorway of a new showhouse on the south road out of town. While making a pillow of my jacket and shoes, I opened the blade of a large knife that

I'd kept with me from North African days and stashed it handily in the folds of my pillow. This was a practice I would follow on every subsequent night of sleeping outside on this six month trip; which was the far larger proportion of my time spent underway. By the next morning, at ease with my good start, I felt purged of irrational fears and ready to proceed in the manner of all earlier trips, as though not a beat had been skipped between any of them.

The thing I had not imagined before I came here was the peacefulness of the small lowland towns and the silence of the sparsely populated countryside. Between scattered events of excitement and interest, an enduring blandness would develop, but even when this were the case, there would never depart an underlying sense of danger that persisted throughout the entire journey which, rather than cause me great discomfort, turned out to be by far the most thrilling element of this whole South American trip.

Having slept at around dark I was up early in Ica and just when on the point of searching for breakfast, I heard the sound of a bouncing empty trailer on the sun melted road. I wafted an aimless thumb more as a token gesture and was amazed that it pulled over first time. On being told that the ride would take me to Arequipa, about 300 miles further south I figured that this whole journey was going to be a breeze. But this, it turned out, was to be the last of my beginners luck for a significant while and one of the few personalable encounters, on what was to be a long hard journey.

The driver was a fair-haired youngish fellow descended from the Christians of Lebanon. I told him of my travels through that region in recent times and brought glad tidings of it, not through expedience, but in honest truth, which put him in good spirits for the rest of the day. Somewhere along the way, through a landscape of little change, we pulled in at a roadside clearing where there seemed initially not a lot to see and, on recalling my recent experiences in Turkey and Iran, I may have suspected the onset of something quite rum. Nearby was a tall pylon, painted in anti corrosive orange, with a viewing platform atop, which appeared to be the sole reason for this parking area. I followed the driver to the base of a zigzag stair and was soon 40 feet above the ground, being invited to look across a plain dusty landscape, to which I feigned a light interest. And then, as the driver bade me look again, I started to pick up distinctive markings on the desert floor, running on into regular shapes. Long fingers on a hand spread forty yards in length, a huge conifer tree at an oblique angle, the body of a lizard untailed by the passing road. It was the Nazca Lines.

I'd known of this place of course as one of the most intriguing sites of South America, but had figured it would only be viewable from a circling plane. Now here it was spread before me like a grand sepia map. Further out there would be grander images of birds and animals, a human figure 200 feet tall,

170

roadways as wide as runways and parade grounds spread across fifty miles. People like me who thumbed rides and kipped out in a sleeping bag didn't generally go in for chartering light aircraft, but were I to visit this site again with less financial constraint, I would undoubtedly have spent wisely in taking the 50 quid, 20 minute flight. Yet the view from the sky would only be a part of the experience and a distant one at that.

Close to the base of the tower was an unguarded area where you could then walk to the edge of where the markings began. I was struck greatly by how shallow the impressions were, they being rarely more than a foot in depth and seemingly dragged into the earth with some kind of ploughing tool. Composed of little more than heaped up dust, they looked barely able to resist a puff of wind, let alone a flood of running water. I did read recently that an occurrence so mundane as five continuous days of rain could see them washed away forever, which conjures up a rather eerie cosmic thought. As the flourishing period of this site ran from 200 BC to 700 AD and hardly a grain of sand has moved since, it highlights the level of stillness and dryness that must have persisted here during that near 2,000 year period. Half the known history of the world gone by and barely a whiff of disturbance.

Every ancient site on earth, which has no contemporary written history, is subject to much speculation and the Nazca Lines are no exception. Theories regarding their original purpose range from the ultra scientific to the superstitious daft, but the

171

most reasonable proposal would be that the site is a huge celestial calendar, once used to predict seasonal rainfall from the Andes, which would be of considerable help in agricultural planning. The theory that rarely escapes mention however is the one that is equally the best known and most commonly derided. This is the argument put forward by the Swiss German writer Erich Von Daniken, that this area may once have been visited by beings from another world, who left traces of their landing ground and were honoured locally by the creation of these images, that were so huge, they could only be viewed at the time by people in a space ship. It became known as the proposal which suggested that God, in these parts, was an astronaut. Around the more studious types, such a theory is viewed with little beyond disdain, but how many of them I wonder would secretly have wished it was they who had first devised the notion, published it in readable form and walked merrily away with a huge retirement package?

When finally we did arrive in Arequipa, it must have been the early evening of following day, as the rush-hour traffic was brake-lighting in long lines around the streets of the town, as it probably does now through most hours, every day of the week. On the way to here, it was likely we had slept half a night on the sheet awning by the trailer headboard, which would have kept us away from the boulder-strewn earth or the cramped confines of the driver's cab. On parting company at the busy kerbside, my erstwhile compañero had embraced and then, with a rasp of two-

172

day stubble, kissed me on both cheeks in a rather emotional farewell. I don't know what kind of impression I'd made upon him with my brand of phrase-book Spanish. Perhaps he had me down as someone on a slightly more noble life-course than the one I presently was on, but whatever the reason for such gestures, it was all a bit mush for me and got me up the high street a bit quicker than otherwise.

As I toured the central suburbs with my eye out for a cheap room, I began to feel once more that strange sense of disengagement that I'd rarely experienced in other places before I reached Lima. The layout of town was appealing enough in a Spanish provincial way and despite its being a growing conurbation, there was always a fresh air feel about the place, as every route seemed to lead towards a nearby solitary volcano that appeared to fill the end of every rising street. Yet there was something quite unreachable in the common atmosphere here; a noticeable barrier that would check the advance of any expressive warmth. In pining after communication I may, for a while, have taken the whole thing to heart, believing it directed only towards myself, but I quickly observed that the rapport between people generally was not so much through spoken words, as it was by a series of eyebrow movements, pursed lips, blinks and gazes. I mention this in particular relation to Arequipa, not because it was the sole example of such a phenomenon, but because it was presently so visible here and, by the time I had ascended to higher altitude country, it had become such a daily feature as to be hardly noticeable.

The reasons behind the taciturnity of people of this region is generally put down to the harshness of Spanish colonial rule, which was followed by continuous decades of oppressive dictatorship, though it is also now believed that life under the Incas could have been as brutal as anything which followed and with this in mind, it may always have been wise here to have kept one's counsel. Thanks however to a revival of interest in Andean culture, a renaissance has begun in the area of pre-Columbian ceremony, which is gradually restoring confidence among a society which had always been taught to think little of itself. The dawning age, alas, came too late for the people of this generation and so, lacking the time to hang around for any glimmer of its arrival, I was moving on from Arequipa, leaving behind the quietest big city that I would ever likely encounter.

*

Continuing my journey from here, I had been intending to turn away from this temporary shift to the hills and to make my way instead down the long Pacific Coast into Central Chile. My aim, it appeared, was to blaze on for as far south as it were reasonably possible to go, before rolling up the Atlantic side of the continent in a giant vee, perhaps returning to the Central Highland districts after two or three months on the road. It was thanks to either God, or the spirit of the Nazca space invaders, that I eventually didn't take up this option, as it would have been a grindingly hard trip had I done so. Directly over the border, beyond a strangely fenced-in no man's land of a couple of miles, there lay the most northerly Chilean Town of Arica. Founded upon mining and with conveyor tracks that ran to near every shipping berth, it had now been developed into some kind of Freeport, which would present, as in most other duty exempt places, a great deal of confusion over what you could actually buy, and to where you could carry it.

The continued stretch of desert began here to take on a new name and became redder and dryer in nature, to the point where it was said that, in some parts of its large expanse rainfall had never been recorded, not just in the time since weather records have been kept, but in earth core samples, mine deposits and through the examination of ageless geological specimens. No rain, ever. This capacious thought rather carried on from the unruffled nature of the shallow lines at Nazca, though beyond the vastness of it, there was none of the present day romance of deserts I'd seen elsewhere. Here were no palm-treed oases or ancient cultures still bound to their camels, just the desert itself, glaring bright and devoid of whatever life that survived on little more than dewdrops. Toward this direction it was that I wandered beyond the last of habitation and laid down my gear for the long road ahead. Apart from the route by which I'd recently arrived, this was the only way out of town by road.

Had things gone truly to plan, I would have been away from here with a long swift ride and committed to thousands of miles of flat lonesome travel. A southern crossing of the narrow Andes would have taken me through weeks of Pampas straw, to the cultivated hills of Southern Uruguay, wondering the whole while when this long awaited adventure would show some real signs of life. As it was, I remained the rest of the day in some God forsaken spot, where I probably ground my teeth and cursed the few passing cars, before wandering some hundred yards to sleep in the desert.

A restful night on the sands and a clear cool early morning had allowed me to summarise events of recent times where, beyond the shock of finding myself actually being here, there was only a glimpse of Nazca and the incongruity of revistiting memories of Lebanon, to break up the chain of monotony. As I ambled back to the edge of town in search of food and drink, I considered the prospect of many miles of the same, not realising then how well favoured we could be by an occasional setback. Over toward the wall of mountains I looked and remembered at that moment a light comment I'd heard from someone along the way. A man who'd given me a short lift into Arica had asked if I were taking the following day's train up to La Paz and I told him that I wasn't. The service departed at 10 am on only one day a week which, unplanned as it was, just happened to be that particular Friday and so, having risen early, as then was my habit, I felt it was only natural I should check it

176

out. Which is how I came to find myself, not on the long road to Santiago, but at the small tin-roofed rail station, a ticket in my hand for some low priced, non reserved carriage and with this slow firing journey about to really begin.

As people mooched around the platform, you would have never thought that any of those present could be caught up in anything more vibrant than standing quietly in huddles. A few weather-beaten Chilēnos from up-country farms stood separately in close neighbourly groups, while the bulk of what crowd existed consisted mainly of mountain Indians, trilby and bowler hatted beside huge luggage bundles which, were they ever unknotted, would probably roll out into an entire market stall. Some fifty yards down the line, there stood a row of dilapidated carriages, with doors wide open and in clear need of removal to make way for our own train. But when a diesel loco shunted onto the far end to reverse them fully under the station canopy, it turned out that this was our train after all, and we piled in

The seating was plentiful enough, with a well worn plastic padding we perhaps then should have appreciated more, and within reasonable time of the scheduled departure, we began to move away at a rolling pace which, once beyond the station confines, never seem to increase. As we achingly progressed through steep desert hills, we moved gradually into a different zone of damp cloud and drab vegetation, where you could sense real mountains out there somewhere, though the base of each was so broad it was hard to feel yourself amongst them. The raw images of bold engineering were there on view, as the train curved sharply around high precarious bends and you felt the journey could become one that would be memorable for its visual content alone. But soon it was cold mountain dusk, with time for snuggling up warm. While whatever lay outside became lost to us all.

*

Deep nutritious sleep while seated upright in a moving mode of transport is only achievable I believe, in cyclic terms of minutes and it must've been in a state such as this that I reached the Bolivian border on a black-as-pitch night, at some unlit railway siding where, in perfect time with our arrival, all hell broke loose. Before the train had even come to a halt, it seemed that several people had leapt to the ground and among the scurrying to and fro, it sounded as though there were some lively struggles taking place in the total darkness outside. Panicked voices shrieked ways of escape, while others, in commanding tones, demanded they be followed. Scuffles broke out and groans ensued, not of the kind to suggest a serious injury, but more like an indication that someone had been nicked. Leaning tentatively through the sash window, I could see little beyond black shadows against a solitary light-bulb some sixty yards ahead, which glowed doubtfully orange above the door of a grey rendered hut. All alighted passengers were now making their way towards this point, while those still onboard began to gird up

178

their garments like warriors adjusting armour. I followed the now nervous queue to the carriage exit that opened to a single vertical step, below which there was no platform and from where it was a long way down.

Inside the customs hall, toward which we had all naturally herded, the air was electrified by blinding illumination and staccato directions from those in charge. A bedraggled line of Indio travellers moped against the wall, with the light in their sleepy eyes, while in the foreground, by their feet, lay the bed-sheet bundles from which they were rarely separated. Some of these had now been busted open to reveal a slithering content of plastic shampoo bottles, hair-dye and various other bathroom-cosmetic items, the exposure of which had reduced their erstwhile owners to a state of despair.

Even knowing of Arica's status as a duty-free port, it still came as a surprise to find myself on a train full of smugglers. With hindsight now, it may seem clearly obvious that people would be drawn in by the offer of cheap goods, regardless of the fine-point rules of their homeward transportation and perhaps this was the true and cynical ploy. It had the ring of that English cross-channel thing of the mid 1990's, where people were suckered over to Calais on the promise of legally cheap booze, only to have it impounded and their cars mechanically crushed on the way back. It was all a filthy wretched business which appealed to, then penalised, those hard-up individuals who were the only ones desperate enough to try it. At last, reaching

179

the front of the queue, my passport was handed across and then passed sideways to an English-speaking officer who took me quite by surprise, first of all with his loud barking manner and then his pronounced Afrikaans accent. You wouldn't for sure know why he was here, but there may have appeared among these isolated hills, a longer term future for someone who lamented the approaching end of South African Apartheid.

Back out in the cold night air and onto our continued journey, things took an unexpected turn, as the fairly standard look of our 1950s Chilean carriages had been replaced by something of an entirely different vintage. A line of ancient conveyances appeared, with vented bulbous roofs, looking like something out of an old Western film, while at the very rear lay the tiny wooden cabin reserved for our own class of passenger which, in what light there was available, appeared to be a green former guards-van with sliding shuttered panels for windows and a small chimney pointing out of the roof. A flight of cast iron steps led to a weathered door, like the entrance to some old garden shed and on wrapping my frame around its wedged open gap, I took a short step inside to find the place absolutely heaving.

The only standard seating lay in the form of two long benches that ran as a fixed installation along each side of the interior, which were by now occupied way above their design capacity and between these, in what once had been an open floor space, lay a sea of sprawling bodies, propped-up or lying upon

180

mounded heaps of blanketed luggage. From the precariously
awkward spot in which I stood you could hardly see a bare
floorboard and so, accepting the conditions of several earlier
such train rides, I simply lowered my luggage into the small
space between my feet and sat on it.

It had seemed a long night already, with only half of it
gone, but things were not about to pass away peacefully just yet.
Our recommencing journey, by slightly different mode, was
accompanied by a surprisingly heavy clunking noise from
beneath the carriage floor and I figured we were running over a
broadly extended range of track-crossing points, but when this
ran on far beyond the normal distance, you came to realise that,
not only were we riding on a rather ill-maintained rails, but the
carriage we were in had absolutely no wheel suspension
whatsoever. To avoid the vibration was completely impossible,
for while seated straight, the shock would run right up your spine
and when taking respite to lean on folded arms, it would merely
shortcut directly from your feet to your forehead. But
eventually, through a state of noise numbness, we were able to
drift into some bearable kind of slumber.

It would be somewhere in this zone, partly asleep and
half comfortable, perhaps even beginning to warm to my
surroundings, that I became gradually aware of a whisper that
was running around the carriage; which turned quickly into a
rustle of activity and then a full blown panic. In the turn of an
instant, the previously docile crowd had leapt into a wild frenzy

181

of luggage re-arrangement, where bathroom consumables were stuffed up shirts, down bras, inside sleeves and under bowler hats. The dreaded word, passed from one corner to another, was "*La Contra*" and beyond a last second or two of tense silence, we were soon to find out just who these feared *Contra* were, as in they burst, three young men in faded blue uniforms, trampling in boots over people on the floor and grasping aggressively at personal belongings. Carefully wrapped bundles were torn apart, with their contents spilled across the floor and any items deemed to be above the listed quota were simply spirited away. A chain of customs men waited by the carriage end door, forming a handball gang for this profitable nights' work. I most vividly recall one frail old gent in a straw hat, holding on to one end of his sheet-bundle as these rough types hauled it away from him in a series of wild tugs. His piteous cries I can still plainly hear, shouting, "No! No! No!"

Once *la Contra* had pillaged as much as each could physically carry, they made their rapid escape, away from the whimpering poor and the scene of their further impoverishment. In exiting single file through the door by which they had entered, they had to step over my shoulder in order to continue along the aisle and as I was naively less obsequious than the local Indians in retreating from their path, the last man out took exception and aimed a short kick toward the base of my back. With barely space to afford a decent back-swing it was not a kick to cause great damage or even severe pain, but loaded with just the right

182

amount of contempt, as though moving a dog away from the fireplace.

At last, as the dust from the raid had settled and members of the third class poor had been left poorer still, those who had been fortunate to remain undisturbed, with their soap-bar shaped breasts and shampoo bottles for shoulder pads, began now to adjust to a more comfortable passage and sighs of relief were expressed for most of the way round. For those who had not escaped the damage however, such as the now distraught old man, it was a time to contemplate their ruin right before the public gaze and after one glance in their direction, you knew you had to look away.

Though we were not then familiar with the notion that a short burst of power-rest may be as nutritious as an hour of normal sleep, we nevertheless must have used it to survive the cold hours of night, in the midst of which we met with one further encounter that, following what had gone before, was taken largely in stride by the now beyond caring passengers. What may initially have alerted us to a change in circumstance was not the dragging sound that our carriage made as it veered along the railway track, but the moment of priceless silence that immediately followed it. We had come to rest on some high windless moor, perhaps in the lee of sheltering hills and the peaceful relief seemed to send us, for a while, into a deeper slumber. When I eventually did look up, I noticed that the sleepy crowd had barely raised a hat brim from their eyes and, with torch lights now flashing outside, I must have been the only one to depart my seating place to go and take a look. In a becalmed atmosphere, beside the darkened track, there stood a small group of mechanically-minded men, who knew exactly how things presently stood. The rear part of our train had become de-railed.

Dragged offline in a black middle of nowhere, we at least had the benefit of some quiet rest to catch up on until, an hour or two later, another train rolled along from the rear, pushing some kind of crane and a row of bright arc lights. A degree of loud maintenance was carried out and before long we had the very odd sensation of being hoisted aloft, to sway for a while in mid-air, before being lowered and crowbar-guided onto the recently departed tracks. It was a rescue mission the type of which I had never heard before, nor ever have since. A passenger public service run off line, lifted back into position and with about sixty people still seated onboard, not one of whom had bothered to disembark.

Underway once more, we could rest in the feeling that all was back to normal by the reassuring sound that had accompanied our initial departure from the border. That of the loudly reverberating din which had emanated from the bed of the railway track and resounded now against the roof of your scull. Clunk, clunk, clunk, all the way to La Paz.

On the train's arrival at its upper terminus, there was barely a trace of any large city, or even that of an outer suburb. A single-house rail station backed onto a high open plain, with a few widely interspersed peaks looking like sails in the distance. As we descended our carriage at a point where the platform didn't reach, I recall seeing a small brass plaque attached to the entrance to the next compartment, to say it had been built in Gloucester, England in 1905. It was a slightly better kept and more modern version than the one we had travelled in and marked the divide from third into second class.

Beyond the end of tracks, where building gave way to spare ground, a line of collective minibuses faced away into some unseen distance and on walking towards these, with the train behind us, we became suddenly aware of a vast spread of boiling mist that lay in the form of a lake just a few feet below our altitude. It was unusual to see such a sight devoid of protruding hills or church towers and being the widest such expanse of earthly space we had seen since departing the desert, it looked most strange. At last, in a proper padded seat with an upright back, like the ones to which we'd once been accustomed, we set off for the shore of this sea of cloud whereupon arriving, we plunged straight in at a steep angle to become embroiled in a grey landscape of winding road and tin-shack housing, shining dull and dripping with fog. Following a few doubtful moments over whether this had all been worthwhile, the view below us suddenly cleared in a parting whisp, the floor of mist became a heavy roof and in the great bowl 3,000 feet below us appeared the nearest perfect landscape of urban terracotta you could possibly imagine and one of the most stunning city entrances in the world. Which was a far grander impression than any it would make on us at ground level as it happened.

Down eventually in the heart of La Paz, I took a room at some traveller place I'd heard of somewhere down the trail, which was usually the way it went on these plan as you go kind of trips. To reach there from bus stop square you had to hike up a cobbled hill, weave across a crowded market and then climb three flights of hotel stairs which, after an overnight ride on bare floorboards, preceded by a doss in the Arica desert, made you sharply aware of the effect that altitude could have when travelling directly from sea level to twelve thousand feet. Becoming breathless in the weirdest way I can remember, I staggered the last few steps up to my quarters in a collective shared room containing three other beds. Not caring who or even what occupied them, I spread myself on the luxurious cotton mattress and slept, for once without a dream. When I re-awoke it was already mid evening and the room was beginning to stir with resident guests.

On a journey not packed with foreign visitors it is easy to remember who you meet, but I would have remembered these people anyway, as they were a fairly eclectic and in one or two cases, an interesting bunch. A young Swiss German fellow, who looked like Carlos Santana, had bought himself a new guitar that he was studiously learning to play. Nothing wrong with that of course and a great way to chill and entertain. Except he played nothing more than the same twelve-bar turnaround over and over

186

again, without trace of variation, for three days! He told me of some urban myth he'd heard about a bunch of Soviet soldiers, who had, for unknown reasons, left blunt razor blades in the wooden model of a pyramid and returned a day or so later to find them amazingly restored into a brand new sharpness, as if they'd only just left the factory. By-passing the possibility that they had been swapped in the night by some practical joker, this suggested that a miracle power had been at work and the people of the Egyptian Bronze Age had been in possession of some lost knowledge, which modern humans had become somehow unaware of where the lost bit had been left. With thoughts of his return home, he was in a mind now to build, or rather have built, a house-sized wooden pyramid and live there the rest of his life, no longer with a head full of sheep wool and ganja, but waking up sharp as a Russian razor blade each day.

A French Canadian woman, with braids in her fair hair, spoke English very well but with the heaviest of accents, maintained as she said, 'so that people will know I am French'. She could play guitar far better than the Swiss bloke and sang a song called, 'Esta La Vida,' which made every aspect of life seem crushingly fatalistic. Through means of astrology, she said, it was possible to define someone's personality by merely connecting it to their date of birth. Which left us wondering whether the wisdom learnt through life-experience was now worth anything at all.

Finally, as if accustomed to being late, in-walked a third person, small, breathless, habitually rushed in his manner who, while remaining still, was not especially striking in appearance, but who had a certain air of involvement that had you thinking of him many years afterwards, hoping that it had all turned out for the best. Mike was from Alberta, Canada and had described himself as an organiser on campaigns connected to public rights issues. His most recent involvement in this field had been with a conflict of interest between some indigenous peoples on a Canadian reservation and the planning team of a proposed hydro electric dam. This case had resulted in the project nevertheless going ahead, but in a far more sympathetic way than it normally would, which is the usual objector's victory. In tandem with this activity, he had produced a dozen or so articles for a liberal Toronto newspaper, a practice which he had hoped to continue on his travels through Latin America and though I wouldn't have put him down as particularly left wing in a change-the-world sense, he was very much drawn towards struggles between the big and the small, the powerful and the weak, and those with a loud voice, against those with none at all.

Throughout the countries of South America of this time, where only one state, Ecuador, had a democratically elected government, there would be acres of ground for research into such matters, provided you were willing to take on the high risks involved. Mike, it seemed, had been more than willing in this respect, especially right here in Bolivia, where he'd gathered the most dramatic tales in some of the most hair-raising circumstances, which usually produce, in their way, the richer sources of copy. He had liaised at secret rendezvous with outlawed radicals, been driven blindfold in the backs of cars and met with organised or solitary rebels who had been pushed to extremes by that one powerful source which is a complete mystery to their enemies; the harsh and simple facts of their own daily lives.

He read the tracts of interviews he'd carried out in recent days, some of which were obtained in places quite close to this room. Their words would be hard to corroborate in terms of source reliability, but having spent some time with Mike, I could safely vouch for his own degree of plain honesty. Their opening tone went right to the heart of the matter.

"It was a torture. It was a terrible torture. They bound my hands and feet. Put a hood over my head. Immersed me in a water tank until I thought I would die. They touched me with live electrical wires. Burned me with lighted cigarettes".
It went on in the same disturbing, yet fascinatingly intense manner.

This small revealing sample was merely a pocket extract of a much larger body of material that Mike had gathered from the troubled world into which he had willingly descended. In identifying himself closely with these areas, carrying hand written notes about his person, even reading them aloud to complete strangers like myself and then publishing abroad under his own name, he was putting himself at great and some might say senseless risk. I wondered later if those for whom he put his own neck on the block would do the same for him, should the relevant circumstances arise, and I rather doubted it.

To some of this local area, the Mike of that time may have appeared as an inexperienced meddler and someone who was very dangerous to be around, while others might have viewed him as well intentioned and fairly harmless. In his own mind however he could have been aiming at something altogether more exalted. It could be that the zeal which motivated him was driven by an heroic craving, to be liked not just as one of a crowd but to an elevated degree and for everyone to recognise what a terrific good guy he was. The thing which led me to believe this was the most innocent of several tales that Mike told me, relating this time to a small encounter at a country market, up in the hills of Guatemala.

Amid the usual scene of blanket stalls and traders in bright shawls, there was one lady seated behind a huge pile of carrots. For some way to the left and right of where she was situated there were several other women similarly clad and selling exactly the same thing. This led Mike to the question we all have asked in these kind of circumstances, as to how a person could make a worthwhile living in the face of so much nearby competition? Filled with sympathy, as was the way of his nature, Mike wandered over to the lady and, in the grand spirit of generosity said,

'Señora, I will buy all of your carrots. Every single one.'

He didn't even know what he was going to do with them had he bought them. Probably hand them out free to passers-by, which could, I suppose, have had some temporary effect on the local market economy. But it seemed like the right thing to him at the time, with not a negative side to it. That was when the lady brought him down from the clouds with a shake of the head and a pitying expression of her own.

"Hombre", she said, "don't be silly. What am I going to do for the rest of the day if I sell you all my carrots"?
She obviously enjoyed the company, maybe even the banter of being there among her mates, some of whom may also have been her relatives and it could have been the perfect escape from all the other aspects of her daily home-life. Mike was quick to laugh at this and recognise that a mean-well attempt at improving someone's lot may actually be taking them away from a circumstance in which they largely prefer to remain.

On a following morning, moved by some conversation we'd had on a previous day, Mike and I took a short bus ride to the dry edge of town, in order to hunt down and bring back a rather large piece of cactus. Amongst others in our room, we had been discussing some types of ancient mountain ceremonies, which tended towards the use of local plant life in inducing an out of body, possibly even an out of mind experience. This practice at one time was considered to be of some spiritual

191

significance, but when popularised by writers such as Aldous Huxley and later Carlos Castaneda, it was merely seen as a good way of getting wasted.

Being as we were, around the culture where these things commonly occurred, we felt compelled to locate this famous substance, with a vague intent that one of us might actually try it. Mike himself wasn't too sure about this, but acquainted as he was with many indigenous ways, he knew not only where to procure a prime crop of this living product, but also how to extract, in the safest manner, the one ingredient that made it work. And so it was that we found ourselves now in a parched outer district, within a low hollow by the National University, where there existed a distinct stretch of landscape known as the Valley of the Moon. Named, quite clearly, before the surface of the Moon became better identified, it resembled more the backdrop to a clichéd cowboy film than anything else, with dry-gulch cliffs and spiky clusters of vegetation as high as a man on horseback.

Our aim here, in one of the quieter spots we could find, was to search among this tall maze for a plant in full flower, which was no easy task in light of the several-year breeding cycle of this species, but upon our being successful we were then to take either a stubbly button from the end of a huge branch, or failing this, to dislodge the entire branch itself, which we would then transport back to our room. Comparing this now to the pruning of a simple house cactus you begin to appreciate the difficulty produced by scale and having dealt with the elevation,

192

the four inch spikes and the toughness of the material, it felt about as easy as stealing eggs from a crocodile's nest. Eventually however, having braved a few sharp scratches and with a determination born of having come this far, we were able to dislodge, through sweat and pain, a piece about the size of a muscular upper arm. With this at last in our possession, we were disturbed for a moment by a college janitor wanting to know our business and with some personal doubts over our legal position, we wrapped it swiftly in an old denim jacket I'd had with me, before scarpering swiftly to the return bus-stop. With a little more presence of mind here we may have retired to some other quiet place where, with a careful bit of carvery, we could have removed some of the cruel armour that protected our specimen. But things being as they were, with a perceived threat to our rear and the bus nearly upon us, we merely made a dash for the approaching downtown service and dived onboard.

Reluctant as I am, in these times of insurance liabilities, to offer candid safety advice, I still feel sure in saying that it is not the best idea to get on a crowded minibus, standing room only, travelling through lurching traffic, whilst hanging one-handed onto a giant log of cactus. As our vehicle accelerated away from its standing start, those of us unable to obtain seats were pitched rearwards like ship's passengers in the face of a giant wave, but then in the loss of momentum caused by change into second gear, we were propelled suddenly forwards, some in a controlled fashion and others, particularly those with hands

193

pre-occupied, catapulted ahead, directly into the person in front of them. In my case this was a heavy-skirted woman in traditional clothing who let out a loud yell, before turning to face me with an angry burning glare.

Apologies were profuse as I scrambled to hold the offending object as far out of harm's way as were possible, but now, in coincidence with alerting one passenger to the nature of our hazardous cargo, I noted that, through the flimsiness of my jacket material and the tightness with which I held it wrapped around my fist, the cactus spikes were starting to protrude in the form of a medieval barb and a large zone of empty space began to appear around us. I tried resting it on the floor, where it slid with the changing speed of the bus, then in an overhead luggage rack, which was marginally too full. I placed the load on top of a seat headrest, from which point I nearly crowned the gentleman seated below and was eventually forced to hold the item at the lofted height of some shiny pole, trembling in my arms, failing of strength and praying to reach journey's end before getting lynched.

At last, along the spacious town street, we raced towards our room with the prize carried at distance like a full pail of water, but as I passed a stranger by a narrow corner I held it more closely, to avoid a collision and in doing so, received my own share of what the lady
on the bus must have felt. Beginning to pace uphill, with my arms and legs at a healthy stride, I swung the item back hard to

194

collide with my upper thigh, which gave a sensation rather like that of being stabbed. Not just with a pin or one of those fluffy-ball cacti that you would see on bathroom window ledges. Just stabbed.

In the relief shelter of our own room we recovered enough composure to settle down for the evening, but impatience got the better of us and we were soon running through the process that Mike had somehow acquired knowledge of. It was a complex business that would be highly unwise to attempt by means of mere trial and error, which required the removal of all spikes (better late than never) and the most meticulous separation of each distinguishable layer of the plant material. Without giving out too much instructive detail, what I need to explain here is that, once the brittle outer layer of the cactus had been removed (without trapping it painfully down the back of your fingernails, as we were prone to do), the thing most importantly required was to scrape away the gravelly white inner core, which contained the poison strychnine. With this in mind, it might be well to question now whether it really is a good idea to risk the hazard of an ingested substance of unknown perceptive or bodily affect, but as it turned out, the greatest danger was posed not by the toxicity or potency of the material itself, which was eventually predictable enough, but by the challenging circumstances of the place in which we found ourselves.

At this part in our co-operation, Mike and I went off along different lines. I think he was vaguely interested in the drug culture thing as a fashionable trend, but wisely preferred to keep himself in better shape and with the clandestine-political business going on in the background he would require full concentration at all times. And so, having carried out the preparations and reduced our visibly threatening item to a few limp marzipan-like strips lying on a cold windowsill, there they remained, in the hope that a pale sun would dry them out. Which, at this high altitude, of course it never did.

The whole thing might have gone down as just another mildly eventful day, with no greatly memorable outcome had not, upon the point of someone's departure, a certain new guest checked into our four-bed room. This was a young Brazilian named Pepe, who had travelled several days from his home in Rio and spoke in hallowed tones of something called '*El Tren de la Muerte.*' The Death Train. Here was a means of transport which, were it anywhere near your line of travel, you would just have to take, be it only for the sheer merit of association. Although the actual journey, in normal mode, was no more of a risk than many already mentioned. Its present notoriety, according to Pepe, was due to the popular practice among some people of riding on the roof in order to escape the stifling carriage heat on long hauls through the jungle. On a journey lasting through day and night, this would lead to bouts of idle dozing, with the inevitable results. (A note I discovered further to this relates to a yellow fever epidemic in the 19th century, where trains exiting the jungle regions were commonly loaded with corpses, but the update version was the one more relevant to people of today). Pepe told us a tale of quite recent times, where a fellow had rolled from the roof in a state of slumber and was quite fortunate to land, barely injured, into a patch of soft ground. Being something of an outdoorsman, he had managed to survive alone in the deep forest for nearly a week until the returning train picked him up. Which resulted, for him, in a rather enjoyable and sometime lucrative spell of national celebrity.

Our newly arrived guest from Brazil made his self easily at home in our company, as most people usually did and before long, considering perhaps that I was male and European, he began to speak to me of his passion for Brazilian football, then in its highest ascendancy. It was rare to talk of Brazilian sport in these days without soon bringing up the name of Pele, regarded by many as football's best ever player, but in the strongly expressed view of Pepe, during his time of watching the game Pele was not even the best player in Brazil. That honour, he said, should have gone to Garrincha, a skilful winger of Botafogo FC, a major force in Brazil's 1958 and '62 World Cup wins, who suffered from inherent ailments as a child, had tough luck with injuries and was probably just as ill-served by poor medical and personal advice.

I was fortunate, as it happened, to see them in the same side at Goodison Park in the '66 World Cup, a game in which they both scored from free-kicks and on that performance it was hard to put a leaf between them. But Pele's career went on much longer, with a greater degree of consistency and it was he who was rightly judged to have made the most indelible mark upon the world game. In team sport however, where people form preferences for one side or another, it is common for unbreakable attachments to develop and it came as no surprise to later discover that Pepe was, in fact, a die-hard supporter of Botofogo FC.

Comfortable soon with our surroundings, Pepe began to mooch around the room and, on finding his way over to the window sill, came upon our carefully prepared handiwork of earlier times. On noticing the strips of cactus, in what for most would have been an unfamiliar form, a smile of recognition came across his face. 'Ah, San Pedro,' he said, giving the substance its common local name and began to prod with his finger for its state of readiness. He asked of our plans regarding this material and on being told of our mini adventure at the town's edge, Mike's reluctance to continue the business any further and my own wish to experiment but only if accompanied, he, the barely met stranger unbeknown to me an hour before, said, 'OK. I'll do some with you tomorrow then.' And so we did.

When attempting to ingest a material that nature has deemed to be inedible for humans, it would always be best to proceed with the aid of some kind of masking agent, or a disguise against the taste. Shredded fruit might help, or a slice of honeyed bread and this is where a bit of careful foresight might

198

have helped us. Without even a dry crust to accompany them, our six slabs of near-toxic vegetation presented a most unappetising sight, but having come this far, there was to be no whimping out and so, like a couple of starving pelicans, we simply leant back our heads, tipped the stuff in and shook it down, like something likely to escape at any second. My God, it was foul!

Even while strongly overriding the senses and with a determination to chew for dear life, it was still a race to get it all past the taste organs, but eventually, with faces screwed in anguish and taking desperate gasps for fresh air, it somehow all went down. Having nothing with which to compare it, either before or ever since, its flavour would be hard to describe, but the digestive effect was somewhere between eating raw tree-bark and drinking washing up liquid. Pepe ran to throw his up straight away but I, like someone who'd paid good coin for a posh crap meal, hung doggedly on until the shuddering urges had passed.

Once the worst of the nausea had begun to clear we decided, as recuperating people often do, to take a walk outside in the cool air. Time had passed enough and, by our own reckoning, the Doors of Perception should be opening wide pretty soon. Along the damp cobbled streets we examined our senses for a sign that some change was taking place. Perhaps a twinkle-reflection that hung in the air a trace longer than normal, or a dash of colour shining brighter than daylight, but as we wandered we began to tire at the taxing high altitude until, during

199

a moment's pause, we turned to look at one another, seeming to realise at the same time that it was a false start. Nothing was happening. Nor was it ever likely to do so. It was all a great disappointment.

With abject shrugs and philosophical smiles, we decided to turn it all in. Pepe to some other business he'd had in mind and I to a refreshment stall on the way back to our room. I was beginning to cramp now, in a slightly unusual way and, in order to take a casual breather, I parked myself upon some stone steps overlooking the Plaza de San Francisco. While huddled there, I came to rest my gaze upon a small group of women traders who were seated on the open pavement nearby. Their bright patterned shawls gleamed vibrant as though lit from within and their long hair flowed like freshly poured black paint. In the recent rain pools close to where they sat, the colour from their clothing ran in a snaking maze, as though oil and water had caught the sun. My tired spirits were lifting now way beyond common optimism, to a point where I felt this to be the best trip ever made, to the most magical of all places.

A cop directing traffic in the middle of the road had earlier appeared a shade menacing, but now he seemed to wave his arms in humorous fashion at the passing cars and swivel his hips like the singer in some camp rock n roll band. The broader than necessary cap on his head, even the holstered gun, tied Western-style with a string to his leg, looked now to be fit little more than as comedy props. I looked across to the Baroque Latin

200

church, devoted in name to the square's adopted saint. Its Romanesque window displayed the finest of craftsmanship, which appeared to become ever more intricate the longer you stared, until it pulsated with mercury-silver light and its stained glass panels began to roll and spin like the segments in a kaleidoscope. Yes, unmistakably, I was on one.

Turning back to where the trading women had sat, the scene now was hard to recognise from its former state. Colours rushed across the pavement as though the ladies robes had melted and were flowing away down the street. A row of faces beamed healthily like ceramic glazed ornaments and as I lingered awhile, I became aware that I was gawping and so moved on. I came to a square nearby, called the Plaza Murillo, where a pedestrianised area of large flagstones lay bordered by shrubs and found there a bench on some ornamented raised ground. From here I could look down upon a gang of playtime shoeshine boys, who ran barefoot, five-a-side behind a ball of rags. Whenever they passed the ball long or took a shot at goal, the image cannoned out like that snooker sequence that once appeared on TV and which became, unwittingly, the benchmark for how much a person was hallucinating. The leaves of nearby lime trees were turning the tear drop shape of Paisley patterns and their hearts had morphed into purple spines, as though I had developed the senses of a grazing insect that felt attracted to deep ultraviolet. It was coming on rather strong now. Despite the recent exertions, my tiredness was difficult to gauge, as there was always something new to revive and drag me on. But what I ought to have done then, whether rested or not, was to remain right where I was, beside the freeze-frame football match and the colour-dripping trees, to hang onto some of the composure that I would shortly wish I had.

On one long side of the Plaza stood the building which, for many years, had housed Bolivia's national seat of government. Grand as it was, the main attraction appeared not in its architecture, but the degree of its status, which had many district visitors arriving in a steady stream to have their photos taken outside it. Directly across the road from this, on a ramp of earth that fringed the park paving, stood an old gas lamp, now wired to the electrical mains. All the old features were in retained however, from the fine moulded base to the windowed lantern and that most frequently admired aspect these days, the upper cross-bar. Which may once have held the lamplighters ladder, but would now take a nice floral basket. I noted that this one fairly common object was drawing more attention than any feature in the entire square, notwithstanding the historic halls of government and so, in curiosity towards this one aspect, I wandered across to take a closer look.

On approaching the rear of a small huddle, awaiting turns to view this seemingly fixatious spot, I could see that, attached to one side of the base, there was a brass plaque of around A4 size, around which many people congregated and, on peering closer, I could make out the name of some past

202

Presidente, with a 1940's date. But beyond that I was at a loss. On the point of departing and wishing to look back at the watching crowd, I wandered to the other side and there, as if for my benefit alone, lay the same plaque translated into English. It read:

Gualberto Villaroel Lopez
President of the Republic of Bolivia
was hanged from this lamp post
by an angry mob
21st July 1946

Aarghh! What a ghastly vision to bring into one's thoughts. I could almost see him dangling there on an old piece of rope with his eyes on stalks and his bulging tongue gone black. It was hardly the picture to present yourself in such over-receptive circumstances and with being alone as well. I beat a hasty retreat toward the haven of my digs and whilst heading there did happen to cross the busy market, which I'd glanced at on my first arrival in La Paz. It was named locally as el Mercado Negro and was said to be where much of the stuff from the Arica train ended up. Though I have enjoyed the vibrancy of many markets in my own country and around the world, here was a rather subdued affair, with many pre-packaged and plastic hanging objects, but it gave me the opportunity to recover some of my earlier serenity.

With panting breath from the uphill hike, not to mention recent vivid alarms, I sought a quiet spot by the market's edge,

203

from where I could gradually bring myself back into the settled pace of things. Here however, rather than finding myself on the happy side of the street, I discovered I was at the desperate fringes, among those impoverished individuals with nothing to sell and the destitute disabled left to fend for themselves. The appearance these people displayed was not intended to disguise or make light of their misfortune, but to bring it strongly to everyone's attention and a mixture of stumps, deformities, splints and murky bandages met my gaze, alongside their crude crawling means of perambulation.

One old gent in particular had a very distinct appearance, with a kind of long horse-face, at the centre of which a giant and yellowed front tooth protruded, sabre-like through a gaping hair-lip. By the influence of my present state, I began to stare at him in rather tactless fashion and then, either through his rightful indignation, or my wild running imagination, his cheeks turned suddenly flush, the cruel lip began to curl into a snarl and while the tooth turned into a hissing spout of saliva, his visage became the ugliest human expression I had ever seen. It was time to leave.

Back at the room, away from the bother of fright-inducing scenes, I captured my thoughts in a more controlled manner. Some of the sights in our recent couple of hours had been rather unsettling, but the main area of difficulty had been the steep cobbled terrain, in thin-air conditions and, with some respite from this, I began to regain a hold on my surroundings.

The sharp contrast however, between swirling events taking place outdoors and the flat plain features of my white painted quarters, caused time now to run into a kind of waiting period, where nothing would happen unless you created some movement, or surrounded yourself with busy patterns. I had no desire to test myself further against the teeming conditions of the street and was of a mind to turn down a dimmer on things, but one of the most critical features of this type of experience is that, once you feel you've had enough, you can't simply control the effect with a switch and whether blissful moments arrive or ones that make you hold onto your hat, you simply have to see it out to the slow winding down.

There were a number of natural products that were said to act as an antidote, one of which was the drinking of high concentrate orange juice. I had bought a carton of this on my way back from the market and whether believing it to work, or in some psychological need for reassurance, I guzzled it down in haste. While burping long and loudly I experienced the repeat taste, not of crushed South American oranges, but of that overpowering and now never to be forgotten San Pedro cactus. Swooning at last onto my sunken bed with thoughts still running wild, I closed my eyes into a fiery starburst and eventually slept.

When I awoke it was to an early evening glowing still with traces of unnatural light, but one in which the outline of objects would remain immobile long enough for you to trust their physical boundaries. A couple of peaceable staying guests had

205

made their appearance and later Pepe turned up. He said that the stuff he'd taken had hardly affected him, perhaps due to his having thrown it up more or less straight away, but I, who'd held onto it in the manner of inhaled smoke, had felt a much greater impact; though not always of the kind I would have wished. In some ways my mixed bag of experiences here could have been a blessing in disguise, as the more turbulent moments may have discouraged me from developing a practice that it would be dangerous for a traveller to undertake, and this was to be the last of my mind-bending experiences, either on the road or anywhere else.

It may appear to some that, in drawing attention to these escapades, I am either promoting or discouraging such practices, when in fact I am doing quite neither. But one piece of advice I would gladly offer is that, having found yourself on the verge of such an activity, it would be best to pursue the normal cosy practice of stoning yourself in some comfortable place, perhaps among friends and surrounded by the familiar pleasures you would prefer. For to render yourself vulnerable in the high altitude capital of a mean dictatorship and wander alone through wretched scenes of poverty and memorials to past atrocity, with yet a faint grasp of the language, is a course you may happily avoid. In whatever other challenges you take up, be kinder to yourself than that.

At one end of the symmetrical bowl in which La Paz sits, there lies a narrow outfall gap which seems to represent the spout of a ladle through which departures from town may pour away south. A few miles beyond this point, as the land tilts upwards, you may come to a plain that would match near exactly the one by which you had recently arrived. The surroundings here bore no resemblance to the hectic dual carriageway exits of other capitals in the region, in which roaring vehicles competed for space against plywood pushcarts. But with the sprawling city now muffled from sight, the way ahead took the form of a quiet two-lane track, through a tussocky wilderness, in which the wise majority of people sought neither to build nor to reside. The change in atmosphere between downtown and here marked not so much the contrast between town and country life, as the boundary between two climatic zones.

In this treeless land of frequent high winds, where the drab grass grew thicker than heather, the llamas had to graze a path in front of themselves in order to move around, while the large birds flew so high in the air that it was hard to take a guess at what species they actually were. Way on down this road, through the red earth land that led to Argentina, the track would turn to compacted bare earth, which some wild motorists would see as a golden opportunity to drift, rally-style, around blind outcrop bends. Even the most careful of drivers here would steer one-handed into narrow corners while pressing the horn with their free other, which typified an attitude of carefree fatalism and the best you could wish for was a deliverance alive, which at last we narrowly achieved.

On our descending from the Andean Altiplano, we paused briefly at the cold rocky towns of Oruro and Potosi, neither now a picture of beauty, yet both with a history of fabulous wealth, beginning once with rich silver mine deposits, which petered later into barely sustainable tin. Around this area it was that Mike had picked up some of his tales of life's raw justice, where miners worked for two dollars a day, average life expectancy was nine years underground and the widows of deceased victims gathered re-saleable ore from slag heaps, in the absence of any pension.

It was reported that an old-style work indenture system had been in operation here, where employees were allowed to build up large amounts of debt at the company store, on the written agreement they could not terminate their employment with any credit outstanding. Nor, in the event of their untimely death, may their relatives make any claim for either future support, or compensation. Some sections of the industry had virtually all their staff entrapped in this way, which turned their working term into a short life sentence, in conditions of hardship and penury. Such a scheme of operation in the late 20th century was not only outrageous, but somehow strangely engrossing, like a throwback to the days of Leveller revolts and early Bolshevism, where dying on your feet was the brave man's preference to life on your knees. There were revolts here also, but ones that were famous not for the fitting justice that ensued, but for the cruel manner in which they were repressed and the

208

harsher dictatorial rule that followed. Such as the time when a workers' radio station was closed down, not by a court of injunction, but by a mob of soldiers bursting in and shooting everyone dead.

Out into the high level countryside, where the problems of urban life seemed to fade through the mist, I picked up a long truck ride on the second day out, which took me from the edge of Potosi right down to Tarija near the Argentine border. In this part of the Upper Andes, where busses were infrequent and the weather often wintry, it was the accepted rule to have to pay for rides in trucks, rather than hitch them; which worked serviceably well on the whole, especially for the local drivers who, encouraged by the chance of extra profit, would not only stop for all comers, but often go miles out of their way to pick up an extra fare or two. The two men in charge of this particular vehicle, the driver and his mate, had been fairly diligent in this respect as, by the time I ascended the covered trailer, there existed already, between the low roof and the high cargo load, enough sprawled out passengers to make up a decent enough travelling away team. The enterprising zeal of these two fellows may have been something to admire in the spirit of the time, yet it was a pity you couldn't say the same for their basic driving skills.

In the way of things on a long journey such as this, we were not unduly worried by the screeching of tyres, as we hared around each new bend on the last of our road-holding limits. Over months underway, through all the various rides, you

209

became immunised against the occasional madcap situation, and if you worried about every likelihood that lay along the track, then where would you be? Certainly not out here taking your chances alone. It was only when the road surface changed from smooth tarmac to soft red clay that the alarm bells really started to ring, as our fully laden vehicle, sixteen tons empty and now piled with sacked farm produce, began to simulate the actions of a swerving speed boat, rather than something bound by highway rules and though the trip thus far had been an entertaining one, with people in the back rolling into one another in fits of some merriment, it became rather more disturbing when the faces of those around us, who would have been used to this kind of thing, began to turn grey with fear. We had barely a few more turns of road in which to contemplate this point, before the inevitable happened.

While descending through the air, our sense of weightlessness seemed to go on forever, as we spread-eagled ourselves against the canvas roof awning until, in a floating mass of bodies and hard mango sacks, we all came down in a heap. A screaming engine revved in neutral, until someone had the sense to turn it off and, as I searched my senses among the general mayhem, I patted my limbs for missing parts, before checking on the well-being of others. By some sublime miracle no noticeable injury had befallen anyone, apart from a whack that I myself had taken on the knee as I collided with the wooden side panels and while coming to terms with this, I was able to drag myself towards the opened back-flap, peering beyond which, I could now see the departed highway about thirty feet above us. A heavily ploughed set of tracks ran to the edge of where we presently lay, in a muddied lake of recently deposited rainwater. Buried to the nuts.

To wade ashore was some effort through the soft base of our pond, with a swollen joint that was more painful to extract from the mire than it was to stand on and it was looked upon not well that I felt unable to offer assistance in removing the vehicle from where it presently stood. But the men, who seemed to have been through this kind of thing many times before, set calmly now to work in collecting rocks and laying a trail from our tyre tracks to the shore. Which, in a surprisingly short time, allowed us to escape not only the flood pool, but eventually, by a different route, the ravine itself, and lay us miraculously in the right southerly direction.

Thus did we continue, now in thankful silence, running no doubt through the same scenarios: of how things had happened and what might have been, had the balance been tipped just a fraction the other way? If the vehicle had rolled upon landing, to trap us beneath its load, with three feet of mud and water hindering our escape; if we'd left the road not here, but at one of the earlier, steeper points, into some gully of rocks, rather than a bath of soft mud; or into a deeper pool, with a competitive battle for escape, to see who could be first to breathe in air again? The turn of events here could have taken any kind of course, between blithe avoidance and total disaster. Which is right where the goose bumps began and I realised then that, had I used up one of my nine lives as a teenager while falling off a bridge in Manchester, then here was another one gone.

As for the cause of this mishap, the driver himself, there was not a trace of contrition about him as we waited to depart. As though the whole event had been a blameless passage of fate and, once back in the cab, he continued to slew at speed around bare earth bends, like some delinquent juvenile in a knocked-off hatchback. It left you faintly ambivalent about whether justice one day might take its course, but the only discomfort with this thought was that, rarely do such incidents occur where innocents are not also involved.

To descend unscathed at last from the trailer was a relief indeed, but no sooner had the tail lights faded into the distance, than I was confronted with a further taxing situation, as the darkness into which I had been plunged became so instantly complete that I couldn't even see the ground on which I stood. I had requested a drop at some angled road junction, where the way ran left to the town of Tarija and straight on towards Argentina. While the truck had been idling beside us and I had paid my couple of hundred pesos, I could see, by the headlight beam, a parallel line of shacks at the turn-off yonder, but now only memory could guide me as I shuffled my feet along, barely raising the soles, until I arrived at one of the strangest places to

212

which my journeys have ever taken me. For here was the village where no-one ever spoke.

In the glimmer of light that filtered through the clouds, I could see I was drawing close by the dark shadow of rooftops against the paler sky, yet no crack of light shone, either through an ill-fit door, or even a window shutter. There was no sign of street lampposts, nor the humming presence of electrical power and not a flicker, this far into the hills, of that all-pervasive media, television. For though the hour was not yet late, the whole village lay bolted-in and sound asleep. Other than the fortunate absence of barking dogs, the one other congenial feature to be found among these rough buildings was the covered boardwalk that ran along one side of the street and, tiptoeing carefully so as not to wake the world, I edged onto its creaking surface, rolled out my usual gear and slept.

Under the low cloud of the following morning, I awoke into a grey light, as the noise of an opening door latch grabbed my attention and I peered above the folds of my sleeping bag to see a broad local woman in brown working poncho and grey bowler hat. On shuffling into the open, she had begun to unravel some items from a bundle upon the floor, the most notable among which was a large Primus stove and while she engaged in this early ritual, I dozed once more into fitful sleep.
By the time I came to be fully awake, the air was sweet with a hot cooking scent and fearing now a morning rush of walkers across my floorboard resting place, I rose to gather my

213

equipment. I wandered now to what had become a breakfast food-stall by the roads' edge and took up the one choice fare of watery cocoa and some rather decent porridge, scooped both in old enamel tins. With an unusually large helping of each, I crouched by the quiet, unpaved verge and began to indulge myself. Had I known how affordable was the price, I would have ordered an extra bowl of porridge as it was that good, but having once entered into payment I was too shy to backtrack and so moved on. When I'd asked the lady how much it was, she raised a thumb and single finger pointedly held together. It was two pesos.

Further along the wooden walkway, large garage-like doors began to open and I wandered into a grocery store, to make some purchases for later in the day. Here again, in response to my *quanto questa* was a manual sign of raised digits and I departed for the road.

Beyond the last of village houses, on the way out south, a weight-levered toll bar had been set up in order to keep the government soldiers on top of their case. In wait for the passage of the next available transport, I remained among a growing band of locals for maybe a couple of hours, exchanging not a solitary word and while doing so, became increasingly aware that hardly a flicker of communication was passed between anyone present. In fact, going back to the previous night and the silence of dogs, I began to feel that, had dogs actually been, there they may have followed the habit of their keepers, and offered hardly a bark.

When Che Guevara had come to this district nine years earlier, struggling for support and heading for eventual defeat, he had described the local *campesinos* as 'impenetrable as stones.' They had never displayed a glimmer of trust in him, or me, nor thousands of others just like us. Which kept it all from getting a bit personal. Eventually there came along a flat-bed green lorry, with a gaggle of labouring-types, buttock-clenched onto the open trailer. On hearing my first spoken words since the previous day, a firmly assured, *"Si, atras"*, a driver's thumb was pointed rearwards. I was on the trailer-back and out of here. Away from a place where people kept their big traps shut and on to another, where they rarely ever did.

*

Of the journeys that I have undertaken, fairly all of them have been carried out by many other people. A few trips, such as the mountain-bike ride through a newly opened Vietnam, without yet a suitable travel permit, was one that had been accomplished then by very few outsiders and to cycle from Bombay to Calcutta on a bed-end of a machine with rod brakes and sit-up-and-beg handlebars was not a very commonly performed feat. But much of the rest, like the hippie/gringo trails and backpacker routes of later years, would be completed by hundreds of thousands then and tens of millions later on. I can't be sure whether the following statement would qualify as a major

215

boast, but from the very earliest part of my travelling days right up to the present, I have never met, or even heard of a solitary person who had hitch hiked around South America. Passing now into Argentina to undertake the lowland southern half of this 6,000 mile road trip, I was about to discover why.

The most widespread view of South America during these times, particularly among those who had never been there, was of a continent beset with political turmoil, where yearly revolutions brought stronger repression each time and where you needed only to step from your door to become prey to street robbery. There were persistent rumours of large scale genocide in two countries in particular, but these were still being described by some as Leftist smears. Barring the faint likelihood of being drawn into these affairs, the greatest imaginable threats seemed to come from getting caught in the crossfire of some local dispute, or being mugged while out on the road and left destitute. In a few notorious parts of the region, such as Coastal Brazil or much anywhere in Colombia, these dangers could be viewed as being quite genuine. But for the remaining thousands of miles, especially across these wide open plains of the south, the most immediate difficulty on a daily basis was in merely getting a ride.

Away from the haunting atmosphere of the High Andes, with its thin mountain air and a culture more difficult to grasp than a wisp on the breeze, the journey now began to level into one where events would creep by, to be later slowly analysed, and arresting encounters that hit you in the eye became notably

216

more rare. Aching long stretches of plain similarity would attend a trudging slog where, rather than dwell on present surrounds, we would always look miles ahead and wish we were already there. Some images however did stay in the memory, to mark where we were and recall where we had been.

Ten foot cacti in a red sandstone desert distinctly marked a fresh landscape on the instant you crossed the border, as though cultures and nationalities were decided upon such things. As the country levelled out, the brief desert ended and you ran into a strange Spring-time of greenery, where muscular red cattle splashed shoulder-deep across flooded fields, to feed upon a soup of watercress lilies. Pink flamingos waded the drying puddles, while further on south the spread became one with our preset view, as hundreds of miles of prairie were roasted to sepia straw.

Around the bland villages of these dust-blown regions a vivid image might flicker into view, of huge roadside stalls selling all the same fruit produce, country boy urchins waving live armadillos at passing motorists, or vultures in the branches resting with one eye open, as people dozed beneath the shade of trees. In a country like this, huge and thinly populated, to assess the mood in passing would be no easy task, but to have caught no hint of the things then greatly amiss, you would have had to be shut off from the world and deprived of all perceptory sense.

It is true that the focus of interest for faraway foreigners was directed then towards Chile, where not only had large scale

217

human right abuses occurred, but a democratically elected government had been overthrown by military force, openly supported by a controlling foreign power. But in the view of those closer to here, there existed, in Argentina, a far worse situation of repression and murder than anything occurring elsewhere. As in most totalitarian countries there prevailed an atmosphere of suffocating stillness, where the powers of state had extinguished much of communal life. It was on a rare couple of occasions that I came face to face with the historic truth, of which everyone later had such a strong opinion, but which, at the time I swear, hardly anyone uttered a word.

Somewhere down towards the more populated centre of the country, around Santiago del Estero, or it might have been Santa Fe, I found myself thumbing a ride by the heavily barbed fence of a military barracks. The camp, as I recall, was a very low-tech affair, with little more than a cluster of creosoted huts surrounding a lush sports area. At the main gate, further back along the road, there had been armed guards in white military helmets, banded in sky blue and a large hanging banner making some bold proclamation along the lines of Pro Patria. But here was devoid of all sound and activity, with not a soul on parade.

I had not been there long when there came along a low army jeep, open-topped, with a couple of Argentinian soldiers onboard and, as it was slowing towards me, I actually stuck out a thumb thinking it was going to give me a lift. Their present

218

purpose however was only to check on my *documento* and enquire as to my travel plans. In light of the country's recent record regards the military versus general public, I may have appeared a little nervous, even though I had done no wrong, but their business was merely a routine one and before departing, they informed me politely, that I could no longer remain there, as the camp perimeter was still a military controlled area. I moved on.

Wandering as I did, about a mile further down, I came to a small village of dark timber houses, set in a crescent high street that ran off and then directly back onto the new highway. Feeling, I guess, that it was nearly time to eat, I took the short detour in, to replenish my stock of food and while doing so, could manage to see most of the way to where the road rejoined the main route at its far junction. The scene along the village was a fairly typical one, with someone doing a bit of work out front of their property, a young family at play in the quiet street and at the furthest end, an old wooden grocery store with a drop-leaf canopy, perched on poles like a Bedu tent. The store seemed to be trading normally as I made my approach and everything appeared as on any ordinary day. But as I drew closer and people became aware of my presence, I thought I noticed a visibly shy reaction from the people, as the property repairing individual retreated indoors, the family began to gather themselves away and one last tiny infant was dragged from the street. The store, which had been wide open a few moments

219

before, was now being closed up in haste, as though an urgent errand had just been remembered and strangely, as I arrived at the already narrowing doorway, a baton of white bread was handed to me through the darkened gap, before a key was firmly turned in the lock. The place was shut.

Perhaps the whole sequence was a mere coincidence and everyone had reached an urgent moment at precisely the same time, but putting the pieces together ever since, of the nearby military camp, the heavy political climate, my appearance then in bulrush-coloured clothing, unkempt hair and beard, even a khaki rucksack (but no black beret with a red star on the front), it may have encouraged some to keep a clear distance in case the law were about. In far less critical circumstances than these, I have often learned that if public audits are to be carried out, they nearly always focus more heavily, at beginning and end, on the places right outside the auditory headquarters. It faintly appeared as though this place had been given some kind of going over, to what degree I couldn't yet imagine, but through conversation later on, I might well have been able to figure out.

Much further along in my journey, having visited a few similarly governed countries to the east of here and become by now rather de-sensitised toward this autocratic kind of rule, I travelled once more through Argentina, this time in a lateral east-west direction. During the intervening spell of a month or so, I had made conversation in my own language with just one solitary South American, a fellow I'd med in Brazil's Paraná Province, on my way out to the Paraguay border. In fact, during the whole six months of this journey, I came across only nine South Americans with whom I could converse in English. Apart from the very few travelling foreigners I'd met along the way, my means of communication were in a rapidly developing Spanish and a surprisingly frequent amount of German.

The following encounter was luckily with none of these, but with a rare type of individual for these parts who, speaking English well and having travelled far, had an honest and clear view of his own country far removed from all the jingo and Panglossian tone that you normally heard along the way. This was a young Argentinean fellow who, having recently returned to his homeland from a spell in the U S, was in that state of lucidity where comparisons can easily be made between one's own place and those witnessed further afield and where the faults in one and remedies seen in others, can't help but come to mind.

As we drove along in the featureless countryside, somewhere near the town of Mercedes, he spoke on in that way people do when steering ahead and not caring who would listen, as if rambling aloud to themselves. In recognising the vast wealth in resources of Argentina, he set it beside the southern half of the US, a land of similar natural resource and while one was in an undeniably healthy economic state, the other was run near to bankruptcy. He spoke of the rampant corruption that was present in the government of Argentinean towns and cities, the wildfire inflation of 250% a year, which had recently reached 40% in one single month. The culture of greed and egotism that existed within the fabric of political life and of people in a potentially wealthy land who were working hard just to eat. What if it was true, as most people here liked to say, that Argentina was the best country in South America? Compared to the world at large, that wasn't saying a great deal.

'It was.' he said, 'All a mess.'

I could see where he was coming from with most of it but, being a foreign guest, I didn't want to throw too much weight of my own into the argument. Sensing an opportunity however, I couldn't resist probing gently towards the subject which, I was told, was dangerous even to mention here in public, namely the alleged disappearances of multitudes of people over the previous five years. At this he fell momentarily silent. He'd heard the stories, he said, and had largely refused to believe them. He had even defended Argentina's record abroad on this very subject. But shortly after his return, something had happened to greatly change his view and now, while coming to terms with this, he didn't really know what to make of the situation.

It was while visiting some old friends, whom he hadn't seen during his long time away, that he came to a quiet farming area on the edge of a low rise country village, typical of the ones of this region. On reaching the isolated spot, which he was quite sure to be their address, he drove past several times in confusion, unable to spot any visible house and upon leaving his car, could

222

find only a pile of rubble where he was certain the building once stood. In some perplexity, not yet running to panic, he called at a few properties nearby, but when people shunned his approach, his deep suspicions began to arise. Eventually he could find just one individual who was willing to give him some run-down on the alleged event, before he too departed, afraid of being seen in communication. The tale that the fellow told, either from first-hand witness or through roundabout hearsay, went roughly as follows.

What had recently passed, said the local man, was that a heavy military vehicle had arrived in the night, possibly a tank or something else on tracks, as you could still see the marks from where it had arrived and slewed to depart. The noise it made was enough to make the ground shake but, knowing it was the *militar*, no-one would dare go out and take a look. Following some further loud noises, the business was done and no report was ever made of it. Not an item on the TV news, nor a paragraph in the local paper. Nothing. The end.

So there you were, no caricature image of the victims being tied to a post with a blindfold and last cigarette, just a 80mm muzzle shoved through the letterbox and Bang! Even with rumours abounding it was still a shock for this young man to find it true and right there in front of him. People had been dumped from helicopters and bricked into garden walls, but the reportage of these may have been mere exaggeration and, even if true, you never think it is going to come around your way. As

223

with others I would meet in future years that had met with similar situations, if he hadn't seen or heard the evidence himself, he never would have believed it.

The most nagging aspect of this event, both for our man at the wheel and now myself, was not the apparent early death of these young people, who were perhaps not really close friends of the story's narrator, but the fact that, according to him, they were not even particularly left-wing, let alone dangerous revolutionaries. They may have possessed a few fashionable books of the time by champagne socialist writers from France or elsewhere and even had clench-fist posters or pictures of Che Guevara pinned to their walls, but by the account of those who knew them, they were little more than hippie students going through a protest-against-everything phase, while posing not the slightest threat to anyone.

And thus it ever was in cases of this type, where purges and witch-hunts have progressed under their own momentum. Those with a despotic hold on power would root out their true enemies and dispose of them in ruthless fashion. But once this had been accomplished they would not hold back, but merely continue like compulsive psychotics, to remove all traces, even of those who had shown merely the slightest hint of resemblance to their nemesis. A horde of mad disciples, with their own bag of personal issues, would compete against each other's zeal, until it was difficult to recognise what originally was intended or at

224

which point it had all gone too far, with not one brave enough to say 'Stop!'

From Torquemada to the Soviet Gulags it was ever much the same, a giant monster lumbering across the land, with less of real control the further it developed and none to take the blame when it was all over.

Those who had Argentina's Junta down as a more ravenous beast than Chile's were eventually proved right, with a fatality count more than six times as high, but it all ended flush at last, in a predictably dry stalemate. Which left us finally with two inescapable truths when reflecting upon such times, from which people could never dump their memories fast enough. In mass cases of genocide, a lot of innocent people get to die, but very few guilty ones actually get prosecuted for it.

Before the two main outflows of the great southern jungle roll into the River Plate, they run in a hundred mile parallel, to form the near island province of Entre Rios. Here, in the quag swamps between Rivers Uruguay and Paraná, lies a pulsating, creaking land of hidden perils, in which the normally dangerous highway is by far the safest place to be and where strong silent mozzies have the power to bite through corduroy. For much of the way ahead the road seeks what natural elevation there is, or rides on hand-shovelled banks from generations ago, but at some stages it drives straight in among the tall reeds, to nose its way through a series of causeways lined with measuring-posts, that told you how deeper in the swamp you possibly could

225

be. In surrounds such as this, similar to many of the region, I found myself on foot, beyond the urban clutter, on a straight highway, where I felt more confident of a worthwhile ride.

Arrived at last in the near ideal spot, I began to loosen my straps and lower my small pack to the ground, but while doing so, happened to notice that, in the road ahead, what I had earlier thought to be an old piece of discarded rope, was actually a live snake basking happily on the tarmac. There was nothing greatly unusual here, a brief start maybe, but no cause for alarm. These things were found all the way along the Pampas highways, usually rolled into leather alongside much of the rest of observable wildlife, but this one seemed fresh enough, with its wet drab skin glinting in the sun and gave us a warning, on this sleepy hot day, to still remain alert.

I made a quiet diversion toward the opposite side of the road, but when almost there, I spotted another snake, maybe twenty yards ahead, which made me veer again to the side from which I'd earlier begun. Soon, while making more progress, I saw a third and then quickly two more, until before long I was swerving both ways through decreasing gaps of space like some footballer on a jinking run. In some places there were communal groups of the things, engaged perhaps in some time-of-the-year ritual and where this was the case, I was forced to take a rather heavily weighted leap in order to clear their territorial range. This, for a while, did reassure me, as it made me feel as though I were taking some control, but quickly I realised that, rather than

226

bringing me to safety, it was merely leading me further in toward the serpents own domain. Behind me I could see the dozen or so snakes whose paths I had so far crossed, while up on ahead lay at least the same number, with perhaps many more disguised within the grey haze of the distance. With swamp and tall reeds obstructing my escape either side, there seemed no end to it. It did occur to me to beat a retreat back the way I'd come, but as I looked rearward once more with a view to doing this, I could see that the bog creatures I had earlier cleared were now alerted to my presence and I felt compelled to push on ahead.

An irrational phobia of any known living creature is something that has never affected me personally. If you have all the facts to hand beforehand you either protect yourself appropriately, keep a good distance, or simply accept whatever risks there may be. The situation here however was one quite different, in that, not having the knowledge to be aware which snakes could possibly be of harm, I was consequently scared rigid by practically the whole lot of them and now here I was, on a narrow causeway pressed close into a slithering mass of their company. There was neither a stick to be waved nor a rock to throw and, as I continued in my outwardly controlled way, I felt the goose bumps rise across my scalp and was consumed by a feeling of purely reasoned terror.

Eventually, after what seemed like a lifetime, but which was probably ten minutes, there came along the first passing car which, perhaps on second thoughts of the driver, pulled up about

227

thirty yards ahead of me. It was a tiny Fiat 500, only going six kilometres up the road, but more greatly appreciated by me than if it were a limousine trip around the world. As I leapt inside in a state near to hyper-ventilation I babbled half-coherent to the driver, not on the subject of our destination, but on my soon to be departed surroundings and the ordeal I felt that I'd undergone.

'Serpientes,' I said, pointing rearwards, 'Mucha, mucha serpientes!'

'Yes,' he said, in his bored country way, 'There are a few.'

*

When a country starts becoming known as the Switzerland of South America, you have to be highly wary of exactly what it is being compared to. Torquay is not really on any branch of the Riviera, nor is Blackpool, in all seriousness, a Northern Las Vegas, though when set beside Preston it may arguably appear so. For Uruguay however, to have become widely regarded in these terms reflects something altogether different. It means it has come a hell of a long way in relevantly recent times.

From the precise moment when European rationing was abandoned beyond the end of World War Two, the bully-beef factories of Uruguay, with their supplying ranch-farms and wide range of supporting services, began to suffer great decline due to a tail-off in demand. This led locally to a general lowering in living standards, high rises in unemployment and all the social and political ills that go with reduced wages, scarcity of opportunity and malcontent voices agitating for some kind of instant change.

Partly in response to these circumstances and perhaps also inspired by popular moods elsewhere, a small band of extreme Leftists began to make their presence felt, with what originally were a series of revolutionary-aimed stunts. The group, the Tupamaros, who had taken their name from the Inca rebel Tupac Amaru, were most notable in their early stages for robbing banks and then giving the money away to the poor, which sounds like a very noble gesture indeed, until you consider the effects on investment, business and employment prospects for people at large and had they achieved any level of manageable power, it was unlikely they would have done the country any long term favours.

Once the authorities had liquidated a few of their members in rather heavy handed fashion, the new rebels replied with a few assassinations of their own and it all blew into a tit-for-tat period of urban guerrilla warfare, in which the image of both sides was heavily tarnished and where no-one could really win. The rulers then in power felt suddenly vulnerable under the open laws of democracy and drafted in a range of emergency measures. Public gatherings were restricted, some people found their free movements severely curtailed, a few loud street

229

protests ended in tear gas and as expected, the Junta moved in. It was into this stifled and silently oppressive atmosphere that I entered the country, somewhere between Christmas and New Year, at around the half-way stage of the dictatorship period.

Following these low times, and particularly since the end of military rule in the mid 1980's, the all round health of the country has improved dramatically, a situation that has come about not by any measure of extreme politics or via economic miracles, but through a calm governing hand, a greater development of efficiency in long haul transport and by that most revolutionary of all game-changers, a simple inflationary rise in the world price of commodities.

On my travels, prior to making this journey, I had always been aware of the approach to national boundaries by the sight of parked-up trailers and container lorries at the roadside, often for a mile or two in advance. In all the South America I saw of this period however, I can recall not one occasion of there being any such scene and in several cases, there would be no line of waiting traffic at all. The precise location of my entry into Uruguay from Argentina now escapes me, but the means of doing so remains quite vivid. It was on a rope-hauled pontoon, decked with wide planks that were just about able to support the weight of small trucks, as we were silently dragged across a placid stretch of narrow river. Such was the provision at not only this, but one or two other significant international borders.

230

There did exist two standard bridge crossings into this western side of the country, one at the town of Fray Bentos and another at Paysandú, plus some quiet narrow highway out west to Brazil, which I later embarked upon. But even at the more standard crossings here, you felt as though your own passing was a rare event, like you'd just woken someone from their drowsy routine and it does now occur to me that the most heightened activity I saw in overland trade between two countries on this entire trip, was on the smugglers train between Arica and La Paz. How we can appreciate now the life-sustaining efforts of those highly enterprising, yet poorly rewarded Indios.

The sudden burst of summer greenery that met you as you rose from the riverbanks into the finely proportioned hills of Uruguay was a heartening sight when set beside a thousand miles of sun-dried Argentina. Here the hedgerow quartered land of gentle slopes all running to some water's edge, put you in mind of North-Central Europe, or places even closer to home. Though town to town distances were not great in comparison to the New World norm, the waits for rides could be rather long, but I eventually made it down to Montevideo, riding much of the way in the back of a white pick-up, with my hair tousled in the wind and a heavy scent of mown cattle-grass in the air.

A companion of mine for much of the way was a fourteen year old black kid who had been labouring on some up country ranch-farm and was hitch-hiking his way home to see his family for the New Year holiday. He told me he'd been

231

employed as a gaucho, though at that young age I think he'd barely got a smell of the stables, but there was always time and he certainly had that on his side. I shared out my food with him at some roadside verge along the way and quickly wished I hadn't as, by the time we arrived at journey's end, he followed me around like a chick after its mother hen and I was forced to dive onto a downtown bus in order to reclaim my freedom.

As a capital city, Montevideo was by far the most quiet that I had so far visited, though this distinction would pass quite soon to a place not far down the line. The recently relaxed curfew here had left people with a residual habit of staying in rather than going out to celebrate and the Festive period felt more like a general strike than a public holiday. The urban silence was dramatically broken on New Year's morning when a massive and noisy drum ensemble samba'd its way through the neighbourhood streets. But this was the only such acknowledgement I had seen in what was not only a sedate period in the country's history, but also very austere times.

In this side-track part of the continent, where little favourably had developed in over a generation, there was one feature at least which had emerged happily from the long times of recession. Like grand old buildings that survive threats of demolition through a lengthy lack of funding, a similar thing had occurred in the world of vintage motoring. A government in unopposed authority, under severe financial constraint, had sharply restricted imports to those items which the country could

232

only really afford and this had brought about a booming revival in the mend-and-make-do of ancient machinery. There were vague similarities to Cuba and 1970's New Zealand, where people kept cars forty years from new, because of lack of fresh availability or high import charges. But this was a situation apart. On the everyday road here you would see Model T Fords from between 1915 and 1929, ancient Pontiacs with wide running boards and flapping canopy roofs like something that Elliot Ness would have used when chasing Al Capone. Cars built by companies that had folded half a century before and on one occasion, a convertible open-fronted thing, where the centrally placed steering suggested it preceded the regulations of left or right hand driving. The one thing that I can appreciate the most from this memory now is not simply the appearance of these early motor vehicles, which can be viewed in many a designated museum and at classic car meets all over our own country, but the fact that they were running around here on a routine workday basis, carting bales and the occasional puzzled looking animal. During this period there would be a feeling among some Uruguayans of faint embarrassment at the continued presence of these old jalopies along the national highways, as though their country had lagged too far behind the rest. But as time has gone on and things improved, there has become a great pride in ownership in the ones that have still survived, especially if a family had owned it from years ago. As though, perhaps, it were a part of their own historic struggle. Like the old horse drawn

233

plough in the garden, behind which one's grandsire had laboured.

The number Treinta y Tres is an unusual name for a town. So called in honour of the thirty three martyred patriots who established national independence here in 1825, it looked like a place where very little had happened ever since. The only notable rustle among the downtown avenue trees was caused by our own arrival in a rattling 1948 Fiat truck, which was powered by an engine of such raucous volume that the silence felt like deafness when you got out. On the far side of town, after a tiring day on the road, I thumbed at the few last passing cars, while keeping an eye out for a sleeping place among the shadows ahead. I had been there not long when I was startled by the presence of someone who appeared to arrive from nowhere, but who must have approached through the formidable fence of cactus that paralleled my side of the road. This was a youngish fellow, bare headed, in local police uniform, who engaged me in a manner I now recognise as painted-on cheerfulness and as our conversation developed, began to probe gently as to my plans and personal origins, in an ever more inquisitive fashion. Satisfied eventually that I was of no great threat, he moved on to the subject of where I was going to spend the night and, perhaps lulled into a false sense of security by his easy manner, (as I'd never before met a cop from around here who didn't look like a high security prison guard) I must have offered some off-the-hip reply such as,

234

'Hell, I'm just going to crash in some quiet place right up there ahead. Probably behind that cactus fence, if there's level room enough.'

At this, he offered me a free place round at the local police station which, in that naive moment, I thought to be a damn civil gesture. And so, back towards the direction from which the young man had reached us, which was indeed through the cactus fence, we were led, across some bare land, towards a plain low building on the side of a slope.

Inside the town nick things were surprisingly low key. The scarcity of furniture on the hard tiled floor made the place seem echoingly empty, which was highlighted by the steel tips on the policeman's shoes. The air of silence here suggested a town of law abiding souls, or one with a population living in dread of such establishments, and a solitary other officer, staffing the main desk, stared blankly on introduction while greeting his friend. A conversation began into which I was gradually invited, but though things at first went affably, they changed quickly into a protraction of the roadside questioning and from there to a full body search, with my luggage tipped onto the courtyard floor. Things turned a little tense for a while, as I feared I may have written words too frankly in a scrappy diary I carried with me along the way and the discovery of a large folding blade caused some concern, until I explained that it was used for scoffing my dinner, at which point it was put back with some distaste.

The most unnerving aspect of this part of the encounter however was that, while the contents of my luggage were being spread large, the taller of the two officers, he who kept guard over the desk and had so far communicated little, began now to entertain us with some handy tricks, featuring his own conjuring skills and a tiny kitten he'd picked up from around the yard. At one minute intervals he would raise the animal to around six feet height and turn it over on its back, whereupon he would release it spinning towards the hard cement floor. The mild creature just about managed to get four legs in position before crashing to the ground and shivered violently, even though the evening was warm. This brought cackles of laughter from the tall man and a cheesy compliance from his companion, which became ever more strained as the repetitions went on. My own initial urge would have been to tell him to pack it in, but I wisely resisted this as I was selfishly willing to see the cat continue spinning rather than do so myself. To divert the attention from this scene, I enquired vaguely as to how things were in the life of a cop around these parts and was informed that everything here was *tranquilo*, which was a popular term used among South Americans to describe circumstances in which all non-tranquil elements had been run to ground. As this was said, the tall one leaned right over me, cat in hand and pointed a thumb rearwards towards his own chest, while uttering words to the meaning of,

"That's because of us, *like!*"

They both laughed heartily.

236

Before there was time for much else we arrived at that stage to which I had most greatly looked forward since the instant of my departing the main road. This was the moment when I should be led away to that longed for luxury of a solitary cell, clean and tidy, secure from all weathers and provided with that one feature which is most sorely missed in its absence, a soft sheeted bed. Along the courtyard walkway we went, to a point where a door had been left opened outwards and beyond the threshold of which lay the true source of my expectations. Peering inside I could see nothing at first, but with eyes accustomed, began to make out a couple of narrow air vents at the angle of ceiling and wall, from which a few shafts of outdoor sky had managed to pierce the utter darkness. In the absence of fittings or furniture there was just one feature that strongly presented itself. This was a four inch diameter hole set level into the bare cement floor, the stench from which was overpowering. Realising now that I had little further say in the matter, I stepped in and on finding a spot less fetid that the rest, began to roll out my sleeping gear. The cop in the entranceway had become now a prison screw and while searching my bearings beneath the graffiti of some tortured bloke from Paysandú, I lay back and gave a signal for the slamming of the door. I was banged up!

Within a short while I had managed to blank from my mind all the kind of things that may have occurred in that place, but as the vent light faded and I was left alone with my senses, I couldn't escape the all-pervading stink, which had a power to

237

instil its own kind of numbness. Shuffling around in search of cleaner air I may have edged my gear a little closer to the ventilation holes under the roof corner, but there was little use in lying next to the walls, as people in search of a toilet had simply pissed into the corners and its residue had crept along. In the whole of the night I don't suppose I'd slept more than an hour and in my state of tired delirium, began to doubt first of all my own capacity to measure time and then whether I would ever be let out again. Eventually, in the blackest hours before dawn, I could resist no longer the urge that I had hoped to withstand until daylight and I was forced to rise and relieve myself. Taking careful aim at where I remembered the facility to be, I urinated long and hard until, right at the end of my slash, I heard a hollow sound within the watery hole that told me I'd finally hit the spot. No wonder the place stank.

At last the new day arrived, in narrow filtered form, and I was glad for the arrival of an early work shift, who let the full light into my room. With neither the time nor wish to acquaint myself, I merely bolted straight past, scrubbed my face and teeth under the standing pipe and made a dash for the road, as though pursued by wild demons. The physical side of the memory stayed with me for quite some way, like the taste of traffic fumes from a busy main road; though the residue in this case was not of carbon monoxide but stinking wet sewerage, and it felt for a while as though I'd departed with a piss-soaked baby's nappy around the lower half of my face. In fact, as long ago as the event was, I find myself taking shallower breaths even now as I think of it.

*

On immediately crossing the border from the mosaic landscape of Uruguay, Brazil announced itself in pretty much the way you would have expected from preconceived images of the place, with a tall swathe of primeval forest, where birds called out like howling monkeys and the air smelt rich as the scent from a million grow bags. In parallel line to the travelling road, an obsolete bridge had become swallowed in moss and what lower greenery there was grew heavily dark, as though attuned to the level of shade. It was an ironic picture of how things had once existed, as the forest petered out not far down the road, to never reappear in more than a thousand miles. From here onwards the land took on the distinct character of the type of people who had colonised it; early 19th century immigrants from a then impoverished Italy and later arrivals from post war Germany. The scene evoked some recollection of distant lands visited, but on harking back to the forested border area, it brought to mind what must have been before, when all the trees were giants, wildlife roamed free and jungle tribes lived right down by the sea.

I had accepted here that communication could soon be a problem, as I had channelled all my efforts into learning Spanish

239

and my knowledge of the Portuguese language was even more scant than my food-related Italian, but as this short leg of the journey progressed, I discovered a surprisingly common outlet for conversation through a medium which, at that time, I had known better than all three of them together. In the late nineteen forties and into the early fifties, a significant migration had occurred into this region, of people fleeing the hardships and haunted memories of a shattered Europe. The greater proportion of these had been from a ruined Germany and as a result of this, up to eight million people, in Brazil's three most southerly provinces, used German as their first language.

For the ones who remained here it would be better not to dwell upon the German economic miracle that had left most other economies trailing in its wake and I couldn't help wondering if those who had jumped ship when it appeared to be sinking, were now regretful at what they later could have had. I offered this point to an old German fellow I met along the way, who was well settled in the town of Porto Allegre and he put me straight in an instant. Life here, he said, could be as good as anywhere, if you made it so. The work was rewarding, weather was fine, football was wündershöen and despite what hardships people had endured along the way, it was still a lot better than Germany in 1945

While embarked on a long journey such as this there always comes a time when a strange sense of disorientation arrives and the most likely moment for it to be recognised is not

240

when drawn into circumstances ever more uncommon, but when thrust suddenly back into a world you knew well, but thought you'd left behind. I have heard of Welsh speaking travellers in the depths of Patagonia being suddenly surprised by indigenous natives who addressed them in the purest Cymraeg. It was an event they described as akin to being hit in the face with a cup of cold water, a reminder of who you were and how foreign to this place. My own experience in this respect came about near the town of Nova Petropolis, on the way up to Curitiba, in the vehicle of a swarthy looking individual who was possibly of Portuguese descent but had, out of convenience or courtesy, fluently learned the language of his close neighbours, the Germans.

I recall we were on a winding road through a very distinct region of hills that were equidistantly spread with a plantation of oil palm trees, looking like the model of a children's play-set. It was while lost in some thought, having already made our introductions, that the fellow tilted his head slightly towards me and asked, right out of the blue, if I had any knowledge of the small Lancastrian town of Rochdale? Rows of mill-worker terraces beneath a range of Pennine hills, an image of flat caps that no one now can ever remember anyone wearing, a famous music hall actress who was very well loved and a large, characterful MP, now under some suspicion. I was not of that precise culture but yes, I knew of the place. It was about the breadth of a city away from where I originated and being never

241

the most stunning of locations on an international scale, I wondered why he should ask of it. It wasn't, he said, due to his having close acquaintances in that far off spot, but simply that he was the manager of the local Co-op store and had built up a fair interest in the movement, which was founded right there in 1844.

I felt temporarily proud of my loose regional attachment to Rochdale and wished, for a moment, that I actually was from there, so I could feel prouder still. It set me off on a warm trail of early shopping memories, where loose cheese was sold in greaseproof wrapping, customers shared a dividend from the company profits and everything was carried away in brown paper bags. Which clashed rather heavily with my present surroundings in a sub-tropical land, near a Greek named town, in company of a Portuguese descendant, who was speaking fluently in German. I reminisced indulgently for a little way further on until, at some quiet road junction that parted our ways, I shook hands, opened the door and stepped out again, back into Brazil.

To some lesser degree, this perplexity as to which country we were in carried on for some way further, as we passed by villages where it was announced that Nederlands was hier gesproken, as though inviting us in to share a rendition, and one small plaque which simply had a painted Norwegian flag on a wooden board nailed to a tree, that either meant something similar, or simply marked the location of the remotest émigré. By slow measures however, we worked our way through the rural provinces of the south and in towards the more densely

242

urbanised areas, where it began to resemble the kind of land I had come to envisage and lately, rather fear.

As the country farms became more securely guarded and small towns clearly overcrowded, the signs of greater hardship would appear, with ragged labourers trudging home at day's end and tall Africanesque women walking the roadside edge with hugely precarious loads balanced on their heads. Towards evening, as I trailed from some tiny town in search of a quiet place to crash, I noticed that oncoming pedestrians would pointedly cross to the other side rather than pass a stranger while dark was approaching. For a while I quite enjoyed this power to intimidate people, but it also spoke plainly of recent troubles and meant that sleeping places should be selected with great care. I had never fallen for the idea of a Brazil in permanent fiesta, where women danced around with bowls of fruit on their heads, but had I done so, I would have been swiftly disabused of the notion here, where everyday life was as tough as anywhere else.

The time that I felt I had truly arrived in Brazil and no other country was when it finally began to rain. And boy did it rain. The sky had been overcast and sultry for a couple of days, to the point where a strange kind of twilight would envelop the afternoon and when eventually a large loud splat hit the road nearby, I turned in the belief that a huge kind of bird had done a dump from great height. It still seemed a puzzle when the same occurred within seconds in several spots close around and I thought we were undergoing an air raid of this kind, only to

243

realise soon that the slaps on the tarmac were actually large drops of water, which became another and then many more until, within moments, the deluge came down in a roaring crescendo. I have seen rain in monsoons and on the edge of typhoons, but there was never any like this and, after one experience, it caused you always to monitor the distant sky, to consider how well prepared you were and how soon you could escape if necessary. In this particular instance I was damn lucky to be within a hundred yards of some garage roadhouse providing cheap cubicle rooms, to where I could rush as the storm came on. By the time I'd made it there, through rebounding knee-high rain, I was soaked to the core of everything I had and was glad of the steamy hot atmosphere in drying myself out. It brought home to you here the reasons why the forests were so thickly matted and the rivers immensely wide.

If, when faced with two potential danger sources, you decide upon one that turns out safely in the end, it could never have been anything but the right choice. I had intended from here to hitch my way up the coast through the urban sprawl of São Paulo and on to Rio de Janeiro, where Shrovetide carnival was shortly due to begin, but on measuring my travel progress against what distance I'd yet to cover, the recent signs were not greatly encouraging. 800 miles from the border to Curitiba had taken me 10 days to hitch and over the whole period since I entered Argentina from Southern Bolivia, my progress had been barely more rapid. The famous Madis Gras would start in three days

244

time and there were still five hundred miles to go. At this rate I'd be arriving there just in time for the post-match tidy up. It was with a heavy heart just then, that I chose to halt my advance in this direction and head instead west toward the more placid environs of Paraguay. Never to know exactly what I'd missed, it could have been the very best of times, or the worst of all mistakes. Being cost-minded, as I then largely was, and taking my chances alone on the road, the subject of accommodation was something to be hardly considered until each day's end. But I wonder how I would have fared among the swarm of a million visitors, in a city with no spare rooms and hardly the space to roll out a mat.

From my earlier days, I retained a natural optimism that, no matter what obstacles lay ahead, we would always somehow find a way through and bad news stories were only relevant if the same fate befell you. But reading later in a Peruvian magazine a report of this year's event, it stated that, during the actual days and nights of the Carnival, a total of 165 people had been killed in a series of incidents, ranging from drunken brawls, to street robberies and revellers being run over. It was, the article said, about average.

By some ironic turn of fortune, at the near instant of my heading left, off the great northern road, I obtained a superb 500km lift that took me to within walking distance of the Paraguayan border. Had I got such a ride along the way I was previously heading, I would have been half way to Rio and in

245

with a chance, but there was no turning back now and no point contesting the rules of Sod's Law. Through an undistinguished landscape of dull shrubs and rampant wild cane, we rode along now in the company of an excellent Brazilian fellow of around early thirties, who was of noticeable good health and took an interest in most things. His fluency in English was fairly decent, which provided some release to me as, apart from with a couple of travellers I'd met at the Montevideo Y.H., I hadn't spoken in my own language since mid Argentina and my encounter with the young acquaintance of the *Desaparecidos*. Here there were to be no brutal revelations however, as our man was happy as Larry, farming some green spot among the Rio Grande hills.

Preferring to travel during the safer hours of daytime, we took a cheap room each at some lodging place beside the road and arrived at our destination the following early morning, at the three-way border town of Foz do Iguacu. A prominent feature of travelling nowadays is that you can research your journey beforehand in all manner of easy ways and choose an itinerary that you feel will exactly match your personal interests. One drawback to this however, when compared with earlier times is that, a pre-organised schedule might keep you away from the many other wonders that you could merely discover for yourself and exclude you completely from those rare moments of grand surprise.

My precise frame of mind when approaching this short journey's end is now rather hard to conjure up, but I would likely

246

be caught in a cycle of continually pushing ahead, possibly road-tired, yet looking forward above all to the exciting moment of entering a new country. I was loosely aware of some great natural feature quite close to here, having been told to watch out for it while back in La Paz, but as I'd never met a soul who could give me a first-hand description and living then in a world where such things were not broadcast on a continual loop, I was of a mind to roll straight on to Paraguay and pass it by altogether.

When I mentioned these thoughts to the kind driver, he let out a shriek of alarm and though his exact words are now beyond recall, I could never forget the reaction that followed, as he leaned over the steering wheel, accelerated hard and drove me at high speed towards the gateway of the place that he insisted it would be a massive crime for me to miss. Once arrived, he repeated near exactly the conduct and advice I'd received on approach to Postojna Caves, in Yugoslavia those many years before, as he pointed straight ahead and commanded me to Go In There! Even staring hard on my back so I wouldn't balk at the entrance fee. May God bless the fellow now wherever he may be, for what a mighty omission this would have been.

Most celebrated features of the natural world are rated either by their dimensions or inspirational qualities, as though a chart were designed to fit each category. Occasionally however the ingredients required to satisfy all parties come together in one very special place, to provide a rare experience of visual appeal and raw power. Such a spot is the unrivalled phenomenon

247

of Iguacu Falls, which lie between the borders of Brazil, Argentina and Paraguay. Here, at a horseshoe landslip across an otherwise unremarkable stretch of river, there exist a set of cataracts that display a more varied quantity of visual charm than probably any site across the world. At either side of a mammoth drop, there run a chain of watery chutes, ladders and raging cascades that seem to envelop wherever you stand like a wrap around screen. The experience however is not merely that of the average bystander, as you become embroiled in the thunderous atmosphere of sound and mist to the point where you are immersed in the action as near as safety will allow. You may question how people can become transfixed by the simple movement of water, but the cataract here is not the only marvel, as the scene is enhanced by a hundred mini rain forests clinging to rocks between the gushing ribbons. Hordes of butterflies swarm the bushes in bloom, while the sky comes frequently alive with the flight of tropical birds As a physical spectacle it sits somewhere between the brute force of Niagara and the atmospheric enclosure of Victoria Falls, but as a picture of beauty it stands alone, with its flora and fauna rainbowed by sunlight through that all enveloping rush. When eventually I was able to drag myself from this marvellous place it was only through leg weariness and a fear that I would miss my border crossing of that day, but by then I had already captured the colour, the noise and even the damp, earth-smelling spray that would last me out of Brazil.

*

For a traveller of long distances, the memory of any place will remain strongest only in the shape of what it appeared during the time of their passing by. A destination may exist in some form for the duration of only a summer, to be described at large as though that time had never passed, but when circumstances prevail over exceptionally long periods to hold a country into some odd kind of time-warp, you find yourself describing not so much the fleeting moment of your own passage, but a central part of the nation's history, which becomes more memorable the odder the tale may be.

The story of Paraguay begins in a common fashion for countries of this region, with a swiftly won independence around 1811, followed by fifty years of benign self-sufficiency. It was toward the end of this period that a very striking passage of events began to occur, where Paraguay's rulers, either worried by the sabre-rattling behaviour of their close neighbours, or becoming victim to their own wild ambitions, embarked upon a bold expansionist programme where they would attempt, by military means alone, to extend their rule into territories then occupied by the citizens of Brazil and Uruguay. In this way would they increase their claim to a share of the Atlantic coast.

249

Such a scheme, had it been fully successful, would not only have opened up Asuncion to a much wider trade, but allowed Paraguay control over all navigable tributaries of the River Plate, thus establishing itself as *the* major power in the region. This was a prospect far too daunting, not only for the established business orders in Buenos Aires and Montevideo, but also the up-country trading stations, who faced further levy on their transported goods. Under these circumstances it was that the War of the Triple Alliance began, a senseless escapade from Paraguay's point of view where, for six years of wretched slog, they fought alone against the far greater powers of Uruguay, Brazil and later Argentina.

Most modern observers, reviewing this conflict from afar, would tend to empathise with Paraguay, who fought pluckily and often heroically against its three larger neighbours, but considering that it was actually Paraguay who started the war in the first place, it must go down as one of the most futile military campaigns of all time. By the end of this draining encounter, the Paraguayans, who were rallied by the slogan Vitoria o Muertre, were confined largely to the latter and the country lay in ruins. Only one third of the population remained alive, ninety percent of all male adults had been killed and their own sovereign territory, rather than increasing in size, had been reduced by almost fifty percent. While the surrender terms were being drawn up, it was only upon the insistence of Brazil that Paraguay remained as a nation state at all, in the hope that it

250

would form a buffer against any future Argentinian ambition. Chastened then in status and doubtlessly haunted by the traumatic experience, Paraguay was left to mourn its losses and begin the very long process of recovery.

After such a catastrophic set-back in its development, one might think that all future rulers of the country would be highly disinclined towards further military action. But it was barely beyond a generation that Paraguay was wilfully involved again, this time in a more justified dispute, in which it gave a far better account of itself, but where the end result was just another fruitless, no-win situation that summed up the pointlessness of nearly all military undertakings.

Some time in the early 20th Century a group of geologists, employed by a foreign oil company, had discovered the light presence of hydro carbon deposits on the south eastern slopes of Bolivia's foothills, which led soon to their development on a small commercial scale. These promising early signs, as they often do, produced a fever of excitement, where expectations vastly exceeded realistic hope and, motivated in such fashion, Bolivia, which had lost its entire coastline in an earlier conflict involving both Peru and Chile, was encouraged to redeem itself by laying claim to Paraguay's northern province, the Chaco Desert.

The fall-out from this money driven dispute was the three year Chaco War, a doggedly fought campaign which cost, collectively, another hundred thousand lives and was remembered largely abroad for the startling fact that each side in its turn was openly funded by a large multinational hydrocarbon interest, Standard Oil, for Bolivia and Royal Shell, for Paraguay. It was rather like the business of young lads being encouraged to box one another's brains out by stable-yard owners, for the sake of local pride and a Lonsdale Belt, while some commercial interest ticked over quite nicely in the background. By the end of this mutually draining episode the original claimant was forced to accept terms and the Chaco was divided, three to one in Paraguay's favour. Yet herein lies a cruel twist in that, though Bolivia's small part of the disputed territory did provide some quantity of natural gas that was of marginal productive value, Paraguay's larger share never produced anything at all which, in light of their territorial success against human losses, must go down as one of the most hollow victories of all time

Living in fairly anonymous fashion throughout this period was a young army officer who, in strange echoes of World War One, would rise to become one of the continent's most notorious dictators. This was Alfredo Stroessner, a son of Bavarian immigrants, precociously bright enough to become the country's youngest ever general, but very much a man of his own harsh times. Here was an individual who would mould the country as a bulwark against his personal fears and then hold it in such a state with his last ounce of will. From the very beginning of his tenure, when newly installed dictators are liable to flex their powers, Stroessner declared, not a state of emergency but one of *siege*, as though every border were surrounded by the worst of demons. By swiftly altering the national constitution to suit the ruler's needs, this official mood of paranoia was stamped for renewal at a regular frequency of every two months. For the next thirty five years!

Somewhere in the midst of this frozen period was where I came in, two thirds of the way through the most unyielding of regimes, where people in ripe old age had never seen a ballot paper and the denial of basic human rights was seen as a patriotic chore that protected the public from itself. On a continent then renowned for its many revolutions, these years of absolute dictatorship may have provided the basis for a stability that was not enjoyed by the likes of Chile and Argentina, but it was at the cost of much that we would normally call life. Through armed men on the streets and informers in the place of every tenth grown-up, the regime had banned any human gathering that would vaguely resemble a party, stifled most open forms of conversation and removed all ingredients for what people would basically regard as a chilled-out good time. With not much beyond work, eat and an early bed to look forward to, life then in Paraguay must have been like waiting for the world to end, while knowing you'd never get to heaven.

For a city of its great size Asuncion was probably the quietest such place on earth during this time. Commercial trade seemed to be based upon the most local of supply, where everything was moved on the backs of tiny lorries and further

253

traffic, where it did exist, was a mixture of forty-year-old buses and ancient pick-ups with slatted planks along their trailer sides. Evening activity was typified almost entirely by people heading home rather than going out and for much of the day, the large square below my hotel room displayed all the liveliness of a quiet village green.

The cheap place towards which instinct had guided me was called something high blown like La Plaza or El Grande and it looked certainly to have had a grand past with its sweeping main stairway, pigeon hole check-in area and high ceilinged quarters that led through tall windows on to some open street balcony. The room I was allocated was truly vast and must have been a top of the range suite at one time, but now the practicalities of life were seen to be squarely recognised and it had become a two quid a night dorm with a clutter of lightweight beds scattered around like pulled up chairs. In significant need of rest I holed up here a few days as I enjoyed the price and in a strange way, the static surrounds themselves, which I hadn't quite appreciated enough in those more peaceful moments.

Having slogged long days by the roadside on my way up from Montevideo and tired myself at the Falls of Iguaçu, I was drawn here towards the long bouts of inactivity that the place seemed to suit and was warming quickly to the present setting. I was often attracted by these surrounds of faded grandeur which had greeted me at various points along the way, not realising of course that such diminished traces were the only

254

type of grandeur I was then able to afford. It was in such an atmosphere as this, quietly unruffled and fitted well to afternoon slumber, that I found myself, on day two of my stay here, stretched at rest on my wadded bed, as a still humidity filled the room. The couple of Paraguayan blokes who had spent the night in near proximity had awoken early to go about their business and the place was now empty, awaiting fresh arrivals. It had looked uncharacteristically like rain, in what was the middle of a dry summer and I felt a warm breeze starting to blow through the louvered shutters, peering beyond which and across the quiet square, I noticed a very strange thing. It was a bird, possibly an urban sparrow, which had flown in peculiar flapping haste across the palm tops, as though in some search for safety only to fall suddenly from the sky, like a stone to the ground.

I had barely the time to dwell upon the oddity of this when the real drama began, as the French style windows flew inwards with a loud slap, shattered glass took off in random directions across the floor and large globs of horizontal rain smacked the far wall about thirty feet away. Crouched into a sheltered corner, I watched on in a kind of numb disengagement as the furniture began to levitate away upon a ripple of blowing waves and had there been curtains or blinds of any type, they would by now have been lying parallel to the ceiling, as the wind screamed in.

Heaven knew what would have happened had I stayed there much longer, but fortunately I was saved from ever finding

255

out by a beckoning hand from the landing, which guided me, via hall and stairs, to a darkened lower level, where those more in tune with events had begun to make themselves busy. The once welcoming atmosphere that had greeted my arrival in this foyer was now completely contrasted by one of endemic fear and men heaved against the giant front door with their feet slithering on the wet tiled floor. I have to confess that, on hearing first mention of the word *hurrican,* I began to feel a sense of real excitement and may, for a moment, have worn an expression of daft indulgence. But sensing now the anxieties of the small crowd, I began to share their deep concern, if not easily their defensive chores.

After some while the men with their shoulders at the door began to tire and I was offered my own spell of heaving duty, but the crowd of replacement volunteers became so tightly packed that I could barely put an arm in one place without reaching for steadiness somewhere far away and so I merely leaned to in symbolic fashion, like some useless moral supporter throwing in their token gesture. For an hour or more the winds blew on and then, in that post-climactic way of all storm-endings, the scowling din and occasional passing thud of debris simply ceased to be. The stifling humidity that had preceded the whole event was soon followed by a cool breathability, as people began to peer about, count whatever blessings remained and trail away to uncompleted tasks, perhaps wondering now if they were still worth the while.

My own thoughts went back to gathering up my few possessions which, when last seen, had been propped neatly by my bed at the window. On approach to the room, I had never expected to find things exactly as they had been, but neither was I prepared for the scene now through the half-opened door, as what appeared to be a floor space swept clear of furniture turned soon into one where all beds, mattresses and broken bits of shuttering were laid in a heap at one end, as though a giant hand had clutched everything together and then flung it hard against the far wall.

Somewhere in the midst of this mangled pile lay my own luggage, far heavier now than when I'd last lifted it and no longer quite holding its shape. I began to wring out its contents like wet washing, while vowing to nevermore travel without a bin-liner protecting its interior. Digging down into its sopping heart, I pulled out an early travel diary I'd been keeping, which I then considered to be a combination of brilliant and truly remarkable. Its ball-point writing had now turned to pages of indecipherable sky blue and, perhaps just as well, I never did get to read it back.

The world outside our disordered lodgings seemed to be having one of those strange total eclipse moments, where one day had ended only for another to begin within a moment. The public at large however were reluctant to test this new air of peace and as I recall, not a solitary bird took to flight. A notable feature of hurricane storms is that in the swirl of their progress

257

there may exist an eye of gravitational calm which can fool some into believing that the real danger has passed. Those people unaware of this fact, which presently included myself, could be caught out by a returning blast, which would bring back with it all the debris once departed. But innocence, in this one case, had won out over wise caution and the storm really was over.

It felt oddly unreal to be walking the capital's streets in the height of the day, with not a human soul for company. Once-raucous vehicles lay parked in silence by the roadside and barely a sign of life had yet surfaced. Eventually though, a few faces began to peer from the doorway shadows and cautious eyes looked towards the sky. A mood of recovery began to take hold, but in the midst of this, it was easy to recognise the physical survivors for whom great thanks were in order and those unfortunates for whom it was not.

On the corner by my digs, a busy fruit and veg trader began to haul down the planks that had boarded his shop front and seemed to show defiance in being the first to open. His polished produce was stacked in easy to handle boxes that became soon a street-facing stall and here was a man prepared for events. Some way along however a cigarette vendor, one of those with his wares shelved upon a large board that was supported on a stick, in the way of a double-bass, was crouched low by the gutter, in search of his scattered wares. There couldn't be many saleable items left now among his meagre stock and on watching him grasp bitterly at a saturated pack of Lucky Strikes,

258

I wondered if he had reserves elsewhere, or whether this really was him wiped out? His deflated, end-of-the-world expression and the sad hunch of his shoulders, suggested something of the sort. And thus it ever was in events of this kind, where strong things remained upright and weaker ones get blown away. Life's natural storms are nearly always better ridden by those in safe houses with sturdy walls around them, while those on society's edge, have even what little they own taken from them.

Back at the cheap lodging place, very little had actually changed from the moment I'd walked in, fresh out of Brazil. From the upstairs landing, a man was sweeping a cascade of water and broken glass, which fell without warning onto the tiled floor below. But apart from this, the mood was not much altered from that of other days, where the daily facts of life were accepted with a faint smile and a shrug. Up in the room the beds were still in car crash mode, but unlike the similar montage-type of stuff that you see in art galleries around the world, this was not just a pile of old crap fit straight for the skip, but a temporary store of furniture that would soon be put back into service and with a careful eye for the best pieces available, I was able to pull away a completely un-crooked bed-frame and a partially dry mattress, which I managed to drag re-united, towards a sheltering wall. There, away from the hazards of unswept glass and stray splinters, I stretched out my limbs before simply falling in with the local mood of the hour. I went back to sleep.

When the time arrived for me to leave here for good, I did so in a way that was far from expected. I had been looking at Argentina for a few days from my room-front veranda, as its river shore appeared between the walls of various tall buildings and occasionally a grain boat, with tall sky blue and white funnels would appear, representing one of its national shipping lines. As things often do in a straight line view, it looked near enough to walk there in a matter of minutes and with a skip across the nearby bridge (wherever it happened to be), I should be back on its territory in no time at all. On approaching the riverside, however, I became at once baffled by the complete absence of any suitable crossing point to the other side and upon looking the considerable distance each way that it was possible to see, could find no trace there either. I was wondering which way I would have to head off first in order to footslog my way towards the next outward route and not wishing to embark upon some fool's errand, I turned to a passer-by, to inquire of the whereabouts of the nearest bridge that would take me beyond this western side of the country. The fellow that I approached I can remember quite distinctly, not so much for his appearance, which was kind of tall, rangy and hard-worked, but by the wounded intonation in his voice as he stooped down from his height and replied,

"No hay puente, señor!"

There is no bridge.

We were here in the capital of a long established nation, at the point of an international frontier, facing a stretch of river that was no wider than the Dee beyond Chester, which had been successfully spanned by 1st Century Romans no less. Yet in such a place we stood, waiting for the age to dawn. It was certainly a sad measure of Paraguay's development during that period and also its brutal isolation which, coupled to Argentina's lack of interest in the place, could indicate how one country might consider itself the best in the region, while ignoring the type of standards achieved further afield. I shook my head and hardly heard the following directions, which took me in some confusion down a roughly-paved alleyway, towards some large black gate, beyond which a slim river-pier provided the sailing point for a tiny wooden ferry-boat. In this fashion it then was, beneath a wide canopy roof and trailing my fingers in the waters of the Rio Paraguay, that we chugged smoothly across, like in some re-created film passage of Edwardian life. Out of a country long frozen in time and over to another, living through times it would never forget.

For many years afterwards I could hardly hear mention of Paraguay without conjuring up this image of a benighted country, as unlucky in its history as some people have been in love. Land-locked and consequently impoverished, surviving through the never ending conditions of a nineteen-thirties-style slump. Things are not now as they were before however, nor will they ever be again. In the early nineteen eighties, after one of the most extensive construction projects in history, a massive hydro-electric dam was commissioned on the stretch of river that separates Eastern Paraguay from Brazil. Though the ecological and human disturbance it engendered may not have been to everyone's liking, when once constructed it brought about a far greater national improvement than any left wing revolution or rightist coup could ever have achieved. Though the debts incurred were a long abiding issue, the electrical power generated was not only sufficient for Paraguay's entire domestic needs, but also left a huge 85% surplus, which could be sold on to bordering neighbours at significant profit. The dusty, small strip of a town that had lain at the country's eastern border, once named after a vain dictator, has grown through its project connections into a booming modern city of steel and glass, accounting for 60% of commercial GDP in South America's fastest growing economy. Where once it was seen that a few wealthier Paraguayans would sidle from the country in order to buy luxuries elsewhere, it was now the case that foreigners would flood to here, in what had become an up-market, duty-free shopping haven.

The momentum garnered by this solitary development has spawned other similar ventures along the Rio Parana, bordering Brazil and Argentina. Asuncion has long since acquired its super modern bridge, taken for granted now as bridges always are. The material status of nearly every single person in the country has vastly grown and with such

262

improvements has come a far greater freedom as, at last, after 182 years of national independence, Paraguay was able in 1993, to appoint its first ever democratically-elected government. This huge transformation has come about not through brow-beating force or political dogma, but by the peaceful means of economic growth. Hydro-electricity here has changed everything, in the way that more polluting sources of energy have changed the world elsewhere. A state that had resisted so strongly the forces of democratic will, has found now it can no longer afford to be undemocratic and finally, after decades of hardship and isolation, Paraguay has made its full recovery from the long pain of Chaco and the Triple Alliance War.

*

Crossing fresh borders, either into new countries or parts of old familiar ones through which you've never travelled before, is near always a great source of optimism. At such times you may cast off any troubles which may have beset you in the place you are leaving, with a hope that none will follow you on. My own minor difficulties were in the laborious business of simply hitching rides, which had been a drawn out affair for much of this southern journey and by simply crossing the Rio Paraguay in a converted pleasure-craft, I thought wishfully that my luck would change. I needed traverse only a narrow strip of east-west Argentina to reach the Chilean coast, from where I would soon head north, back up into Peru. The thousand or so miles, with just one good day's travel in among the average dross ones, should see me there in just about a week. In a surge of optimism however old lessons can easily be forgotten and thus do they have to be learned all over again. It took me a fortnight.

The tendency to feel sorry for oneself took over here for a while which, in light of my decent health and the fact that I was travelling for free, seems rather unkind to the circumstances, but even in such relatively fallow times, there could be passages of event that you would barely encounter in any other form of travel. A roadside siesta beneath a shading tree brought inquisitive wildlife to my side and I awoke with a live vulture peering straight into my face, from about a foot away. As I swiftly rose in my own defence, I recall that there was no flight of panic from the carrion eater, but merely a couple of slow hops back and a hunched expression of apology as though, if dialogue were possible, it may have offered the word, 'Sheesh!' Even when standing bolt upright in a more threatening pose I could affect no instant departure, as it merely beat its way calmly to an overhanging branch and stayed there in case I should suddenly changed my decision on whether to peg it or not.

Where the land rose up like a slant tectonic plate toward some faintly distant heights, the plains of straw revived suddenly into a carpet of lush grass that must have seemed like a mirage to the poor up-country farmers who struggled perennially for good animal fodder. Pleasing to the eye and no doubt to its proud

264

owners, it arrived with a new sense of dread, as I was still filled with a phobia of such low places after my terror in the swamps of Entre Rios. In such a summer landscape it was that I scanned all horizons to see nothing but this knee-high growth running to every visible direction which, in my present state of caution, left me with little option beyond remaining at the roadside all night, should no ride arrive soon.

Eventually, with shadows fading into one and the fields disappearing under a sea of black, I came upon an avenue of tall poplars, angled away from my route and with the faint outline of an overgrown cart-track running between them. At some safe distance from the road, I wandered in to find a pair of hollowed-out wheel ruts, into one of which I rolled out my gear and there I lay, with pendulous heads of grass brushing my face, as I attempted rest. With a mozzy coil well on the burn, my other great concern here, beyond that of snakes, was that some homeward farmer might use the track during the night and my faculties were attuned to the sound of a whirring engine and bright headlights bearing down, which might force me to suddenly flee. What I did encounter however was something so greatly unbargained for that I was barely able to react until it was nearly upon me.

Reposing for a while in a state between slumber and adapted discomfort, I began to sense a rhythmic noise, which I thought at first to be either the onset of a dream or a light throbbing within the depths of my ear, but as it grew louder I

265

could make out the distant sound of a horse's hooves, beating at pace across the bare earth somewhere very nearby. It began as something quite spooky but then, as the volume increased through the pitch darkness, it became something more alarming. It was on this track for sure, there was not a light to be seen and it may or may not run straight over me. The measure of how many thoughts one may conjure up in the space of four or five seconds is a difficult thing to quantify but, in the course of this short time, while the pounding grew stronger in my direction, I was able to consider whether it really was coming this way. It unmistakably was. Would it jump over me in the darkness? Most likely not. And lastly, right at the death, should I start rolling aside in this last available split second, in which I lay bound and defenceless in my sleeping bag and about to let out a loud piercing SCREAM?

A very underrated element is blind panic, which is something that should never be omitted from one's own survival kit. It might lead to the odd temporary loss of dignity, but it will get you out of a lot more tight spots than it will get you into. I must have raised my voice at one of the few available seconds remaining, which would allow the rider to haul in the reins and stand his mount at broadsides ahead of me, at a distance of no greater than five yards. In whatever light there filtered through the tall trees, I could now see them both, in a steaming cloud of sweat and heard the man's voice, breathlessly cursing.

"What the fuck are you doing there?", he shouted.

266

I mumbled something half thought out, in a foreign tongue, about my travels on the road and a need for sleep, in which I doubt he was the least bit interested.

"I nearly fucking killed you!", he said, a truth I could hardly contest and with little further to say, he tiptoed the horse around within inches of me, stumbling over the grass central verge that ran between the tyre tracks, before belting on, full speed ahead, into the black tunnel of night.

I have mulled over this near-miss incident several times over the years and never having mentioned it to someone who really knew about horses, wondered what actually would have happened had I merely curled myself into a ball and not let out the un-manly scream? Would I have been dashed into a pulp by flailing hooves and left there to suffer in my final hours? Or would it have all passed off like a Keystone Cops car chase in some perfect dovetail of non collision? I was familiar with the idea of horses being reluctant to step upon prone riders if they could actually see them, but that was related to National Hunt racing on the daytime TV, while here was a tree-lined track where even the starlight struggled to break through. And what of that fellow racing alone at madcap speed through the unseen wilds? Was he totally off his head? Or was he one of those who had calmly thought things through and decided that it were better to be totally alive for one minute than half dead for fifty years? As my heart now diffused it's thudding beat through the crown of my skull, I had no wish for either choice at such a late hour,

267

when I would much rather have been sound and peacefully asleep.

On the watershed side of the lower Andes, the arable landscape, particularly at this summer February time of year, appeared richer than anywhere there could be on the entire southern continent. The late seasonal branches weighed low with every type of fruit you would wish to gather and ripened nuts that would make a healthier diet than the one we had recently known. Peaches, apricots, everything we would think of as a luxury, was hanging here in abundance, including those huge sweet dobbing grapes which, until then, only seemed to exist in the most expensive of shops. It provided a strong temptation for living off the land, despite the inconvenience of the land not being our own.

On eventual sight of Mendoza, at the edge of this thousand mile plain, the feature that first caught your eye was not the cypress-dotted town itself, but the wall of sheer rock that rose from behind it which, from great distance, could be mistaken for a part of the sky itself. From ten miles off there appeared not a hope of advancement through this granite barrier, but on closer approach you could pick out movements on an engineered road, which must have followed the trail of mountain goats. The pass through here, though a daunting prospect when looking up, would bring us quite soon to a different large city and another desert, on the Pacific Ocean coast. En route to this place we would brush the shoulder of Mount Aconcagua, at 22,831 feet, the highest peak on the entire American continent. With careful acclimatisation and few real technical challenges along the way, it would be a steady climb to the top, according to those who had recently made it. It was alas, another good opportunity passed lazily by and during the days when we were suited more to accomplish it, we would regretfully never return.

*

High altitude roads through South American countries are filled with more than their fair share of hazards and coupled with the sparse availability of cheap rooms, plus the fact of truck-lifts being about the same cost as public transport, I decided to break a two-month sequence here that would matter to no one now, but which seemed to me at the time like a huge cop out. I caught the bus. While travelling in the company of people who never spoke, I felt that the journey was suddenly over and I was back in commuter land, but it got me to Santiago in the afternoon of the same day, feeling as though I were stepping off at exactly the same point as that which I'd embarked.

If there was any merit to be gained from this misted, side-on window view of things, it must have been during the long descent into Chile, where the tortuous lasso of a road contended strongly for most hair-pin bends on a single mountain pass, but a further point of interest, strange be it to say, was in the change of climatic landscape, not just over a single day, but within the

269

space of a couple of hours. The American continent, with its high west-coastal ranges, appears to have been given near monopoly on these compacted regions, where you can rise from lowland fields, through rocky passes and between walls of cut snow, to descend at last onto a scorching desert. I found myself eventually in some strange orientation on the edge of Chile's capital, overlooking its hazy sprawl and focused my immediate attentions elsewhere.

I had neither time nor the inclination towards embroiling myself in a lately developed city such as this when, within seemingly easy reach, there were places of far greater interest. From almost the moment I left the Highlands of Bolivia to wander these southern states, I had pined for a return, not only to that haunting landscape of the Central Andes, but to the strange mystical culture it possessed which, even when nothing happened for hours or days on end and people rarely spoke, you felt always that there was some hidden kind of spell in the air. The inland districts of Peru presented a similar kind of image at large, with perhaps a few stronger features thrown in and it was a region I had so far passed by. I reckoned I must only be a week away now from its southern borders, but as with most of my other timescale calculations on this long drawn-out trip, my estimates must have been about three-times over-optimistic.

The low strip of land that broadly foots the Western Andes creates a wide featureless plain, where the last of arid crags fall shy of the not-too distant sea. At certain changes of temperature, a few miniscule drops of water may come to rest, which might seem like a deluge to the few creatures that do survive here but otherwise there is hardly a damp patch, nor even a waft of humid air, in what is regarded broadly as the stillest and driest place on earth. As a measure of how long-dry this area is actually considered to be, there are some parts of its vast expanse, variously known as the Secure, the Puma and the Chico, but largely by us as the Atacama Desert, where rainfall has never been recorded, not now, not ever, even in archaeological records that have analyzed sampled evidence from the last three million years.

Some broad scale historic facts might make a place more interesting than it would normally appear and also a trip-wire camera kit, with months of photographic patience applied, may highlight the point that we are never truly alone, but in the normal light of day this could feel like the emptiest place imaginable, with none of the romantic elements found among dry lands elsewhere and in the few small areas where strong changes did occur they tended to be created by surface mineral content, rather than historic human activity. In the course of time however, while inching through this desolate gap between mountain and sea, a few faint traces would come to light, not quite of present life, but of difficult past ones that had been spent out in this arid wilderness. Small towns of fallen timber, lying askew to their derelict pit-heads, spoke now of exhaustion in all its forms. At the few open driveways to operational works, rarely

271

a vehicle entered beyond the rusting signs, while rather more eerily, none ever seemed to leave. Way further ahead, the cheap mine operations of much earlier times bore no protective barrier around their open shafts, which were hazard-marked only by splashes of copper green and at last, where the road ran deep into coastal bays, twin jetties lay idle beneath a framework of pulleys, where nothing moved now but the grey Pacific waves.

Someone once told me that real memories are never forgotten and that once something is consciously recorded in your brain it never leaves, but the hardest thoughts to rekindle are always those of how you viewed somewhere prior to your actual arrival, before your ideas on the place had really settled. In the case of Chile however my own recollections are quite clear, as they fall much in line with those of the watching world during that period. In September 1973, a Chilean government which had once been freely elected, was violently deposed in a rather well organised and distantly plotted coup. Nothing out of the ordinary there, in a region of bi-annual revolutions, except that this particular overthrow was known to have employed strong logistical support from partners further abroad, pretty much like the sponsored conflict in the Chaco of forty years before. The common outrage at what had occurred may soon have died down, were it not for the long drawn out business which followed, that was described locally as a Dirty War. This was not so much a two-sided armed conflict, but simply a

272

widespread programme of state sponsored murder, set in place by the newly incumbent government.

Having eventually run out of domestic victims, the practice was carried on elsewhere, as a number of dissident exiles were assassinated in cities across the globe. The scheme was part of a much wider plan involving several Latin American countries, including Argentina and was co-ordinated under the codename Condor, from CIA headquarters in Panama. Beyond the issues of the lately ended Vietnam War and the ongoing Apartheid regime in South Africa, this was one of the most widely discussed world topics of the day and due to the visible evidence of large scale liquidations, notably concerning events in the National football stadium and the overthrow of a perceived democracy, it was towards Chile that much of scorn was directed, despite matters elsewhere being at a far more critical stage.

While travelling through both neighbouring states in close proximity of time, it would take little more than a scratch below the surface to see that it was Argentina that had progressed much further along the road of civil genocide, but the most remarkable thing I discovered in these two countries was that, despite wide beliefs to the contrary, of a whole country succumbing unwillingly to the iron heel, a large proportion of people, perhaps a quarter of the ones I would meet, were not in strong opposition to the situation at all, or in the way it was developing. On becoming aware of this, it was with great caution

273

that you would skirt a conversation on these subjects, as you could meet overly strong opinions from surprisingly unexpected quarters. Which could have been why, in general, there prevailed a tight silence on all but the simplest of matters?

I had met, in Argentina, a man whose friends had vanished into smoke and been in a village that had closed up like in a Western gun-fight, while later, around Ecuador, I would meet an individual who, during military service, may have actually been doing some of the executing himself, but in the main there would be no revealing encounters here. That was, of course, until I had a very brief and surprisingly comfortable passing moment with an associate member of the Chilean Military Junta.

Some days further along the road, in the lee of some ravine of fire-brick red, I picked up a strange lift from a vehicle so grand in outward appearance that I was initially in two minds as to whether it was worth raising a hopeful thumb in its direction and was truly amazed when it pulled over beside me. Long, low and wide, in a high-polished black, I hadn't really noticed until climbing inside, that the leather-seated rear interior was large enough in which to hold a business conference, while upon the front nearside wing, the small chromed aerial, which I had thought to be related to an in-car radio, was in fact a tiny flag pole. The gentleman driving was a cultivated fellow who spoke a decent level of English and when I remarked that he seemed a little over-educated to be working as a humble chauffeur, he

274

replied that he had, in fact, given the chauffeur the day off and he himself was an Admiral in the Chilean Navy. He further told me, I think by way of an introduction rather than a boast, that he was a member of the Fuerza del Armas Council, which presently governed the country.

Having heard many of the tales associated with this group, I at first held my breath, while pondering the ramifications should our meeting not go well, but the fellow seemed decent enough on a personal level and we began some kind of conversation. There must have been a hundred questions I could have gently forwarded at this time, but being wearily tired from nights of rough sleep and perhaps at a stage in my life where I lacked the savvy to negotiate tactfully such straits of peril, I passed over the situation rather lightly. It was rumoured (with justification, as it turned out), that people had been bricked into walls and chucked out of high-flying helicopters for taking the wrong conversational line and I feared that my own artless efforts may go similarly astray.

In the end, it was my own reply to one of the gentleman's questions that brought out the most telling moment in this brief engagement as, in response perhaps to my visible unease, he asked me plainly what people in other countries thought of Chile? I was more than wary of the rules on free speech here at this time, particularly when uttering words of criticism and told him so, but I was reassured that this was a private conversation right in the middle of nowhere. And so,

invited to go ahead, I told him straight out that in countries
where I'd recently spent time, i.e. France, the Netherlands,
Germany and through liberal-type newspapers in my own
country, the general consensus was that Chile, like Argentina,
was presently a country run by a minority fascist dictatorship,
that had murdered thousands of its own people. He seemed
genuinely taken aback.

'My God,' he said, 'is that how people really see us?'

'Yeah,' I said, 'to anyone who takes an interest, it pretty
much is.'

The silence that followed was not one filled with threat,
but of someone turning over a truth that they had either
overlooked or deliberately kept at bay. Perhaps he'd convinced
himself that recent bold moves by the military government had
been a lesser course of evil and their cause had been essentially a
noble one? The means they employed might have been
condemned in some foreign parts, but the country had been on its
way to the dogs at the moment they stepped in and in the purely
economic sense, they had staved off a national disaster. Why,
they were practically all heroes!

There were many earlier factors into which I'd never
deeply researched at this time, such as how radical Leftist groups
had brought retribution upon themselves, as in Uruguay and
Argentina, but in this long unequal battle between a military
government and its people, did he really believe that the
summary execution of up to four thousand civilians was rightly

justified? At that moment, either by nature or wilful effort, I think he really did.

While years have passed, I have gone over this event a number of times, not necessarily to understand the wider background, but to weigh up its relevance to my own presence. Was this a noteworthy incident or just a mere ripple in the breeze? A real dice with death or a flickering detail in a panoramic landscape? In terms of consequence it could've been nothing at all, yet now I think of it, there was one thing I could carry with me from here that might be significant, it was in the handshake. Throughout this period of my on-the-road days I had always followed a European Continental practice that I rather admired, where drivers and hitch-hikers would shake hands on parting; for one to thank the other and perhaps receive wishes of good luck in return. Which is undoubtedly what would have happened here.

This Junta-appointed fellow, in his state car, must have encountered all the main players of Chilean politics during this period, plus many of those of similarly governed states and when met, would have greeted them in the customary fashion. This in itself brings forth one rather unsettling thought. In bidding a thankful and innocent farewell, did I unwittingly shake the hand that had shaken the hand of one of South America's most notorious dictators? If this was indeed the case, then I can only hope that, in moments of private audition, Augusto Pinochet was

277

following the same practice as on public state occasions and that he was always wearing gloves.

A few days and not many miles further on along this quiet desert road, I arrived at another point where the shadow of danger passed closely by, but unlike on the most recent occasion, where I couldn't be sure whether the threat was genuine, here I really did feel as though the earth was about to open up and swallow me whole. By the edge of some failing settlement, where only the stragglers and the roadside cafe people stayed on, I found myself, around early dusk, beside a small adobe church that, were it not for the slant sun blazing against its windows, would have blended indistinct into the earth from which it had risen.

At this hour, with the day almost gone, I would have been searching the onward horizon for suitable bedding-down places in order to avoid a fumble in the dark and the sight of any kind of prospective shelter would have been most welcome. The sanctuary of a barely used church would fit the bill quite nicely and, as well as protecting us from the mild discomfort of desert dew, would keep out the early morning light for an hour or two more, until such time as the rest of the world had risen. Soon it was then that, by some self-contrived opening and while stealthily avoiding attention, I found my way inside, to a dusty, benched-lined interior, where everything you laid hands on made a loud creaking sound and the mud floors were worn concave every way to the altar.

It would have been by the flicker of a lighted match and then the memory of what I had seen, that I arranged my things upon the earthen floor, before settling down into a heavy sleep that was vividly remembered, not for any dream that appeared within, but by the abrupt way I was awoken; which I recall as like being hauled from the lowest depths of drowning. I had never known a state of wakefulness like the one I then experienced and thankfully have never done since, as the earth rippled beneath me and I arose from one surreal state of consciousness into another; which felt like a dream within a dream. I had really thought at first that my heart had developed a strangely uneven beat, or my body had given over to some wild spate of convulsions and it was only moments later, as the material dust came to settle, that I began to realise what had happened.

On picturing myself in the midst of an earthquake I had always imagined (in vain secrecy), that I would be the coolest customer around. Keen in my wits, quick on my feet and perhaps with a bit of time for a one-handed spot of casual heroism right there at the end. How different then the reality, as I lay in the strait-jacket of my sleeping bag, fixed into a trance and feeling not the least brave but strangely, with not a trace of any real fear. In re-summoning these circumstances, I am reminded of a tale I heard much later on, about an adventure faced by David Livingstone on his wanderings through Africa where, out on the savannah trail one day, he was attacked by a solitary lion.

279

The beast had leapt on him from behind and shaken him violently by the neck, as dogs often do with a rag and the effect of this was to both stun and release the fellow of all worldly cares. In the brief passage between then and the time when a couple of African bearers beat the animal away, Livingstone had experienced a moment not of terror, but of tractable calm. Being a religious man, the Great Missionary had regarded this phenomenon as God's merciful way of smoothing a path into the after-life and by a similar measure, this earthquake disorientation could have been Heaven's own local means of preparing myself should the roof shortly cave in.

With this having clearly not happened, I gave thanks for my own continued survival and comforted perhaps by what I was sure was the end of the affair, I merely snuggled up and found my way back to sleep. Had I been more wisely informed on these matters however, I may have rolled up my gear right then and made a safe bolt for the exit. In line with my unabashed confidence over the high winds in Paraguay, I was totally oblivious here to the possibility of close repeat events, or aftershocks, which may bring forth the same if not a greater degree of peril. In blissful ignorance of this I was able to rest peacefully, until a grey morning light began to struggle its way through the dust-coated windows.

On preparing myself for the next day's departure, I peered around this place, now looking strangely new and noted that, beneath the icons and behind the benches, a number of wide

280

wall cracks had been created, clearly over the course of time, which gave testimony both to the common prevalence of such events and the building material's capacity to withstand them. At the base of some of these rents however were pyramid piles of fresh soil, four inches high, which would be a record of our most recent episode. Before leaving I grabbed a scoop of this mud-brick dust and ran it through the fingers of one hand. Its odour brought back the memory of an old school potting shed.

Out into the real full morning, I picked up a swift ride which was well convenient, as I had neither food nor water and there was none nearby. The driver who took me along was a stocky middle-aged fellow, bald and jet-black haired, who drove a bullet shaped American car from the nineteen fifties, which rather resembled his own image, as pets and their owners often do. He spoke decent English, having spent time up in Chicago and due to this, I was able to compliment him fully on the fine upkeep of his streamlined classic. Our conversation, which couldn't have been much regarding scenery, would have largely concerned the direction we were taking and certainly, after the meeting with the Admiral, would not have veered anywhere near politics. But there was one other issue that was burning on my lips, the mentioning of which was simply too much to resist and so, without further ado, I cut straight to the heart of recent events.

'Did you feel that earthquake last night?' I asked
He looked temporarily baffled.

281

'What earthquake was that, my man?,' he replied.

'Well, *the* earthquake,' I said, 'It began at around ten o'clock, ran on for what seemed like a minute, shook the ground wildly and left some cracks in the walls. *That* earthquake.'

'Naah,' he said, 'that wasn't an earthquake, a tremor only. Bloody hell no! If it's an earthquake, half the houses fall down!'

I felt a great sense of deflation, as though my great big deal of an event had been reduced to a piddling pile of dust and while sniffling through the remainder of our short journey together, I peered at every isolated structure along the way in the hope that just something had collapsed, while mercifully sparing its occupants and causing expense to none other than huge corporate businesses, who could well afford it.

In defence of my earlier great excitement, it was perhaps understandable that for a person lying on a bare hard floor, rather than a raised mattress, a tremor would have been felt in much greater intensity and even on the low scale that it was, maybe Richter 2, 3 or 4, it would have made significant news elsewhere. But in this narrow strip of a country, where the Pacific plate spears in from the west to flip up the Andes, to call this rumbling disturbance an earthquake would be like telling a Brazilian that Mancunian drizzle was real rain. Though far removed as it was from the falling walls of Jericho, it was enough to enlighten me on which was the safest place to be in the event of an earthquake. Right out of it.

282

A couple of nights before my final departure from Chile, I bedded down upon a rocky hill overlooking the twinkling lights of Antofagasta. While lying in the dark, on some smooth surface that ran into a tip for old road material, I was witness to an innocent seeming event, where two men in a low-sided pick-up pulled in off the road, halted close to where I lay and began to create a large bonfire out of heaps of paperwork. As they stood glowing and shielding their eyes against the chest-high flames, I pulled the sleeping bag over the white of my face to avoid detection, and continued my rest undisturbed. By morning time, the evidence of their activity was merely a pile of tissue-thin ashes, with a few burnt folder-clips and I departed soon, unaware yet of any great anomaly.

The distance from Antofagasta to the recently known town of Arica was around 720 kilometres, through one of the least hospitable parts of the Atacama, where few signs even of ghosts existed and judging by my recent rates of progress, I was in for some hard slog. But at what seemed to be the very height of my difficulties, I was denied the indulgence of a wallowing bout of self-sympathy, as I was there with one single truck ride in the course of a whole long day. The driver who brought me this great stretch was an earnest, sincere fellow of not advanced years, who had strong opinions against the military rule which seemed, for him, to have become closely personal. Being un-fluent in the language I could delve not closely into this with the right level of sensitivity, but what I could gather was that, beneath the quilted cover of his truck's gearbox, there was enough documentary evidence to get him presently shot, or to bring certain people to justice, come the day.

The uniform tedium of our long straight journey was only briefly disturbed, firstly by a three-toed rhea, running yards ahead like some daft rabbit in the road and later, when I was asked to take a photo of the driver standing before a towering road sign. The point of which seemed to be to record how many kilometres we had travelled from Antofagasta, (700). But for the rest it was just a battle to conjure up some worthwhile thoughts, while not showing disregard to the driver by simply falling asleep. Only when approaching the town of Arica was it that we were reminded of our real purpose and that we had not warped into some Mars-like other world, where all days and seasons were the same. That was when the retrospective worries began, as the fellow asked me where I was going to stay.

Being on a kind of loose, not to mention low-budget schedule, I told him that I had no wish to enter Arica that night, but would be happy to be dropped off on the desert-edge of town, where I might bivvy out in the open and showing him my rolled-up sleeping bag, displayed my intentions to such effect. At this he firmly shook his head, telling me that it was not optional to remain outside, due to something called a *queda* and that I would definitely need to be staying indoors. I wracked my memory to find the meaning of this half-familiar word and

284

eventually found it in the latter pages of my traveller's dictionary.

Queda: / *To remain; rest in one place; a curfew.*

'A curfew?'

'Yes,' he said, ' a curfew.'

I was suddenly alarmed.

'And this curfew,' I asked, 'Is it only in the town of Arica, or in all of Chile?'

'All of Chile,' he said, 'from first dark until daylight, seven days a week.'

'What happens then if they catch you outside?' I asked.

'Peligroso,' he replied and made a click-clicking motion with the trigger-finger of his right hand.

I got the message, which became rather scarier once it had fully sunk in. I recalled, when I thought of it, an incident that was reported a few years previously in some home-based newspaper, of a pregnant young woman in Santiago who, feeling that her time of child delivery had arrived, made a rush into the street in order to find assistance. In her panic, she had failed to follow the emergency procedure of draping a white bed sheet from an opened window and she was gunned down. The soldiers who took her life were exonerated from blame, as they had merely followed the rules laid down under the government guidelines. This however had been in the twitchy period immediately following the coup and I was somehow convinced that such circumstances could no longer prevail. If this rule had

285

indeed been in force during my nearly fortnight's journey from Santiago, then it surely was a moment for chill reflection and even the driver gave a shudder on my behalf. Fortunately, at last, for my own peace of mind, I was able to observe correctly just one final night of the curfew, as this kind fellow allowed me to remain in close proximity to his parked-up truck and while he dozed alone in the cab, I lay in the sand below, settling my swirling thoughts and trying to achieve some worthwhile slumber.

Perhaps my course had not sailed so close to the wind after all, as the desert villages were lightly populated to the point almost of abandonment and had the military there busted you, they might only have thrown you into a piss corner for the night, as in Uruguay. But what then of those two fellows back in Antofagasta, with their bright bonfire, visible for miles? Were they in possession of some special exemption from curfews and if so, why? I wondered whether they were the kind of people to whom you would like to introduce yourself in the dark hours of night and I rather doubted it. Finally, I mollified myself with the thought that, while large nets are cast wide to entrap their primary victims, there would always be room for tiddlers like me to wriggle a way through. I slept.

*

In a one-day respite from this long desert slog, I rested at Tacna, the first southerly Peruvian town, where seasonally running streams had painted with green, this normally dry side of the Andes. Before the white facade of a Spanish church, a small garden was criss-crossed by a pattern of hedges, in imitation medieval style and around here, the working weary and those with some leisure to spend, bided their time beneath the shade of their wide-brim hats.

I had eagerly awaited my return to this less formal atmosphere, in what we might have called the Third World, where people were less likely to flaunt their tokens of material gain, or weigh you up according to how worn your clothes were. But in more immediate terms, there were two specific reasons why I should yearn so strongly for this moment. One was the generally lower cost of things here, and, with a huge 40% devaluation in the local currency having taken place during the recent months of my absence, it would make things a whole lot cheaper for a while, until rampant inflation should eat the whole lot back. The other reason was one of a more personal nature, in relation to that one feature of Peruvian street-life that I had missed rather more than expected and only an early re-engagement with, would mark my true return to the country.

In a corner of this garden area, worn grassless by the passage of feet, came the wafted smell of steam cooking, which drew me in to a hub of slow activity, among which I was able to peer onto people's dinner plates and make my choice, before

287

legging over the wooden bench, with its uncommonly pneumatic tyre suspension where, elbowed in beside others, I made my happy reconnection with the memorable bicycle restaurant. If the fayre this time was not right up to standard, it mattered not so much, as the pleasure was in partaking of the event itself. Which seemed to say, if not welcome home, then certainly welcome back.

Perhaps impelled by these few Spring-like shoots at Tacna, I'd decided on enough of the changeless desert and headed onto the greener side of the mountains. Arequipa, in passing, seemed no longer the quiet backwater, when set beside the stillness of Atacama and through a quilted patchwork of hills, I descended soon to the shores of Lake Titicaca. The waterfront town of Puno was low-rise and sleepy then, with a swathe of red oxide roofs, overborne by a tall cathedral. More recent years of rural migration have seen its profile rise in skyscraper fashion and the population increase three-fold. Its commercial life will certainly have risen in kind, but you wonder by what measure the quality of life has also changed and it would all depend, I guess, on who you should ask.

The main stop-off attraction here, as it was and will always be, surrounded the string of floating, man-made islands that existed somewhere offshore and the boats, built sometimes with reeds, that plied the waters thereabouts. To those I'd met who had paid their fares, it would be either a true revelation, or the most retentive of tourist traps. I avoided the need for making

288

such choices through my lack of spare time and funds, though had I made the crowded trip out there I dare say I would have stolen away, to grab a few moments of the place alone. A lake, by itself, holds no great fascination for me, as I would always find myself drawn away towards the surrounding higher ground and whether a certain lake (being this one in particular), was the highest such on earth or another was the lowest, made no special impression. My resources would be spared for a couple of more worthy destinations not far down the mountain rail-track, towards which we had been drawn by hearsay and reputation, only to find, in rather uncommon manner, that both were markedly better than we had previously imagined.

The reason that Cusco can amaze even the most jaded of worldly travellers is that, on the slow approach through its surrounding landscape, there is barely a hint of its likely existence nor, on the length and breadth of the continent, is there anything quite like it. On first sight, from the open end of its long, populated valley, it appears as would a spa town in some Middle European country, while down in its heart stands evidence of a more definitive Spanish past. But the one area of real fascination lies not in its scenic location, or the upright imposing structures within it, but in the thin crust layer of paved ground that remains below your feet, which occasionally would extend to a foot or so of rising foundation or, in rare cases, an entirely preserved wall. Here were left the last few traces of what may now be, had it been allowed to survive, one of the great wonders of the ancient world.

Running along one side of the old Main Square and part way into the corner of another, there ran an arcaded row of stone buildings, terracotta roofed and shaped in rugged lime, which reflected a picture of pure Latin Europe. Within this small, world-of-its-own enclave, there existed an atmosphere entire, with its hourly moods that seemed never set against quite the same backdrop. At early dawn, the place would be shafted with horizontal light, which ran through the vapour of traders' cooking and then, as the breakfast stalls departed, the shops would unroll onto the forecourt pavement, their wares as bright as a paint box. By mid afternoon, a few busking players may appear, to blow base tunes down their pan wooden pipes, while later, in the mid evening bars, an entirely different crew might tune up, for what would be a likely more sophisticated set. Finally, in the glow of primus lamps, the day would seem book-ended by the familiar street-vendors, selling not this time husky porridge, but peaceful good night cocoa.

The rest of the square was given over to those classical-type buildings of a certain period, which initially represented one culture's victory over another, but which were now looked upon as an attractive regional blend and were variously spot-lit in the evening, to emphasise the fact. It's true that these civic and religious halls contributed their lot to the atmosphere of the place, set in plain contrast against the jarring colours of local people's clothing, but in the wider scheme of things, this was barely more than a veneer of recent times, a widely spread but rather thin disguise. At the latter end of trading hours, or in very early morning, as the stores began their working day, a clearer view could be made of this old heart of town and what had gone to make up its present form. Along the arcaded pathway, polished by passing centuries of so many rope sandals, the flagstones bore signs of adaptation from uses elsewhere, while in a number of established buildings, walls that were clearly medieval had been placed upon foundations of a markedly different origin.

Not quite beyond this central vicinity stood a high stone wall, unconnected on either side, which had been allowed to remain, for no apparent reason other than to showcase the unusual skills of those who had built it. Its separate components were selected from randomly sized pieces that had been shaped to fit into place on a one-by-one basis, rather like the pattern on a large chocolate Easter egg. It displayed at once a great level of finesse in its jointing workmanship and what seemed initially to be a muddled degree of thought in forward planning. On some hills nearby, a matching example of this style had prevailed, probably because its stones were too large and remote to be carted elsewhere and finally, as if the method had gained some kind of wider approval, there were domestic-looking buildings of a later date, which had been placed by selection on such foundations, as though this practice were now the chosen thing.

291

The most notable historic feature of the colonisation of the Americas is that much of it was carried out in an age of very low enlightenment and often by the type of individuals who, though undoubtedly brave, were themselves a product of their own brutal times. In addition to the regretful slaughter and years of forced human misery, another projecting feature of this time was the cultural ruin which had taken place, where artefacts once held sacred were thrown to the fire in the name of holy zeal and objects of immeasurable importance to history were reduced to ingot lumps for the base value of their raw materials. In the spirit of that age, it was as though everything which had gone before was inferior and ungodly, while all that followed was better and somehow more divine. It would take longer than the days when it would have been relevant, but a few facts did eventually surface concerning this once disregarded building pattern, that would prompt reappraisal, not only of its worth, but of the foresight and wisdom of those who had produced it.

In the year 1950, the district of Cusco was shaken by a large earthquake which destroyed up to one third of all buildings in the town and its immediate vicinity. Of the properties that remained undamaged, a high disproportion were of those that had been built either in the ancient pre-Columbian style, or erected later on the foundations of such earlier works. It then first began to seem that structures of this type, formed of asymmetrical stones worked tightly into place, were more likely to roll against one another and re-settle, rather than collapse en masse, which made them, centuries before any similar such discoveries in Japan, a much safer option in a region periodically beset with seismic activity. It marked something of a turnaround in people's opinions toward these indigenous peoples, who were for so long lightly esteemed and said much for their earlier disregarded measure of intellect.

When places you have visited because they were considered to be off-beat, much later become a part of the mainstream, it fills you with a rather mixed set of feelings. On the one hand, you might develop a private sense of pride at having been in on things before they became heavily over-visited, while on the other, you may experience sadness at every later picture you see, showing images to suggest the old atmosphere has departed and never will return. In a wandering life, this type of situation will occur so many times over as to be barely countable and while it is comforting to know that the people who live and work in these districts are at last receiving some of their dues, it is a sentiment forever accompanied by a nagging sense of loss.

I was lately at another famous travel destination on the far side of the world where, as in the case here, visitor numbers during recent years had increased by up to five-fold. It was plain easy to see that, since my earlier visits to this location, transportable light business had been driven off the streets, practically all features of original character spruced to resemble the extensions of a shopping precinct and every web-advertised hotel, providing but the basic requirements, seemed to have received a slap of pastel paint on the walls, a towel for a carpet, some new boutique name and fifty quid on the price. If some improvements had been made, they had been bought at the cost of most other things that the place had originally offered and you wondered whether it were part of a purposed intention to banish from their midst the kind of visitors whose business had popularised the venue in the first place.

Back in Cusco's heart, down a dog leg lane that ran off the central plaza, there existed a squat, low-rise *pensione,* of a quite distinctive nature. Converted to a Latin style of courtyard villa, it was constructed mainly from huge smooth stones of random size, which were said, by the proprietor, to have been laid during Inca times. Whether this was actually true or they had been transported, cannibal-fashion from another place, it was difficult to tell and it may have been of some advantage to have taken a peep around the better rooms, to follow this interest up. Being unflushed with the necessary however, I was directed instead towards the more humble quarters, which were situated, in rather novel fashion, out in what had been the central courtyard area. Into this space was built a section of wooden-shack housing, the corrugated roof of which just about butted-up to the more appropriate terracotta of the original building and rather un-complemented it, as would a tarpaulin shed to a grand old house.

294

The rooms themselves, devoid of door-locks, (notwithstanding your own), opened each into a cemented floor space, partitioned with painted pink boarding, the top foot or so of which, on not quite reaching the ceiling, was finished off with a rolled out band of tight chicken wire. This open topped design, though lacking in the qualities of peace and privacy, created a unique atmosphere, in which there was rarely a dull moment. My first reaction on entering my own allotted coop was to lean back at the cage-like ceiling connection and utter loudly, 'What the f-ing hell am I doing here?' This was a statement repeated in near identical fashion by every incoming guest to arrive while I was there. From the tone of their voice and regardless of the language you could guarantee it was exactly the same. The partial presence of walls lulled people into a false sense of being in their own private space, rather than a sectioned up dormitory and conversations from several rooms apart could be clearly overheard, whether you wished it or not. Occasionally people from adjoining quarters would join in the chat, getting briefly to know their neighbours and perhaps departing without ever having actually met them. In all truth it was a jerry-built dump of a place, but the worn wooden panels and shaky construction seemed to ooze a class of their own, like a battered old nightclub where a great deal had passed through. There would always be something of an outward nature going on and, when it did, you were never too slow in knowing about it.

295

In the room directly next to my own, a large acoustic music ensemble, or perhaps two such groups jamming together, would go through their numbers for an evening spot at some bar down the road, route information would pass to and fro, other people's adventures would whet your appetite for future times and though the obvious fire trap nature of the building was always something to be wary of, it would be remembered by the majority of those who stayed there as one of the great traveller hotels of the region.

I wouldn't like to make a guess at what the place was actually called, as the name may recently have changed and with there being several hotels in that corner now, I may end up praising or damning the wrong one. But those who were there during that time would never confuse it with anywhere else and so it was that we and many alike, would advance from this spot into the nearby hills, to find among the overgrown rocks, the ruined traces of a faded culture and reach at last, a site whose name could never be in doubt were you to be spun around three times and taken there blindfold.

Whichever way you chose to approach or depart from the ruins of Machu Picchu, it would always make for a truly momentous occasion, from the time that you departed your digs a.m., to the moment you returned, wearied with wonder. A forty mile trek through jungle hills may be the ideal way to approach this stunning location provided, of course, that the weather was visually clear and you could be sure of passing there unmolested.

296

I avoided this choice however, due to the cost of hiring in proper gear and would be further discouraged now by reports of overcrowded routes and bandits along the track. But there would be no regret at having foregone the opportunity of the well-worn Inca Trail, as I wouldn't have missed the rail journey out there for anything.

Some types of passage by train, especially those in the poorer countries, are largely memorable for a communal spirit that develops among the passengers, as they impart freely between themselves and often towards yourself, but in the company here of a silent population who presently weren't engaged on any wild smugglers trip, this was never going to be the case. In other places, an excursion may be livened by the surrounding view, though to be honest, I feel this could be taken in better by other means. The thing which really caught my eye here however was something similar to the fascination I once had with the structure and purpose of roads; it was a feature within the actual rail track itself. To travel on the perfect railway line is rather like riding across the perfectly designed bridge, uneventful and largely taken for granted. Throw in a touch of precariousness however, with perhaps a bit of Heath Robinson and you start to get the recipe for a more interesting journey. Which is all fine and dandy so long as you don't have to do it on a daily basis, throughout your working life.

The line that ran out of Cusco heading for the Urubamba Valley took you between high bare hills and

eventually down through a wall of forest, where the view
extended hardly beyond the width of a railway carriage. The ill-
maintained rolling stock in which we were huddled and the slow
diesel engine that hauled, us completed the make-up of a journey
where early arrival was the only matter in our thoughts. That was
until we found ourselves confronted by a decent-sized mountain,
around the sides and through the bowels of which there seemed
to be no way onwards.

What followed then was a strange turn of events, as we
rolled into a siding at what seemed like journey's-end, only to
roll out again in reverse at a steep upwards angle, a feat that was
repeated perhaps a dozen times in stop-start fashion, until our
progress resembled the reverse movement of a dish through
water. While this strange process was taking place, which must
have taken half an hour to climb three hundred feet, I noticed a
chancy collection of improvised moves which accompanied its
advance, as levers were pulled at track-side, not by people solely
designated to do so, but by individuals who had jumped down
and then back up each time from either the brake van or the
driver's cab, depending on which way the train was headed. From
a one-off travellers point of view it had a quaintness about it
rather like those farm gates you have to keep opening then
closing behind you on very minor country roads, but it was a
laborious effort that eventually made you tired just to watch and
a major concern in the long run would have been the safety of
the brakes.

I understand there is at least one similar mechanical feature somewhere in the Himalayas, which may have been built when project money was tight and if so, it could be the last remaining one in the world as the Cusco-Machu Picchu line, since some years ago, has been re-directed. To the relief no doubt of the point-changing driver and his similarly employed brake van mate.

On disembarking finally at the ruins station of Aguas Calientes, the trend of slightly hairy journeys was continued, as we boarded a battered minibus with a huge crack in its rear window, that took us at jet-climbing angle, up a zigzag hairpin road of such loose gravelly surface that we had to take a run at it in order not to slide back. This carried us at a worrying pace of always too fast, until we arrived at last in a patch of pure air, among carefully cropped forest lawns, before a narrow stone gateway that leaned, in earthquake-damaged fashion, slightly off square.

In terms of architectural quality, the ruins at Machu Picchu present nothing to rival the highest of human achievements. Nor are their known historic details anything that would inspire you towards great or noble thoughts, anymore than they might fill you with a morbid kind of horror. Yet they draw people from across the world with a stronger magnetic pull than any other place in South America, due to a visual quality that is shared by very few sites on earth. Because, in their steep shape and jungle mountain location, they look exactly as a lost ruin should.

Rising from dark overgrowth at the base of the valley, the site opens out into a well-cleared ridge of luminous green that runs on towards a sugarloaf outcrop of mildewed rock. Here is the image that would remain for life with most people, as it is not only the first view on arrival and last on departure, but also makes up the package of near every photographic collection of the place that you will ever see afterwards. Among the physical ruins that straddle the ridge lie the decently constructed gable ends of stone houses, well terraced fields, known points of heavenly alignment and suspected ones of barbaric sacrifice; which, for some, is where the real interest begins, while for others it marks the point at which it gradually subsides. For in the broader picture of this place lies a magic that is totally in keeping with its shrouded mystery and should anyone break the code of the past to reveal answers to every outstanding puzzle, then I would wish they keep it quietly to themselves and leave me in peace, with the awesome memory of this breathtakingly wonderful site.

The switching ride back into Cusco felt not so strenuous in reverse, even though the roll down the steep mountainside was probably fraught with more danger than on the way up and the overall climb back to our temporary base was hardly of note, compared to the near 11,000 foot drop that followed it, to the inescapable desert coast. On the way there, through the descending hills, we took a days' rest at Abancay, randomly selected for no reason other than it seemed to provide the typical ingredients of a Peruvian rural town. If such were the case, then life was fairly hard and the pleasures simple for most people in those days.

At the place where I stayed, the road fell away on the opposite side, down a steep hill to open country, from the direction of which climbed a regular stream of pedestrians, as though walking miles into town along a mountain track was more common here than riding a bus. To help people through the day there seemed to be a high reliance on coca leaves, as there were huge bales of the stuff at the local market and though people toiled well in their manual labour, there was not one among them who looked able to afford a decent second set of clothes.

At the local flea pit cinema, of an early evening, I went to see an old Marx Brothers flic from around the year 1940 which, right down to its rude country audience and low entry fee, must have been played in near-authentic period conditions. The grainy film showed heavy signs of its travels through the ages and the old reel snapped about six times, which was fine at first, as it brought the lights on and gave opportunity for the popcorn and soda traders to make a few more sales. By slight coincidence, I had breezed on some light grass shortly before, which would give me a right fit of the giggles and while the local audience remained stony silent, unable to make much of the subtitled dialogue, I sat alone in a half disguised state of apoplexy.

The real hysteria however developed by several degrees each time the film reel broke down, as it often re-commenced at a completely different place in the story. The trio of comedy brothers could be one minute bouncing in the back of a Western stage coach and then, within seconds, transported to a raucous saloon, where whisky glasses slid long along the bar. As a gentleman raised a drink to his lips, he would be suddenly wrenched away to a hotel room, where a man burst in to finish a sentence that had begun on horseback in an Indian raid, but which ended at a smart ball, where someone kissed the arm of a woman who was wearing huge long gloves. As things went way beyond the sublime and all hope of a coherent screening disappeared, the audience of normally placid Indios suddenly started clapping and stamping their feet, while shouting,

'La Plata! La Plata!,' meaning give us the money back.

This brought at least a trace of seriousness to the circumstances and you kind of felt for the poor projectionist, stressed-out in his baking cubby-hole, who at last contrived some kind of high-speed ending, with credits too fast even for a super-scanner to read. Which sent a message from management to audience of, 'Thank you and good night. Now clear off.' The money bag was probably already out the door and there would be no refund today.

302

Back on the dry side of the hills, along the carretera I'd once followed down, I passed once more the faded girders of the look-out tower from which I'd viewed the Nazca Lines. The weary old driver, carrying me north, barely raised a glance as I mentioned its relevance and I realised how fortunate I'd been when meeting the Lebanese truckie who went out of his way to bring it to my attention. Once more at Lima, I had to offer a wry smile at how tame and unthreatening the whole place appeared, by comparison to how it had seemed on my first arrival. The tar-wet road that always hissed beneath passing wheels, the single cloud that ran to every horizon, the steam smell of cooking in the street, even the boy urchins riding the fenders of buses, getting drunk on fumes and feeling in that one single moment, as though life were really a child's playground. Each gave an air of strong reassurance that, if all was not exactly well, then it was exactly how it was expected to be.

During the day or two that I rested here, before giving the road its one final hit, I called in on the airline agency, to make a request that my return to Europe be brought forward by a couple of weeks. My six month budget had been dented slightly by events that should be always anticipated and I was now running close to broke. I departed the office that afternoon feeling reassured on a person's word and, as with many such periods of looming difficulty, never thought much of it at the time. It was the last occasion ever that I would leave such

303

premises without nailing down every corner of an agreement and fighting with great tenacity to get as much of my way as possible.

By the northern town of Trujillo, on the way to Ecuador, the scattered remains of another lost world lay hidden beneath a millennium of drifted sand. Its gradual rediscovery over the next twenty years would re-emphasise the point that, ninety per cent of world archaeology is thought still to lie underground.

*

Through the last few miles of coastal Peru, a faint sprinkling of fresh green began to brighten the arid land until, on the almost precise moment of crossing the border, we rode into a completely different world of climate and vegetation, as though the national boundary had long ago decided upon its own location. The dry thin mountain ranges that had run half a continent's length shed their waters now suddenly west, to nurture the land with seasonal rejuvenation. In days far gone, a primeval forest had stood here, the type of which we would presently cherish, but the view now, if one could rise high enough to obtain it, would be of an endless crop of rippling banana leaves, parted like a Biblical sea by a stretch of the Pan Am Highway.

On the upland side of these grand plantations there rose a type of country rarely seen beyond this South American region,

304

where it seemed that farmers had climbed to heroic heights to create an agrarian patchwork which, between its various stages of ploughing and cultivation of the black soil terrain, produced a rather absorbing skyline. The steep rising ground lead soon to a serious mountain landscape, where the clouds on volcano tops made you wonder whether things there were really cooling off there or actually smoking, and you wished for an early passing before much else became apparent.

On the back of a white pick-up we sped along, with billowing shirt and tousled hair, feeling that momentary sense of freedom these things strangely produce, and then huddled soon to the headboard through a bank of cold mist, towards some high altitude frozen town. I was riding in the company of the one other hitch-hiker I would encounter, (young Uruguayan kid apart), on this whole long journey. A fair-haired Argentinian fellow named Oscar, who had travelled from home via the Chilean road, on his way to a mad rendezvous with someone he'd met on holiday. He was now minded to return by the more interesting route, through mountainous Peru and into Bolivia, a plan I was happy to recommend as highly preferable. Despite his speaking a fairly good English, I still found it hard to warm towards Oscar, though he did afford me one ray of enlightenment, that would always re-surface in my thoughts whenever mention was made of his home region, during its most difficult time.

Spending, as we did, a couple of days travelling together, there would have been time aplenty to have discussed many of the issues of the day, some of which may even have concerned the life of Oscar himself, but whenever I tried, gently as I thought, to broach these close-to-home matters, I was met with a surprising response that suggested a complete indifference to the past. By his appearance, Oscar would have led people to believe that he was a hip young fellow, with his shoulder-length hair and easy going manner, but I caught a sense, perhaps due to his age and occasional demeanour, that he had done a spell of national military service and regarding the severe circumstances in which it would have taken place, I wondered in what state of mind it had now left him.

We might have been having a half conversation, where one side was keen to discuss a certain issue while the other clearly wasn't and I may have mentioned, without actually knowing or understanding much about them, the name of the Personistas, who were said to have been particularly targeted during the recent military crackdown in Argentina. At the mere mention of this name, Oscar rather took me by surprise by spitting forcefully upon the roadside verge and swearing in a loud manner, pronouncing a torrent of unbridled hate. I can't recall my exact words to him at this stage, they being likely some unpolished remark to the effect that the military forces, if reports were true, had killed off thousands of them already, but I can

306

remember precisely his cold reply as if it were spoken again at this very moment.

'Well,' he said, 'they're not killing them now.'

And that was it. Bang! Bang! Blink twice and it's gone.

Apart from this cold insight into the thoughts of one engaged individual, Oscar did provide some service of a practical nature in that, being obviously fluent in the local tongue, he was able to conjure us up a cheap room each at some box-wood hotel that I never would have found, out on the edge of Riobamba. This was a three-storey, tinder-dry place of bare-plank rooms, that had the clothes hanging facilities of a garden shed. Whilst checking into my own tiny quarters, I noticed a pair of bare wires protruding from a hole in the wall by the door and instinctively dodged around them, even though I considered it highly unlikely they would be live. Towards dusk, I decided to draw the shutters in, (I can't recall there being any window glass) and before doing so, searched around the room for some kind of light switch. Oddly, I could find nothing of the sort and on extending my quest into the outside corridor, nothing there either. And so, after a brief rummage in my dictionary for the correct word for switch, I made a trip to the reception desk and informed the young man there that, while there was a reasonable sized bulb in my room, I could find no relevant way of turning it on. At this, the fellow stared at me as though I were an idiot and on raising the desk-flap without an 'excuse me,' strode forcefully past, up to my room and grabbed hold of the bare wires, which I now noticed were twisted into the shape of two hooks. These he shook irritably, as if to highlight their clear presence, before balancing them precariously together into some form of circuit, which produced a warm orange glow in the low powered bulb. As he turned to go I was on the point of offering him my thanks, but he'd already shot a glance back in my direction, which seemed to say, 'What d'you mean no light switch? What the hell d'you think *that* is?' Eee, what am I like?

For the large capital city that it was, Quito seemed most unusual in that it wasn't one of those alienating kind of places where, after a couple of days, you were gagging to escape into the open countryside. Renowned mostly for its high altitude and near equatorial location, it was noted also for having the best preserved colonial centre anywhere in Latin America which, though terracotta-ed and cobbled in outward form, still retained the strong basic elements of its pre-Colombian origin. Had you travelled upwards through the mid-range of the Andes it would have put you in mind of Cusco more than anywhere else, but unlike the old Inca capital there was not so much the country feel of surrounding green hills, nor of course was there any Machu Picchu. What there was however was an incongruously slow pace engendered by uneven streets and thin mountain air, a solitary church to compare with any temple in the world, plus a surrounding wilderness that would leave lasting regrets were it not extensively explored.

The Jesuit shrine of La Compañia de Jesus, in Quito's otherwise plain main square, is a beacon-like feature of Spanish Baroque, which is perhaps most unique for having had a fortune lavished on it that would normally have been spirited away to overflowing coffers elsewhere. Funded by a profit from the world's richest mines and embellished, one suspects, by re-cast artefacts from an earlier classical period, the elemental value of treasure, along with its high degree of artisan craftsmanship, make it, to the minds of many people, the finest such display in all the Americas. Were you not in the least inclined towards religious belief, the luxuriant mood of its gold-rich interior would still invoke some humble form of reverence, if only towards those who so skilfully created it. The signal it conveyed was one of trust in an omnipotent power, while perhaps at the same time highlighting the missed irony of huge wealth-disparity.

Hypnotised as we briefly were by the flickering light of devotional candles on gold panel walls, we came away with those mixed kind of feelings you have when visiting the best of stately homes: glad to see the preservation all under one roof, but wondering just the same how many lives had been lived in penury to make it all possible. The outer lying buildings of this district were of a markedly reduced nature (and those further afield, even more so), which led you to imagine that, had a city like El Dorado actually existed, it would have been just a cluster of palatial premises surrounded by impoverished hardship.

309

Although most of my travelling days and a high proportion of my nights at this stage were spent in the open air, I was never truly engaged then in what people would call the outdoor life. This would cause later regret as variously mentioned, but although we may rue the opportunities that slipped away, we are consoled with the knowledge that we did actually take things quite about as far as they would go in the circumstances and the unattained summit, as non-successful climbers like to say, would always be there for another day. My fixed purpose at present was to cross over one remaining border north, before heading back for Lima to call it a day. There was one more country that lay in range of my depreciating funds, but from this direction came the most discouraging of news, from media reports to recent first-hand accounts, which rather than deterring me, strongly drew my attention and I realised then that, though I had not yet regained any level of fitness, I was not one of those to turn pale at the sound of a few menacing tales; for had I been so, I never would have left home in the first place. It was perhaps for this reason that, though fear had risen more than at any time on the journey, turning back now was never an option.

*

For most people to whom I'd mentioned it, hitch-hiking alone into Columbia had seemed like the most dangerous course

310

imaginable, but once I'd settled myself beside a road much like any other, it all calmed down into simply enjoying the mild buzz of where we actually were, and what we did. To this kind of travel there is always a random element, which adds to its levels of peril and excitement, but in the open countryside here, surprisingly beautiful as it was, the risks must actually have been far lower than in most other regional parts, especially when set beside the likes of Medellin and Bogota.

At the provincial large towns of Pasto and Cali a strange time-warp mood had settled upon the classic houses around their sleepy central districts. Here were the kind of places where some long ago boom must have occurred to have funded such grand developments. With whatever product that had once been the rage now spent to its last however, they had grown in population size only in direct contrast to their declining wealth and seemed to be surviving way past their profitable heyday. Not all decline is permanent however and in searching recently for updates on these two places, I am astounded at the skyline transformations that have lately occurred. Where once a spread of drab suburbs surrounded a flaking three- storey heart, there now stand reflective towers that seem to have risen in some kind of competitive race and where dusty streets had harboured battered old taxis and tricycle food stalls, there are swish boulevards packed with the latest in modern conveyance. The multi dollar billions that had financed this huge layer of growth must have come from something rather more profitable than the traditional bananas and tin, but whatever it was, moral, legal or otherwise, I wonder if those whose lives were transformed by it really gave a damn?

In the years before this great bonanza, when money went round in the more usual way and drugs were something that came only from a dispensing chemists', the main concerns of people, beyond earning a basic living, were in avoiding the effects of general crime and hanging onto what was rightfully theirs, either by powerfully protecting themselves, or more commonly, by not displaying too much of what they had. The effect of muggings at knife-point, house break-ins, even armed hold-ups within your own hotel, had created such a fearful climate throughout the country that it seemed the only way to avoid falling victim to this type of occurrence was to stick a wardrobe across the door of your room and hide under the bed. During the six months I spent roaming the lands of South America, every person I met who had travelled through Columbia had been robbed of at least some possession and every person that they had met in turn, had been robbed also.

The tales were stark and unforgettable, of cops being complicit in the criminal control of areas where robbers operated with impunity. Gangs of small street kids (the notorious Niños de Bogota), who would drag down larger prey like a pack of dogs, before escaping into the ginnels with whatever they had been able to grab and one other story which hit much closer to home (possibly even a tale I heard *at* home), where a young fellow had saved up 700 quid through various hard labours, flown with the money in cash directly to Bogota of all places, only to be held up in the back of a taxi and left penniless before he'd even reached town. In this latter case, the fellow did at least receive some sort of rescue in that a kind local citizen had taken him in, helped him to contact the police, his embassy, the airline etcetera and sustained him financially until such time as he could be repatriated. Finally, back at the airport, much sooner than he had expected, he was bidden farewell by this Good Samaritan, who had spread his hands wide and uttered the memorably frank words,

'Well, that's South America, Señor.'

I often find that traveller tales are the most revealing, though you can't always tell how they have developed during their several times of re-telling, but as if to confirm the widespread prevalence of these freely occurring incidents, I did read in a broadsheet liberal newspaper sometime after I returned from this journey, of a number of similar cases that related to the bidding stages of the approaching 1986 World Cup of football. As the article stated, Columbia had originally been hot favourite to stage the event and a large team of delegates from football's world governing body (FIFA) had been dispatched to tour the nation's facilities. Support was strong both outside and from within the country. It was clearly their fair turn, the deal was almost done. At the last moment however, with an announcement due, the awarding was suddenly cancelled and the honour instead

313

handed to Mexico, even though it was they who had hosted the event as recently as in 1970, four tournaments previously. This was clearly a fall-back measure due to a lack of late alternatives, as it had been reported back that Columbia was not really such a suitable venue after all. The one issue that had tipped the balance regarded security of foreign personnel and their belongings, as found to the cost of several FIFA delegates. During their brief tour of the country on their official business, 70 of the smart blazered gentlemen had been robbed.

On hitching both into and back out of Colombia, I was aware more than anywhere else of the constant threat of robbery, which is perhaps why I'd saved this part of the trip to the very last. I realise now that there was rather less possibility of being turned over in quiet country districts, especially for someone who'd been six months on the road and looked now every day of it, but I was fired up well against the prospect nevertheless. I may not have had as much to lose as the hapless fresh arrival at Bogota, but going through the difficulty of finding some distant British embassy while suffering the effects of starvation was a hardship I could do without and it would take just as long to pay back a repatriation fee as it would to save money for another trip. I wasn't slaving my guts for the prime benefit of some local toe-rag bandits and so, whenever parked at the roadside verge, I would collect a small pile of handy-sized cobbles against which I would prop my luggage. A couple of these in the teeth would have been a fair enough discouragement for anyone with a knife,

314

but in the end it doesn't usually come to that. Robbers, in the main, are a predatory, cowardly lot who would walk a mile from a real stand up fight. They would rather simply move on and find an easier target elsewhere.

*

Back down the road up which I'd recently travelled was the beginning of another head-down homeward trip. At some half-asleep village on the way through Ecuador I witnessed the clichéd appearance of a drunken Indian, with the most full on stagger I'd ever seen. While reeling across the whole width of a broad pavement, it appeared as though he were performing some slow unrythmical dance, while playing wildly on an upright piano. It brought the secret smile that these stereotypes always do, though to be fair, it was the only such example I would see, either here or anywhere since.

In mid Peru once more, I bagged a ride from some Croat-Yugoslav bloke who described the present government as *medio communistas,* which just goes to show that, no matter how much of a far-right military junta you manage to create, there is always a bit further you can go in order to satisfy the real purists.

Then, at last, I was back in Lima, not quite so tame now, as in addition to the shaky nature of my return flight reservation, there was some tension in the air due to a plebiscite election that was taking place, which allowed those in power to

315

run a rigged-up public vote for a one-party field, in which there were only two permissible answers, yes and yes. Those who weren't voting any kind of yes were holding a fiercely lit meeting in the central Plaza de Armas, while around the square, a cordon of visored, club-wielding soldiers waited their turn for whatever came next. I walked boldly in at first, with a sense of fascination and then, as though realising the no-joking nature of things, picked my way out again, pursued by a cold attack of the goose bumps.

At the tiny downtown office in which Agencie le Point had situated themselves, the mood felt familiar and most welcoming. Even though the brick interior walls were painted a drab grey and the solitary window looked upon nothing more than an neighbouring outside wall a foot away, it was with a sunny day, chipper feeling I entered the room, having outlasted the trip in a manner I'd fairly hoped for. Now all the random elements of travel could be put aside, as I could rest assured of a certain ride home. At least across the most inhibitive part of the distance.

Behind the steel, rubber-top desk, a lone Frenchman sat, puzzling over some handwritten list as though it were a difficult crossword, the answers to which would somehow fall into place if he only looked at it again. We'd met before he and I, just a couple of weeks previously and had parted on cordial terms, at least on my part. But now, as my dog-eared ticket lay near the page before him, a similarly crumpled look appeared on the man's face, as though he were wondering now just how he was going to fit all this in? I stayed quite calm, even a little smug, on awaiting the completion of what would be this final formality, but as the silent pause ran on, longer in fact than I expected the whole business to last, I found myself suddenly fallen into a great mood of doubt and began to develop that gnawing sense of unease which, from now and forever, would always accompany me as I walked through the door of an airline ticketing office.

In the modern world of travel it must be one of the most commonly recurring ironies that, in the highest-tech forms of transport, there is the lowest percentage chance of either getting anywhere, or finding your way back. When last I left these offices, I was certain I'd placed my name on a flight departure list for a definite set date, but now I seemed to be tumbling out into limbo, onto another sheet of paper full of scribbled names and pencil revisions. It brought to me then the sheer worthlessness of fine words without a solid piece of evidence, that would banish the need for all trust.

'But you are right at the top of the wait-list,' said the man with fobbing reassurance.
I was far from reassured, I was livid.

Of the many features of a travelling life, the ones of occasional hassle and inconvenience are certainly the most inescapable. Where most things arrive through fate or the patience in trying, you tend to become philosophical about logistical problems and at such times, a set-back may bring about

317

a new situation, with a charm all of its own. My difficulties here however were compounded not only by my present naiveté, but by my wild budgeting of the previous few weeks. Knowing full well that local currencies were fairly valueless outside of the region and perhaps also encouraged by recent huge devaluations, I had been blasting my remaining cash as though it were going out of fashion. Which meant that, beyond a small dollar-stash which I'd kept to sustain me from Zurich to home, the scheduled flight departure date would find me all but skint. I could survive on the open road when apples fell easily into your hand, or even tolerate the streets of a modern big city around the haunts of the wizened old bums, but this shanty-town suburb thing, where everyone saw me as a wealthy interloper, was a whole new ball game and more than a little scary.

Before leaving the office, I attempted to forward my case in plain terms, but as the tenor of our dispute began to rise, I found myself at some disadvantage, with having to argue the point in a mixture of Spanish and French, in neither of which I was fluent. The list of altered names that lay on the table left me feeling madder the more I looked at it, but at the end of the day, there was little I could do beyond making a bad situation a whole lot worse. The way that matters had been allowed to drift from me here, brought forward a difficult situation that would only have occurred somewhere else down the line. In future days, I would be minded to check all assurances time and again and make that responsibility my own. This, however, was not yet that time and I departed the scene in a cloud of the worst anger, the kind which is pointed wholly at someone else, but which ought to be aimed directly toward yourself.

A couple of days later, at Jorge Chavez Airport on Lima's dry outskirts, I stood by a check-in desk which resembled a bar at ten past closing time, as its majority custom had departed elsewhere and the regular staff began to gather belongings for their own short journeys home. With a quarter hour still to go before final takeoff, a small cluster of us huddled around the remaining open channel, in an atmosphere for which the word tense would seem barely fit. The office Frenchman's reassuring words on my place in the waiting queue had kept me fairly calm up to now and on account of this, I had tipped away my remaining *soles de oro* on uneatable craft-souvenirs. But as the true moment drew near I began to realise how exposed I was, in a position between safe passage towards home and a week among the stray desert dogs. It had become time for long deep breaths and puffed out cheeks. At last a woman came forward with an A4 sheet, held onto a clipboard and, in a clear announcing voice, began with the following statement.

'Now will begin boarding of the wait-listed passengers.' I could feel my heart beat inside my ears. A name was called out, unfortunately not mine and a grinning face lurched forward to claim a card, before disappearing in haste through the wide gate beyond. A second name. My eyes met the floor as my stomach drew towards it. A third name, still not my own. I could hardly breathe now, as if I were on the cusp of a gigantic fall. Finally, as though from some echoing distance, my name was called.

'Derek Arthur Hudson.' Position number four. So much for top of the wait-list!

Bursting forward to clutch at a boarding pass, I fumbled my luggage onto a tall-sided trolley, before scurrying like a rat through a deserted exit lounge and by the time I was clasped into my restricted-room seat, the aircraft door was already being closed, with a hissing clump that altered the pressure in your ears. Phew! I'd made it.

I may recall now how I heaved a massive sigh at this last-second departure, though I might have preferred not to record the actual fact that I would have exhaled in carefully controlled whispers, so as to hide my nervous hyper-ventilation. And that's just why these seat-of-your-pants, low budget deals are for the young and resilient, rather than the old. You can laugh about it all afterwards and talk as though it were a great big adventure, but you have to be sure that your heart can stand it first.

Chapter 7

Africa

Sometimes you'll never admit how much something really bugged you until you've gotten over it, but completing the South America trip, after earlier failed efforts, was certainly a weight off my shoulders. Overlooking the things I urgently needed to address in my personal life, such as health, fitness, and a sound career, I prepared only for the near future, the most pressing urgency in which was the clearing up of another failed travel attempt, that concerning East-Central Africa, and it was towards this aim that I set about my usual task of finding work to raise the necessary. Funnily enough, at that time and for way into the future, I never saw this as making any kind of sacrifice.

By some chance meeting, I found my way back into commercial decorating, which was financially more rewarding and though still a bit of a grind, deterred people at work from talking to me as though I was dead from the neck up. It was, in the wider scheme of things, the tiny beginning of a huge change in my life, which would take me a million miles from what I had previously done. Not only in my own obscure life were things in the mix however, but in the area of international travel and consequently the world at large.

It was difficult to know from where the move began, whether it was through the development of the worldwide web, or that people simply got tired of paying too much and someone saw a gap in the market, but what really got things moving, whether intended or not, was the development of ever larger planes which, once the major airlines possessed them, created the scramble to fill all the extra seats. In order to address this issue, a number of agencies were engaged whose sole purpose was to vend out block packages of tickets, bought at consolidated rates, which were now available at jaw-dropping discounts. Initially it was only the smaller airlines who adopted this practice, or those who were already committed to low cost operations and though the scheduled departures and list of destinations was not yet quite so extensive, the prices were truly astonishing. A standard return air-fare of the time from London to Nairobi, for example, was around £460 sterling, yet a one room agency off London's Regent Street was offering the same destination, via Moscow, for £220. It was as though someone were giving you the return half of the ticket for free, while throwing in a few quid spending money for good measure. You couldn't even hitch-hike there for that.

Round the world itineraries would soon become advertised as a stock part of the airline trade. People who you never considered to be the least adventurous would head away on some intrepid jaunt, leaving their jobs and worldly cares behind, while some would decide, all things considered, that it actually made more sense to decamp to somewhere warmer for the winter, rather than stay at home and freeze. The globe was being shrunk in size to the point where some were even calling it a village and once the trend was set, there would be no turning back. As mobile technologies developed and a few cartel issues were levelled out, people could make their own arrangements from any room in the house and budget flights became more the norm than actual regular services. Huge planes ran largely to capacity, extra ones were engaged to accommodate the growing demands and, while business enjoyed its resounding boom, we in the know became smugly self-satisfied.

In common with most other areas of human development however, not all of this was beneficial in the long run. Noise and pollution levels rose in proportion to the extra traffic, peacefully idyllic spots could never remain so for long and most alarmingly of all, the region of the earth's stratosphere which absorbs most of the sun's UV rays was said, by those who kept an eye on these things, to now resemble the appearance of a Swiss cheese. The fault it seemed, lay not just with the profiteering airline companies, or the fat cat investors who sponsored the operation, but with a greedy public who hankered after such affordable deals, i.e. every single one of us who has benefitted quite happily from the recent revolution in public transport.

I begin to see now a huge shift in the tone of public pronouncements over these type of developments, where everyone, from major fuel producers to Fred Bloggs, is eager to polish up their eco friendly credentials and I smile my secret

323

inner smile. It brings to mind that circumstance of long ago, when the inventor of a certain high explosive method, appalled by the negativity his work had attracted, decided to leave a trust fund that would reward the various benefactors of mankind. With the world being what it is, would they still have developed dynamite and aeroplanes if people had known of all the potential drawbacks? You can be sure as hell they would.

*

Landing suddenly from out the sky, alone into East Africa with no look ahead arrangements and having not travelled gradually overland, was an unusual experience to say the least. In faint echoes of my earlier such arrival in Peru, there seemed a prevailing sense of unreality, as though changes had occurred much faster than my thoughts could keep up. Yet, in the midst of this disorientation, there were incongruous signs of familiarity in the gentle traffic flow of a fifties English town, with cast iron road signs on black and white poles, a zebra crossing between flashing Belisha beacons and, along Nairobi's wide main street, a row of blue blossomed jacaranda trees, that provided a welcoming entrance to a busy Woolworths store. In a further reflection of my most recent trip, the quiet beginnings here ran on for a while and it was only in unexpected circumstances, not this time on a run-down railway packed with smugglers, but on

324

the shattered streets of post-Amin Kampala, that it would spring suddenly and vibrantly into life. The most commonly circulating tales regarding Africa during this time were pretty much as they are now, with an emphasis on scary or bizarre events and very little concerning the matters of everyday life. All seemed fairly calm in Nairobi however, at least during the daytime and particularly during this affluent stable period, before people started referring to it by its later name of Nairobbery.

At the 'thirties style youth hostel, off the steep Ngong Road, the interior was bedecked in a period style of old varnished wood, which seemed to make every indentation a reminder of someone's former presence. Among the resident guests were those who had travelled through every nearby country you could wish to visit and their conversation, whether engaged in or merely overheard, would leave you more reliably informed than what you may have gleaned from half a year of reading books. From what I could swiftly gather, before jet-lag consumed me, the road ahead would be littered with dangers and obstacles unlike anything encountered before, but should you survive the trip, as some here had done, you may then be filled with a lasting glow of warmth, holding no visible regrets, nor would you recall any long stretches of the journey where little seemed to be going on. For here, in Sub-Saharan Africa, from crowded city to mellow country road, there was never a place to be found where nothing ever happened.

A rather laborious, though necessary chore during the early part of most long trips was to make a tour, usually on foot, around all the embassies and national government offices whose permitry you would require for onward travel and, while hardly trying to do so, you would find yourself drawn into the daily business of local everyday life. At such times you would meet all kinds of people, from those who would normally not engage in public conversation, to those who would never cease to do so. And of course, there were always the hustlers. Down the wide primary course to Jomo Kenyatta Avenue, where defunct flower bins, turned now into ash trays, marked the entrance to Woollie's, I fell into conversation with a local fellow, not greatly older than myself, who wore that tired hungry look which, in those days, I could instantly relate to. He had recently, he said, walked from the shores of Lake Victoria in the hope of finding work, but had so far met with no luck. Today he had tramped among the outer-lying districts where the big houses stood and, as tomorrow was Sunday, he wouldn't be trying again until the day afterwards. He hadn't eaten since Thursday, was sleeping rough in the local bus station and five shillings would see him right, at least just for now. Being none too flush with money, I handed him eight bob and, on watching him wearily drift away, wished I'd done more.

Shortly afterwards, perhaps even within minutes of the same incident, I would be walking alone up the long hill towards our accommodation, when my stride was matched by a bright young fellow, smartly turned out who, upon my taking up with his cheery conversation, was joined in pretty short time by two like companions. There followed another woeful tale, a rather more fabulous one this time, of dramatic, possibly historic migrations across Northern Uganda, retreating armed forces still loyal to Idi Amin, dragging with them an exodus of destitute refugee. Cases of stragglers being summarily shot, rather than being allowed to desert and of university students blending with nomads, in order to cross the Kenyan border. It was a hair-raising account of undoubtedly real events, but a compilation of several people's experiences, rather than the true property of those now relating it. They wanted forty eight quid, either between them or preferably each and it was an opportunist scam.

Back at the hostel, almost everyone I spoke to on the subject had been approached by the scammers, but not one had fallen for it. For such a thing to last any length of time there must have been some encouraging dupes to keep it going though. Perhaps those staying down at the expensive hotels? Among these youth hostel dwellers however, who spoke favourably about open-handed wealth distribution, but could make the same tea bag last a month, they surely had to be joking. Upon one point of the Ugandan tale however everyone did agree, in that conditions in the country, as described by these individuals, was a fairly accurate one, and things there were far worse in its presently tumultuous state than at any time during the Amin regime.

Around the travel permit sections of the national and consular offices of Nairobi, my enquiries threw up more obstacles than there seemed to be green lights for go. But as in many cases of stilted progress, the alternative routes ahead began to reveal some intriguing options that, by journey's end, you felt you wouldn't have missed for the world. A feature of this period was that the border between Kenya and Tanzania had been closed for several months, due to Kenya's unease over Tanzania's overthrow of Idi Amin and its military control of his now leaderless country. It was rather surprising however, that the frontier between Kenya and Uganda had continued to remain open, even though few would use it, due to the hair-raising reports presently emanating from that region. Flights were available to several points south, which was an option that many people took up. But to me, the idea of using short hop air routes on a planned overland journey, apart from the disheartening expense, rather negated the whole object of the exercise and if you took this course to its full degree, then you might as well jump on a plane right around the world, without ever getting off.

The last alternative lay in an oddly directed journey which, in order to bring you south, led you in fact west, along a huge horse-shoe route taking extra days, maybe even weeks to cover, which would leave you eventually only a few hundred miles south of where you presently stood. It would involve dirt road travelling through the presently quiet lands of Rwanda and Burundi, before bringing you to the shores of Lake Tanganyika,

328

from where you may continue your travels eastwards into Central Tanzania. The main drawback with this plan however, was that it would mean crossing the one region which presently filled us with the most dread, an area which we were advised to avoid at all costs (at least by those who had never been there), but from where the general feeling, among those who had actually made the journey, was a kind of secret pleasure, like a slow burning excitement that you couldn't quite put your finger on. And so it came about that, owing to our own financial constraints, coupled with the stimulating idea that it was actually a bit dodgy, to Uganda it was.

If you were to travel along the main northwest road of Kenya, which takes you past the teeming shores of Lake Nakuru, you would witness eventually the spectacle of a rolling green landscape, falling suddenly into a wide rent, which near resembles the crown of a large loaf that had become stretched and burst upon opening the oven door. Here, below the steep escarpment, lies a broad expanse of land, flat as a sea bed, upon the furthest reach of which could be seen the faint trace of a blue hill range, pretty similar in height and feature to the one you were presently leaving behind. It gave you the feeling of having descended into the widest such trough it were possible to behold by human sight alone. Which is slightly ironic, as it is witnessed here at one of the narrowest points of its entire length. Regarding a feature such as this, it may be reasonable to assume that great rivers had been in force at some earlier time, or even glacial

329

activity, were it in a more northerly place, but the powers that had created this seismic feature were altogether more fundamental, being the huge tectonic forces that pull whole continents apart. For this was the Rift Valley, running in name beyond the length of a country or, if you would recognise its greater geological course, from the shores of the Dead Sea, to the lowest tip of Lake Malawi.

There are many places where untarnished rural surrounds make it difficult to believe that a major city could exist so very close by, but here the sense was greatly heightened not only by the steep valley walls, but the proliferation of large wildlife animals within a few hours memory of Nairobi's crowded streets. Buffalo, zebra and wild antelope roamed the sepia plain, while families of giraffe, in transit from one cluster of acacia trees to another, would stride in file along the road's edge, unconcerned by passing traffic, but causing alarm to stationary hitch-hikers. There may be areas where this sight is diminishing, thanks to the sprawl of new-build settlements, but what will happily prevail in the remoter parts of Africa, is a surprising frequency of wild animals appearing randomly from the bush, largely on lesser used roads and, by journeys' end, this had become one of the most charming features of the entire trip. Road crossing lines of baboons, quizzical ostriches, nervous gazelles, even a red elephant coated in clay, at the mud rolling end of dry season. It was certainly handy for those on low budgets who were undecided whether to book a standard safari

330

tour as, by the end of your several months travelling, you would have seen most of the wild life anyway, as it conveniently came out to meet you.

Some few miles along, beyond the far valley wall, the landscape turned back to a deeper green, where freshly turned soil smelt richly damp and, among the fields of chest high crops, almost everything that grew seemed valued for its sheer bulk weight. Somewhere among the shading leaves there would be circular huts of lattice and mud, topped heavily with dried palm fonds. From the open doors of these, parents would smile as their kids shouted *'jambo'* and *'habari'* at the passing foreigner. In some town along the western road, where I'd checked into a wooden room above a raucous cafe, a sudden power-cut brought us a moment of merciful respite. While wandering outside here, to avoid the stuffy claustrophobia, I found myself still in a world of utter darkness, but surrounded now by the sound of shuffling feet, the owners of which I could make out no further trace. I was beginning to submerge now into this slowly enveloping journey, where events would open before me and scenes close behind, as though I were a swimmer through space across a distantly familiar land that, by the time you really knew something of it, would be like nowhere and nothing else on earth.

*

331

Beyond the small town of Bungoma, at Kenya's western edge, a long line of flat-bed trucks waited their turn to cross the open border. Among the vehicles heading outwards, not one was carrying a trailer load, while those few returning were packed high, to the branches of trees. It seemed Uganda was importing little beyond a few bare pallets these days, while exporting cheaply everything that could be moved. In the shadows of trucks and between the pop-up food stalls, illegal money changers conveniently loitered, carrying rolls of cash the size of your fist and offering ten times the official rate for Ugandan shillings which, despite what delusion the government hung onto, was the open market price for a currency in free-fall.

Barely twelve months before, after eight years of madcap rule, Idi Amin had been forced to flee and coincident with his having done so, the gates of the national reserve had been flung open, to leave an already impoverished nation all but penniless. The antics of Amin, when viewed from afar, were received with plenty of amusement, but as you got closer to the lives of those who were sorely affected, the thing you couldn't miss, beyond the cheery tales of survivors' bravado, was a deep sense of horror. Three hundred thousand reported dead, the main forces of business driven abroad and what survived of the state-civil apparatus left to resemble the remains of a village jumble sale.

With the help of dissident Ugandan exiles, the Tanzanian army had moved in and following a brief shooting

332

exchange that had not quite extended into all out war, a degree of order was imposed, the type and effectiveness of which all depended upon whether the soldiers had been paid that month, and how much looted booze they had managed to put away. Whoever came next into power (and some were saying the Tanzanians already had their chosen candidate in waiting), they would have their ready-made scapegoat for the present shambles and a handy excuse that, before things improved they would have to get a whole lot worse. Which they most certainly did. Commonplace murders, armed looting, highway robberies in all directions. This, aligned to shortages of everything and a near constant cut off of power and water, conveyed the feeling that, not only was no-one really in control here, but those recently elevated into such positions were, by all accounts, the ones you had to be most fearful of. The details of such conditions had been widely mentioned long before my arrival in Uganda, but even so, it presented a set of circumstances never wholly appreciated until you found yourself suddenly in the midst of it.

The moment of travelling into a newly visited country is something that rarely sticks in the mind, as your thoughts are cast forward to some fresh point of arrival and yet another set of personal experiences. Here for once however, was a marked exception, as I rode along in a loud Kenyan truck, in the company of a cheerful driver and his companionable mate, who was brought along, I guessed, either for security reasons, or to help pile the trailer as high as all those I had seen driving out of here. At about forty miles in from the border and having just crossed a narrow bridged section of the Upper White Nile, we passed a long tract of land, where a slightly withered crop of maize grew near high enough to cover the whereabouts of a standing man. I may have been staring idly at the road ahead or searching around for all kinds of imagined peril, when all of a sudden, from the plantation at my nearest side, there leapt a quivering dancing figure, painted like a ghost in white ash, with his bushy hair on end and shaking forcefully in one hand some kind of animal's tail. For clothes, he wore little more than a waistband wrap and beyond the bold amulets that enclosed his ankles and wrists, his most lasting memorable feature was a pair of wild bulging eyes, which, along with his vertical hairstyle, gave him the appearance of being filled with a permanent electrical charge.

This was at a time when Apocalypse Now had been doing its cinematic rounds and, having both seen the film and read Conrad's literary source, Heart of Darkness, I was primed already for jumping out of my skin. On noticing my distress, the driver asked what the problem was and, as I pointed rearwards to the ashen figure, they both let out cackles of laughter, before one of them, wiping his eyes, informed me it was only some old juju man chasing the demons out of a farmer's field and really no harm to others. There was no duty to believe any of it, so if the farmer was reassured and the Witch Doctor earned a few shillings, what was there to worry about? On hearing this, I was relieved to know that Uganda's recent decline hadn't actually taken it back as far as the African Dark Ages. As we travelled on I managed to recover some of the composure I'd lost, though not quite all of my dignity and I realised then that, in response to this upcoming stage of the journey, I was not so cool as I'd thought when crossing the Rift Valley, or departing the calm outskirts of Nairobi.

Even for a city of lurid rumours, Kampala was far worse in appearance than anything I'd imagined. There were business premises black and gutted almost a year after being laid waste. A Caltex petrol station had been burned to ruins beneath a dome of twisted girders, while close in proximity, what had once been a large multi-roomed store, was stripped out completely to resemble an empty hangar. The sign above what had once been its door announced the name of its last proprietor, Amin Trading Co.

Somewhere towards the edge of the shattered centre, having survived the direction of drifting sparks, there stood a tall building, rendered with grey cement which, though rather brutal in appearance, was in possession of a perfectly warm heart. Its name was evocative of rustic huts in wildlife safari parks, rather than a fortress among this urban wreckage. It was called the Tourist Lodge. The patrona of the place was a large African woman, not yet middle aged, who brought joviality into almost all situations but who, at certain times it was said, could be quite a formidable force. At the height of the looting period, when the only street marshalls were armed soldiers out looting for themselves, she had famously confronted a group of invading Tanzanians, who were intent on robbing the hotel and all its guests. After a brief verbal stand-off, it was they who had backed away and the property was spared.

The lady displayed a kindly attitude toward passing young foreigners, perhaps with a commercial view in mind, but also because she genuinely enjoyed their company and if those in budget mode decided the rates were uncomfortably high, there was a space prepared on the roof where people could stay for free. The simple word free could reverberate an enormously long way in a region where travellers roamed and as a consequence, it became heartily frequented by people from all parts. A Canadian fellow had cycled the Sahara on his way down from Europe, since when, he'd taken to hauling his bike on the backs of lorries. Two American girls had volunteered on some aid project to the famine- hit north. A woman had blithely worked in apartheid South Africa, filling out eye prescriptions for a minority population, while others had toured the Moon Mountains near Zaire, to gawp and gaze at the wild gorillas.

Their tales were similar to our own of the time, being those of people who had seen yet little, but figured they knew a lot. But the most revealing stories were the ones related by the few Ugandans who had taken refuge here, up above the line of random rifle fire. A couple in their early twenties, who had eloped due to family differences, were living in a wooden tent

336

that looked about tall enough for a person to sit up in. They spoke of the early moments of Tanzania's invasion, when the night had flashed with blue-white cannon fire and the buildings shook. During Amin's time, they said, it was very dangerous to oppose the government, but if you kept to yourself you were basically ok. Now everyone was under threat and even to walk the course of daily life seemed like a lottery.

The occupying forces had the security of their own barracks and a fit supply of food rations, but in regard to passing the time they had not been catered for at all. There was a rumour that soldiers hadn't been paid for three months and tales were rife of armed men in battle fatigues committing robberies and much worse, during the curfew hours of dark. In response to these charges the interim governors had claimed that some local ruffians had dressed themselves in fake army uniforms and were tarnishing the good name of innocent recruits. Yet it was harder to explain how the robbers had also acquired the precise make and model of standard issue weapons and that they were often seen scarpering from a crime scene to retreat through a military camp gate.

Some stretches of time, especially on a long journey, can blend together and seem like one passing moment, but short days such as these, from the cheery world of Nairobi Youth Hostel to a Kampala hotel rooftop via the zebra grazing Rift Valley, the freakish sight of the medicine man and the fire scarred streets through which we'd passed to get here, seemed

337

not just a journey across distance, but through a full page of history. As I eventually fell into a tired, open-air slumber, I heard a short sequence of three loud *crack* noises in the near distance, as though someone were slapping two short pieces of wood together, which caused me, at the time, little thought of concern. I later came to realise that it must have been the echo of gunfire, which was a sound I would hear for every night of the ten that I remained in Kampala.

At the break of dawn, with the curfew elapsed and the night time bandits either well caught or safely asleep in their beds, it was time to accustom ourselves to new surrounds, which meant discarding all traces of unreasoned fears and turning our attention directly to the source of real ones. Before long however, as in many such circumstances, a sense of ease and familiarity began to set in until, not only were you no longer peering anxiously around every new corner but on return trips from walking into town, you couldn't quite remember whether you'd already passed a startling feature such as the burnt out Caltex station, or if the few cars you'd seen on the road actually had fitted headlamps or front windscreens.

The most pressing task I had to perform here, once my border-obtained stash of money had begun to run out, was to acquire some more notes in the local tender and I recall returning from such an expedition with huge elastic-banded wads concealed about my person, feeling as though I'd just blagged a wages van. In some contrast to this scene of plenty I did hear a

338

tale of an English couple, slightly before my time here, who, in the right and proper manner, had walked into a local outpost of Barclays Bank (Africa) Ltd, with a pile of twenty pound notes, intent on changing them into shillings at the official rate. Across what must have been an otherwise deserted exchange counter the clerk simply stared at them in disbelief, before waving a hand towards the door.

'Don't be silly, man,' he said, 'Go and change them outside. You'll get ten times the rate out there.'
Could this have been the last time ever when someone received the best available financial advice from a public bank?

In light of how things were in this town, the crumbling infrastructure, the dangers, not to mention the harsh condition of some people's lives, one might have expected a constant pall of gloom to have descended upon the place, but as so often occurs at times of common hardship (and greatly more so here), a downhearted spirit was considered something to be strongly resisted and a feature rarely seen. A wartime mood, recalled in the histories of many a country, was present here with its own strong local twist in that, people displayed a game determination, not only to get on cheerfully with the business of life, but to live it as though the next day might never arrive. Which, for some of them, might well have been the case.

A shoot-on-sight- curfew may have erased all of nightlife, but that hadn't dampened people's appetite for a right good time and the bars, the ramshackle shebeens and the open-front dance halls merely switched their working hours from dark into the light. Once the early morning shift had been completed and the matters of normal survival made as secure as they could be, people cast off their daily worries and began to live the moment like party heroes. Bottles of Kenyan lager littered the wet table tops and when that ran out, a local substitute was brought in, brewed from green bananas, which was served in plastic mugs scooped full from blue chemical storage barrels. Decently accomplished bands played the plectrum-sounding African music that locals typically wanted to hear and people danced in pure abandon, to a sound that was power-amplified by a stage near full of interconnected truck batteries. Never mind the state of nearly everything, for right now, here, between the hours of one pm and six, Kampala was the hottest most happening town in East Africa.

By the end of the day, had not the matoke beer taken over the senses, we could idle back to our rooftop space and from there view the strange spectacle of swiftly emptying streets at the approach of dusk. Any open sound now would be highly discernible, such as a passing army lorry, an exchange of rifle fire, or like the time when a jeep came clattering down the road with only one headlight in place and not a solitary tyre on any of the wheels, just bare steel rims on the uneven road.

It was normally around ten pm when the shooting began, which may have had something to do with army meal times and shift changes, or the true cover of darkness for thieving

340

activities. But much of the firing now was restricted to idle target-practice at static objects and with a memory for what had altered, you could find fresh examples on your way out each morning, of bullet-riddled road signs, or splintered tree trunks. Occasionally, during the small hours, a real gun battle would start up, perhaps when a proper job had been planned, but this was becoming more rare, either as a result of tighter military discipline, or due to the fact that all areas of worthwhile plunder had been well and truly stripped. The gun shots of late had dwindled to around a dozen or so a night which, as I was reassuringly told, was relative peacetime.

In the settled-down evening period, between our banishment from the streets and readiness for a rough night's sleep, it was common to find yourself, regardless of the company, in an atmosphere rather like that of a quiet social gathering, but simply without the refreshments, chairs, or any form of electrical power. It rather reminded you of such nostalgia-inducing moments elsewhere, in which candles lit the public buildings and everyone felt as though sailing along in the same communal boat. At times like this it felt quite natural, without even having spoken to the people directly, to know where everyone was coming from and to have some idea of their future plans, which made it a great opportunity for all kinds of information gathering, travel related and otherwise.

A Ugandan gentleman, who lived beneath a tarpaulin sheet bivvied at an angle from a roof-top water tank, had been

341

there longer than anyone could remember and recalled when people first took flight from their homes, to shelter wherever they could. I didn't pry into the circumstances of his own departure, as the subject may still have been too raw to touch upon, but on the events of the earlier unrest he was most forthcoming. The neighbouring store, with the name of Amin above the previously situated door, had always been a prime target, he said, as it was commonly believed that, though Idi himself hadn't owned the business, it was in some way connected to members of his family. When Tanzania launched its coup invasion and Amin's remaining loyalists fled north, a security vacuum had appeared which developed soon into a state of complete lawlessness. Soldiers, either invading foreign ones or returning exiles who joined in the wave, had become 'big' on their possession of supreme power and had begun to walk away from stores with armfuls of goods, simply without paying.

Whether this was the start of events it is difficult to say, as there appears to have been an inevitability about the whole episode, but the catalyst that really sent things out of control was when a liquor store got busted open and the booze was passed freely around. As armed young men got filled with drink it became a case of follow my leader and grab what you could, as the whole business part of town got trashed, with local civilians joining in. The petrol station was mob-raided purely for its fuel, but when someone ignored the incompatibility between petrol fumes and lighted cigarettes, the place went up like a bomb.

342

'And who was doing the looting?' I asked, wondering what kind of mob it would take to cause such wholesale wreckage.

'EVERY-body,' he said, 'It was like a chain of ants carrying white sugar down the road.'

I tried to picture the event, with local nuns, country vicars and that tidy gentleman who reads the TV weather-forecast, carting stuff away in traditional top-of-the-head manner, which was perhaps not entirely his meaning. But whoever it was that darted through the ruck to shop while stocks lasted, they would've had to be fairly fleet of foot to have beaten the soldiers and the cops to it. From prized work tools down to the last pickings of rice, it was now all gone. It was suggested to me that, on my next trip into town, I should pass by the Central Market and witness there, the high proportion of near-new goods being offered for sale at the second-hand stalls. Miniature electric cookers, vacuum cleaners, hair dryers, basically everything that didn't run on charcoal and which represented all the gear that people had looted in haste, but had no particular use for. The place was awash with the stuff.

For the first clear moments of each day the sun would rise gently in a soft glow, before rising above our rooftop, to be capable already of sweltering you out of a tight sleeping bag. To those already accustomed to its line of trajectory it was just possible to find an extra line of shade beside some nearby obstacle, (though not behind the water tank which the Ugandan

343

man, with great foresight, had already taken), but in doing so, the extra half-hours' respite was never really a gratifying one, partly as we'd already had enough by now of the hard deck and also due to our awareness of being strangely and rather spookily overlooked.

Upon the flat coping stones that topped our surrounding parapet there would often perch, either alone or in small groups, the hunched, staring figures of giant marabou storks. Growing up to four feet in height and completely untroubled by any form of presence, they seemed at first a happy addition, as though a feature of the surrounding wild country had come to pay us a visit. That was until I discovered these were in fact a rare carrion eating version of that species, who had likely mistaken our prostrated bodies for a spread of tasty corpses. It rang an echo of that Argentine incident with an over eager vulture and an occasion elsewhere when someone also thought that I'd died sooner than I should, but there were to be no signs of disappointment in this case, as these well fed monsters could always fly away to gorge themselves on rich pickings elsewhere. They would never starve for carrion so long as things remained as they were round here.

Later, whilst in town, I actually did pay a visit to the central market and there, sure enough, was a blanketed ground adorned with the kind of goods earlier mentioned. Among the futile objects with plugs and sockets however were a few items of more relevant use, such as the doors and window-frames that

344

had been ripped wholesale from people's houses in heaven knows which neighbourhood or town. If your property had been denuded in this manner you knew just the place to go, where you might even be able to buy back a piece of your very own stuff, knowing that you wouldn't have any of the problems associated with cutting it to size, as it would just slot straight back in.

Of all the stark images to meet me during my time in Kampala, there was one which stood out more memorably that the rest and which I can visualise right now, as I feel strangely honoured to have witnessed it. Though fortunate, I suppose, to have survived. It would have been about two thirds of the way through my stay here, as I walked back from some late afternoon errand, that I ambled down a side street off the main drag, attracted either by the pulsating beat of music or the cooking smell of street food. This trail of the senses brought me soon into the heart of a lively night-club area, where four o'clock in the afternoon had the lubricated atmosphere two in the morning. Around the clustered pavements lay the usual array of obstacles that these places attract, with makeshift barbeques grilling the kind of entrails you would never tackle sober and shelled peanuts steaming under a layer of doubtfully sourced rags.

From the doorways of discos, couples who'd met just five minutes earlier would slink off together wearing that look-ahead expression they normally do and I wandered in myself, not to engage any of these trades in particular, but to purchase a single smoke, which was then a fading habit of mine. Strolling as

I was, with not much else in mind, I heard soon a friendly voice
at my shoulder which said,

'My friend, my friend, where are you going?'

I turned to see a young soldier in battle fatigues,
wearing a smile as wide as his face, who was making such a
pronounced stagger that you had to fall in line somewhat with his
movements in order to speak to him. With a lolling head that
looked ready to take his body to some crumpled corner, he rested
his arms upon the side-slung barrel of an AK-47, at the firing end
of which was the large green cone of a live rocket grenade. I
took a pace back, giving myself time to sharply breathe in, but
not wishing to cause insult by hasty departure I answered, as
calmly as I could, that I was off to buy a cigarette. Fancying a
smoke himself, he decided he would become my companion and
so ahead we went, me walking he stumbling at double the
distance, while in front of us the crowd parted like a sea of
blown leaves.

By the upturned cupboard drawer of what now
represented a tobacco stall, I tapped myself out an imported
Rothmans King Size and began to light it from a smouldering
rope, while handing over the shilling it cost. The soldier
followed suit, but only to the point where payment was due, at
which he simply turned tail and walked away. The cigarette
vendor stared bolt ahead as if powerless to complain and it was
not difficult to see how the fellow had got so drunk in the first
place. For who would argue the toss over the price of some

346

smokes and a gallon of beer, against a man with a bomb-loaded rifle?

On eventually managing to extricate myself in the politest way I could, I made a hasty dash for the hotel roof, where I had only the carrion eaters to worry about and from then on I packed the incident away, hardly having the opportunity to mention it to anyone since. Throughout time however I have thought of this incident in a variety of ways and my latest form of recalling it is of when imagining I held some autocratic power over the whole world, just long enough to change things exactly as I wanted. The sad ending to this fantasy would always arrive at the realisation of one insurmountable problem. For means of implementing such a dream, just where *would* you get the staff?

Despite us having viewed Kampala initially as a place you'd want to swiftly pass by, it was not rare, for those who stopped off here, to remain an unexpectedly long time. Even a week on an asphalt roof had flown swiftly by, with always some new turn up, plus trips out to venues of recent or historic interest. But as the time for departure drew near, I figured I needed the boost of a couple of good night's sleep and so checked into a budget hotel I'd heard about over near the red earth market. The place, I think, was called The Mukwano, and was so well affordable that I wondered why, for the purpose of comfort, I hadn't made the move over there days earlier. With some hindsight, however, I could feel glad that I'd stayed on the roof for as long as I did, as it was not long before I missed the immediacy of people coming and going, with the sounds of the street below our parapet. For the sake of calm convenience, the people here seemed not half as involved in their surrounds as the ones I'd just left and I felt right there and then, that one vivid phase of the journey had come to an end.

One fellow here who been putting his self about, but who was presently in a subdued mood, was a weary Japanese cyclist, who had been laid out by malaria. Some guests at the hotel had been tending to his needs and from there I gathered that he might now be of a mind to throw in the towel on his trip and sell his bicycle. Not really being committed to such an idea, but using this as a way of opening a conversation, I asked him if it were really true that he would part company with the bike? At this, a stark change overcame him, as though power cables had been attached to his formerly fading batteries and he rose to a bolt upright position to yell, in a high, slightly crackling voice, Nevah!

It always rings the bell of amusement when a fine example turns up of some stereotype of which you'd long been aware, as I'd heard they could be quite fanatical in their ways, these long distance cyclists.

Within direct view of our front hotel window and attached, as if part of the lay-down market, there stood an open air bus station, or rather a track of worn clay where vehicles pulled in to allow their door-hanging conductors to bawl up a bit of custom. With all that had been going on here recently and how

348

more unpredictable things were in the outer suburbs, it was considered a gamble too far to run through the ambush corridor that ran into open country; though this hadn't stopped us a day or two earlier when we'd hitched to Lake Victoria with some girl I'd met at the hotel and walked much of the way back beyond Entebbe. The main cross-country route was a different matter however, with a promise of richer pickings that attracted an altogether more organised type of robber and those wild things who did fancy risking their necks along this open stretch of road, usually took a fifty mile bus ride out to the town of Masaka, before starting to hitch.

While preparing my morning departure from this latest hotel, I happened to peer through a window towards the market bus station and while doing so, noted the slumped figure of a large African man in an empty shop doorway across the road. He had the appearance of having lain there all night and presently the early business of day was continuing around him. Although it would be a rare occurrence in this part of the world, I figured he was some kind of hopeless alcoholic or a reveller who'd simply gone too far on a night out, which would leave him feeling sorry when he came to his senses. It was only weeks later and three countries down the line, that I met another traveller who'd passed this way around the same time and who could give me further news of the man in the doorway. It turned out that, when someone had tried to rouse him at last from his apparent slumber, they found he'd been dead two days.

From the quiet roadside at the far edge of Masaka, my thoughts on the way ahead were crowded out with nothing but visions of danger. A pile of roadside rocks may have reassured my sense of safety in South America, but here they were nothing in the face of a bullet. I looked to the distant hills, which may have been a part of another country, and wished I was there already. The most common of hazards in reality however, tend generally to lurk when you think you're on easy street and in tune with this drift, my sense of high fear soon dissolved into one of the most placid and agreeable days, beginning with a long swift ride on the back of a hired lorry, in the company of a large Ugandan family and an occupied coffin.

The one laid at rest was a young sister of the family, only in her twenties, who had sadly died while under treatment in Nairobi and was now being transported for burial in her place of origin. The passenger I had noted beside the driver in front was a dog-collared clergyman, her brother, who was set now for a ceremony he'd wished he would never have to perform. Whenever the truck braked or accelerated hard on the bumpy road, the trailer would pitch like a boat at sea, which caused all aboard to roll wildly about on their side-facing benches. The coffin, however, remained gladly in one firm position. Despite the poignant circumstances that had brought these people together, the atmosphere was generally a good spirited one, which boded surprisingly well for the journey ahead.

In the far west of Uganda, where a season's worth of untended growth could disguise whatever had occurred on any bare piece of land, we picked our way cautiously through what had been the earliest scenes of Tanzania's invasion. I had been set to receive a picture of devastation far worse than any I'd seen in Kampala, but was surprised at how tidy the place now appeared, with any pillaged buildings picked clean as a dry skeleton. In the absence of doors, window frames and even roof panels, the properties had lain open to the elements, which allowed the spread of fresh grass, grown high across the earthen floors of once lived-in rooms. It gave an indication here of how the scars of catastrophe could return so soon to plain images of normality.

On taking leave of Uganda, it had been expected I would heave a sigh of relief at my safe survival, but what I really felt above all was a deep sense of sadness, as though realising there would never again be a place quite like it. For there was a strong humanity here that shone more noticeably through all that was greatly flawed and which brought always hope of a brighter future. Reasoned and well balanced optimism had never been in short supply for a land with rich natural resources, where the high altitude warm climate favoured growth of any kind. Yet the obstacles to progress were still huge. At the northern heart of the country came recent news of a potential oil bonanza, while mineral riches were known to abound, but commercial development would require the draining of giant swamp areas

351

and the installation of a worthwhile road network, which would face the immediate barriers of wildlife preservation and the natural reluctance of investors. In other words of course, it would never happen. Meanwhile (and for a long while it has been), Uganda remains as one of the poorest half dozen countries in the world, with a potential wealth to match almost anywhere, but with realised assets that could only be lashed onto the back of a flat bed truck and sold out to Kenya.

*

Along the last miles of Uganda and on into Rwanda the condition of the largely unpaved road was something of which you would marvel to see, but never wish to drive on. Especially in a vehicle that you owned yourself. There were washed-out sections from last years' monsoon that were so wide and deep it was considered acceptable to allow vehicles to find their own way through, rather than repair them and thus was the road made passable again, more by the sheer intuition of motorists than by any organised maintenance. With traffic infrequent as it was, the international highway resembled sometimes a broad hiking trail, above the bare earth surface of which tree branches would knit close together in an archway tunnel. Even to someone who would not walk for pleasure, it would be hard to resist an urge to round each new corner and before you'd even noticed it, you'd done a half decent march by the end of each day. The restraints

352

of money and schedule alas, meant that lifts must be taken and when they were, the more rapid progress resembled often the type of buffeting, lurching experience you may smile about afterwards, but not particularly enjoy at the time.

Having foot-slogged the last nine miles to the quiet border, I was of a mind to bed down in the bush while a trace of daylight remained, but before I knew it, the kindly customs men had bagged me a ride all the way to Kigali and so, on we ploughed for three hours more, covering eighty miles, consigned to a late arrival. The people who took me along were a group of Kenyans in charge of a convoy of brand new pick-ups in bright orange, that were being delivered overland from Mombasa docks. Not so enamoured as I with their crossing of Uganda, they now nursed their valuable cargo along a dry corrugated track, where some of the craters matched the height of a car roof. At last, about twenty miles before our evening's destination, the road evened out into a two-lane strip of narrow tarmac, way-marked with traffic signs in French. It must have been about as far as the old colonists had got in developing the place.

Rwanda's capital had the simple functional appearance of many towns that had sprung up in the mid 19th Century, with a symmetrical grid of streets dividing rows of plain houses which may have been mop-thatched at one time, but were now roofed with more reliable, yet less engaging materials. Its main central hub lay not in the traditional form of a market or main square, but along the spine of a narrow hill, where lay most of the civic

353

buildings.   Below this level, on either side, there grew an ever
more crowded jumble of yards and makeshift buildings, from the
vicinity of which came the workaday sounds of garage
compressor tools and the constant tapping of plennishing
hammers, that turned large oil drums into domestic pots.

After Kampala, almost anywhere would seem to have a
more restrained air about it, although the mood here was much
heightened by an unmistakable coldness, not just in the damper,
high altitude climate, but in the reserved and rather sniffy
atmosphere that seemed to prevail. If you spoke French, which
was the common second language, people would either stare
away elsewhere, or answer you in mumbled tones and the only
time a greeting smile would appear was when it became clear
that French was not in fact your normal means of
communication. I'd made note of this trend at earlier times in
North West Africa, which was expanded upon here if it were
discovered you were only a passing visitor, rather than a long
term resident.

It may have been a pity for the few foreigners living
here, that notable divisions had developed through possibly no
fault of their own, but the issues of this place were inevitably
compounded, not only by recent colonial rule, but by a matter of
much sorer point in that, the late foreign rulers, when appointing
their local administrators, had recruited largely from an able but
distinctly minority tribe, who had maintained their governmental

354

control up to the present day. This would be the cause of much trouble later on.

Away from these areas of festering concern, the setting which surrounded Kigali was actually a quite pleasing one, with wide plantations of banana running out into lush jungled hills. It gave the place a feel of what it was originally meant to be; a small country town governing a wide administrative area. I hadn't planned my journey on any seasonal considerations, other than I had worked in England and by the end of Summer was ready to go, but the timing suited me well here in that, my only encounter with an African monsoon was in a place where the rains from the west just about encroached upon the dry period of the east and I was able to shelter out whatever inconvenience came my way by hiding in the foreign council libraries and in my shared common quarters at the Catholic Mission.

This latter was a throwback institution to a time when people were taught to know the importance of fixed regulations. It was run by an order of obsessively strict nuns in starched-white habits and Flemish head-dresses, who ruled their domain with a rod of iron. Despite their severe nature however the ladies devoted a diligent effort toward their every task, which brings to mind the sad fact of so many wasted efforts in this region, as I heard that during the later times of great trouble, their years of service were rewarded with the worst of harsh treatment, including even murder.

355

When the time arrived to depart from here on my way toward the southern border, I did so with little regret, as it had been cold, damp and more than a shade uncordial. Yet despite these obvious features, there was never the slightest trace of what disasters would follow. I would like to appear wise and say that I saw it all, the signs of simmering resentment between district neighbours that would explode one day into the worst of tribal slaughter, leaving a million dead and causing trauma to most of its survivors. The truth is, there was never anything but a serene peace, where the movement of people and goods continued with a fine grace. A bit like the atmosphere in Burundi, where such incidents before and afterwards had left hundreds of thousands dead, or back in Uganda where only the present day seemed to matter. And that was just it with this amiable, fatally attractive part of the world, where life could seem as mellow as the evening sunset. Until Wham! The place was alight.

The southern route to Burundi's border weaved its way through a scattering of hills, so alike in their symmetry that they appeared all tipped from the same upturned mould. I rode to the town of Butare in the back of a bouncy pick-up truck, which had been leased to some Dutch voluntary project and stood with my hands on the header bar, my face to the wind. For the last fifty miles the road had been diverted, due to some structural collapse, and we were guided onto a track so remotely out of the way that we found ourselves being driven through people's front gardens, scattering family dogs and chickens in our wake. From

356

the summits of hundred-foot hills, you could look down through the plantations of trees, towards grass roofed farmsteads, from which damp smoke gave signs of home life and as the route twisted on, it left an image that remains until now, the most beautiful stretch of road I have ever seen.

*

Burundi was a country that shared plenty of landscape features with Rwanda and most of its national history, having been virtually the same state for nearly a century, first under German rule and then, following World War One, mandated to Belgium. On one point however it was notably different in that its people, particularly those in the remoter country districts, impressed you as the most instinctively good natured you were ever likely to meet. To be among them was to be completely disarmed by their placid charm which, had you not remained in some way alert, might leave you perilously vulnerable, as I would soon find out.

Like my late arrival into Kigali, I reached Burundi's capital, Bujumbura, at the end of a long day, having ridden a route which could have matched the splendour of Rwanda, were it not stolen by the encroaching night. Upon first making town I had enquired for a room at a few hotels, to find them either fully booked, or way outside my normal price range and now here I sat, upon the entrance steps of some incongruously swish car sales depot, wondering which way I should turn next. It was a windless, calm evening, with the heat of day largely gone and I was perhaps a little overcome by what I had recently seen of the landscape, the warmth of the people and just the simple fact of my arrival there. Contrasting with my normal desires of ever moving on, I felt as though I'd arrived somewhere that I precisely wanted to be and saw no reason other than to happily remain. As the few late trading shops began to haul in now their noisy shutters, I happened to be approached by a friendly African youth, in formal attire of white shirt and office trousers, who spoke to me in a kindly voice.

'My friend,' he asked, 'What are you doing there?'
I told him, rather airily, that I was waiting a while longer until the street became quiet, so that I could roll out my gear and perhaps snatch a few hours of peaceful rest, right there, until dawn. At this he threw his hands up in horror.

'No, no!' he said 'You cannot stay here. There are so many thieves. They will kill you!
I looked at him puzzled, as if wakening suddenly into cold sobriety.

'Come with me,' he said, 'I will help you find a place.'
It can take, sometimes, a couple of months on a long journey for you to become completely spaced out, but only a few seconds of genuine danger to snap you out of it. Travelling alone in random circumstances, often as the only white face for miles and making acquaintances along the way who you felt could be

358

friends for life, had you remained. Witnessing scenes that you'd only read of in stories and places that few from afar would ever know. Yet there was greater volume to these parts than witnessed through my passing glance and not all of it was good. And so I followed the young fellow, first of all to a couple of Mission dormitories, at which there was no room, and then to the National University campus, where I managed to park myself, for one night only, onto someone's living room floor. I departed the next morning, not quite rested, nor nearly as grateful as I ought to have been and it is only much later on, in recalling this moment, that I began to appreciate the great significance of such a small encounter, not so much in regard to anything that actually happened, but towards several real possibilities that never came to pass.

We had heard already the murmured tales of cataclysmic unrest in this region within the recent past, the most memorable thing of which was the fact that it had been near totally ignored by the outside world. During a time when the East-West power struggle was our major concern, with other conflicts raging nearer to home and without the kind of instant picture relays we have on the news today, it seemed as though these events had barely occurred. Historically of course, we have become aware that, over a wider period of time, perhaps ten years before and after my visit to this region, up to a quarter of a million people had been massacred in some form of racial and tribal conflict, within the close proximity of Bujumbura. Being now in possession of such knowledge, would you still wish to sleep outside and alone, right in the middle of a place like this? I think not.

The following morning, having parted from the revising students, who didn't really want the disturbance of my company in any case, I made my way onwards, unappreciative then of the great value of just a plain ordinary day. With a grey reflected light ahead of me that signalled the onset of a giant lake, I pursued a winding track running between forest and shore which presented, unbeknown to me, the last real stunning route of this entire journey. The timing of my exit must have coincided with some early morning market, as the departing road was alive with barefoot figures, carrying bought or unsold wares gracefully aloft. Among the good-natured crowd was a young mother who, in the usual sign language, asked why I didn't carry my rucksack on my head in the local manner. I pointed to the child on her back and asked roughly the same question. Which went down not too bad in the circumstances.

Before we travelled much further, the way ahead became affected by some road collapse up yonder and we were faced with the choice of either turning back, or beating our way over freshly trampled ground. Providentially however, some family of local fishermen had set up an impromptu ferry-service to carry people on to the point where the good road began again and so in we piled, to be rowed through the choppy inshore shallows, in a long wooden vessel with huge flattened oars, by

360

men who were powerfully up to the task. I hadn't seen much in the way of strong wind throughout the day, but perhaps the waters had been affected by pressures elsewhere and there was a lively roll running across our line of progress. With no full sleep since the Mission at Kigali and being fairly light on food into the bargain, I suffered a pallid queasiness throughout the half hour trip, which I managed to keep fractionally under control. Had I failed to do so however, I wonder how many people, if any, I would have told about such a loss of dignity? The intrepid worldly traveller, sea-sick in a rowing boat on Lake Tanganyika?

*

When you reach a highly anticipated border crossing, such as that between Burundi and Tanzania, to find nothing but a couple of bell-tents and an old desk parked outside, then you know you're in the world of resourceful make-do. Yet there was still something to admire in the way that things had been made to work here, by moving the Customs posts around. There was an atmosphere at this one spot that was so surprisingly relaxed that, once you'd passed through both sets of passport formalities, you could flit freely back and forth between the two territories. With the onward transport on one side and the tea-stall on the other, you would stand there taking your refreshment, whilst not only conversing with the affable border guards, but also the gang of Zairean carpenters, who had established a boat-building yard

361

right beside the trees they'd recently felled. Hence the suitable site clearing.

On account of the remote forests through which I'd lately been travelling, I somehow expected Tanganyika's shores to be more of the same, but as I continued, I became ever more surprised by the scale of development here, spreading for long ways around each inlet bay and capable of drawing in all kinds of maritime traffic. I had followed the recently gathered border crowd to an improvised jetty, from where we'd ascended a frail wooden plank, onto some rusted hulk that had once been painted white and by that means did we chug on down to Kigoma, a sizeable town set quite back from the visible lake's edge.

Kigoma gave the impression of a place that had been built up in quite recent times, certainly not beyond a hundred years, but oral tradition would have it that, long before the great explorers came here in the mid 19th century, it had already been a crossroads of some significance and, as meeting places often do, it had retained its marketplace atmosphere, as people hailed local visitors in the street, as well as yourself the distant foreigner.

It was around this point in the journey that I began to recognise what a fortunate mood of goodwill I was riding along with, created not only by a natural cheeriness of the locals but by the great efforts of many who had come before, giving up their time, youth and labour for not a cent in profit. Of the rides I'd hitched since departing Nairobi, a fair proportion had been from people working on some aid project or other, and the good deeds

362

of these individuals had brought great credit, not only upon themselves and their respective countries, but somehow reflectively upon the rest of us. My own readings then of Africa's past, where not regarding the lives of discoverers and pacifying missionaries, was centred upon the history of slavery, commencing in times of Arabian expansion, profiting through tribal war and developing eventually into a large European-led industry in the 18th and 19th Centuries. Though this had occurred to much greater levels in West, rather than East Africa, I was still expecting a fair degree of grief on the subject, and was surprised not only that I didn't, but by contrast, was afforded a high amount of the credit earned by others. In various parts further along the way and beginning at just around here, I became addressed variously as Doctor, Sir, Teacher and Bwana, which was incongruously flattering for someone with a professional reputation then for merely slapping a few coats of emulsion on walls and ceilings. Still, it was better than being called a lot of other stuff and a heartening rebuff to the moans of those who said our overseas involvements were merely money-chasing exercises, that had brought benefit to no one locally.

Towards the end of this trip, coming away from a newly independent Zimbabwe, I had seen the kind of things that could be achieved here through a steady course of development and began to sense some of the optimism that people in a past generation may have felt when deciding to throw in their lot with such a future. It began to dawn on me then, and forever afterwards, of how great were the prospects for this region and how many the opportunities that had been thrown aside. Of how richly beneficial it could have been if people had worked together, Africans, foreigners, tribes and nations, over a prolonged and stable period, rather than have the grasping, hoarding free-for-all that largely took place. Due to the various aspects of human nature however and the assorted gathering of motivated rivalries, it never could have happened.

In those normal times when the Kenya-Tanzania border had been open, the main route south through this part of East Africa had run along a parallel path some hundreds of miles to the east of where we presently were. To regain that travelling line and continue on our intended way, we would now need to pass through a thinly developed province, in which there was but one major town. Through dry thorn bush, along a road sparse with traffic, it was a distance not impossible to hitch, but one that would be, I was told, very time consuming to do so. In view of such a prospect, and for this one stretch only, I resorted to a form of transport that may now provide some points of interest in our own time, but which I then came to not think well of. I caught the train.

The line that ran east from here towards Dar es Salaam had been installed by the Germans sometime in the late 19th Century and when first opened must have provided the smoothest form of transport ever seen in this region. Generations of use beyond its original design capacity, along with low levels of maintenance investment, had not been kind to the service however and with many further years of the same treatment, I shudder to think what it may since have become.

At Kigoma's old railway station, looking transitory in wood and tin, but still standing after a hundred years, the ticket waiting times were famously long. You could spend more hours in a queue here than it would actually take to cover the journey itself, as people would wait from six a.m., at a tiny office window, that didn't even an open until three in the afternoon. Unlike the January sales however, this was no communal jolly, undertaken by a few quirky individuals, but a scramble for seats by people in urgent need to carry out the tasks of life and had you not been there in early attendance, you may have found yourself waiting to no avail, behind a line of hopeful passengers that was longer than the average train.

In this pool of common suffering, where every standing, crouching position had been tried to the point of exhaustion, things could actually become quite companionable, with strangers in the queue becoming soon on first name terms, but if the waiting time had taken most of your day, you did begin to wonder how your stamina would last the rail journey itself, which began shortly before sundown that evening and ran on through the following night.

Somehow, between recovering from the slog through Rwanda-Burundi and building up my dander for this overnight continuation, I managed to grab the time for a little side hike, to a place of greater than expected significance. The village of Ujiji, by the shores of Lake Tanganyika, was well known as the place where Henry Stanley first met David Livingstone, on November 10th, 1871 and greeted him with the words that rightly presumed his identity. The renowned spot was indeed still acknowledged by a tall monument, showing a map of Africa with a cross at its heart, symbolising the faith that Livingstone had fostered in the region.

A little further on however, barely a couple of minutes walk and often found quite by chance, was another monument: small, possibly bronze and barely knee high, it drew far less notice in the devotional sense, but was no less momentous in terms of history. It recorded the moment, just fourteen years earlier, when John Speake and Sir Richard Burton had become the first two white men to set eyes upon Lake Tanganyika. Two greatly influential passages in the story of this massive region, occurring within close time and barely three hundred yards of one another. It rather belied the notion of Africa being a continent then where all was darkly lost and suggested more a territory with trade routes well established, though not widely recognised beyond each local district.

At the other far side of town later that day, through spangled rays of late sun, the train was on its way. It would have been hard benches all round in the cheaper sections, softened perhaps with the contents of your luggage and pretty soon the thicket branches on either side would close to a tunnel of pure darkness. Within the carriage there were dim orange dim lights, by which you could see your own tired reflection in the hauled-up window and people who had been in the queue for hours that day were beginning to fidget and wish already for the end. An occasional campfire in the night outside threw a flickering image that you'd not really caught in real-time vision, but left you with a sense of something you'd regretfully missed.

From a small store by our point of departure, I had bought a weighty national newspaper (two days old after its journey from Dar es Salaam), in which I began to read a timely article on the present state of Tanzanian Railways. It reported, rather disturbingly, that of the 137 bridges which existed within the national rail network, only 36 of them, on recent inspection, had been found to be up to the required standard. It went on to state that, during the previous 12 months, a total of 91 significant train accidents had occurred in Tanzania, while some form of carriage de-railment had taken place at an average of twice a week. It was a bit like buckling up your seat belt on an airport runway, with a storm raging outside and an airplane disaster movie showing on the TV screen. There would be no copping out now however and rather like those many rough journeys of the past, so long as it was negotiated with the least of bruises, it could be looked back upon not only with a degree of survivor's pride, but even a small amount of pleasure, once the physical aches had abated.

From a traveller's point of view, a ride upon this low level, crowded form of transport, so long as it was not repeated to excess, could be an engaging experience and here was to be no exception. At some long halt upon the way, where it seemed the train was in more need of refreshment than the passengers, I wandered the busy platform, among the steaming urns and sticky things wrapped in leaves, until I came to a shaded waiting area, which consisted of a tall wicker gazebo, looking like a sale piece from some country house auction. Among the few faces inside, was the one of an obvious foreigner, a student from Germany and as you often do in these circumstances, I found myself falling into immediate greeting and conversation.

The young fellow was studying medicine in Bavaria and though I never found out his name, I did discover, during this fleeting encounter, things of far greater interest in the present passage of his life. He had, he said, been volunteering recently at some up-country clinic, where the most striking of many things apparent was the disparity between those who believed primarily in modern medicine and those who did not. Regarding the ones in the latter category, the small town surgery had been inundated daily with people who had first treated themselves with traditional remedies, such as wild herbs and mud poultices, or paid a visit to one of the juju witch doctors, who would attempt to cure by rattling charms and sticks of fire. These crude measures would often leave the patient in a worse state than ever and the toughest task faced by doctors at the clinic was in

368

clearing up the complications, before addressing the original ailment itself. Our young man here, headed one day for his own charge of responsibility and by now being probably much of the way through it, had no time at all for these superstitious remedies, not as a complimentary treatment nor even as a placebo. There was a time, he said, when such practices had been carried out by people who were searching for real answers to local problems, but since the advent of modern cures, these types had all moved on, leaving behind only a shadowy scene frequented by a charlatan ragbag that would fleece the gullible poor, whilst making them more ill into the bargain. It was, he said, a degenerative medicine, providing no visible benefit, while creating much harm. And of course he was right.

Another feature that had caught this man's attention and one I would be reminded of much later on, was the unusually high presence here of Cuban doctors, on overseas aid projects. Here was a situation that differed rather a lot from the norm in that, the attendance of these most worthy people was not quite on a voluntary basis. It was believed by many western foreigners and whispered by a few Cubans themselves, that rather than work here willingly, they had been pushed into service by the promise of more favourable prospects if they complied, and far less favourable ones if they did not. Which seemed like one of those heavy handed offers that you couldn't refuse. Often isolated in language and deterred from mixing socially by politicised minders, they were denied any recuperating home leave during their two-year stint of service, lest they should find some excuse for not returning. With no family visits allowed, even for those who were married and having to endure the feeling of being constantly under surveillance, their one consolation, if it was such, was that their financial allowance was of a sum so piffling that it prevented them from ever turning to drink.

More than a decade later, rather fitter and more direct in my aims, I made a 1,000 km bicycle ride through the centre of Cuba and among the few people I got to know well, I made reference to this situation, of Cubans working in Africa, a practice which had since largely waned. What puzzled me by now, I told them, was how a poor-ish country like Cuba, which I found to be no more visible in wealth than Tanzania itself, could conceive the idea of sending people off to Africa, to build and assist in all kind of things, from military projects to medicine, when there were at least as many development issues to be addressed on their own doorstep? And no, they couldn't understand it either. Unless it was, as a few sceptics have pointed out, just the prevailing influence of someone with a mad ego, who craved the world stage to such a degree that he would let his own country go to rats for the sake of it. Which rings a few loud bells back home, now I come to think of it?

Once this brief association with African trains had come to its early morning end I found myself in the quiet town of Dodoma, a collection of cement rendered buildings set upon a plain grid of streets and surrounded by a patchwork of dry-thorn

370

scrub. It was only when checking through the usual media channels, on how the place had lately developed, that I recently discovered this had now become the new capital of Tanzania and I began to wonder if there were some kind of competition secretly arranged to attach the highest possible profile, to the site of least charisma. When I think of the cities that have had their capital status removed in favour of new-town developments elsewhere I picture characterful places such as Rio de Janeiro, La Paz, even Melbourne and, to some extent Dar es Salaam, but who can devote barely a trace of feeling towards the insipid creations that have replaced them? I would like to say that I have fond recollections of Dodoma and always had it marked down as a place to watch out for, but the truth is that, by the time I'd hiked to the edge of town to lay my bag by the dusty roadside, I could remember already hardly a thing of it.

To be on the open road after an overnight confinement of some discomfort was a relief indeed. There were no wearisome crowds out here, nor frustratingly long queues and you could pull away from the trail on the moment you'd had enough. While thumbing a ride you were, to a large extent, dependent upon others, but compared to routine transport out here, where you were squeezed in for a set number of hours (and possibly unbargained ones beyond that), it gave you a powerful feeling not just of momentary freedom, but of actually being more in control.

371

The surrounding land presented now a massive change from the green highlands that had run from Kenya's west, and reflected an image more commonly recognised as typically East African. The fields of yellowing grass, the animal corrals of mounded thorn and the portly baobab trees in marching solitude, provided a powerful backdrop to this heartland of tribal tradition. Where the daylight shone through the seasonally bare scrub, you could distinguish the shapes of rolled lengths of tree-bark, that men had fashioned into bee-hives, and placed there in order to harvest honey. Against the skyline of a hilltop, or along some country track, you might see a newly fashioned one on its way out to the bush, slung like a quiver from some countryman's shoulder.

The way ahead now was turned into a salmon pink strip, not of baked mud as, had earlier been the case, but of crushed-up spoil, from some open-cast iron mine and with vehicles so scarce on the road, people would simply walk about their business to town, to school and over the hills, on tracks to who knows where. The Masai had kept to their old way of life in this wandering sense and you never seemed to see them but they were travelling to somewhere, near always on foot. Their male youths were supposed to take off once in a while on some adult rite of passage, where they would travel on their own wits before returning to marry. It was only at these sorts of times that you would see them mount a public bus, in full regalia, to stand, spear in hand, by the rear entrance steps and when the conductor

372

requested their fare, stare hard back with an unflinching grin. Apart from this single kind of mischief, I never saw them once ask anyone for anything.

Beyond the modest town of Iringa, the road turned back to tarmac and though it was only a single each-way lane with heat-rippled edges, it was not to be undervalued, as it represented the main international trunk route between Dar es Salaam and Zambia's Lusaka. It brought us before long to the border-crossing settlement of Mbeya, where I made one of those unforgettable errors which, the sooner you make them, the less chance there is of them ever being repeated.

Most of us, at some time or other, find ourselves in the situation where, in having tried to save money, we have incurred far more expense in the long run. Like the crap cheap product that lasts five minutes, or the stop-gap measure that doesn't quite fill the gap, it can often cost more to remedy a situation than if you'd gone for top quality in the first place. Whenever this occurs there are always many areas in which to apportion the blame, but the most suitable place to begin is near always right there, with yourself.

Mbeya was a typical border town in that during the daytime it would seem like somewhere that had suffered a commercial by-pass, but by night it was absolutely rammed. An intensifying element in this frequent situation was that the nearby border posts, on both the Tanzanian and Zambian sides, were only open during normal office hours, which meant that beyond dark each night the place would be full of people scratching around for a place to sleep. It would also create a circumstance common to many other such transitory halts in that, no matter how well or badly the passing guests were treated, there would always be roughly the same number of arrivals tomorrow, the day afterwards and so on into the future. Accommodation was scarce, prices high and as always in such unavoidable stop-off places, the bandits were out.

Among the handful of flimsy hotels that I checked, just off the central streets, only one had a room to spare and this at about double the rate I'd been accustomed to paying. I tried to be smart and turned it down in the hope of a better deal elsewhere, but when this failed to develop, I was loathe to swallow my pride in returning to take up the offer and so ploughed on ahead. I came eventually to a bus station, full of people with nowhere to go and parked myself there a while, feeling somehow cosy in the safety of numbers. I had always sought to blend into my travel surroundings, as if immersing myself in the experience and though I was obviously stand-out in appearance, being the only white foreigner in the midst of a hundred locals, I felt I could relax here among the dozing and luggage-slouching figures. I had been received in an easy, cheerful manner up to now in near every place I'd been and even where danger lurked, I felt that local people had gone out of their way, in order to guide me from it. It seemed that another small adventure was about to begin,

374

where nothing could possibly go wrong. Which is right when it usually does.

In the middle of a dim-lit waiting hall, along the line of a concourse that would, by day, be busy with foot passengers, I found a wide empty space, by a Victorian-style roof pillar and there rolled out my gear in preparation for sleep. In making final arrangements I cross-plied and re-attached the straps of my rucksack around the column, as a guard against snatch theft and tied an alert string to the shoes beneath my pillow. While lying then in a state of welcome rest, I recall an overpowering sense, not of anxiety but of easy security, as though right in the middle of it here was just where I wanted to be. It may have been the air of contentment that brought me a sleep so deep that I was oblivious to the shuffling noise around me, having little care for what made it, and for what must have been an hour, I enjoyed the blissful peace that we sometimes briefly achieve. That was until the smooth voice of an African woman brought me awake with the softly spoken words in my ear.

'Oh mister, they have run off with your things.'

On scrambling from my bedding and onto my feet, I glanced towards my luggage to find it unexpectedly still there, but now having an oddly deflated look about it, as though its innards had somehow been drained out. At the left-side panel from the front a long jagged cut had been made, running from top flap to the aluminium base and though every strap and tie-up was still in place, the contents had all gone. I let out, at first, a natural curse of anger at those who had perpetrated this act, but once the rage had subsided, largely through a lack of its own stamina rather than reason, I was left with sense of mortification at having been turned over so easily in a very public place. I'd been travelling a number of years by now, in a few rough and ready locations and to be done in such a fashion had me looking like a naive fool. The thought that a row of passengers had sat idly by while all of this took place was even more galling, but I guess that people just didn't want to get involved in such things, especially where sharp knives and razors were involved.

In formal manner, I reported the incident at the local cop shop, not for insurance purposes or any real hope of recovery, but as a means of preventing it's occurrence to others and here my present distaste for all things local became rather tempered by the offer of a free cell for the night. While reeling off my list of disappeared gear to the large man at the desk, I realised what a threadbare set of kit it actually was and how it would be near as much disappointment to someone dishonestly receiving it, as it would be for me losing it. There was no camera, as in these days I was scornful of the photo-clicking brigade on their two-second visits and preferred to drink things in with my own eyes. For the rest, it was just some road-worn cheap clobber from somewhere like Millets and a cluster of second-hand books. The objects most valued by me at that time were the shoes beneath my pillow, the wallet in my trouser pocket, my trusty sleeping bag and the unappealing sweat-soaked

376

pouch that hung around my neck on a cord, just long enough to nestle out of sight. In this was my passport, my stash of travel cheques and the ticket that would get me from Nairobi back to London. Perhaps I wasn't such a naive fool after all.

In the course of time, I put a brave face on things, bought some cord, a giant hook-needle and sewed up my bag. The well-used clothing was quickly replaced by similar gear from second-hand market stalls and perhaps swayed by the local trend for all things garish, I even ended up with a pair of comfy-fitting trousers in some bright shade of red. Much of the memory of my set-back and any shame attached would eventually fade, but there was one regret that still carried force for some time afterwards. I really wished I'd paid double whack for that last vacant hotel room.

*

Should you cross at the main border point coming south towards Lusaka and rather than continue straight ahead, take an immediate ninety degree east, you would arrive, before you even became accustomed to the new country you were in, at the frontier of yet another territory. It would be a bit like that mid-European thing, where you could drive round in a circle through five different countries in a single morning. The journey through Tanzania had been agreeable enough, though I've generally found that flat open land, pleasing as it may be to arable farmers, is not always the most exhilarating through which to travel. The central route through Zambia presented a landscape of similar kind, which had given it at one time, the rather presumptuous title of Breadbasket of Africa. But in travelling on, I felt we could be in for the long stretches of quietness we had experienced on our recent South American travels. The good news ahead came almost entirely from the south east, where jungled hills swept down to the shores of a partly swimmable lake and from which direction I'd been hearing great reports from a while back. So Zambia could wait, in favour of this one country which emits good messages even now whenever mention is made of South Central Africa.

The one time that Malawi springs most to mind is when hearing of unbelievably high rates of urban crime. Not that it was a land bedevilled with such issues, but because it largely was not. Many and varied are the explanations I have heard for the high prevalence of social disorder within some areas of large cities, ranging from human alienation to perceived poverty and according to some, these are undoubtedly contributing factors. But how can it be I wonder, that in one of the world's half-dozen poorest countries, people may walk around in general safety and private property remains largely respected? Answers may lie in the size of towns and a country life that provides always something to do, but would it be too simplistic to suggest that the bulk of the reason lies within the nature of the people themselves and what they have become? There was a level of crime existing here for sure, but nothing compared to places even close by and though tribal conflict was ingrained into the country's history (as I would closely soon discover), it had been reduced to a point approaching national unity. Overall it would seem a fortuitously happy place, that enjoyed a degree of warmth and comfort that transmitted itself to nearly all those who travelled through it. Which is just how its mood reached me, through tales from over a thousand miles away.

Somewhere along the road, through this strange strip that seemed like a no man's land, but which was in fact a narrow sliver of Zambia sandwiched between Tanzania and Malawi, I met with an extra layer of the surreal, at the approach of a large box-shaped military vehicle, built by Mercedes in the 1940's, that bore no other marking than the balkenkreutz insignia of World War Two Germany. I wafted an arm as it shrouded me in dust and was amazed if not quite thrilled, when it pulled up a few yards ahead of me.

It was with a strange mixture of feelings that I climbed onboard. Glad of a lift, awed by the appearance of this significant vintage piece so far from its place of origin, but sensing at the same time that it was perhaps a little early, even at a generation's distance, to be honouring anything military German from such a period. Not that this would bother the vehicle's occupants in any way, who turned out to be a young Austrian woman who'd hitched along and a pair of wildly energetic fair-haired fellows, who seemed as positively German as it were possible to be.

The ride was to take me the short distance across into Malawi and with everyone being sympathetic towards my recent property loss at Mbeya, I was offered their travelling company for a few days further on into the country. I recall that the banks were on some kind of holiday over the period that we entered, which made changing money a minor problem and wherever they did remain in service, it could be a very hit and miss operation, where the business roamed from village to village, rather in the form of a mobile library. I was spared any great inconvenience however by the provision of free food and accommodation until such time as I could pay them back and though conditions may have been rather Spartan on the floor of their already crowded truck, it felt like some new kind of luxury to me, where the journey was guided for a while by others, who would take us off on little side trips to waterfalls and jungle swimming pools. This contrasting passage of calm allowed me to count my remaining blessings, but along with all the other kindnesses I have been afforded along the way and the moments of unexpected captivation, this may have largely been forgotten, were it not for one extraordinary revelation that came to light towards the end of our second day together.

A most engaging feature of travelling like this for months on end and one that is commonly overlooked, is that whenever you meet others on a similar venture, there are often discussions that take place that would never find their way into the everyday business of normal life. Call it a sense of liberation or an indulgence that comes from long periods in isolation, but most people develop, every now and again, an overpowering desire to either share thoughts or reveal personal secrets that would cause them great vulnerability elsewhere. In these faraway places the outcome seemed to matter rather less, which is the only reason I can imagine that in a moment alone in the back of their decked-out van, while parked in a forest glade, the younger of the two men turned suddenly towards me and declared that they weren't really Germans at all. They were in fact, he said, white South Africans from Namibia, descended from earlier generations of German immigrants. On a recent work trip to Europe, they had obtained, through parental descent, West German passports, which had allowed them to travel at free will on what had been quite a daring journey. Throughout the whole trip they had adhered strictly to the habit of speaking German to one another and all references to South Africa were suppressed.

I have met a few of the less extreme South Africans over the years, who took a great personal interest in the wildlife, landscape and the human culture of Africa and for whom such a journey, secretly and unmolested, would have been their dream. But due to the inescapable facts of the time, such a chance could never come their way. Here now were a couple of blokes who, thanking for once the fortune of their birth, could fly below the radar while their secret lay intact. It put me slightly in mind of

Sir Richard Burton's brave adventures undercover in Arabia in the 19th century and though I've never been a great admirer of anything much that came from the Apartheid era, you had to admire the sheer balls of it. Had they, or Burton, ever been discovered in some of the more volatile districts, they would have been ripped to pieces.

When a place becomes a travelling hub for long distance overlanders, it generally does so because of some special feature not common in the surrounding area. This may be a base attraction of the bingeing kind or, more commonly for those on the long distant haul, some refuge of calm, away from the everyday hassles that pass for normal life. Such was the case with the small cove resort of Nkhata Bay, tucked away at the northern end of Lake Malawi. Here the urban streets that led off the main highway, were largely formed of compacted earth, which gave one the feeling of being hardly out of the bush, and beyond the edge of town, down a clay road overhung with trees, a small bay could be reached, from the sandy beach of which you may glide away upon a crystal pond.

The most fortunate circumstance here, on a continent swarming with harmful parasites, (such as bilharzia), was that the waters of this one district were relatively safe for swimming and following two thousand miles of hard bumpy slog, it had a soothing effect that filled your soul with spiritual calm, while bathing your bones in a bath of Radox. People could roll up here on a day-trip and still remain a week later, intent on departing

382

always the following morning. With the beach a half mile from town and hardly a sign of motor traffic, it was rare to see more than one group of visitors at a time, while for much of the rest it was left to its normal everyday, of local spear-fishing from dug-out wooden canoes. Were you to swim beyond the hazard zone of these, perhaps with the aid of a borrowed snorkel mask, you would find yourself in a fish tank wonderland of bright tropical colours, viewed clearly as through a sheet of glass.

One of the brief moods that this created was similar, in some ways, to those great mountain adventures, where you would find yourself arrived at a point so perfectly set that, were your world to end in just such a moment, then you would die happy. Which is perhaps just as well, because I heard much later down the line of an incident involving a local man who had swum here, perhaps a little further beyond the protection of the cove, having been attacked by a crocodile, which tried to drag him under and his only successful means of escape was to have bitten the animal fiercely on the nose. Still, I never said it was always calm around these parts, but only by comparative regional standards.

Somewhere up among the jungled hills, I had bidden farewell to the undercover Namibians in their Wermacht truck, but they predictably showed up here in this place where people rarely omitted to pause and linger. Their secret was safe with me, but I sensed some regret now at their having let the cat out the bag. A couple of Aussie blokes drifted by, bottles of locally

383

brewed Carlsberg in hand and an attitude incongruously chipper for this part of the world. They told of their great fund-saving jobs down at a weather station in Antarctica, where you worked a full year, with free lodging and saved near every cent you made. They raised a toast to their recent neighbours at the British Antarctic station, who had to remain there for two years at a stretch, rather than just the one.

With several people having come and gone during the time I stayed here, it was eventually my turn to move on. I had restored, where possible, my sources of energy and kitted myself out in second-hand clothes, which made me blend easily with the labourers of the fields, especially when the dust of the road had settled upon them. The way ahead became now strangely dead, for reasons I was slow to fathom, but it eventually transpired, after hours of waiting and walking along a road almost entirely devoid of traffic, that a bridge had collapsed some way back at Mzuzu and the route had been diverted elsewhere. In the wider scheme and with much time to spare, this was not the disadvantage it seemed, as the track now reverted, in surprising fashion, to what it had earlier been, with herdsmen guiding their flocks along the overgrown verges, children playing freely and shy wild animals nibbling their way out into the calm open. Progress in miles was heavily curtailed, but during the few days I was thus delayed, a rather different kind of journey began to develop, one in which I could absorb myself a great deal more and later wished I'd had further time to enjoy. Since my passage through the bush lanes of Rwanda-Burundi, my travelling taste had developed towards ambling long walks, with the odd lift thrown in and in certain memorable areas, where the branches formed leafy tunnels, I could hardly resist each bend in the road ahead, as though it were a magnet drawing me on.

By mid afternoon of my first day from Nkhata Bay, with fifteen miles of foot slog behind me, I came to the widespread village of Mankambira. Wasted now through hunger and honed on the village store, my disappointment was sorely felt when the man there announced in gleeful fashion that, owing to a large wedding taking place in the district nearby, he had sold out of every single item in the shop. I'd seen many such country outlets throughout Africa where stocks had been allowed to run to near depletion, but someone here had managed to go the whole hog and was not in the least remorseful about it.

On noting my obvious fatigue however, the gentleman came up with an offer that was surprisingly kind and way beyond the call, as he suggested, in the most casual of ways, that we should simply close up the shop and take a trip over to the nearby wedding venue, in order to locate any food that may not yet have been consumed. So off we set, from one of those start outs that we never in a million years would have devised, towards something once again that we wouldn't have missed for the world.

The setting for this civil ceremony had been at the centre of a large plantation, that produced mainly the staple

385

crops of cassava and large green bananas for cooking purposes. A huddle of mango trees sheltered a wide clearing, where, upon our arrival, we found a row of small huts raised on stilts, mud walled between their beams and roofed with heaped grass. The mood here now was low key, as the wedding had been performed in fact two days before, but people still milled around, invited as guests and in no hurry to leave. We found ourselves introduced into a small crowd, who appeared to know each other well and soon the man of the moment was brought over into our company. This was a patient, but rather tired looking fellow named Wellington Mwase, who seemed drained by the two day event. I caught a faint glimpse of his wife, a tall-ish, handsome woman of a calm nature. They looked to be a good match.

On walking over here, trailing behind the shopkeeper, I had been consumed by a mixture of shyness and guilt as we were engaged in little more, basically, than an opportune begging mission. But I need have worried not, as, from the moment we arrived, for some reason or other, we were made to feel most royally welcome. Whether there was a tradition locally that strangers at weddings bring future good luck, or it was that our sudden appearance from the bush had a small measure of the exotic about it I don't know, but having passed by these kind of settlements for two or three months now and to find myself suddenly as a guest right at the heart of one, the sense of exotic could not have been more strongly felt than by myself.

Seated as we eventually were, upon some old logs, it was not long before food arrived and following this, through questions about my present purpose and journey plans, it was decided that I would spend the night right there among the huddle of their African huts, while hearing a selection of their handed down tales. At either end of this rather stretched out farm-compound there were two specifically designated areas, one where the women would be exclusively undisturbed (except by their children) and another at which the men congregated, in close proximity to their penned-up animals. We were rested now in a reserve known as the Mpala, near to which some placid brown calves were wicker-fenced in below the floor of a stilted hut; while elsewhere, in what could've been a different land altogether, the friends of the bride shared their own select company. You could see now the one great advantage of this arrangement in that, a lot of talk could be carried on about people whose sensitivities were spared, by their simply not being there.

As the heavily overhanging branches disappeared into darkness, a blaze was lit from dry fallen twigs and there we sat, sharing the encircled kind of talk that camp-fires and long day ends often bring. Notwithstanding the usual queries that were aimed in my direction, the hosts were happy enough to discuss some details of their own lives and spoke a little of their history as a migrant tribe, who had travelled from the north many generations ago. They were, they said, the Tonga people, early permanent settlers of this once-forested land, though what had become of the transients who dwelt here before that time seemed hardly worth a mention.

Things were greatly peaceful here now, but there was one traditional enemy who had harried the Tongas in much the same way as they would have done to the earlier bush inhabitants and these were the Ngoni, a more war-hardened tribe who had been chased out of South Africa by rampaging Zulus sometime in the early 19th century. This had led to fiercely contested struggles over good land and useful resources, which had largely dissipated through the central control of colonialism and beyond into national independence. It would be hard to tell what residual feeling remained from that turbulent period, though in future days I would come slightly closer to finding out.

In this one spot, I enjoyed the easy cordiality and also the filling, mealy food, but one thing above all that was brought home to me was how much I had missed such close contact on my earlier long trip among the police states and paranoid dictatorships of South America. The travelling life was risky wherever you went, but here in Africa there was a warmth you could sometimes feel, as you immersed yourself into a scene, which would have been absent among the closed-in-your-face doors and fearful silences of elsewhere. It was something I was able to reflect upon once more the following night, as I became welcomed as a guest by the earlier mentioned rival tribe, the Ngoni.

On the road next day, little progress was made in terms of miles covered, but at the height of dry season, in such unusually charming surrounds, I couldn't have cared less. I'd walked a way through the early morning before resting on my gear at some long straight, which being quiet of traffic, had soon become a crossing place for timid buck and family chains of blue monkeys. Before long, from the direction I'd earlier arrived, another traveller appeared, a rangy man of late twenties, trudging tired along the crushed earth road and lacking a pair of shoes. At the start of his journey he may have dressed his self quite presentably in a tidy shirt and office worker trousers, but now the dust had got to him and, as I was soon to discover, the cares of life as well. Upon our greeting he made his self easy company in a seated place nearby and soon began his weary tale. He was, he said, on his way to his original hometown of Nkhotakhota, which was a hundred miles from where he had set out and so far he had walked the first forty. He expected to be there in a couple of days, to attend the funeral of some family member and hoped to arrive before the wake ended. As it appeared he was too skint to afford public transport, I asked why he hadn't simply stuck out a thumb and bagged himself a ride, but his answer brought something to my attention that I'd rather missed along the way as he said,

'It's alright for you here, you get lifts for free. But we have to pay.'

It seemed a harsh imbalance, where one could enjoy the goodwill generated by others, while someone was struggling in greater need, but that's just where we were at the time and had it been proposed to me, I guess I wouldn't have turned down my own gain from the situation. I enquired of his travelling luggage and he told me it had been stolen at some place back the way while he was asleep, which drew forth a strain of sympathy and though I was no longer flush, I gave him some money to get him through the day, which made me feel dumb for having depleted my own stash and then regretful at not having done enough. As I watched him depart, determined and barefoot, I wondered how often I would think of him when I considered momentarily that my own life was hard.

Along that same stretch of the way, at a further crossing of bush animals, there came along another to engage our attention. A tidier individual this time, dressed for town and seeming to have travelled little far from it. The conversation began in response to his surprise at my presence, which led to my discovery that the road behind was in fact under recent closure and there would be little through traffic today. With faint chance of a lift and having done a good march already, I enquired if there were any kind of food outlet nearby, where I might stock on refreshments. At which he answered most kindly that not only could he take me to such a place, but may later guide me to the local bus station, from where I might find a more certain way of continuing south.

Through hedgerow trees we then wandered, to the heart of a very small town, which I think was called Chinteche and there found the usual dolloped-out but heartily welcome wayfarer's gruel. I vaguely remember some offer to pay for my meal which, in equally airy memory of the occasion, I hope I must have declined and then we searched for a bus. To find such a mode of transport was no problem at all, as there was one standing idle in a shed just doors away from where we had earlier eaten, but this vehicle had a flat tyre and, in the way of local things, there was not a jack onboard, nor in the surrounding district, with the four-ton capacity to lift it. A car had been dispatched to some faraway town and all should be ready by sometime tomorrow. Providing, of course, that all the right kit was available.

With the afternoon running now late and the spare rooms all taken by delayed bus passengers, my now companion, a decent young fellow named Bobby Siwande, invited me over to stay at his parents' house, which I accepted at once, both as an opportunity of rich acquaintance and a great honour. So to there it was we trailed, through neatly-lined fields of pineapple and cassava, to their Ngoni home. On some way over there, along the earthen paths that wove between the ripening crops, we met and were grandly introduced to the local Ngoni Chief, who bowed low theatrically while bidding as a, "Good afterNOON, Sir"! In his office day clothes of formal attire, he looked anything but the Chief I'd imagined, but it made an impression nevertheless and left me wondering how suddenly I'd gone from playing a hobo in the road, to this diplomatic-level kind of exchange.

The home of the Ngoni farmers, set in its plot of easily arable land, may have been of greater financial value than that of the previously met Tonga, but to me and probably to those with a sense of belonging to such places, the atmospheric setting of the previous day, among the tall enveloping crops and houses that were hewn from local trees, there was a certain type of wealth that would never be obtainable in these wide open tracts, with their tin roofed dwellings of rendered breeze-block.

Away from the modernisms however, there were a few old traditions that were unlikely to pass soon, not least regarding the control of an heirloom object which was always faithfully reproduced as the population grew and kept, by custom, in a position of easy access, right behind the front door of each family house. When the eldest son took a wife, he would come into ownership of his father's spear, which the old man had inherited from his father in turn and a new one would be cast, to hand over to the next in line. Each successively married son, in every settled family, would inherit a spear and thus did wedded life begin, at a freshly prepared house with an old spear, parked without fail in exactly the same place. I have lived in several places where the facts of life dictated that something weaponlike should be kept to hand behind the main front door and I wondered whether there really was the state of truce here that was said to exist. Perhaps, through the presence of such practical safeguards, there actually was.

The following early morning, yet not so early as some would have risen, we made our departure from this place, back through the raised mud paths that skirted the planted crop rows and while wandering there, began to hear the flat-hand sound of many African drums, played slow and lazily together. There was an accompanying cry of ululating female voices, which gave it a kind of soulful air and I was filled initially with glad feelings that such a chance event should greet our passing. Yet this was no grand fanfare to herald our exit, but a mark of respect towards some old man who sadly had died in the night. Siwande's father had visited the gent during the previous evening and now everyone who knew him would pass through his door before the day was out.

At the shed in town, the bus was in a road ready state, with now the most highly treasured rear tyre in probably the whole country. As the vehicle eventually pulled away, revving high at a none too rapid pace, I waved from the open window to my well-met friend and then cast my thoughts ahead towards a more rapid kind of journey. In a knee cramped confinement, with faint view through a dusty window, I would cover, in three hours, more than twice I'd done in the last three days. It was then I realised just how much I would have missed had I bussed it directly from Nkhata to Nkhotakhota, or picked up a ride straight through on a road with no collapsed bridges.

393

The journey onwards, to the one-time capital Blantyre, was none too out of the ordinary for this part of the world, with a lift from some British Overseas Aid representative who described his job as 'giving away tax-payers money,' followed by another from two grand-looking African ladies, in huge flowery frocks and wrap-around head dresses, who made some benevolent call at a leper colony along the route. Blantyre, when we did arrive, was actually closed due to an unexpected national holiday. I supposed that it must be the day of independence, or some other stand-out calendar date, but it happened to be something far closer to many people's heart. It was Mother's Day.

Owing to the holiday period and the homecoming travellers that it brought, spare rooms in town were at a high premium and the only shelter I could find was in a large shared dormitory at the local Government Rest House. I had stayed at a similar gaff on the previous night up at Zomba, where some late arriving drunks had kept us awake and I was fearing a similar repeat. There would be no such worries here however, as we had our own quietener in the room. A burly ex-champion boxer, not long out of the professional ring and well-known, not only throughout this land, but at one time the wider sporting world. This was King Marshall Tetu, an amiable, cheery individual who, as a person, still had plenty to offer, but in terms of his fighting-career prospects, was now all but blown out. He told me that in his early twenties he had held some version of an international title at light middle-weight, but here he was, near twenty years later, dreaming of success as a comeback light-heavy, while training alone in pound-a-week digs.

When I had entered the Resthouse dorm, he was already into his compulsive routine, in a boxing ring made out of shoved-aside beds. Gleaming with sweat like a polished Cadillac, his figure said bulk rather than toned athleticism and his breathing was short due to the absence of any air conditioning. On his raised mitts he wore not the standard sparring or bag gloves, but a pair of foam squares that had been cut from some dormitory mattress and held in place with a turn or two of black insulation tape. There was no speedball, punch bag, nor moving partner with hand pads, so what he hit beyond fresh air is anyone's guess. Perhaps the partition wall?

As he broke away from his round of slow shuffles and shadow routines, he seemed happy enough in the moment and glad to give me a resume of his paid career, not needing to mention of course the great pride it had brought him. He had battled successfully in London, Paris, Copenhagen and New York and was presently hoping to take on a fight in Malawi, against an Italian boxer, which hopefully may return one of them to the level of world title challenger. He showed me a photo of the suggested opponent, which looked a rather dated copy, with an unfashionable wavy edge to it, like a postcard in its own frame and I figured they were both now at the same stage of their lengthy careers. No longer on the way up, but not wishing to look down.

395

There was inkling, he said, of a fight with Victor Galindez, a recent light-heavyweight world champion, but whether this was just an inducement to keep him interested in the game I really don't know. Had the contest ever come about and Galindez been in the right shape, it would have been a ritual slaughter for the benefit of a promoter's profit and people's one-night entertainment. But as it happened, Galindez was to take retirement around this time on the grounds of some eye problem and, having chosen a healthier lifestyle, was ironically killed at a stock car event just a few months later.

Around these parts, the name of the King drew plenty of warm recognition, as I would discover wherever I later went, but here he was now in a fifteen pence a night flop house, devoid of any proper kit and boxing alone, as if in defiance of the shadows he hit. To all whom I spoke of him in my following travels, they had known well of his boxing career, though none would be aware of his present circumstances. I did hear that he'd suffered a big defeat in those recent times, that ought to have finished him for good and that he'd taken a job as a Blues singer in some local hotel, which might pay him just one night a week. But beyond that I was to hear nothing. I would like to think that he quit the sharp end of the game right there and then, but continued with his training routine, which may have been his real addiction and the thing that gave him confidence. I might hope that he'd fallen into some safe steady life, with a job he could handle and the contentment of his memories, but it's easy to envisage the way

396

ahead when you're a million miles from the same personal circumstances. To break away from a life of sport, even for bog standard amateurs who once thought they'd had a chance, is to have a great wedge removed from your soul, but for those who once lifted large crowds, or even whole nations by their own personal actions, to depart from such times must feel like giving up on yourself.

During the course of my staggered departure from Malawi I had attempted to pass through a narrow strip of Mozambique, which would take me to my long intended aim of the newly freed Zimbabwe. Having checked out here through Malawian customs however, I was turned back on the other side by a restriction that had been put in place to keep non essential visitors away from Teté Province, which had become badly affected by famine. Subsequent to Portugal's cut and run departure a few years earlier, it was the continuation of a long period of decline and impassability for this region, leading to major conflict and a legacy of land mines, which did for local agriculture the remaining damage that war could not complete. Blithely unaware of the wider details, I merely cursed my own inappreciable luck and doubled back through Blantyre on a new road into Zambia, along the way of which I had a slightly different experience of Malawi.

Compared to the earlier atmosphere, which seemed like a reflection of the placid lake itself, the mood inland and on the way out through Lilongwe was a rather frostier one which, I had heard it suggested, may be connected to the common appearance on these highways of rich white tourists coming largely from Apartheid South Africa. Whatever image I wanted to be associated with, it certainly wasn't either of these and I was content to hold strongly to my previous good memories, while departing in haste. It was not with complete success however that I maintained my earlier rosy view of this land, as my final impression, if not my abiding memory of it, was gathered out on the road, at some place near the small regional town of Dedza.

I had thumbed a lift off some Swedish fellow who, in convoluted fashion, had emigrated to Canada and later found himself on a Canadian railway project in the heart of Africa. The point of his present journey was not a work-related one however, as he was on his way to visit a foreign friend he had met whilst out here, who had now become needful of some assistance. The individual in question had been recently honoured with a surprise visit from the wife of a most senior Malawi politician, who had called in while he was taking lunch with his family. Feeling that things might get a bit messy if he broke up the party, the fellow sent a message that the unexpected guest should be made as comfortable as possible until the present meal course had been finished, at which point the whole family would come out to meet her. But when that time did arrive, the celebrated lady had already made tracks. With little more time than it would have taken to drive onto Zomba, the fellow received a short phone call through an official channel, telling him that he had 48 hours to leave the country. Our man here was on his way over there now to help him pack. Although one of the starkest of its kind, it was far from being the only such tale I had heard whilst travelling in these parts and would be a reminder to many that, though it may be a rewarding experience to devote some of your life to this great continent, to invest your whole heart and soul in the place might not provide a good return.

*

Across the border, through Zambia, our progress changed from the earlier snail's pace into a more fortunate rate of advance. I met up with a Japanese fellow named Etsuya, who had waited throughout the previous day without getting a lift. I told him this would be the day when his luck would change and sure enough it did, as we scooted three hundred miles down to Lusaka, to arrive just beyond following dawn. Along the way, whilst riding a flat-bed trailer, we were forced to pull over for a few hours and kip on the road between the lorry wheels. A dusk to dawn curfew had been imposed at very short notice, as someone had launched a coup against Kenneth Kaunda. The details were vague, as there was a media black-out on the subject and no newspapers were to be published for the next three days. Which I guess, in its way, was a better form of honesty than the usual plain lies you get at such times.

399

On reaching the capital we took lodge at the local Sikh Temple, as we'd heard from afar that you could stay there for free, beyond a recommended small donation. In most of all cases, travellers responded to the word free more readily than any other and should one of them fall into a five year coma, it is likely that the utterance of such would revive them in an instant. The intention here though was not to provide logistical support to freebie-seeking wanderers, but more to make a statement about the general aims of Sikhism, a purpose in which it largely succeeded. The armed African guard, standing on duty at the temple gates, told us that before they put security on here in recent times, the building would be broken into at intervals of around once a month. Nothing much of value was ever left on the premises, but the thieves would come nevertheless, denuding the place of doors, furniture and even wash-basin taps.

On the subject of theft, Etsuya had plenty to say. as he'd already been robbed eleven times during the year he had spent travelling in Africa. The usual trend, he said, was towards sneak theft, where single items would go missing from a room or a pack of luggage. So far he had been divested of two cameras and replaced most of his everyday belongings, though he had always managed to hold onto his passport and funds. I noted still, however, that he remained a little careless when pitching his tent and leaving it unoccupied for long periods, which suggested he had someone at home who was willing to restore his losses. My own shield against such events was a vague hint of aggression,

400

coupled with an appearance that I was barely worth robbing which, as in the case of Mbeya, didn't always work the trick. Though to be fair, I did find on the whole that when Africans saw you fall below a certain level of prosperity, they leaned away from taking advantage and towards actually helping you out.

On arrival at Lusaka, the most striking initial impression was how bland a place could be at such great size, with hardly an outstanding feature of note. The one strong memory that we took away with us however concerned the paucity of food stocks in the local stores and the alarmingly high prices being charged there. Nationally produced goods were commonly as expensive as they could be in European countries, while imported items from faraway places were often double what they would have cost at point of origin and very poorly kept.

In various parts along the way, we encountered white farmers who had stayed on after independence and lived now in some kind of savage isolation. They spoke, almost to a man, of the decline in public services that had taken place during that time, of the huge frustrations felt in trying to achieve anything here and the opportunities missed, in what they said should have been the main agricultural producer in this central part of Africa. My youthful partialities of the time lead me to view this merely as a load of old WW2 veterans moaning about the superiority of things in their day, but the memory of the battered tins of

401

condensed milk and pork luncheon meat, with their paper labels unfastening from a mouldering surface, would always come back to me whenever I thought of places elsewhere and how they similarly could have been developed, but weren't.

The way beyond Lusaka, in any direction you chose to take, would lead you through wide open country that could have been ideal for agricultural development, had it been better utilised, but which held little of scenic interest. One notable feature that it did possess however, was to act as a huge draining area for the Southern hills of Angola and distant Zaire, whose rain waters flowed largely east in the form of the Zambezi River. Containing many noteworthy aspects along its great route, the most prominent, from our great distance, were that it formed at least one national boundary and had two neighbouring countries named after it. When finally I reached its shores, at the unremarkable little town of Livingstone, I thought I'd done with Zambia almost for good, but was forced to wait an extra day and a half for a very quaint and unusual reason. The border crossing into Zimbabwe didn't open on Sundays. In a spot that I may have passed in a more hurried manner, I now had cause to hang around and better familiarise myself with what is, beyond all doubt, the world's most outstanding natural wonder.

*

When I first set eyes upon Victoria Falls it was from a side-on position at the down-river, Zambian end of things, with the slant sun of afternoon cradling each feature in a warm pool of light and though I can never recreate the feeling at pure will, I recall that I must have drunk in every detail of its hypnotic descent, believing I would never see anything so marvellous again. Grounded for the weekend, I remained roughly hereabouts and when I did eventually depart, was quick to realise that what I had seen up to now was but a narrow snapshot of things from out on the furthest edge and all the best views were to be had from the Zimbabwean side. To achieve this short distance involved more than the formality of waiting however, as a few potential obstacles still lay in our path.

On the morning I rose to finally attempt my crossing of this border, I peeped into daylight through a slot in my sleeping bag to find, upon the dry trail that ran through the trees, a pile of dung about the same height as a dog's kennel. Beyond the initial shock that great animals were on the loose, there came a sense of relief that, whatever beast had dumped it hadn't strolled by in the night, as I may have been heavily stamped upon, or possibly much worse.

There was actually quite some doubt over whether I would be allowed to enter Zimbabwe, as I had neither the sufficient fifteen hundred dollars in fund, nor an onward ticket, but I gave them some old-flannel ruse, I can't remember which, either the one about a consulate in another country having told

403

me that I could enter with less, or the one where I was forced to count out the money and then shout out, 'I've been robbed!' right at the end. But I was eventually let in on the terms of a five day transit visa, through to Botswana.

The customs procedure itself presented a sudden change after the lazy day approach of recent formalities, as I was barked at in staccato fashion by a trio of Afrikaner guards, which rather took me back to South America and specifically the brutish experience I'd encountered in Bolivia. Any shock to my senses was quickly soothed however on departing the customs compound, to be greeted once more by the roaring sound of a falling torrent and that touchable fragrance of dew-soaked vegetation.

The physical landscape of Victoria Falls begins in the form of a wide river, which flows smoothly by a cluster of tufted islands, before descending into a narrow earthquake-ravine. The Zambezi waters divide endlessly into beaded rivulets and tumbling cascades on their 300-foot descent, before taking a sharp flow right at the base of the gully, as though having been thrown sideways onto a moving conveyor. This allows the fortunate convenience, unusual in waterfalls, in that it can be viewed from a directly facing position while positioned on the high river bank opposite. Beyond the tumble of warning signs telling you to Turn Back Now Or Die, you could lower yourself carefully over slippery rocks and through snake infested greenery, into some strange new climate, where permanent clouds are shot with rainbows and the world is fresh as a spring shower.

When David Livingstone was brought to this place, by natives who knew it well, the great man of faith was said to have fallen on his knees in praise to heaven, having arrived at so wonderful a spot. Although we, unlike Livingstone, were not the first of our kind to cast eyes on this grand spectacle and had even some idea of what to expect, we were tempted in turn, if only in our thoughts, to follow some similar kind of course.

On departing here after almost two days, I felt I'd stayed not nearly enough and was glad, in my way, for the closed-border inconvenience. But now in relief at having gained entry and being able to continue the journey, my onward thoughts were directed largely to what measure I would take of this newly liberated land, of which some had offered grave warnings for the future and many had spoken in terms of the highest optimism. Zimbabwe was a country in which justice had finally arrived. The majority population had achieved their voting rights, the proportion of settlers who still believed in the place had gladly remained and at only six months after its freshly won independence, hopes were never so high. Over the following weeks I would encounter many first-hand tales of this region, promoting views as strong and extreme from one another as it were possible to be. Which are the kind I seem to have been hearing ever since. Though highly incompatible with each opposing stance, these opinions did have one thing in common, in that, they all bore their own powerful element of the truth.

On turning again to the open road, I extended my recent good luck with a superb 290 mile ride, all the way down to Bulawayo. I found suddenly I'd joined up with the military, in the wide front seat of a camouflaged Land Rover, assigned to a couple of regular soldiers. The driver was a local Matabele who spoke little, while his companion, a sergeant named Tonks from Solihull, who had been an army man since his youth, was primed to speak at great length. The sergeant was philosophical about the recent political upheaval, seeing it as a natural step towards better development, which would surely throw up its own range of opportunities. Whoever led the country from now on would certainly need well trained soldiers, with proven leadership qualities and with the signs in this direction looking all fairly good, he was for staying.

As we drove along on a perfectly smooth road, by farmlands well tended and small towns maintained with a fair degree of pride, you caught a strong impression of the contrast between here and the countries to the north, which had seemed like a shock to our earlier state of denial, although we'd been told of such things many times on our way down. Those who would highlight and harp on about this circumstance were always accused of being favoured towards continuing in the old quasi-colonial ways, but through a land and townscape resembling parts of Southern Europe, you had to admit that on this single matter, their point was undeniably true. The previous form of rule may have been morally unsustainable, but what a thriving economy they had created and such a fine infrastructure to hand to their immediate successors.

Finally at Bulawayo, the men from the military, whose role in recent events would have been a little too scary to enquire about, dropped me with great courtesy right by the youth hostel door, upon entering which, I stepped into a strange world that seemed like a pan of disjointed scenes from some surreal play. Before I'd even put down the pen that would sign in my details, the old boy at the desk had already given me a rundown of his own name, the English town from which he hailed and the almost precise measure of time he'd been in the country. - Tommy, Leamington Spa, forty three, nearly forty four years. - He had a close companion there, a tiny fellow named Errie, who appeared even smaller than he ought to have done in his baggy safari shirt and turned-up Boy Scout shorts. This fellow would break in soon with his own life resume, of being born to this district, possessing no particular profession beyond jack-of-all trades and having nowhere to go it seemed, beyond this echoing youth hostel.

On initial meeting, it seemed heart-warming that they should welcome me in this way, as if I were truly one of their own number come to bolster the cause, but it soon felt as though they were clinging to me in desperation, as a would-be ally, who'd shared their life experiences, understood their present

407

circumstance and felt exactly the same way about it. Around the kitchen hob and the drinks hot-water tank, I couldn't escape the attentions of Errie, who railed on against African majority rule and the foreigners who, knowing nothing about the place, had worked nevertheless to bring such change about.

'It'll be just like Zambia in a couple of years,' he said, 'where the prices are sky high and you can't even buy soap. You'll see.'

We smiled at his wild anxieties, as we would at some old fogey who couldn't make sense of the changing times, but it must be the worst condemnation of the government's future performance, that he was to be proved correct more than several times over.

In the hostel common room I got talking to a busy American fellow who was on the verge of raptures in describing the wonders of modern Johannesburg, particularly the tidy section reserved solely for Whites. Quite apart from the politics, it would seem to me to defeat the object of travelling in Africa at all. He became shortly joined by a sturdy individual named Brian, from Durban, who was clearly not the brightest spark, but was filled with a congealed set of views that had likely been devised in jest by some light-hearted apologists and then hardened later, in the minds of others. The two, who were strangers to me, greeted each other as long lost companions and began a conversation that was merely an exchange of statements that would either confirm or compliment each other's strong opinions.

It may often draw feelings of fond nostalgia to recall how freely people were able to speak in former days, but Brian's tone was way off the scale even for those times. Were it even printable in our present climate, I couldn't be precise in specific memory, as I tend to discard like dead weights the things which have made me uncomfortable, but I do recall his saying that he wished the US Cavalry had operated in Africa rather than the plains of the American West, in the event of which the overall population here may have been somewhat restricted.

Our blank response to these tirades seemed to spur him on, as though our silence were meant as some kind of tacit approval and I reflected for long afterwards on what further might have been said, had I taken up the argument. But as I would learn here and shortly afterwards, it was much better in these parts not to bring your own views too far out in the open, without checking first on the temper of your audience, as there were many such standpoints around that could be shifted only by strong action rather than words, with much of it heading towards violence.

Around the town of Bulawayo there was plenty to admire in the way the place had been attractively set out, with a tidy and informative museum of natural history, a lovely botanical garden and a penned-in area around the public central park, that represented some kind of miniature game zoo. There were huge enough things going on here away from the tidy civic sights, but in the way that the memory prefers to comfort itself, it is upon this scene that I dwell most when recalling Zimbabwe, as I wonder what became of it all when food ran short and people carted their low value wages home in plastic carrier bags.

The mood among local Africans was surprisingly calm in light of recent events and the reception was a relatively good one, turning to better still when it was revealed that you were not, in fact, a long term settler, but just a passing traveller. Those who turned out to be a less predictable quantity however were the miscellany of long-standing immigrants, or born-here Europeans, who would reveal their various natures in ways you would seldom have predicted.

On the road by the town's edge I encountered a beaming young Matabele fellow who was proudly introducing all and sundry to his brother, a tall khaki-clad individual, who had been a volunteer in Nkhomo's bush liberation army. As the honoured relative stepped out to shake my hand, I was struck by how placid and friendly it all seemed. Which perhaps held a bit of menace in itself, when thinking back to countries earlier visited in this region and how suddenly things could change?

Further along on my passage through here, to the charmingly named town of Figtree, I rode in the company of an African country cop, who was cheerful as the sunshine and bore little sign of stress. Then later, in similar fashion, to the border settlement of Plumtree, with a white Rhodesian farmer and his stocky son, being ferried homeward from some posh-blazered school. This latter pair, on hearing my British accent, closed up

410

like clams and never spoke a word to me even up to journey's end. It was an early warning sign of the undercurrents present in this land, where all versions of recent history were highly selective.

*

From here on I'd intended to mosey through Botswana at a leisurely pace, as it looked likely to be the most southerly part of this particular journey, but while attempting no hurry, it was ironic that I should reach the far country's end in a single day, with a rare combination of travelling fortune. The majority of this 300 mile distance was covered in the company of a Swedish water engineer, in a ride that I hadn't actually hitched but was offered while passing through a cattle fever tyre-washing station set up at the roadside. Already packed into the Land Cruiser rear, among the theodolite stands and ancient ranging rods, were a gaggle of local field workers, one of whom kindly invited me to head for his uncle's house, on arrival in Gaberone, where we might both take shelter. Wherever I was, I would always jump at invites such as this, not merely through comfort or cost considerations, but because, in addition to the honour, it would present me a much closer experience with the journey I was on. Such did turn to be the case here, though not quite in the way I would have wished.

411

Upon reaching the address, which lay down a tidy street of bungalows on the town's northern edge, we found the uncle to be away on some business and his wife, the aunt, at the helm of things. There was a younger woman present, perhaps a niece or daughter, who looked in her early twenties and though the elder woman was merely muted in her greeting, the reception I received from the younger was the most glaring form of hostility I have ever encountered in personal one-to-one circumstances.

It may have been that, due to her age, the younger woman was more attuned to the political vibes of the time, or perhaps she had worked for bullying employers in Apartheid South Africa, or recently similar Rhodesia. Whatever the reason for her strong ill feelings towards me, it couldn't have been helped by my present companion's introduction of myself that had me down, for heaven's sake, as a White Rhodesian!

It was through a moment like this that I could appreciate the happy times I'd had on the way down, but as I departed, glad I'd not involved myself more in this southern region. It left me feeling, through no fault of my own, rather like a defendant at the Nuremburg trials. On my exit through the door it was suggested I might try for a place at the nearby Holiday Inn, which displayed a chasmic misunderstanding of my present circumstances, but eventually I found my spot beneath some artic-trailer, on a quiet industrial park, under low heavy skies and hoped that, should it rain, the rills of water wouldn't run along the cambered side of the road, to where my sleeping bag lay.

412

From here to the South African Republic was no further than a common run into your nearest town, but it wasn't the way for me. There were as many reasons for me not going there as there would have been for others in doing exactly the opposite, but prime among these, as far as I was concerned, was the matter of my own personal freedom. It wasn't simply my dislike for the type of political injustice that existed here then, as not all of those on the wrong side of it may have attracted my full sympathies, while a few of the more privileged may actually have been admired for earning their own rewards. But the problem I had with this odd form of fascism was that, it denied everyone the opportunity to go where they wished, ride in whatever train compartment, piss in any pot and to judge people as they pleased on a one-to-one basis and if this wasn't going to be the case, then you could stuff it. Being a foreigner this far south led everyone to believe anyway that you were either headed to, or had just departed from South Africa and they would only break into a broad smile when you actually stated your case for not having done so. Well, they could all smile away now, as I gladly turned my back.

The respects I paid to Botswana on this fleeting visit were far less than its rightful due, as I merely ran in and out along the main perpendicular map-line, which resembled a much plainer version of Egypt, with a road, a railway and very little else. In this slim corridor of reclaimed desert, lived almost the entire human population of 700,000, outnumbered by cattle at a

413

ratio of four-to-one. Elsewhere across the broad square of territory, there were things of far greater interest, but which required some funding and the time to afford them full justice. Somewhere in the desert there were rocky outcrops where Kalahari Bushmen had marked their territory long before the invading Bantus had arrived. But by far the greatest attraction of all was a natural feature, perhaps unique in the entire world, where a mighty river, rising in the jungled north-west and running in a curve across Namibia, took a wrong turn for the ocean and died gloriously in a huge oasis of natural greenery This was the Okavango Swamp, a wildlife experience so renowned that people would plan their whole African trip around it and prepare for the adventure with true seriousness.

There was a noted presence here of the tsetse fly, a slow moving insect, easy to see and not difficult to swat from your skin, but which, should it be allowed to take a bite, may transmit the highly debilitating illness of sleeping sickness. This was far from being the greatest threat to one's health however, as apart from the usual mixture of wild beasts and snakes, there was said to be present, a strain of cerebral malaria, so contagious that the normal immunity pills could not defend against it and which had affected around half the people I'd met who'd recently been here, plus those of which I'd distantly heard.

In Gaberone I met the Antarctic-working Australians whom I'd earlier encountered way back in Malawi. They told me they'd recently parted company with the Namib-Germans in the

414

Wermacht van, with whom they had toured the Okavango Swamp and up to now, two out of the four of them had gone down with malarial fever; this despite the fact they'd all been taking chloroquine or similar. For someone on my kind of incidental trip, thumbing rides and kipping wherever you could, it was certainly a stage too far, but with the right preparations regarding comfort and safety, it would be the sure way to go.

Hitching back up along the main straight of Botswana was only a shade more difficult than on the way down and within a couple of days, through dry flats and over-grazed stubble, I was back once more by the border through which I'd arrived. Beside a heat-shimmering railway that was shielded from the road by a line of white-washed trees, I picked up one final ride that would take me out of the country. It was an odd looking vehicle that drew up doubtfully ahead of me, white and shaped like a tall box, with a row of tiny windows along each side which, had they been round and not square, would have resembled the port holes on a ship's cabin. As I ran towards it, luggage on shoulder, I noted that the rear door was rather like a sturdier version of that which would appear on someone's house, with a regular levered handle and a couple of cross-bolts high and low. It had also been painted white to match in with the scheme, but was now coated with a layer of desert dust. At front, driving alone, was a tired looking Botswanan fellow, dressed in blue uniform, who said he would take me to the nearby Customs post.

415

Throughout the journey conversation was terse, perhaps due to our respective weariness, but also the strange, elsewhere kind of attention that the fellow was paying towards a rather dawdling train, which ran parallel almost at our side and seemed to be matched almost exactly to our pace. This service, I was soon to learn, was running from Mafeking to Bulawayo and whenever it pulled in at some quiet rustic station, the driver would steer right in alongside and park as close to it as possible. The fellow told me it was his present task to monitor the train on its passage through Botswanan territory, but when I asked him why, his voice trailed away as though he had told me enough already.

Some way down the road, at the side of our second or third railway station, I was asked if I wouldn't mind transferring to the rear compartment, as the driver wished to pick up a work colleague and on my agreeing to this, we pulled over to the side, whereupon we both disembarked and I was led out towards the back. The large cabin door, at which I had only previously glanced, was mainly held shut by a mortice lock, which required two turns of a substantial key to open it and as this was flung wide, I was invited to enter, whereupon doing so, I found the compartment to be occupied by one other person, a local young African, seemingly very low in spirits and light on luggage. I was on the point of making my introductions when I heard the key double-turn in the door behind me and got that soul-sinking feeling that such occasions usually bring.

416

The youth who, for now, was my companion, cut a dejected figure, but though vanquished, had yet the will to hastily relate his tale, as if for him it were some kind of therapeutic release. His hometown, he said, was somewhere among the Shona lands of Central Zimbabwe, from where he had travelled spontaneously alone. He had lately run away from the care of his uncle and had been en route to South Africa, where both of his parents worked. At the first main Botswana halt he had been busted for possessing neither a valid ticket nor the proper documentation and was presently being booted out of the country. The man at front, in charge of the vehicle was, in fact, an immigration police officer, who was trailing the slow train in order to pick up illegals nabbed along the way and this was the deportation wagon. Although neither of us had made any great impression upon the land we were presently in, we were at least travelling out in some style.

*

Back in Zimbabwe I set quickly about crossing the parts of the country I'd recently visited, in order to reach the areas that had strongly featured in recent news items and which tended to be all towards the more central regions. Initially though, I spent a single night in Bulawayo and found hot news being made all around me, or rather would have done, had I stayed awake long enough to witness it. Back at the old youth hostel things must have appeared slightly less surreal than before and not having seen a bed since my last departure, I was able to fall into such a state of comfort as to be completely lost to the outside world. This must have been the reason I was the only person at the place, or starting out on the road the following day, who hadn't heard the raging gun battle that had continued throughout much of the night. The date was November 9th and could have been one of historical significance, if not overshadowed by the so many others, but many here were regarding it as the onset of a new civil war, or the beginning of the country's ruination which, to a certain degree, it was.

In a local city park, at the heart of this Matabeleland, a political rally had been held that was organised by the ruling ZANU PF Party, which largely represented the majority Shona tribe of the new Zimbabwean president, Robert Mugabe. In prominent place on the rostrum was a government finance minster named Enos Nkala, who had harsh words to say, not only about the government's coalition partners, ZAPU, but also the Matabele peoples they stood to represent. In the capital of Matabele territory itself this would have raised hackles even at the best of times, but in the sensitive period fresh after independence, when power sharing promises were being reneged on willy nilly, it was like a red rag to a bull.

Despite earlier assurances to the contrary, Nkala had chosen this volatile moment to announce plans for a one party state, which would leave many of those who had fought for independence, powerless in promoting their own interests. As if this were not enough, the minister seemed to deliberately provoke the crowd by saying the government would, 'Teach their opponents a lesson,' by 'Delivering blows against them,' which led to what seemed to be the desired state of uproar. Before finally leaving the stage, Nkala, as though now drunk on the occasion, declared that he would come back to say, 'Even bigger things tomorrow.' An event, alas, which never did come about as, by then the rising had already begun.

At the moment I hitch-hiked away towards a place that would soon be Harare, I had failed to fully realise the sudden weightiness of the times. The early news reported one person as having been killed in the overnight disturbances and a few more injured, but as media controls were relaxed this soon changed to 44 dead and over 300 injured. Among the travelling public, who seemed to know rather better, the mood was a surprisingly mixed one, ranging from fear to stoical resignation, with a tinge of secret pride in some people that the things of which they had warned were now becoming manifest. The most dangerous view I came across among settlers however, who for once were taking a backward seat, was that this new conflict was a welcome turn of events that would cast their own history into a much better light. But of course, this had never been the case in the past where similar such things occurred and nor would it be now.

Along the open road, during the following days, the mood was an edgy and rather watchful one. I had thought that by merely moving away from Bulawayo the problem would have been somehow left behind, but its echoes had travelled already far ahead. An old farmer named Jack, who may have been a veteran of WW2, berated Britain for not supporting Smith's version of white minority rule, regardless of how it would have isolated us from nearly every country in the world. It was a viewpoint I would hear from several around these parts and suspect of many more.

A subcontinent Asian, fretting over his lifetime business investments, kept a loaded revolver wrapped in a copy of the local Herald, which was wedged against the hand-brake of his Datsun Cherry. He took me to Gwelo, where I met up with the only White Rhodie hitch-hiker I would ever encounter. The young man had been in both the military and police force but was now working in a mine up somewhere by Kariba. In former troubled times he had never left home without a loaded gun. Which is how I prominently remember him, with a pistol in a shoulder holster, bulging from beneath his white tee-shirt.

Before the town of Que Que I rode on a flat-bed farm truck, seated high up on three bales of hay. The old settler driving it leaned out the window as I approached and, on pointing to his African companion, said,

'I've got a rifle in here and he's got to watch it. You can climb on the back if you want.'

Even in such moments of highly exposed danger, I still rode along with an air of fool's innocence, seeing it all as some

420

kind of adventure and oblivious of the true severity affecting everyone's lives. Had I known of the coming times, the scarily erratic governance, the avoidable famine, the murders, the massacres, I wouldn't have been at all brave.

At last, one final ride took me the remaining distance to the capital which, for a few months more, was still called Salisbury. The Afrikaans-sounding driver, on hearing my accent, turned bolt-rigid ahead and never spoke a word all the way there. For some here at least, the age of white colonial rule had ended a way too soon. The main city, during this period, was in one of those strange phases where it represented nothing it had ever been, nor would be again. The talk among many Whites was of fleeing across the Limpopo to South Africa, with hardly the shirt on their backs, or returning to their former countries to a life devoid of the old privileges. A few saw hope in a future here, while others, like the old boys at Bulawayo, had simply nowhere else to go.

The views of travelling visitors, opinionated and more freely given as they often were, varied even more widely, with some accepting the inevitability and fairness of change and others saying that all outsider opinions were merely shallow and from people who had no practical knowledge of the place. Emotions ran high all round and unless you wished to spend all your time in arguments and fights, it was best you kept your own thoughts hidden from all but similar thinking or mild mannered

421

people, who may not have been so widely distributed as one may earlier have imagined.

One fortunate circumstance of my travelling ways during this time was that, due to budgetary requirements and a need to keep my wits about me, I was not much into bars or public drinking. Had I been so I would have doubtless become more aware of the sore edge that was present between open-minded visitors and some of the more hard-line locals. If there was one thing that young white Rhodesians hated more than anything else it was to be lectured by outsiders on the subject of social development and for many, to even hear such matters being openly discussed was enough to drive them into a rage. A number of people, mainly British, had been attacked for merely being present on such occasions and as a Canadian fellow once described to me, it was never a square-up situation between two willing sides, but always a wild hit from a sneaky position, followed by the joining in of several accomplices. A pure cowards attack.

At 80 Baines Avenue, in a leafy suburb of town, a bunch of young fellows, who were temporary residents under the old regime, had rented a large 'thirties house from which, in addition to continuing with their regular day jobs, they ran a change-money business. Their eager customers were a gaggle of passing travellers, looking for the most realistic alternative to the government rigged rip-off rates and nervous business people, who feared that a spiralling economy would take them all down

422

with it. The scheme was all highly questionable in the legal sense, which made those who ran it either some kind of crooks or secret heroes prepared to chance their necks, depending on opinion and one's own personal needs.

Here was a rather sociable, come and go sort of place, with wide associations and a strange atmosphere of superficial cool and underlying anxiety. The main mover of the premise was a bright young fellow of professional qualification, friendly enough but patently hard, who had held strong views on history before he even came to this country and had developed them further during the time in which he stayed. I would hesitate to judge him on the course of his life, as I would never be a party to the details, but I remember him from this moment as a stand-out example of someone who believed strongly in the principles upon which the original colony had been founded. In the fading twilight of these days, he was now prepared to defend such qualities to the very last.

Though we'd hardly become known to one another through conversation, he tore into a rather long potted history of the country's formative years, which was shaded perhaps towards favouring his own views, but was an engaging listen nevertheless. He described a time, about a century and a half ago, when a wave of terror had swept across this region. A roaming tribe of Matabele, who had been driven from Southern Africa in acrimonious circumstances, were in search of new lands to occupy. Various acts of slaughter and scatterings had occurred, as they pillaged through various districts, until they settled upon this attractive open country, where they began to rout the Shona, then lords of much of the land. In a wider sense, it was a continuation of Africa's unwritten history, where such events had promoted the interest of the strong over those of the weak, from the Bantu lands of the north-west, down to the Cape.

The tale of the Matabele is both an heroic and a cruel one, as they grew from a renegade few hundred, expelled from the main body of the Zulu nation, into an even more fearsome force than the one from which they had been ejected. Employing the old Zulu methods of swift movement and constant attack, they overcame every peaceable tribe in their path, either absorbing its members into their own fold, or simply slaughtering all the males and keeping the women of a reproductive age. Any children born of these women would become Matabele and thus did their numbers expand. Cattle were prized as a measure of status, but toiling on the land was considered a task largely for the conquered, as the new masters enjoyed their spoils of war.

At the time of white man's arrival here, around the 1880's, the very survival of the Shona nation was in some doubt, but thanks to a series of colonial battles involving the British and a number of treaties based largely upon commercial interests, a new kind of order was established and some form of peace ensued. In the way that many colonial systems develop, a few local natives were inducted into the governing civil system and, as the Shona had most reason to stay close to the incoming rulers, it was they who were afforded the lower administrative jobs, such as those of minor officials, policemen and jailers. Suddenly the boot was shifting onto the other foot.

Our fellow here appeared most gratified in telling me all of this, hoping perhaps that a new Matabele rising would somehow turn back the clocks and while doing so, cause a re-evaluation of the recent colonial period. But it was a desperate last line of defence. As a detail of the past it was rather like the story in Malawi, where one side claimed that another had usurped the land which they had merely taken from its earlier inhabitants, which is a logic that could be applied to so many turns of event. Here, for now, the arguments were futile however, as this part of history was already done with.

It was a sign of these pressured times that, straight alongside this vivid encounter at Baines there came another, which was more striking still, if based on just one standout statement. It was in the same house, barely the next room, perhaps at a moment when someone else's business was being conducted, that in the chilled way things were carried out here, I was handed a bottle of beer and invited to partake in a game of darts on a board that had been hung on a corner wall. My friendly opponent was an Australian fellow named Harry, whose fair flowing locks and hip language of the times, suggested a cool attitude to match, but which brought a reminder in the end, of a lesson I'd learned some time in the past. To never take such appearances for granted.

We were sharing a conversation which I realise the young man must have practiced time and again and which led us eventually, via Vietnam and Australia's support role there, to the recent Bush War, in what had once been Rhodesia. He spoke with such authority on these matters that I suspected he'd either been closely involved in such affairs or idolised the people who had, as he continued in detail about the mistakes that had been made and the actions he rather wished had been carried out. The thing that grieved him more than anything, beyond the politics and the justice of the recent outcome, was the rather more basic question of how a professional and well-drilled army such as the Rhodies then were, had been given the run-around by what he called 'a disorganised ragbag' and the one glaring reason he put this down to was the constant presence of small kids, playing on the outskirts of African villages.

The role of these minors in the military campaign had been to keep watch for the approach of government soldiers and when such an event did arise, to run swiftly into the village to warn their rebel elders, who would flee with their weapons before capture ensued. It was somewhat similar to how things were during the Kenyan struggle of the fifties/early sixties, where children would run home shouting *Go! Go!* as the army approached. The words *Go Go* translating roughly as *Mau Mau* in the Swahili language. Our man here breathed a heavy sigh at

426

this, as though rueing a grand opportunity which, if not missed, might have turned things right around, won the war for the side that he had favoured and seen minority rule in Rhodesia safely maintained into the future.

'If only,' he said, 'they'd had the courage to shoot the kids, they'd have been alright then.'
And that's just where he lost me.

There was a strong belief then among fresh travellers to Africa, that all who had ventured into this minority-ruled southern region had come back tainted somehow with its self-validating views. Though this may have been true in a wide number of cases, it could have appeared more greatly so due to like-minded people being drawn towards these countries in the first place. For Europeans born and raised into such isolation, it must have been hard to oppose the general trend, but for all those who were able to garner little sympathy from others, there were a few for whom you couldn't help but feel a degree of compassion.

On the road to Fort Victoria, to visit the strange ruins of Ancient Zimbabwe, I hitched a ride with a mild mannered fellow of around forty years, who took me to the town of Beatrice. He had been born in this region, was proud of its achievements during his own lifetime and could see no sense in what was presently happening to it. In his own mind he had always done his best by Africans and for the good of this country. He had volunteered where he thought necessary, provided work and prosperity, yet here were his efforts now torn to shreds and thrown in his face. He had lost a brother in the Bush War. An aunt, plus a second brother had been brutally butchered in a farm incident He'd had a nephew seriously assaulted in most recent times and beyond the constant fear, he was simply worn out with the whole cruel business of it. It was the type of story I'd expected to hear much earlier to be honest, but in these days of slowly advancing revolution, I had never envisaged much of the good being swept out with the bad.

This fellow was thinking of emigrating along with the rest, but was knocked out at the prospect of a new start elsewhere, building it up all over again. He could barely take anything out with him legally, as residents were only allowed to export a maximum of a thousand local dollars and these were now becoming worthless. The remainder of his wealth would be frozen in perpetuity, which effectively meant confiscated, and so he would begin anew, in an unfamiliar land, in a state close to penury. South Africa was an option, but it would be the same there in ten years time and to make any attempt at a stable permanent business seemed like a pointless exercise. As I was left once more at the roadside, the most striking impression I retained from all of this was that, amid the anger, sadness and fatal resentment he and others felt at this time, none of them could quite grasp the certainty of what was happening, that the world had moved on, not much for better or worse in the wider scheme of things, but plain and inevitably, to leave this time behind.

428

On the northern route out of Zimbabwe, through greener fields than I'd seen for a while, I received the sharp antidote to these mellow sentiments towards the old Rhodesia, as I was approached on the road, bat-out-of-hell fashion, by a rampant Nissan Bluebird, which screeched to a mad halt on the instant I lifted my thumb. Inside were a couple of young White Rhodesians, one partly encased in plaster and the other, steering wheel in hand, bearing a loaded revolver on his lap, which he juggled around nonchalantly whilst driving.

On making myself comfortable on the back seat, I looked first to the injured man, who appeared still in high spirits, as though fairly up for anything, then at the gun in the gentleman's lap and thinking perhaps ungenerously that the firearm was of more immediate concern to my own interests, I offered some banal enquiry as to whether things really were so dangerous around here that you should be armed at all times. At this the driver turned round full towards me while replying, 'Nooooooo,' in mocking tone and I guessed the true answer was dependant on what kind of attention you tended to attract.

They had both, they said, fought in the recent war of independence and though featuring on the losing side, there was no doubt the experience had been a huge one for them, not in the negative way that had affected the poor fellow at Fort Victoria, but by stirring a sense of exhilaration they largely retained. They spoke of the affair as though it had parallels with America's involvement in Vietnam and referred to their foes as Gooks, which distorted the image somewhat. Yet despite the broken bones, that had been received in some recent road accident, they were both imbued with a devil-may-care attitude and as one encouraged the other, they careered along the road at a speed not greatly fast, but far too much so for local conditions. Somewhere back along the way they had picked up a straw punnet of plums from a roadside stall and amid the veering action of a one-hand driven vehicle, these were freely passed around.

What happened next was probably a continuation of something that had begun long before my own appearance, as their mad behaviour increased in tone, through a series of wild close encounters with straying cattle, homeward-trailing field workers and women with huge bundles on their heads. Until, right out of the blue, the driver leaned full out the window and spat a large plum stone right onto the windscreen of an oncoming car. I could see the picture of alarm on the face of the African bloke at the wheel, fearing perhaps he'd been shot at, and I turned behind to see him veer off into the dust. As the two in front looked around with expressions of glee I must have offered a faint cheesy smile so as to keep the ride together because, a few moments later, good heavens, he did it again!

It was becoming a little scary for a while, with a pistol wielding driver gobbing stones into oncoming traffic and a man half-killed already, seeming further ambivalent toward a preference of life or death. And so, in order to lead us from where we seemed to be heading, I reached into my bag and took

430

out an object I'd found along the way, wishing to find out what it was and hoping also that it may act as a means of diverting attention. This was a large green fruit, rock hard and almost the size of your hand, which I had optimistically grabbed off a roadside tree, thinking it might be edible. On recognising this, the man in the passenger seat took charge of it in his good hand and holding it forth said, 'Ah! A Kaff orange,' before tossing it playfully like a cricket ball. It was, he said, a kind of wild fruit, favoured by Africans who wandered the bush, but in its present green state, a way off being ripe to eat. With little more interest in the item he was on the point of handing it back to me when suddenly, he stared in a fixed manner at an image along the road up ahead.

'I know,' he said, '*Slow* down.'

All I could see in the tree-less flat landscape up yonder was a solitary African cyclist, peddling along on his old black Raleigh, after a dusty day at some rural job and within an instant, I knew what was about to happen. Drawing alongside, we free-wheeled at about 25 mph which, with the added momentum of a thrower's arm, must have made up the speed of an average pace bowler's delivery, and then wham! Out went the 'orange, some kind of ricochet took place and I turned once again to see, not this time a cloud of car dust heading into the verge, but a cyclist wobbling to dismount, before falling, winded, into the ditch. The two characters in front cackled away like a pair of geese and on we continued, one more image the wiser.

431

Among the many short impressions I received during this double passage through Zimbabwe, there was not one of which you would say that here was the country in a nutshell. Yet somewhere within the mix there ran a consistency, not in the personalities you met, or the type of adventures that had befallen them, but in the underlying feelings they provoked, of how close things were to working out well here and of how, we all eventually knew, they never could. It was probably true that a number of decent Europeans had done more in Africa's cause than anyone born of here likely ever would, but any merit arising from this would have been crushed underfoot, not only by fundamental greed, but by a force of lordly arrogance that came to exist, at government level, in the common workplace and most noticeably of all, in the realm of domestic service.

The traces of this were still clearly visible, not only in Zimbabwe, but in the white settler enclaves that ran up from here to Kenya. People who, back home, would have been just ordinary farmers and their wives, or middle-management railway workers, had turned pompous with pride at their sudden elevations and granded it over their charges, in the ultimate show of snobbery. And now it was someone else's turn to play the big role, without much clue of the responsibilities involved. Flaunting their arrogance in a way we've all come to recognise, they would change years of competent stability into a state of famine, employ political murder as a means of social policy and cause such a scale economic catastrophe as to even overshadow

432

the news of tribal genocide that had occurred in their name. What a mess it all became, a catalogue of governmental failures to match any throughout the ages, an embarrassment to its earlier supporters and another great opportunity thrown aside.

On approach to the border town of Kariba, which stood on a rise by the newly made lake, I noticed a copse of trees in neat plantation form and told the kindly African driving me the final distance, that this is where I would bivvy on my last night in the country. Knowing much about wildlife, he advised strongly against this, as the creation of the nearby power dam had chased many wild animals into uncertain habitats and there were tales of elephant, hyena, lion and cheetah in the district. I took his word and parked instead on a well tended plot of grass, by cultivated trees, and slept like a baby; only to find, the following morning, that I'd camped on the front lawn of some huge grand house and had to scarper quick before the dogs woke up. Passing this tale around over a number of years, I've had a few come-back versions of a similar nature and discovered this was far from being a rare occurrence.

*

An early morning stroll across the nape of Kariba Dam brought me the strange amalgam of calm natural beauty, engineering wonder, a tinge of ecological concern and finally, an unhurried customs procedure, which allowed me on and into

433

Zambia. For a country's distance ahead, there was not much for me to linger on, with food prices high and the landscape plain in appearance. A fair scope existed for arable planting however, and I was surprised to see a scattering of white farmers who had stayed on, post-independence; which I thought boded well for the new Zimbabwe. I encountered a few farmers in lifts along the way who told me, almost to a man, of how much more affluent and well ordered things were just sixteen years before, when a colonial governor had held the reins. A few Africans that I met actually did agree with this, though whether they would really wish a return to those times, with their ill-fitting complexities, I was rather in doubt.

Among the remnant settlers now, the main complaints revolved around the constant uncertainty over their long term residency and of the shifting rules regarding fixed prices on their products, which seemed far removed from any sound rule of business. Onward they struggled however, grumbling and frequently exasperated, like poor country hill-farmers, holes in their pants, holes in the roof, but still hooked on the old way of life.

*

In Tanzania once more, through flat lands dense with thicket, I fell into travelling with someone else for a while and refreshed my memory of the lessons I'd learned from this on

434

several previous occasions. John was a decent enough bloke from some country place in New Zealand, who would try hitching occasionally as a means of breaking up his regular bus routine, but if things dragged on for more than an hour he would leap at the first bit of passing public transport. This was fine for a day or so, as it allowed me to switch off while someone else took all the talk and directions, but beyond that it came soon to outlive its appeal.

I may, at the time, have felt guilty about wishing to escape and do my own thing, but I need have no regrets over this, as I realised later that being in a company of two or more tended to shut a traveller off from their wider surrounds and I felt I was missing out on the encounters that may usually have lit up my trip. I preferred the solitary route not through wishing to always be alone, but because, in paradox, it brought you into much closer contact with the people all around. And how seldom were you really by yourself.

On our pretty much eventless way through the country we rested a while at Dar es Salaam, where you could now obtain a permit to cross the Kenyan border. To process the information on one A4 sheet of paper took around four days of official business, which was still a huge advance on recent times, when you would have either taken an over-priced flight, or chanced another limb through Bujumbura and a still scary Kampala. Eventually, at the north-crossing out of Tanzania, a paperwork

435

technicality led to our easy parting and I moved on once more, with a heightened regard for my precious ounce of freedom.

*

After nearly five months of rough road travel, I wasn't sure I had the energy left to do Kenya real justice, but though my longer stay here came at the far end of the journey and its paths were rather more heavily trodden by foreign visitors, I did manage to feel some engagement with my surroundings, if not quite in the open-road manner to which I'd recently become accustomed. The one great advantage that Kenya had in attracting people from overseas during this period was its great political stability. Aligned to a fantastic countryside of tall mountains, rolling down to a coast of coral white beaches, it had a good head-start on all countries south of the Sahara. Here was a land of well protected wildlife where, had you time to linger, you didn't even have to go to a game reserve to see, as most of the roaming animals, were they not fenced around and dangerous, would be coming out to you. Along the uneven bed of the great Rift Valley there were lakes of salt and fresh water, from which a million wading birds might take to the sky and should you borrow a pair of handed-round binoculars, you could closely witness not only these, but the snorting spume of bathing hippos, who would only make shore during the hours of dark, to do battle with the farmers over local grazing rights.

436

On my way round all of these and other such fine locations, I observed the hard working life of country croft-holders and the big ranch farms on well prepared acres, once foreign occupied, but since expropriated at bargain rates by the new political elite. In the city I'd hastily left, there would be developments taking place even as you watched, with buildings sprouting up, suburbs expanding and in the spaces between, the rambling encroachment of shanty slums. Somewhere within these extremes existed the low rise mix of old-time buildings, where lived either long established residents of town, or the worn out stragglers who just couldn't move on.

At a cheap hotel off the notorious River Road, I checked myself into a collective room which I shared with a sometimes changing, but surprisingly permanent collection of paying guests. Though the residents were largely regulars, there was, throughout the day here, a busy sea change of faces as, in addition to its nightly purpose of sleep, our room served as some kind of meeting place for small time trader-hustlers and local survivors of the street.

There was a Somali fellow here I remember well, who was bright way beyond his present hand-to-mouth status and who traded in all kinds of odd junk. Half Arab and half African, his name was Romeo and described himself as a businessman, though not yet up to the corporate level I guessed. In the corner of the room that he'd chosen to occupy, the walls were stacked like the innards of a garden shed and you feared that, should

437

someone slam the door a little hard it would all collapse and we might never see him again.

A Goan, named Costa, had been something clerical once and behaved always quite respectfully, but he was quietly sad and only scraped money enough for his bed and to buy drink. He attended the Sikh Temple at least once a day, where the communal meal was free.

The one other spot, in our four-bed room, was occupied by Ali, an old Indian Muslim who held very strong views, not likely printable nowadays, but he knew his own mind. He hated every Japanese on earth because of the War and had a tired old girlfriend from the Seychelle Islands, who everyone said had worked for years as a prostitute.

Other characters drifted in, bringing tales not of their own successful hustles, but the alleged ones of others. A small bull of a fellow from Shropshire looked not particularly old, but was approaching that stage where, if muscle had been your only trade, then the young hounds would begin to catch and overtake you soon. He called himself Simba which, in Swahili, means lion, but I wasn't sure if this was either a name he'd chosen for himself or one that people had given him in ironic jest, as he'd been some kind of budding boxer once and dined out on the fact rather a lot. Throughout his grown up life he had followed the trails of opportunity through Canada, America, Australia and finally to here, where he had remained for the last thirty years. He never spoke of any skilled profession and I guessed he'd

438

pissed on his chips once in a while which, with the way things stood in Africa these days, left him with hardly a place to go.

One person, by contrast, who seemed to have everywhere to go and not much time to waste in getting there was a hulking Kenyan fellow, obsessively gregarious and full of split-second smiles Through his habit of chewing *qa*t all day, he spoke in short bursts, as though mowing his audience down in a hail of words. This was Big Stuff, a fittingly named character who would tear into every new quarter with a grand rushing entrance and behave as though there were a world of things going on, when in general there was nothing much on at all. Those who had given him this moniker had done so in regard to his tendency for embellishment when describing every moment of his fairly ordinary life, although he could truly lay claim to the acquaintance of movie stars, having once been a crowd-extra in The Rise and Fall of Idi Amin.

The manner in which I came upon this place was pretty much how I encountered everything else on this and other trips, being purely by chance, as I was looking for somewhere else at the time. But I always wished I'd found it much earlier, not only for its central location and easy affordability, but because it provided such preciously rare moments of insight, which seemed to renew and update themselves each time you stopped by there. It was called the Iqbal and was owned by a family of Yemeni's, who ran the cheap restaurant downstairs. I had a memorable meal here one time of five-shilling stew, where I found that a three-inch long insect had been cooked into the mix. I returned it at once to the waiter, who came back shortly with a suspiciously similar-looking plate upon which a large finger-shy mark appeared towards its edge, as though someone had merely shoved the offending item off at one side and passed it back out again. I ate it anyway as I was starving and should've been grateful I guess that, unlike in some other countries, there was no extra charge here for cockroaches.

Over the following weeks, I criss-crossed Kenya several times between the Mombasa coast and Aberdare Hills, visiting the wild bird lakes and tall ribbon waterfalls, as most people do. But through this time on the common tourist trail, the quirky hotel by River Road remained the central hub to it all and the image I most strongly retain of this period. On my later return here from somewhere up country I discovered that Ali, the Indian, had gone missing and people were concerned for his wellbeing, but the time after that, having come to finalise my arrangements, I found him fresh out of hospital diagnosed recently with cirrhosis. He spoke of Kenya being finished now for the likes of him (although it could equally have been true the opposite way around) and he wondered how he could raise the money to leave. In the company of others, he spoke of the free medical care he could get if only he could make it to England, where they would also provide him with permanent accommodation.

'They even give you money as well,' he said in a high tone of amazement, 'It's true, isn't it?'

And what could I say?

Simba had shifted around a few places during the further weeks of my wanderings and had dossed for a while on someone's room floor like a secret hotel-squatter. But he'd eventually been turfed out over some dodgy change-money deal with a Japanese tourist and had moved down a peg to the Mombasa Hotel, at the rougher end of River Road. It was fifteen bob a night to stay there, which was a saving of two on the Iqbal.

Over the long course of time, I have realised I was most fortunate, even honoured to find this place during a period when it was filled with a mixture of such people in their changeable circumstances and in a rare moment of peace, before the streets became violent or new divisions appeared. This might have been said for my early travelling days as a whole, but it seemed more intensified here, by the closed-in atmosphere of the shared rooms and the contrasting clamour of the city outside. Despite early appearances that were quite to the contrary, there was a respectful sense of order and much to be admired in the way these people held together. There were hustles of course and scam deals for tiny pickings, but nothing really villainous and there was never any steady work, either through choice or because no one would ever engage them. Fairly all of them took a pride in somewhere they once had been, if not where they presently were. They were cheerful at last with merely being

441

alive and you never heard a moan or trace of self-pity from a single one of them. The end of our own journey was fairly well arranged, as things from here on tended to become, but if you had to survive in a place on little or no funds, having blown your dosh and missed on your flight date, as I almost once did in Lima, then you felt that here, among these street-wise survivors, with their deceptively clear wits, it would have been an absolute doddle.

Before leaving town for good, I picked out a rather striking piece of East African art from the junk that littered our room. Romeo and I thought that forty shillings was just about right and its qualities, for me, have shone ever since. Near the leaving time at last, while bugged with uncertainty over my bucket-shop flight reservation and the prospect of a frozen Moscow on the way to my January home, I felt an anxious suffocation far greater than any I'd experienced when departing for Africa in the first place. To alleviate this I made my escape into the next-door flea pit cinema, where I sat through some locally shot drivel and searched hard to find Big Stuff among the background extras.

Chapter 8
China Thereabouts

When changes take place in the world at large they sort of creep along, until it suddenly seems as though a transformation has appeared overnight. My own circumstances were about to alter substantially, due partly to providence and in some degree to my own efforts, but in the area of international public transport the order was about to turn upside down, with formerly small budget operators becoming soon the largest. The effect of this on our present lifestyle was that it moved many of us on from being hobo hippies into becoming bourgeois backpackers, with much of the world within easier reach. It was not however, a clean break from past to future, as we stepped cautiously into this new cattle truck era, mistrusting of the many in-between vendors, yet succumbing eventually in the belief that each new bargain may shortly become the last.

The clearly most welcome aspect of the new long haul flight deals was that we could migrate seasonally between climatic zones, which encouraged us to remain at home in the warmer months when work was plentiful and burst out for the tropics once all the garden furniture had been stashed away. Such a circumstance it was then that led me to jack a job of painting

443

outside on some rough Stockport housing estate, to head for sunny Thailand in mid November which, by comparison, felt like a trip to Heaven itself.

Thailand is a wonderful country with a great winter climate, superb food, a largely respectful population and low crime rate. The culture is fascinating, the architecture distinctive and prices are affordable, while off its various coasts there lie a pattern of small islands where you may still find a glimpse of tropical paradise, should you manage to disappear around one of the few remaining quiet corners. Many other worthy attractions wait here to be discovered, but I've found it often a burden over the years that whenever I mention having passed through this part of the world, I am spoken to conspiratorially, as though I were an authority on the location and quality of girl bars and whorehouses. It's a shame that this one subject overrides all others in some people's minds, when in fact it represents a very tiny percentage of what the country is really about.

Many aspects of Thai life have fascinated me over the years, but the one that has held my attention for longest is the rate of modernisation here over a relatively short time and the contrast between how far back the country really was and how swiftly it has advanced. When I first came this way in the early 'eighties you could cycle on quiet country roads up by Chiang Mai and see giant carts with solid wooden wheels, pulled along by a pair of lumbering bullocks, while in the passing fields, neighbourly rows of women sang shanty-like songs as they

444

worked young rice plants into the watery mud. It was a far cry from the present day, where hell-driven pickups scatter all in their path and solitary farmers tend a multi acre plot, alone with a single rice tractor. I recall the tales then back home of how the elderly were becoming confused and disoriented by great changes in the modern world. But that was only people with a 1930s outlook adapting to decimalisation and the digital age, whereas people in rural Thailand were seeing their lives catapulted from non mechanised medieval into the approaching 21st century and all this in the blinking of an eye. Quite some adjustment.

We must all field accusations of sentimentality when recalling poorer, simpler days, and often quite rightly so, but when I see careworn faces among the busy Sukumvit traffic and people dollar rich but impoverished of time, I realise that among all the material gains, much of real human value has been lost. A common rise in living standards needs to be earned by somebody along the way, which doesn't leave much room for neighbourly assistance and an outdoor singsong.

I didn't exactly throw myself into things on my first passage through Thailand, as I was always intending to return here on my way out and there would be other opportunities besides, with this being a common entry route into SE Asia. I did however view the obvious sites of Bangkok and stopped off at the quiet seaside resort of Hua Hin, merely because it was a half way halting point on my planned route down into Malaysia.

445

Swimming in the discoloured water here as big waves crashed onto the grey sand beach was nothing special when set beside some of the idyllic places I would later find, but it was relatively warm and I never lost my sense of gratitude for this, when compared to my recent experiences of sheltering in a freezing ginnel, as the rain eased off, while standing with a can and paint brush in hand, on Gorsey Bank council estate, Stockport. The dependency on standard public transport had so far kept me from forming any real bond with this trip, but that would inevitably change. I do recall though that on the train ride further south, the view through the carriage window drew me into a richly exotic wonderland and, to shake me out of such indulgent dreaming, there were armed guards on the train in response to local insurgents.

*

For this one time only I felt far more relaxed upon entering Malaysia. The conversational exchanges were easier to follow than from where I'd recently arrived, the lower traffic volume allowed you to breathe the air more confidently and, unlike in Thailand, you could get out on the road and meet a few ordinary people. You could hitch hike. This gave you a far greater sense of freedom and was miles more interesting than looking out the side window of a bus or train. It was also very easy during this period, in fact for the first three rides it took me

446

down to Penang I didn't even need to stick my thumb out at all, as vehicles just pulled up alongside while I walked onto the main highway. As so often happens with this random way of travel, something just sprang out of the blue here that I may never have become aware of through any other set of circumstances. It was a chance encounter that was to set the whole journey alight.

At that time there were many countries that were inaccessible to solo travellers, which have now become more open, whilst elsewhere unfortunately, the same thing has happened in reverse. China then was one of those off limit areas which, in its case, had been isolated since about 1950, due to civil war, revolution, and then revolution within a revolution. Rumours had circulated for a while that this was about to be eased off. The perpetrators of cultural vandalism, the so called Gang of Four, including Mao's widow Jiang Qing, were presently on trial, revisionism was once again being revised and China was edging experimentally towards inward foreign travel. The early examples of this were in the form of guided group tours, which were all rather expensive and on which I wouldn't have been seen dead anyway. We were all waiting for the gates to open permanently, but with the way things were at that time, China being very much into bellicose propaganda and the rumblings over Tibet, we weren't holding out much hope. But then, as so often occurs with significant events, things were to change in an instant.

447

Hitching blithely as I was towards Penang, I think it was on the second lift below Alor Star, that I got a ride from some resident Europeans in a Land Rover Defender. Seated sideways in the back was a young Canadian fellow, flushed with the success of recent adventures, who had lately returned from three weeks of travelling alone in the Peoples Republic of China. I'd been totally unaware of any relaxing of restrictions in this area, but this was fantastic news. An early journey into a part of the world that had been closed off for over thirty years! I was mad with intent to get there before the next Party Plenum changed its mind and for a while could think of nothing else. But first I had to complete the little SE Asian loop I was presently on, before losing myself in other plans.

Malaysia's most convenient advantage is that it has a relatively low population, which creates a rather relaxed atmosphere and allows you to move around with less of queuing and clambering. Apart from a couple of high density zones around KL and Johore Baharu, the Malay Peninsula consists largely of country towns, jungled hills and un-developed beach areas. Even in the most heavily visited region of Penang, you never feel as though you are in anything larger than a localised neighbourhood and beyond the maintown limits, you are straight back into the rural island atmosphere of rice fields and coco palms. Several times I passed through this mainland part of Malaysia, once along the east coast on a bicycle from Thailand to Singapore, but mostly down the other more populated side and each time I did so I would stop off at Penang, which always greatly fascinated me. Along, I suppose, with most others who did the same.

Georgetown Penang is a town of three main cultures, (not including transient foreign visitors), the appeal of which lies not so much in its diversity, as in the distinctiveness with which the variously occupied neighbourhoods have developed. It is noted in some parts of the world that when people are moved to live far away from their indigenous homeland they become, either through sentiment or patriotism, much stronger and more complete in their culture. The Chinese traditions here seemed to be held far more dear than what I would later see in China itself, and it took me quite by surprise to see an Indian neighbourhood such as that around Lebu Chulia, to be enjoying a calm, almost festive atmosphere when I compared it to the clamour of urban India.

The cuisine, that central part of the travel experience, was also rather special here, with a standard to compare favourably throughout the region and a million miles better than that cash n carry sourced Asian food on offer in much of Europe. Finally, in the formal world of architecture, there was much to admire in that, though we had by now seen mosques, Hindu temples and Chinese shop houses by the score, to see them situated here in close proximity, was like making a microcosmic journey through Southern Asia and presented much of the charm itself.

449

The central spine of Malaysia is a place where far fewer people stop, which makes it attractive to some for precisely this reason. The Cameron Highlands, a former hill station from colonial times, enjoys fine winter weather and provides a great opportunity for testing your skills at what would be a rare new activity for many, that of hiking alone through the largely primeval jungle. The trails that run by here are not of the wild frontier type, but a manageable introduction to a fascinating domain. The local peaks rise to a temperate zone at around 6½ thousand feet, though a fine summit view is not to be expected amid a barrier of forest trees and the fine prospect has to wait until the lower returning slopes, where the ground opens out into a wide carpet of tea plantations. Taking this a step further you may follow the narrow rivers and wildlife tracks around Kuala Lipis, where hollowed-out elephant tracks provide the need for greater caution and seasonal dwellings appear at the end of nowhere, temporary home to the remotest of rubber trappers. A few peaceful islands off the south east coast would finally encapsulate the best of my Malaysian impressions, though I never in the world did warm to Kuala Lumpur, a large urban sprawl of few urban charms, made only slightly congenial by comparison to Jakarta. More of which later.

*

I have ample space yet to dwell upon the spectacle of Chinese culture and though Singapore was my first full experience of this and the impressions must have felt quite strong at the time, my lasting memories of the place are of how everything around you was changing at that time and how much more of it has changed in the passage of years since. You could rarely walk far without meeting the distant sight of rising steel structures, or the close at hand din of groundworking machinery. It was a day in which the mobile compressor was coming into its own and people were going mad with air fed guns, bolting one thing to another at speed inducing pay rates. I wonder about the health of those busy Chinese blokes now and whether they think it was all worth it. Perhaps their families do.

I don't know what had disappeared to make way for these ever more sizeable developments, but I do know that every time I returned to Singapore in subsequent years, another favourite spot, that I had set my heart on re-visiting, had vanished beneath the glass and steel towers, or been over-tarted into a state of modern uniformity. Lovely old markets of latticed ironwork, converted then to Chinese food halls, the lively random stalls around Temple Street and the death alley that was Sago Street, where the elderly would go, so as not to bring ill fortune upon their younger relatives by dying in their house. All of these were soon either gone, or sanitized beyond recognition.

I know that the commercial forces which brought these changes about have increased the living standards for most

451

people in the region, and some of the new architecture did take on a vivid charm of its own, but it's ironic that one of the few places spared from this modernising helter skelter, the giant market food hall of Lau Pa Sat, in the new Central Business District, has become one of the most popular spots in the whole mini state. Perhaps in future times a fashion will arrive to return some of the tidied up facades to their former homely condition and the old and the new will be celebrated side by side. For the meantime however, much of what we have seen is a full ahead dash for modern development, creating a time-capsule cityscape of its own era.

The subject of accommodation is a mundane topic to follow in any travel narrative that aims at raising the spirits, but the business surrounding budget hotels, both in Singapore and also in Hong Kong, is one worthy of some detailed comment. Standard hotels in this popular region could be fairly pricey, if not difficult to locate, but thankfully, for the benefit of those on a shoestring, there were the crash pads. These were a series of rented rooms in apartment blocks, sometimes taking up whole floors, that had been filled with bunk beds, with a few small rooms set aside for facilities and reception area. On first approach it may have seemed these would resemble Victorian doss houses, harbouring loads of rough characters, but they were, with a few exceptions, largely well kept establishments and were occupied on the whole by outgoing young people from various nations, doing long trips on limited resources. They were also, as we had found elsewhere, great places to gather upto date information from all compass points surrounding.

One thing that these places did have in common however was that none of them were operating on a strictly legal basis and were therefore unregulated. It appeared that the government had allowed them to exist in view of the financial benefits they would bring to the State in terms of longer staying foreign guests, while not wishing to get too responsibly involved in case anything should go pear shaped. Which was quite clearly a possibility. If a fire broke out below and you were among twenty or thirty people all searching vainly for a fire exit, you could always shrug your shoulders and say, 'Well, there you go. Win some, lose some.' Unless of course, you'd habitually checked all the escape routes on your way in.

Of all the images that I took away from this place over the years, many of them mixed in with scenes of the Chinese world elsewhere, there was one which symbolised nowhere else but the Singapore of that time, where it stood in the world and what it would soon come to represent among the league of rapidly developing nations. It was the scene that met me at sea, on the boat trip out of the place. The next destination on this journey was to be Jakarta and, for those not flying, the standard route then was to take a small craft out to the rickety stilted village of Tanjun Pinang, which lay in the mangrove swamps of Bintan Island, Indonesia's first sizeable landfall. As our boat sailed out, we passed a few large cargo vessels anchored up around the mouth of the harbour and then, moving more into open sea, ran by scores of ocean going ships, spread out like a fan across the horizon. So many were there that it must have taken us an hour to reach the last of them. On later enquiry I discovered that there may have been, at certain times, vessels that had waited here upto a month before finding a berth in port. When set beside the doldrum atmosphere I'd witnessed on docksides at home and in Europe around that time, it was clear to see the way things were shaping up.

Fast forward a number of years, to possibly the last time I was in Singapore, I was expecting again to see this spectacle, but on looking seaward I could spot not one solitary ship on the outward horizon. A chance image I picked up from the deck of a local tour boat allowed me a lengthways view, through what had become the new maritime port of Singapore. The sight there really took my breath away, as the poetic movement of overhead gantry cranes and large frontloader trucks dovetailed into a mega-ton ballet that said more than any thousand words, about the value of accomplished engineering and sound, efficient management. It is reported by now that, in line with several countries around the more developed parts of the world, the Port of Singapore can turn around a large container vessel in roughly one day, even though the volume of traffic has several fold increased. Upon such basic means of transference are economic miracles delivered.

On the face of it, the passenger boat trip from Tanjun
Pinang to Jakarta should have been fairly straightforward but, by
the rules of local transport, barely any journey in Indonesia was
then a simple matter, as I was soon repeatedly to discover. The
grand vessel that sailed by Bintan Island bound for Jakarta had
actually begun its journey at Medan, in Northern Sumatra and
was far too large to pull into any harbour close to Tanjun Pinang.
Consequently, in order to pick up passengers coming down from
Singapore, it had to anchor in shallow waters out at sea, at which
point we would approach in a series of small boats and board it
from the side. Our craft, though one of the first to leave the
beach, was the last to pull up alongside the main ship and this
must have irritated me to the extent that, rather than wait in the
long queue for embarkation, I simply climbed on the roof and
scaled the side of the ship with luggage in tow, to arrive at mid-
level of an already teeming deck.

Any companions I'd acquired along the way were now
lost in the melee and for a while I was alone with nowhere to
camp. But a bunch of Indonesian students soon made a sliver of
room available for me and I rolled out my gear to lie down on
the deck, which seemed to be the norm. Most people around
were agreeable to accept my company, though not all, as I was
later to discover. Being rather shy of losing my place, I hung in
there for quite a while, until a bursting urge overcame me and,

becoming familiar with the floor plan of the ship, I rose to chance a piss. And here is where the reason for this preamble about a simple ship boarding becomes apparent. It was in the bathroom facilities.

I've been in bogs all over the world, some where your departing turds were halted in a logjam with an existing seat-high pile, others where you crapped out of the back of a moving boat while being careful not to let go of the lifesaving handrail, one where the edible pigs ate my diarrhoea as it ran down the exit chute into an open drain, several where a hole in the ground had to be located in the dark, (without taking a slide into it) and many more, where it seemed that one deep breath could be fatal. But I've never come across the like of the one on this Indonesian ship. It would challenge a film noir maker's imagination, unless perhaps they'd truly experienced the same.

The washroom entrance was formed by a large metal door, with a step-over about a foot high, which suggested that this passenger boat had been used in some cargo based capacity, perhaps in another country. Inside was a broad open room, split into two levels, at the upper end of which were urinals, wash basins and about four toilet cubicles. Heading for the stones and bursting for a slash, I had to tiptoe my way across the floor through several piles of crap before reaching my intended spot, only to find that all such fixtures had not only been crapped in, but also down and around, as though mimicking how someone taking an urgent piss might miss the target. I went over to the

456

cubicles and found the toilet bowls there full to the brim with hardening, dried up shite. The wash basins had also been used in a similar fashion. Anywhere that people could perch and squat had been dumped upon, provided there was foot space either side of the piles. People had crapped in the corners and subsequent visitors had moved outwards until the sewage was nearing the doorway and, to cap it all, a thin layer of piss rippled gently across the check-patterned floor, as the ship changed its position on the maritime waves. I guess I must have then pissed against the wall and cleared off, but I do recall that when I was forced to make a return visit, (for this was an overnight journey) I simply stuck my knob through the open door from the gangway outside and pissed as hard as I could to maintain the distance.

Many years later, when this memory was well buried, I had a strange and most lucid dream. I am not one to normally remember dreams, but this one was so vivid it had me gasping as I awoke. I dreamt that I was in a large toilet area where everywhere I looked there were waves of piss lapping towards me. All the white porcelain fittings had been shat upon to overflowing and across the floor, large mounds of crap were migrating towards me like mop headed puppets drawn in on a string. I was puzzled by this for a few days, as dreams often seem to reflect our fears, or random recent memories and I could think of no personal connection to it. But then I remembered this experience afloat and from that I can only guess that it was some kind of long delayed flash-back. It was a bit like Marcel Proust's petit madeleine cake memory, only darker and with crap.

What we needed after a passage like that was a fair dose of fresh air. What we actually got was the city of Jakarta. In many ways over the last 50 years Jakarta has been an enormous success story, with a surge of employment opportunities, expanding trade and significant regeneration. Where it hasn't quite succeeded however is in the area of infrastructure, in maintaining services that would keep pace with the extra public requirements brought on by all these rapid developments. I couldn't go into the details of everyday domestic life here with a great deal of authority obviously, but the one area that caught my attention immediately was the poor state of the urban canals and rivers.

Jakarta sits on a delta created by several estuaries that converge here, plus a number of artificial waterways, built during the Dutch time to alleviate flooding. Most estuaries require constant dredging to keep levels under control and canals need to be regulated and refreshed by a constant gentle flow. In Jakarta this had not been the case over many years and the result was a black stagnant network of trash-strewn channels, filled with ill bred mosquitoes and dying rats, that created an overpowering image that was difficult to escape from. I heard recently that a program has been launched to clean up some of these waterways, many of which had received no attention whatsoever in more than forty years. You could use many strong and pointed words

458

to describe how this situation was allowed to fester for so long and no doubt accusations in that part of the world are flying to and fro. But raw human nature, if allowed to run unchecked, will normally favour the quick buck aim of large real estate projects and leave any outer lying problems this may create to someone else.

With my tourist visa running for only one month I had to be selective with my movements here and the choice was between heading east to Bali, or north west up through Sumatra. Java seemed a bit too populous and busy for me and the tale of Bali, according to many who had earlier known the place, was that it was all screwed now and nowhere like what it had been. To the north west was a lesser known quantity and I guess that's what must have drawn me in. There are many wilder ways of travelling through Sumatra than the one I took and I regret not having the means to explore many of these, but the route I chose was engaging enough and one of those hard won passages that are always the more gratifying. My most abiding memories of this region are of the difficulties presented by the central highway running northwards through the island and of the few havens of peace, the pleasures of which were highlighted by the surrounding circumstances.

Much of the main interconnecting road system in Sumatra then was unpaved dirt and one rough section, between Palembang and Padang, was viewed almost with reverent awe by first time through-travellers. Journey time between these two

459

locations is now about 18 hours on a well metalled surface. Back then it took 43 hours over two days and three nights on a trip that must, at times, have been quite hellish. The upgrade in road surface has obviously been a boon for local commuters, but for those of us who would pass this way but once, the smoothing of the route was just another little piece of the old traveller magic lost. There was one memorable spot where, during periods of heavy rain, it was required for a rope to be run out from the front of the bus, looped around a large uphill tree and all the passengers would be invited to haul it up the slope, as the engine roared and the bus slithered along to the summit. On our time through here rainy season was just beginning and we managed without the rope, merely having to get out and push at the rear bumper. This, I later realised, was not wholly without risk as, should the bus roll backwards on gear change, then it was rolling heavily in your direction. It was not a thing to greatly bother me at the time however as, rather than an older person's sense of safety and caution, we merely saw it as an exhilarating moment in the journey and what most people talked about for long afterwards.

There was also a ferry crossing on this same route where the bus, with 20 passengers onboard, was rolled onto a floating bed made of planks and narrow boat hulls, to be punted across a shallow river with large bamboo poles. But, when compared to the thrill of an 18 ton vehicle competing with your own strength on a slippery hill, as you darted to escape from its backward lurch, it seems hardly incidental.

Though we often rose-tint our memories and bury the bad, it is fair to recall that a lot of the towns through this way were not the type where you would dwell, other than for pure necessity. The prime example of this for me was at Padang, where everyone seemed to overcharge by about 100% and people were otherwise not friendly, or just quite unhappy within themselves. Added to this, it was a poor coastal town and the waste disposal system seemed to be largely dependent upon how far the daily tides came up to the shoreline. There was one murky encounter that befell me early in my stay here which seemed to set the tone for the whole place, but which in long hindsight has come to be more greatly valued as a re-tellable tale.

It was in the very basic room I stayed, after a heavy trip from Palembang and just about to collapse on any available bed. I'd asked some young fellow in the street of a cheap hotel in town and he had guided me to this place, only to enter the room uninvited behind me and wouldn't depart until I'd paid him for the service; which you had to become wise to at some stage in these parts. The room had a tubular steel divan and a bare floor, which was ok by me. It also had wooden partition walls that ran to within a foot of the ceiling, the remaining gap being filled by three sides of rolled out chicken wire, a style I'd only ever witnessed once before and that in South America. I took the room immediately because I was too tired to look elsewhere, but

461

as I was making the arrangement, I noticed the odd angle of a chair that was standing in the mid floor space, looking as though in a state of imbalance, but which actually had one of its legs jammed into a wide hole in the floorboards. A damn strange place for a chair I thought and immediately pulled it out, placing it gently against the wall.

I needed to nip out for a bite and a small beverage before launching myself on the welcoming mattress and so, having paid the room fee, I departed for the street, padlocking the door as I went. On my return about twenty minutes later, I was confronted by the freakish sight of about three rats clinging to the chicken wire high up inside the room and with the obvious necessity to enter there myself, I swiftly unlocked the door and began making the loud clapping and foot stamping noises that you usually do to hide the fact that you are actually a bit scared. At this point the rats zoomed down the wall at high speed, ran across the floor and hot tailed into the void underfoot, in a swiftly moving queue, whereupon I picked up the chair and rammed it back in its apparently rightful location. And there you have it, the ideal way to bodge a cure for a local spot of rat infestation. Find the point of entry, pick up the nearest wooden chair and bang it straight in the hole. Once done, sleep well.

Some of the nicest places I've been have usually benefitted by a contrast with somewhere I've visited immediately preceding and such was the case with the small upland town of Bukittinggi which, after Padang, was like walking out into fresh

462

Springtime. Surrounded here, by electric green hills covered by low bush, the country market gleamed like a picture postcard and the produce on sale spoke of wholesomeness and health. Every deal seemed surprisingly straight and everyone looked cheerful and happy. We've probably all witnessed this situation much nearer to home, where we've wondered how such a place could exist so close to less favoured parts and remind ourselves that this was still the same country.

From hereon was another hard 17 hours of grinding road travel, with loud blaring music that kept the driver awake and denied the passengers a wink of slumber – prime among the reasons I've never taken fondly to public transport in such regions. A reward was at hand however, as it usually is in these hard slog kind of journeys and we eventually rolled up at Parapat on the shores of Lake Toba. With a 3a.m. arrival and nowhere open, I simply bedded down in the faintest of starlight on the pebbly shore to await the early dawn, a ploy I was advised never to repeat for fear of violent robbers. Yet I survived the darkness and awoke to a natural revelation of cathedral-like splendour.

Lake Toba sits within the caldera of a super volcano that created the largest known earthly eruption of the last 25 million years. The multi megaton explosion said to have occurred here, deposited ash as far away as Southern Africa and led to a volcanic global winter that may have considerably reduced the world's living population. At the very heart of this lake lies what may have been a resurgent dome of this collapsed volcano which, surrounded by crater walls of nearly 4,000 feet and sheltered glassy waters, provides a peaceful Shangri La, that contrasts most sharply with both the present grind and bustle of North Sumatra and the climactic events of the prehistoric past. It was to this now peaceful spot, a 21 mile strip of buffalo grazed greenery, that I was presently headed. To Samosir Island.

The transport, I remember, was a small wooden boat, fitted with a low revving outboard motor and, with the water being near enough to trail your fingers in, I found myself, even though super tired, almost hallucinating with the sublime beauty of it. Here you had that strongly reassured feeling that you often get among fine mountain scenery, where you sensed that, whatever else in the world might change, the outline of this landscape may never do so. Which was perhaps just as well, because heaven knows, much of the rest of this place was about to.

My digs on the island were in a low rise building at the village of Tuk Tuk, which was fronted by one of those tall Batak houses, with high peaked roofs and upward curving eaves, that resemble the horns of a water buffalo. Things were quiet then, with just a couple of resident guests, though I could sense a drift towards tourist savvy expedience, as a teenage member of the hotel family was selling dope to guests and then disappearing with money owed, while his 12 year old younger brother was collecting hallucinogenic mushrooms on the hillside to serve the same purpose. But compared to all the places I'd so far been on

464

this trip, it was still a haven of peace. We had been the only boat on the lake coming across, with I the sole passenger and when I later went out for a lone reconnaissance around the top end of the shoreline, I saw just four cars in the whole day. Up and over the island was a nice two day walk and kids along the way would ask you not for coins or baksheesh, but pens and writing paper, which you were more than happy to prepare yourself for.

It is an inescapable sentiment for surviving travellers of my era, but when I see images of this and other such places coming back to me through various media, I recognise little beyond the unaltered background hills. The boat journey across here now is on a large steel-hulled vessel and there are at least six trips a day. The shoreline village more resembles a growing town and the Google map shows bars and resorts around all neighbouring inlets. Yet the stunning caldera is still there, the sheltered blue waters where bathers glide and there's possibly a swathe of open country on the island summit from where you could view and begin to feel all of this.

A place is yours only for the moment of your visit and some of that you might get to keep in your heart, but it has a life and necessity of its own and the developments that occur may be happily accepted by those who come afterwards, who find it hard to imagine the world without them. My ideal is not a permanently deserted region but one where services are just beginning to appear and the place is still fresh, but one can't complain if these become eventually overrun, because let's face it, it was the likes of us that dragged the hordes there with us in the first place.

On my way back to the mainland shore I boarded the same boat, not alone this time but with one other passenger, an Australian bloke who would have welcomed a few disreputable hangouts on the island. But that's his story and we all have our trip to do. From hereon the journey would move away from rural serenity and into heavily built up areas, but it was non the poorer for that. I was going to Hong Kong, to try my luck on entering a quite recently opened up China.

*

Flying into Hong Kong's old Kai Tak International Airport was a never forgotten experience, especially for those lucky enough to have obtained a right sided window seat. The long approach was scary enough, as the plane twisted and turned to get onto the right track and, as it flew lower, it appeared we were about to plough a burning furrow through a spread of packed residential streets. Almost at the last however we made a banking 45° turn, which brought us face to face with rooftop water tanks and TV aerials, before levelling through a narrow urban gap between short tower buildings, where it was clear to see hung out washing on the balconies and, it was somewhere claimed, the flickering blue light of television sets within apartment rooms. The landing was generally a smooth one, but

466

the excitement did not quite end there, as there was a strong roar of reverse powered brakes to prevent the craft ending up in Victoria Harbour, as the far end of the runway jutted out into the sea.

As buildings encroached into this space cramped area of Kowloon, it was finally decided that this old 1925 airport should be closed and flight operations moved to Chek Lap Kok, on the side of Lantau Island, which in 1988, did become the case. The move no doubt was greeted with great relief by tortured Kowloon residents and apprehensive pilots alike, but for those who travel for just a bit more excitement, it was as if yet another light had gone out from the world.

Though changes in the world may come slowly or fast, almost any visit to a distant foreign place will fall into its own unique time slot. I have visited Hong Kong several times since, on my travels to elsewhere and I realise that this first occasion I stopped by had its own period conditions. The handover from British Colonial to Chinese mainland rule was still some 15 years away and I never really felt the pressure of this from where I was standing, but in the zone of commercial activity I could see it was something of a riot. Perhaps fearing the uncertainty over future changes, everyone here seemed eager to make money as fast as they possibly could and, with the long hours that people worked and their demeanour in doing so, their urgency was clearly apparent.

This was a time of huge growth in local commerce and the authorities were struggling to deal with the problem of unlicensed trader stalls invading the more central business districts. Vendors were a splash of colour to us wide-eyed visitors and the cheap tacky wares they sold were often of great convenience, but they were a plague to the regular businesses, who had paid their rates only to find these characters blocking their shopfront displays and as for keeping the pavements clear, it was a case of stand in the logjam queue or walk into the busy road. It was here one time where the stall I was browsing at suddenly had the covers put on and was wheeled away as the permit police were closing in and I was left standing there holding a yellow plastic watch that I hadn't paid for. It lasted me about three days.

What all of this signified of course, the loosely controlled building developments, the locally made goods on sale everywhere you looked, not to mention the street food stalls hampering your steps, was that Hong Kong was heading towards some kind of temporary gold rush, with the usual assortment of winners and also rans. Nearly everyone, it seemed, wanted to be either a wholesale manufacturer or a super salesperson and, though it appears a long way from tat on a stall to a mansion on the hillside, some of them actually did make it.

A strong example of how commercial activity was prepared to fill every corner here was revealed to me the moment I arrived at the place where I was to take up my first temporary

468

residence in Hong Kong. This was at the Travellers Hostel, a crash pad on the 16th floor of a tower block called Chungking Mansions, on Nathan Road, Kowloon. Out front were the usual array of street stalls, nicking the light from the windows of legit businesses, while inside on the ground floor was an old fashioned shopping arcade, trading in everything from supermarket groceries to fashion clothes and tourist knick-knacks. Impromptu foodstalls with their scarper-quick furniture lined the pokey side alley and beer was for sale at the back arcade entrance. There were two sets of elevators at opposite corners of the block and by the one that stopped at my destination, the odd numbers, a queue had formed to enter the lift. This momentary captive audience was far too good an opportunity to miss for one rather enterprising (or desperate) salesman, as there he stood, with a tall wooden pole attached to a long board, across the front of which were held about twenty pairs of really cheap looking shoes. A possibly tempting sight for someone whose socks were just beginning to make contact with the bare paving.

After a first day of roaming the territory in search of a Chinese visa, first of all at their own Embassy and then at the PR China Travel Service, I eventually discovered that the duty of issuing them had been farmed out to a travel agency that was actually right in the entranceway of my own digs on the 16th floor. The wild goose chase was far from a wasted one however, as I began to get the feel of Hong Kong, which had an atmosphere about it that I could recognise straight away as being something special. From the swish business district of H.K. Central, along the shopfront workhouses of Hennessy Road, on the clanging 1890s trams and the ever crowded Star Ferry, the place had a buzz that I have never experienced in any other place either before or since. It was as though everyone here, from the supercharged marketeer to the humblest brush hand, was out to make something for themselves, without waiting for it to fall from the sky. The positivity was exhilarating.

Back at the digs on a Friday afternoon I applied the visa and was told that it would be ready by Tuesday at the latest, which gave me opportunity to check out a little side trip I'd heard about whilst out on my rounds. This was the short island hop out to Lamma Island, a 30 minute sally out from H.K. Central Harbour. I'd been travelling in traffic since departing North Sumatra for an overland slog up to Bangkok and though my mind had been blown by recent surrounds, I was ready for a change in volume. Once I'd stretched myself out of the boat on arrival and walked a few yards away from the jetty, I felt as though I'd gone deaf. There were absolutely no cars on the island. Many people don't realise that Hong Kong, away from the bright lights, can also be a place of wooded streams, singing birds and hiking trails; but if you had to stay here for a long while, say a few month assignment, or for life, these are the places you would probably come to treasure, although it might

470

be the memory itself you would later treasure, because such spots are filling up fast.

The return trip over to the busy end presented us with a different view of this rapidly developing enclave, as it took us back in the direction of where things might have begun. From the same jetty I caught a different boat this time, which took us to the south side of HK Island and into the suburb of Aberdeen. Crowded beneath the tall inland buildings were a mass of parked up sampans and house boats, while along the shoreline a random collection of shacks clustered each wooden jetty. This would be pretty much how Hong Kong began as a settlement, with people dwelling near or actually on the water, while making their living from fish and trade along the nearby Pearl River. A view such as this is best taken in whole and from a distance, which was the grace of arriving on a calm sea, with the deck of our boat a couple of feet above the water line. A circumstance that was gratefully accepted..

Back at the crash pad my visa was ready and I chose my means of departure. There were three options available and I went for the middle one which, being a broken journey up to the Chinese border at Lo Wu and then by local train into Guangdong province, was about 60% cheaper than the tourist through train from Kowloon. But I missed the real trick of the day, which would have been to take a public service boat up the aforementioned Pearl River, from Tsim Sha Tsui Harbour to

471

Guangzhou. What a great way to enter a still unmodernised China this would have been.

Before my departure north, there was still enough time to witness one more revealing aspect of Hong Kong that would leave me, at last, with my strongest memory of this weird and wonderful place. It began with a fit of exasperation as, after a short trip outside, I returned to my digs to find that both sets of elevators had packed up and I was faced with the task of mounting thirty two flights of stairs up sixteen floors. I was less than superfit in those days, but I still took stairs two at a time and hiked around a fair bit, which I guess was my saving grace, so off I set, full of pace and determination. After about four floors I was beginning to blow a bit but then, as I slowed down, things began to get rather interesting. Upto now I had passed, I forget in which order, the entrance to a place selling baby clothes, a huddle of people assembling plastic watches, somewhere running up fake designer jeans and a plastic radio factory. Further ahead there was a floor of hotel apartments, a crash pad, a calculator production line, some shoe works, some boxed up alarm clocks, a tailor's shop, another hotel, some shirt place and, further along to our own floor, another crash pad and a travel agents. The whole place was a business centre, industrial estate and cheap accommodation complex perched on top of a teeming downmarket shopping arcade. It was a veritable beehive. Here was the seed from which Hong Kong's recent prosperity had

472

grown and, though such relentless endeavour wouldn't be everyone's idyllic choice, you had to take your hat off to it.

*

At the outset, my entry into China was a very low key affair, as though I was waiting for images to hold onto, but with little success. That wasn't the way things turned out however and for the further that time ran on, the impression was to become a long slow burner. Through the broad window of my hard seated rail carriage things appeared a lot less affluent here than I had earlier imagined. Dirt roads wound their way through uninspiring villages of low brick dwellings and the flat landscape was a patchwork of randomly mixed crops that spoke loudly of manual labour. In the cement-rendered city of Guangzhou, made greyer by the overcast seasonal weather, the boulevard life had a provincial air, as wicker brooms and wheelbarrows were wheeled around by an army of municipal workers. Peoples' non uniform clothes were in a well worn state, rather like my own poor elders in the austere 1950s, but many were either in military khaki or blue baggy overalls, with the ubiquitous red star on the cap front. I'd checked into a dormitory full of foreigners right opposite the railway station and was soon out for a wander, totally thrilled to be here, but wondering what the hell to make of such a notable place that, so far, had little to offer, beyond dim electrical lighting and long red banners.

473

The first place I approached to get my bearings was Shamian Island, a sand bank in the Pearl River that was conceded to the traders of Britain and France from the mid 19th to mid 20th centuries and which gave the city its Western name of Canton. This I could relate to with some faint knowledge of the Boxer Rebellion, the opium trade, gun boats on the river and the forced opening of foreign commercial business. The district then looked rundown and dilapidated and in dire need of some miracle rescue, which fortunately does happen from time to time. The cityscape was not much to hold your attention, with low rise housing over towered by unadorned blocks that we would always associate with functional Communism, though there were a few classical structures dotted around, preserved I guessed, not for religious importance, but as features of a surrounding park. Beyond this, the most remarkable images I could gather were of what was on sale. Skinned dead dogs in the market place and hardly much in the uptown Government Store. Things would gradually draw us in however, through some of the people we met and by the country landscape that totally absorbed us.

The first person I spoke to at length in China was a fellow who had found himself a long term victim of the Cultural Revolution, launched by Mao Tse Tung in the mid 1960s and which ran on until around 1976. The stated aim of the project was to preserve Chinese Communism by purging capitalist and traditional elements from society. A feature of this wild drive, one that blighted the lives of about 10 million ambitious Chinese

474

youths, was the Down to the Countryside Movement, which took people from the comfort zone of professionally trained jobs and the student life, to the rice fields, bamboo plantations and mountain pastures where, for a statutory two years, they would see how the other half lived. Some people, especially those too old to be roped into such a scheme, might say this was an idea worth following up, as it may encourage a few of them to try washing the pots once in a while, but the real downside to this heavy handed approach to social engineering was that, not only did the hard working country peasants and the urban smartarses famously fail to get on, but when the two year period had ended, many of those temporarily misplaced could not return to their professional training or university studies.

Our man here, perhaps in his late twenties, had missed out on the second half of his university education and was presently driving a truck for the Diamond Lock Company on $4.50 a month, which wouldn't get you more than nine days lodge at the cheap dorm I was staying in. By studying in the evening after his driving shift, he was working harder than most of the hallowed proletariat in order to retrieve what he had lost, but it was going to be a long road back. In circumstances such as these, a level of bitterness could be forgiven, and making it harder to bear was his inability to loudly protest, but he was far from alone. Beyond the death of about a million people and the destruction of historic artefacts from the classical past, here was one of the most hurtful aspects of this mad upheaval, as the economic effects of forced movement were enduringly damaging, while those sorely touched by it became known as the Lost Generation. Some in China still theorise that Mao and his mates launched the Cultural Revolution to divert criticism away from the failures of the Great Leap Forward program, which featured a communal tinkering in food production that killed 30 million people through famine. If so, it must go down as the highest price ever to have been paid by a public, in order to save a few political careers.

From Guangzhou my plans were fairly flexible and I allowed myself to be talked into travelling to Kweilin, a famous landscape beauty spot on the Li River, which was a bad idea at first, but a huge blessing later on. Though Kweilin then was a low rise sprawling city of few eminent features, its surroundings, on a fine day, were a pictorial wonderland. A strange phenomenon here combines an otherwise flat terrain and meandering smooth river with a cluster of tightly packed conical hills of karst limestone, created probably as undersea coral mounds, now deformed and made far more interesting in appearance by acidic water dissolution. Here is the scene featured in a million works of Chinese art, from traditional paintings, to porcelain vases and modern dinner plates. Tall craggy rocks with arched bridges from one outcrop to another, people along the river with decorated parasols and blossoming trees beside a stilted house. It's muse was all out there somewhere, but thanks to the seasonal damp weather and the

476

mist as high as the rooftops, I could hardly see a trace of it. I've hiked up to many a hilltop with no view and the consoling term that mountaineers use is that 'the mountain will always be there again,' but hell, I'm not. Especially in South West China! Still, I compare my setbacks to those of others. Like the person I met in the US who drove a thousand plus miles to the Grand Canyon and could barely see the end of the street. Their loss was a proper sickener and this, to a far lesser extent was mine.

While staying a couple of days longer in Kweilin, unsuccessfully waiting for the weather to clear up, I put myself around town and near walked myself to a standstill. I was becoming warmed to the local atmosphere by now and rather than feeling the gloom of Guangzhou, with its grey cement walls and its brow beating political banners, I observed that the people here were rather prone to visible outbreaks of cheerfulness. It was some contrast to the competitive anxiety that drove Hong Kong, where the natives were far richer of health but poorer of time. But perhaps it was just that everyone was at nearly the same material level, basically skint.

A few people, from time to time would hold you in conversation in the street and become quite effusive in their chat. Such a one was the plainly dressed elderly gentleman who had taught Americans to speak Mandarin in 1930s Shanghai, had lived four years in Hong Kong and ten in San Francisco. He spoke English, French, Russian and a collection of Chinese dialects and should have gone far, but 1949 caught him in China, in the territory unoccupied by Chiang Kai Shek and so here he remained. In 1950, English teaching was scrapped in favour of Russian, but by 1958 the two Communist Titans had fallen out and he had to revert to teaching English again. It seemed, listening to him and others, that so many peoples lives here had been like corks on the waves, subjected to massive changes between war, peace and social upheavals.

To change my own traipsing activities I rented an ancient bicycle and rode along the crowded boulevards, where the cyclists seemed to outnumber both the motorists and pedestrians combined. It was never a scenic journey but one possessed of a strange thrill, as once you found yourself in the centre of a lane, it was impossible to turn left or right because of people immediately either side of you and you just had to carry straight on, nearly forever. If one person fell off it would be a peloton like pile-up. But they never did.

Later I got talking to a gentleman who just wanted to practice his English, which can often turn out a lot less thrilling than it seems. I did pick up one memorable snippet of information from the encounter though. As we stopped outside a huge government bookstore in our suburb of Kweilin, I was told that, though many famous books in the English language were on sale here, I, as a foreigner, was not allowed to view the interior. It turned out that in line with much else of foreign design here, copyright fees had not been paid on any of it.

478

Though my passage through Kweilin did have some disappointment attached to it, the direction I took brought me eventually towards the best part of this and many another trip, which all centred around a three day journey out of Chongqing. The direction I was following had to take me back to Macao and Hong Kong on the homeward trail, and the northward turn I was about to make was part of a huge loop which, when looked at later on the map, made a paltry free formed rectangle on the huge expanse of China. To cover by rail, one quarter of this vaguely four sided shape, took me 39 hours.

A lesson I would always remember from this journey was that, if you ever take a hard sleeper on a foreign train, make sure your lower bunk is not directly over the rear axle of a carriage, as the railway sound of clickety-clack etc, has a far less romantic ring to it after many hours of the same and by arrival time it could feel as though your head had been run over. It was at times a very pleasant journey however. I had noted already on my brief travels through China that every plot of spare land I'd seen had been turned over to agriculture, rather like in wartime rationing days. The landscape was starting to rise up now and show this off to better effect and as we rode along, the sun danced up and down the hillsides among the yellow oilseed rape crops and the reflecting rice terraces.

Chongqing then had not undergone the huge skyline change that has become common among large Chinese cities and the picture I have of it was of a place that was not yet rundown,

479

though not quite run up enough to do so. It was Socialist era architecture again, with people huddled in concrete apartment blocks, sharing their closely aligned lives and grassing one another up. The strangest thing I encountered here was the curiosity with which locals received foreigners in their midst. Despite our knowing that the country had only been open to solo travellers for a matter of months, and this wasn't quite on the main beaten track, it was still a surprise to have people stop and stare at you in the street, either by themselves or in groups. My most colourful memory of this comes from the time I was enjoying some soup at an outdoor cafe on my way out of here. There were crowds of people waiting to board the boat that would take us together some way down the Yangtze and every one of them appeared to be staring in my direction. Though slightly disconcerting as it was, especially while eating, I was kind of used to this by now, having endured it elsewhere, particularly in 'seventies India. But the real fun came when it was time to settle my food bill. I had just changed £100 at the bank and the highest denomination banknote I had was worth about £3, plus a ruffle of smaller bills. The wallet I had them in was so bulky against my waistband that I could hardly bend to sit down and as I pulled it out to pay, opening it up like some high roller at the casino, a big 'Oooooooh!' went up from the crowd, as though a lower league cup side had just shaved the crossbar of their elite Premiership rivals in the FA Cup 3rd round. I flicked out a three quid note, hoping it would more than cover the price

480

and was faced with even more public shuffling, as I received a not inconsiderable amount of paper change. The soup was just about 3p.

From this point, soon began what was then one of the greatest short journeys on earth, a slow sail down river, lasting 3 days and 2 nights, through the Yangtze Three Gorges. This was a trip designed not purely for tourists, but a regular boat service from Chungking to Wuhan. But, if you had only come along for the passing view, you could stand on the upper deck roof for most of each day and be totally amazed. Which is roughly what I did. The first day out from Chongqing was sometimes special, but nothing compared with what was to come.

The grey river was bland as we departed and a blanket mist that had enveloped the pier, seemed to grow thicker as we entered the cold morning countryside. Enveloped within this, there rose a mixture of images that seemed present to only ourselves, as a sampan rode in our side-wake, powered by gangs of standing, shouting men, hauling hard at very long oars. Somewhere in the distance there had been the ringing sound of hammer on quarry chisel and the load that had held the boat low to its gunwale, was probably a product of the same. Faintly through the mist, then vividly clear, a range of significant peaks stood terraced to their summits, in tribute to generations of honest hard labour. I counted the terraces in the time that we passed and had reached around forty, before the summit was lost in falling cloud. A little while later, an ancient junk bobbed into

481

our view, with its wooden sail-frame and russet brown cloth, defying for a while longer the convenience of quick start motors. And so that was my day. Something to fill your eyes as you closed them in sleep, and we hadn't even got to the Three Gorges yet.

Conditions on our boat were good, even in the 4th class. There was a clean 24 bed dorm and, as there were only eight of us, we could loll around in spacious luxury. Out in the passageways the 5th class passengers slept on a hard cold floor, suggesting there were some hardy characters around here, though for how long they would survive in such a state was anyone's guess. I had travelled for a while with a German bloke called Manfred and there was a Chinese couple from Hong Kong. Manfred was very blonde, with bushy eyebrows and a great 'tash. Some small kid came into the sleeping quarters and started screaming at the sight of Manfred before running to hide in his mother's clutches. The cartoon image of a deceased spirit in Chinese comics is usually of a pale faced person with white hair and eyebrows. There hadn't yet passed too many foreigners by this way compared to the main trail elsewhere and the kid thought Manfred was a ghost!

Early evening we pulled into some riverside town, as we would several times along the way and went ashore out of curiosity. These places felt like the real country China, where everything led from the fields to here and the town had the air of a huge farm storage shed. There were no fancy temples or tall pagodas, but I feel I should have appreciated these places more at the time as, beyond the veneer of red banners and political lobotomy, they had a touch of the medieval about them.

Without the benefit of a local weather forecast, it was with great surprise that we rose the next morning to glorious bright sunlight. We'd been travelling in clouds since Guangzhou, but as the day became fuller we found ourselves gliding into gorge number one in conditions we earlier couldn't have dreamt of. Being the highest up river gorge, Qutang had the narrowest passage and also coincidentally the steepest sides. Bushes grew from the crags in places and its five mile route saw the recurrent contrast between the dramatic and the softly picturesque. It was rated locally as the most spectacular of the three, but I guess all those who said so were well familiar with the rural Chinese landscape. For me the greater wonder existed further down. Before we exited its tight confines we were to encounter the sight of a thirty foot raft of giant bamboo logs flowing rapidly on the ravine current, while being guided by standing men holding long oars and barge poles. Its cargo was a thick layer of stone blocks, which meant it had come quite some way from the sound of hammered chisels and you felt that one false turn could have taken the lot down. Hence a clear sense of danger on men's faces.

Following shortly on our exit from Qutang we entered the second of the gorges, the 25 mile long Wuxia, which seemed near impenetrable on approach, but which ran on wider as the

483

river progressed. I actually began to enjoy this a bit more, as I had found my way through forbidden quarters onto the roof and from here I would appreciate the journey in reverse order to the accepted fashion. In contrast to the earlier tight confines, the landscape became much broader and the rugged mountains made us feel as though we were heading out into the wilds, rather than being on a route that would take us to Wuhan and some on to Shanghai. Agriculture had tailed off a little here, as the ground was probably too rocky and it seemed like the kind of area where you would have looked to have put on your hiking gear.

Finally, with the sun beginning to slant from the west, we came to Xiling Gorge, the longest of the gorges at around 49 miles. The reason I found Xiling the most attractive may have been the time of day, or even the time of year. It was a clear Spring afternoon and the low sunlight shone over our shoulder onto everything before us. The green and yellowing crops had a fluorescence all their own and the orchard blossoms blew orange and lemon scents faintly into mid water. The view was much more expansive here at a lower, warmer altitude and the hills rolled rather than towered. But the tameness of the landscape was compensated for by the awe inspiring work that had gone into it. The scenery of open country, I feel, is always enhanced of interest when the generations have been labouring on it, and this was a work of art.

I don't know how long I'd been on the boat roof but it wasn't until the last mile of the last gorge had been completed

484

that I realised I'd become numb. Soon we were at a point to the north west of Yichang, where a large power plant straddled the river. There was a canal-type lock system beside it which, through a series of manoeuvres, lowered us about fifty feet onto a wide expanse of water that looked like a turgid lake. We continued some way, hardly able to see the distant shore of what was a flat plain landscape, and it was over. One of the greatest days of travel in my entire life.

There is many a postscript to the story of the Three Gorges and more will be written in the course of time, but the central event of what brings us to date with this region is the construction of a new dam at Sandouping, about 27 miles upstream from the earlier build at Gezhouba, Yichang. This later project has brought forward every kind of response from high praise to passionate criticism, which of course, equates to much controversy. The work of construction displaced 1.3 million people, flooded historical sites and erased famous beauty spots that had been lauded by the poets as far back as the 3rd Century B.C. The flooding caused by damming has raised river levels by 90% in some areas, which has widened the base of valleys and lowered the majesty of its bordering peaks. It caused an increased risk of landslides (constantly under review) and obviously had a traumatic effect on the ecology and biodiversity of the district.

Among those who have to live within its daily sight however, there are many, perhaps a majority, whose views lean much to the opposite. In 1954, huge floods in this region were responsible for the deaths of around 33,000 people. In 1988 again, with better defences in place, about 4,000 people were killed in a flood which adversely affected 180 million throughout the region. The Xiling Gorge, which lies closest to where the new dam is situated, was once renowned as a shipwrecking area due to rapid shoals, numerous reefs and odd shaped protruding boulders, all of which have been removed as hazards. The river is now a safer cargo and passenger shipping way and the hydro power has seen China attain its economic goals, which have hugely increased national prosperity. Everyone would agree that it has been a huge upheaval for all concerned, but that's the way things have been here for the last 90 years, since General Honjō first invaded Manchuria and, when transition does take place, nearly everything in China involves massive numbers. I was fortunate to travel this way before these great changes occurred, but after ten minutes of viewing online photos of what the place looks like now, it is easy to forget how once it looked, and the whole valley, from the boat, on a clear day, with the western sun at your back, still looks exquisitely beautiful.

Some journeys can be over long before you get back home, but this one still had a message to deliver. It was not in the run down city of Wuhan, which then had a population of 4 million but has now grown to 11: nor was it the train ride back to Guangzhou, about the distance of a full bottle of rice brandy away and a restless nights' sleep. It was however in the turbulent

486

bus trip from Guangzhou to Kung Pa, on the Macao border, which revealed to me more than anywhere else, the striking difference between where a developing China was then, compared to where it was headed.

The five hour ride to Kung Pa took me through the kind of districts I had so far not seen in this part of the world, where unpaved highways ran through villages of tiny cramped houses, walls were uniformly sand washed and every window blown with dust. Four river crossings were made on makeshift transport ferries, which spoke of an infrastructure that was way behind the developed world. Fast forward to now and the various economic zones that straddle this region, it barely seems recognisable as a part of the same continent, and great credit must go to the human efforts of labour and organisation that brought all this about. It may seem now that this country was like a coiled spring, waiting to leap forward more effectively than any 5-year government plan. But I must say, that, at the time, there was never a trace of it.

*

The ornamental archway of Portas do Cerco was surrounded by spreading trees as I entered Macao. The regulations in China, though cheerfully applied, had been many and various, which continued to bear upon us right to the end. It was clear that I had just crossed a border between separate

487

worlds however, as there was no one around at all to check my documents on the other side. They were probably deep chilling under a sensible shade somewhere. I found a cheap room on a Latin avenida, which took me back a bit, and went out for a short walk which, within little over an hour, had taken me around the whole northern half of the territory. There was a hillside appearance about the townscape and the rococo basilicas seemed to compliment the sea-facing Chinese temples, while the plazas and balconied streets left you in a kind of geographical limbo. It reminded me of Spanish Ceuta in North Africa, where you didn't seem to be in any particular country at all and much of the history included people who were headed for somewhere else, but had stopped off here accidentally and sometimes permanently.

People like Henry Davies Margesson, from Surrey, who, on the eve of his return to England after a residence of 23 years in China, drowned with the sinking of his ship off Yokohama in June 1869. Three American sailors in 1849 lost their lives in consecutive weeks, two falling from aloft and one unexplained death. It seems they didn't get along too well on that ship. Say no more. The Protestant cemetery had been a tempting diversion, but when it got to the piercing details of high child mortality in those days, it was time to move on.

The museum and gallery were shut for repairs, which was a shame, because they had there some of the works of George Chinnery, an English artist who had been given free local reign in the early 1800s. I came to love the works of these Orientalist travelling painters, like Captain Cook's artists in the Pacific and those who tramped the Arab lands depicting water sellers on the spot. The works of highest artistic merit will be the longest survivors, but for me it was more in the historical value. They were of scenes that I would have loved to have witnessed firsthand. But only for the view and a bit of passing chat, not the hard shipworm of getting there.

The trip to the casinos was an excursion in itself. I wandered through the halls of the posh Hotel Lisboa with people greeting me smilingly as though I was going to be the perfect mug punter, before I blended anonymous into the crowd, interloping quietly in my chancer's clothes. They wouldn't be making much out of me today, I needed this shirt to get home in. The old Floating Casino in the Outer Harbour was rather my form of entertainment. A bit nearer the bottom end of the scale, it was rather like a casino version of Sha Tin Racecourse, with people scrambling excitedly around one another and waving money while trying to get a bet on. I had hoped to watch the roulette for a while, but couldn't get near enough the table to see it.

Finally, after a brief moment that had been filled to an age, it was time to leave Macao, a place that had seemed like several other places but which, in the end, was only itself, and even that in a much passing phase. I was on the slow ferry boat to Hong Kong and a very fine thing it was. Hulky and dawdling, it allowed you a deck borne, sea spray approach into Hong Kong Harbour, which is one of the most spectacular places in the world to sail into.

*

Back in the old colony there were always things going on. People were talking of doing paid courier trips to other Far Eastern countries, taking goods that were deemed within the law. But you only had a day of turnaround in each place, which might kill my appetite for visiting them in future and I doubted they were all strictly legal in any case, as future discoveries would confirm. It did however whet my appetite for a future journey out here and the flight deals that were beginning to appear on bucket shop window boards offered up a kaleidoscope of possibilities. I was still very much on the hook.

My image of Hong Kong had broadened after visiting China and, in addition to my admiration for the degree of public endeavour, I saw that it was also a muted, unsmiling place, rather like 1970s London, where people were neither over hostile nor faintly friendly, just look ahead busy, and I instantly missed the real personal contact and humour of the country Chinese. You can't have it all ways however and practically all my contacts here were with other travelling foreigners who, at this stage, were all eager to hear my accounts of travelling in a freshly opened China.

490

One who memorably wasn't was a fellow so well on with his own tale that I was loathe to interrupt. This was a slightly unkempt American bloke with a crazy smile (perhaps a temporary phase), who was prone, if not yet fully addicted, to some hard-line drugs. He had recently been wandering in the Golden Triangle when he was kidnapped and held hostage by the Shan United Army. The leader of this group at the time was Kung Sa, then reckoned to be the world's No 1 drug baron, responsible for nearly half the smack in New York and, on being brought into the presence of the fellow, our man here, rather than tremble in fear, almost bowed down to him in adoration, as a crack addict might if introduced to El Chapo. It was clear from his report, that the pair had got on famously well, so much so that when the ransom money was paid (allegedly) and it was time to depart, Kung Sa gave the fellow a letter he had written to then US President Ronald Reagan, just in case he happened to see him in McDonalds. The letter was in a sealed envelope which was quickly whipped away by debriefing agents on his release, but it was probably an offer to destroy drug crops in exchange for financial aid (but with the drugs never actually getting destroyed), or some other law protected way of selling drugs, such as existed throughout the region. All in all it was part of the adventure and, if pushed, the fellow would probably have said, 'That's one part of the trip I wouldn't have missed for the world.' As, when following a close shave or an unexpected piece of excitement, we all usually do.

There were several parts of this trip of which I would have said the same and much more so for the journey as a whole, but I was drained of the adventure spirit for now and headed for home. I delayed only a week in Thailand to wait for my connection and, to spend the time well in what was now a fine sub tropical clime, I headed for a tiny island near Rayong, which was then a little paradise, with pristine sand and gentle waves lapping beneath the stilts of your bamboo house. There was no mains electricity on the island, no road, no TV. or video screens in the cafes, just people meeting and doing their thing. And people really talked to one another around the beach bungalows, sharing travel experiences or seeking the knowledge of others at the beginning of their own adventures. But that's the start of another tale, of how things would change through unplanned, unsustainable developments and some places would turn into Benidorm, while others to dereliction. Further along it would become someone else's paradise and, as we now know, that subject can fill its own bookshelf.

Chapter 9
Japan and Hitching USA

It was nearly two years later when I returned to Hong Kong. In the meantime I had steadied my earning capabilities to some degree and spent a short while travelling in the tightly repressive countries of Communist Eastern Europe, which was not a great deal to write home about, and so I didn't. I had intended to stop travelling altogether by now and address the issues of my long term future, but there were a couple of opportunities I'd spotted out here last time and I just couldn't put the idea aside. Among the proliferation of flight ads in various forms of media was the appearance of round the world deals where you could choose from a very tempting list of stop off destinations and obtain a ticket at a highly agreeable price. Having seen what was on offer on my last visit to this region, I realised I could go one better. I could devise my own.

The main aim of my direction was Japan and the US, but from here I could include, at very little extra cost, Taiwan, South Korea and Hawaii. From the American East Coast I could fly back to London on one of the cheapest per mile flights in the world, upon which you could (theoretically), obtain a seat by simply turning up at the airport and taking off. To arrive at this point I could either take the Greyhound bus for three days, while staring at freeway lanes through a side window, or I could hitch hike across the USA. Which was risky and worrisome, but also an irresistible lure.

A further area of interest to me was that you could offset the cost of the middle part of the journey by buying common retail items in one country and selling them in another at a small profit. It was an extension of the courier service which was being touted around during my earlier stay, except that you merely bought and sold the correct goods yourself. It was a small scale circumnavigation of the protectionist import duties that were then in force, which were designed to revive the Taiwanese and S. Korean economies after WW2 and strengthen them against the threat of Chinese Maoism; yet came to mean that they could flood your market with cheap goods at will, but you couldn't touch theirs. The hustle was just a bit of play acting really, for people who dreamt they were at the high end of world trade, but among the travellers it was known as the Smuggler's Trip and we were the bootleggers. The money for doing it now wouldn't be worth the shoe leather for most people, but back then it made the difference of about a weeks' extra travelling and to have not done it would have felt a bit like wimping out. And so, we gathered together our Sony Walkman, Phillips hair dryer, twin-headed Philishave, a few cans of abalone fish and some Chinese ginseng. I'd buy the duty free booze and fags in the airport. To mask the Walkman as my own and not for resale, I bought a couple of Beatles tapes, which turned out to be some

494

Chinese band singing Yellow Submarine and Paperback Writer. You can guess the result.

Every time you come back to a country you seem to learn something else and such it was here, as I returned from a break at the perfectly rural Lantau Island, now standing under the low flight path of the new Chek Lap Kok Airport. I had checked into some cheap place on Lock Road in Kowloon, which was run by a fellow from Bangladesh. There was a youngish room boy there, also from Bangladesh, who used to sweep the communal kitchen floor with an old squeegee mop and then detach the head and wipe the kitchen work tops with it. I was told that the owner had instructed him never to leave the premises for fear of the immigration police and the poor bloke hadn't been out for the entire two years of his employment there. He must have been going mad! One afternoon on returning to the gaff, I saw him seated on the step outside the front door with his head in his hands, reflecting a picture of desolate anguish. I spoke to one of the longer term foreign residents, someone who had been working on a fly-by-night job there and asked what was up with him? It turned out that, just as the fellow's work contract was about to expire, his family, without his prior knowledge, had hired him on for a further two years and he was stuffed. It looked as though the roof had fallen in on his life. Kept on in slavery by a man from his own country and sold down the river by his relatives.

495

After buying the ticket for my journey half way round the world and packing my items for sale along the way, I heard another disturbing tale, a little more relevant to my own situation at the time, which made me feel glad that I'd bought all my own resale items and would be responsible for selling them on. It was in reference to the courier service which was being advertised in various locations, even within my former digs at the Travellers Hostel at Chungking Mansions and which paid around $200 a trip. Some European bloke had taken a package to S. Korea containing nothing more suspicious than a large box of sunglasses, but was busted at the airport in Seoul on a big rap. It turned out that the frames of the specs were made of pure 24 carat gold and he got 4 years in jail. He told his contacts back in Hong Kong that when he got out he would kill the people who set him up with the offending items. But, putting my premeditated murderer's cap on here for a moment, it wouldn't be quite so easy to carry out a hit in these parts as it would be in a large sweep of territory like North America for example, with all those lovely thousand mile serial killer freeways. The only public way out of Hong Kong, unless you had your own private boat, would be through Kai Tak Airport and you'd stick out like a sore thumb. Once he'd recovered from the impotent rage, the guy would probably accept a small degree of the blame and realise that, though faith is sometimes the only option, it is better to never put yourself in a position where you need to trust people.

496

*

The most confusing thing about Taipei at that time was that, apart from at the major highway junctions, all the corner street signs were only in Chinese. It meant that you had to have a very good memory to get back to your accommodation and a notepad was handy, though some went into full survival mode and took a compass. In future years this would improve in the capital, but out in the countryside it stayed largely the same. A long time later I would come back here and do a cycle journey around the coast of Taiwan and, on my first morning out onto the non motorway road, I discovered that all directional road signs were only in Chinese characters. I had quickly to scramble and sketch a few Hanzi logograms of the places on my route ahead and memorise them as I went along. Which wasn't as hard as you would think really, they being merely a collection of a few straight lines with the odd squiggle here and there.

Taipei seemed a friendly enough place and less hectic than Hong Kong, but the cultural aspect in terms of mainland traditions and historic buildings etc, wasn't as strong as in Chinese places I'd visited elsewhere. Immediately after WW2 the population here was only 6 million and the boom in numbers (to around 24 million), came about largely through the arrival of Chiang Kai Shek's defeated Kuomintang Army in 1949 and the following influx of Nationalist Chinese, fearing Maoist reprisals.

497

Consequently the architectural history is largely post 1950, which means a lot of that lovely grey matching concrete.

The place I checked into was called the Formosa Hostel, which was full of Europeans teaching English and a few semi pro musicians, touring the clubs and dodging the work permit checkers. They all knew where you could flog duty free fags and booze and whatever else, as they'd all done it themselves and I quickly offloaded most of my gear. One of the musicians, an American, spoke quite good Chinese, which very few foreigners did at the time. He told me a funny story about a recent train ride he'd been on in China where the two rough country boys he was seated opposite to were debating over where he hid his money. Was it in his shoe? In a secret coat pocket? Or perhaps in a belt around his waist? Just as the train reached his stop, the fellow stood up and said, 'I've enjoyed very much listening to your conversation, now enjoy the rest of your trip.' They were still open mouthed as he departed along the platform.

Flogging the gear was harder than working actually and I got plenty of refusals at the various bars and corner shops I visited, but once it was done I was left with rather more local money than I'd had on arrival and was restricted on taking it out. That's where the street wisdom of the teachers and semi pro musicians came in and I was soon on one of those great urban adventures that all travellers love: a trip down a murky back alley to face heaven knew what and come away with the problem

498

solved. I'd made enough on the deal to pay for my stay here and probably in Korea as well, which was important to me at the time, but memorably more relevant it got me out and around the place and, by the time I left, I actually knew the way out.

*

Seoul seemed a lot more ordered as soon as I got there and I would realise later that I was arriving into a kind of halfway atmosphere between the busy informality of Hong Kong/Taiwan and the more stand alone reserve of Japan. If asked to make a choice I would say I prefer them both, but at least here you could cross the road a lot more easily and sometimes people would even stop. The accommodation had a degree of continuity about it from the last port of call, as it often tends to do in these cheap traveller places, though the present bunch of schoolteachers, who seemed to spend much of their time around the nightclub/ red light district of town, were a rather more dissolute lot and would find it hard, in their present state, to find any kind of job at all back home.

I still had a few things to sell here, including a new batch of duty free from the last flight and, once this was shifted I was of a mind to take on a bit more luggage, having left home with a near empty bag. I'd had my eye on a half decent locally made leather jacket to replace my cheap rag, but most of all there was a good quality down sleeping bag that I'd long desired and

which was still very affordable here. With this in mind I headed
for the camping and outdoor shops. What I found there was quite
a surprise, for instead of the occasional mooching customer and
a bored assistant asking them if they needed any help, each place
I visited was absolutely teeming with customers, working the
sales staff to their limits. It suggested a strong local attraction to
the outdoor life and, through enquiring further into this, I
discovered that out there somewhere beyond the last trace of
urbanisation was a distinctly wonderful landscape, consisting of
upto 70% mountain country with peaks of five and six thousand
feet, where traditional Hanok villages of a harmonious design
dating from the 14th Century, blend into the valleys in a
thoughtfully planned Feng Shui style. The climate is a warm
temperate, which makes the deciduous scenery attractive to view
in all seasons and as well as the gentle lowland option, there is
also the challenge of highland winter snow. I'd already set my
stall out for Japan and the US on this trip and so S. Korea had to
go down as one of the few countries to which I've paid a passing
visit and never gone back, and I do regret that. But if you do find
yourself here with wisely allotted time to spare and you head for
open country, to visit what many would regard as the real Korea,
then make sure you get there on a weekday as, going by the
crowds in the camping shops, half the active population likes to
get out there on a week-end.

Beyond the courtesy of the people and a few
memorably fermented Banchan dishes, there was not much else

500

that I could extract from my time in South Korea, but the feeling at my departure put me in mind of an old show biz maxim about people leaving the place always wanting a bit more, and that's just how it left me.

*

When I began this travelling life, on a spontaneous impulse, with hardly a bean in my pocket, I never imagined it would take me as far as Japan. It was a dream to go to places such as this, but my God was it worth the effort, and the wait. Everything about Japan fascinated me then, from the futuristic trend of most things in public daily use, to the sacred areas of ancient tradition. There was the strange obedience of the people and their courtesy to both strangers and each other. The roads where no one seemed to break the speed limit and crossings where every single person waited on Don't Walk. People would trail several blocks to bring me to a door rather than point directions and one man even drove ten miles out of his way to drop me outside a ryokan youth hostel. It was said that if you left your wallet in a telephone box here, someone would run after you waving it in the air, instead of doing the same in the opposite direction. People in Western countries make a big thing about those in the Far East being largely motivated by saving face, but when you are in daily contact with these exchanges, all you can see after a while is a whole lot of dignity and good grace, though the obsessive symmetry could take on a bit of a quirky tone every now and again.

On arrival in the airport and even before you'd accustomed your eyes to the sudden glare, you were greeted by a series of audio messages on a recorded loop, telling you to walk between the yellow lines, follow them to baggage claim, stand on the escalator keeping to the left, walk through the hall to passport check, stand in the right hand queue. Most people seemed to know the routine and those that didn't followed the messages quietly and expressionless, but I didn't know whether to rebel or resign myself and say, 'Take me, I am your slave.'

Narita Airport was about 40 miles out of Tokyo and, due to the astronomical price of everything and the reported friendliness by most accounts, I was hitch hiking the whole trip. I thumbed a ride into town from an elderly couple, with whom I shared barely a word of common language. We were just shaking off the tail end of stereotypical jokes then, about peoples' personal characteristics and the funny way they seemed to talk but, as if I didn't know already, the tendency wasn't just the single reserve of one region of the world as, between them, they took the piss out of me all the way into Tokyo and laughed that much they nearly cried. Did I mind?? Did I bollocks.

Thinking I would probably want to continue my journey by train, the couple dropped me off right outside Shinjuku Railway Station and, not wishing to disappoint them, I wandered inside to take a look. Swept into the crowd, I quickly became lost in a strangely enclosed travel city built on five separate levels, incorporating metros, mainlines, elevated railways and shopping concourses that caught the passing trade from about fifty platforms. It took me half an hour to find the way out, which I now feel was a comfortable score, as it takes some people two hours. I'd had an address in Tokyo for a cheap place to stay and it wasn't far from where I presently stood, but it was already full by 4pm and so, it was back into the rail system, for real this time, to take a train to the edge of town and complete one of my first Japanese rights of passage.

It's a novel image, to us in the West, to see rush hour Japanese commuters crammed into urban rail carriages in a seemingly well natured manner of communal shoving, with not a pick-pocket, a yob or an arrogant thug in sight and I couldn't imagine anything of the kind on the London Underground. But the one thing that caught my eye, and something for which you would never find the right kind of staff to operate here, was the neatly uniformed man with white gloves whose job it was to somehow make people thinner, like cramming too many clothes into an already packed out wardrobe. I always thought that, if ever I was in that situation, I would try to be the very last person onboard in order to enjoy the full experience. And there it was, not exactly Sumo wrestling, but it was a tick in the box nevertheless.

I was headed on the Shibuya Line for the edge of town and a longed for break-out west. Apart from a brief escape to

503

Lantau Island on my passage through Hong Kong, I had been in large metropolitan areas the whole time since I left England and even for some while before. I was hankering for a fresh open landscape and a slower pace of life, which brought me to the E1 Tomei Expressway, running out towards Nagoya. A six lane dual carriageway is not normally associated with a sudden outbreak of serenity, but this was a strange and highly memorable experience; my first encounter with a major Japanese highway. On most motorways, freeways, autoroutes or whatever you would call them, you will enjoy a variation in speed between the plodders, the racers and those who wish to maintain a sensible steady pace to keep away from these assortment of fruitcakes, but not here. The speed limit was 100 kph, or 62.15 mph and that's exactly what everyone did. There was no tailgating, no cutting in or out and the cars were so equidistantly spaced that the road looked like the conveyor belt in a cake factory. I was awaiting an end to this warm up lap and expecting a light to change somewhere up ahead so we could all start racing, but no, this wasn't Italy or Brazil, it was Japan and everyday normal. I couldn't decide whether it was a monumental show of patience or a morbid dread of the cops, but it was certainly a spectacle.

In the late afternoon we passed Fuji-san on the right, with its snow covered peak glowing red in the falling sunlight; another climbable great mountain gone by. That nightfall I made it to Shimizu, where I must have just dossed out somewhere, but the following day I was at Nagoya which, with its bright evening

504

lights and whirling signs, didn't seem a lot different from the
more neon addicted parts of Tokyo. I stayed in a wooden hostel
here where I quickly made friends. In the morning when I awoke
there was a note beside my bed, which read,

> Good morning.
>
> It is fine today. I have to go now. I wish you have
a nice trip in Japan.
>
> T. Aria.

It kind of encapsulated the mood I was to encounter throughout
my stay in Japan.

Upto now I had been struck not only by the strange
orderliness of Japan, but by the mad rush to modernity. There
were systems and inventions I had never seen before, which
would soon become commonplace in our parts of the world and
one wonders what kind of innovations they have there now. It
was here that I first saw bar code scanners used on supermarket
checkouts, automatic sliding doors at neighbourhood shops,
where a voice message automatically tripped in, welcoming you
to the store and running through a list of today's special offers.
We all used to freak over these crazy young people taking photos
of each other while sitting at cafe tables, now we're doing it and,
as for karaoke, we all thought it was in awful taste, while many
of us still do. Modern things don't amaze us for too long
however, they either become swamped by more recent fashion
or, in the case of infrastructure, are overtaken by Dubai,
Singapore and Shanghai. One thing that can take us by surprise

however is a bold surviving image of the long ago past, which was something I wasn't sure I was ever going to see in Japan. That was until I came to Kyoto.

For the short stay visitor to Kyoto the images came thick and fast. The Shogun domain of Nijo Castle with its finely decorated fusuma panels, the wonderful setting of Kinkakuji Temple, gold-reflected within its own sheltered lake, the beautifully ornate gardens at Ginkakuji, which could have been designed on painted porcelain and the Zen installations at Ryoan-ji, where people would empty their minds of all earthly worries by contemplating a pile of raked gravel. This latter may have been a spectacle of the audience looking at the spectacle and, as the keepers readily admit, no one really knew what it meant, but there was something oddly mystical going on here. Perhaps it was the calmness brought about by a recreated mini landscape in which there were never any cars, which gave them an escape from the busy street they'd so recently departed.

My own favourite of all these types of experience was at the Shin Buddhist holy site of Nishi Honganji, which was a temple complex of various 16th Century buildings, (but we won't go into all that, as I was just on the point of being cultured-out here,) and it was an occasion that would encapsulate in an hour, a trove of features from Japan's cultural past, from architecture and love of nature, to mysticism and devotion. To me, after visiting a few sights by now, the surrounds were atmospheric rather than something of great beauty, but I was highly fortunate

506

to enter the large dark cavern of a temple building within which there was a low, very broad stage, upon which some black robed Shinshu musicians were just warming up on their collective string, wooden and bamboo percussive instruments. A scattered audience, with shoes in the entranceway, knelt upon the matted floor and then began a musical performance from another world.

The sound was one of humming, chanting and whispering notes, played in irregular timing, as though the space between the notes were as important as the notes themselves. A babble of bright sound would be followed by silence, as though awaiting an answer, or be replied to with its own fainting echo and thus the musicians played on, without rhyme, creating a tale with each new refrain. I got to like 18th Century European chamber music for a while because of its strong connection with the natural sounds of running water, birdsong and the wind rushing through foliage, but this was like Bach without the mathematical symmetry and the nearest imitative thing I have heard to the natural sound of the wild outdoors. I stayed as long as my kneeling legs would allow and absorbed the enchanting sounds, the timeless atmosphere, the concentration of musicians and the engagement of the small crowd, before stumbling off again, as though I'd been ambushed by a thing invisible.

I was sorry to leave Kyoto but, after 3 days there and only 30 on my visa, there were other places to visit and I was on my way. Even the hostel was a little gem, with sliding panel shoji paper walls, tatami floor matting and futon beds stored in a cupboard. To cap my good impressions, I had a fine stroke of luck on the morning of my departure. I had asked a Japanese fellow guest if he could write me a hitching sign for Hiroshima, on a piece of old cardboard I'd acquired along the way and by chance he happened to have a railway pass, in the form of a small book of tickets, which expired coincidentally on that very day. He had two tickets left and needed just the one to get home, so very kindly he gave me the spare ticket and took the trouble to look up in his rail book, the connecting train times, including relevant platform numbers, which he wrote on a note in both Japanese and English. All I had to do was show the ticket and note at the station and I would be directed accordingly. What a thoughtful fellow he was and, by that days' end, I wished I'd thanked him more.

The train journey was nothing like the mad scramble, meet everyone kind of experience I'd had in much poorer countries and people sat quietly within their own space, but the trip itself was memorable for two things. The first was the precise punctuality, which I had been quite expecting but which still took me slightly aback when I came face to face with it. I'd had to change trains at Shin-Osaka en route and the arrival/departure times were just minutes apart, with the second train leaving on a different platform across a sizeable footbridge. I was warned that I may have to run and so it was, as everything arrived and departed within the space of about three minutes, right on schedule. The thing that mainly stuck with me however,

508

beyond this personal detail, was the view from the window. Not a scenic one, nor even edge of town rural, but buildings, roads, factory yards and low urban houses for mile after mile without a break, two full hours all the way from Kyoto to Osaka and Hiroshima. If you needed to know that Japan was largely a coast-populated country with steep mountains inland highly unsuitable for building on, then a scene like this would hot brand it into your memory.

Everyone thinks they know the main story of Hiroshima. An large bomb dropped, a war ended and a huge number of people killed, with perhaps as many to suffer thereafter. But stories fade with the long distance from learning, even among those who have an empathy with the subject and when you suddenly come face to face with the physical lasting images, you often find much of great relevance that you may have overlooked, or simply forgotten.

It was 8.15am on the 6th August that three US B29 bombers flew over the city at an altitude of 28,000 feet, having embarked on a sunny morning from the Mariana Islands 1,300 miles away. The two rear planes carried photographic and scientific monitoring equipment to record the upcoming event, while the foremost plane, Enola Gay, was to drop the world's first and probably second last atom bomb. On releasing the load, the head plane made a sharp turn of near 160° before departing at full speed and by the time of the ensuing explosion it had travelled 10 miles to the north. The bomb fell in a visible trail of flame and detonated

509

around 40 seconds later, at an altitude of about 1,900 feet. According to witnesses the fireball was of a bluish white brightness, a bit like a modern welding flash. Soon afterwards there rose an enormous pillar of dust and smoke, which began to form a mushroom cloud that billowed to an altitude slightly higher than Mount Everest. Then, from half an hour after the explosion, a murky watery shower, containing high doses of radioactivity, fell upon the city for 90 minutes, resulting in further discomfort to the already suffering survivors. For those still able to look above, a rainbow had formed in the bright morning sunlight, that ran through the black rain. How bitterly ironic.

A complex range of afflictions would advance across the district, some dragging on for many years and no one then would know their full extent, but it had been a bitter war, with feelings running high. A land invasion of Japan may have cost 100,000 Allied lives and many times that of Japanese. The fire bomb raid on Tokyo in March 1945 had cost 100,000 lives already and there could have been many more fire bomb raids before the country was subdued. Conventional weapons are no comfort pill, just ask any one of the surviving victims, but there were yet several untold lessons to be learnt from this cataclysmic event, some of which were laid plain at the local Peace Memorial Museum. Photos on the wall depicted human remains fired into brick, pale marks on a step which identified the spot where a victim had been vaporised, curtains form a house two miles

510

away, toasted like the fragile pages of an old book and behind you, in the display cabinets, there were the aforesaid artefacts, along with a lot of other charred remnants and forensic debris. The real weight of evidence however was in the two short films, which described the long term physical and medical effects of the blast. The dead were already dead, but the survivors carried their message into future generations, that those who had been pulverised in an instant may have been the more fortunate ones. Most people these days think that nuclear war would be a simple case of turning the lights out and saying tara! And for many this could be true. The Hiroshima A-bomb was 20,000 tons of TNT, whereas today's thermonuclear warheads pack upto 40 million tons each. If the unthinkable ever did happen then the perimeter of such an explosion would be quite considerable, leaving many grotesquely injured survivors and that's when, on facing such an event, you would wish to be right underneath it, peacefully among the scattered ashes. Like granddad in his favourite walking spot, but without the publicly subscribed bench unfortunately.

Out on the western road again I picked up a lift from Sagá with three young students who pulled into some brightly lit place I thought at first was a rather noisy cafe, but which was in fact a Pachinko palace. For anyone who doesn't know what Pachinko is, it's a kind of vertical bagatelle that was inspired by an idea of what to do with a thousand tons of WW2 army surplus ball bearings. It all seemed fairly harmless, as addictive things

511

initially tend to do, but some would play this with a rabid enthusiasm, leading to heaven knew what decrement on the rest of their time. There didn't seem to be any major financial gain offered and as far as I could see, victory and loss were largely accidental. The strangest thing was, no 'one played it slowly like in Vegas, it was all at a hundred miles an hour, with loads of tumbling payout noise, or pay back in. Not to be left out, I obtained a couple of hundred Pachinko balls and sent them away like rapid mortar fire, losing them in seconds. I think I kind of got the idea of it.

I wasn't intent on visiting Nagasaki, as one heap of apocalyptic information was enough for any single trip, but someone at the last place sold me on the idea and so I paid it a fleeting stop on my way to a more peaceful open country beyond. Having been 92% destroyed in you know when, the attraction here was in the 8% that had remained intact, which was along the eastern hills overlooking the Arikawa sea inlet. Here were the houses and remnant traces of Western traders who populated this town intermittently between the 16th and 19th Centuries. Some English bloke I met there said he hadn't come all the way to Japan to look at Jesuit foundations, Dutch paving stones and old English houses, but I felt there was a significant part of our European past bound up with these sort of places: like the pioneering spirit of adventure, which sadly has very little outlet these days.

512

Being here you couldn't really avoid the obvious however and, in the company of some Australian fellow, I took a local train to the epicentre of the second A-bomb, where stands a tall black marble memorial. It was a long trudge from the last stop and the weather was hot and tiring. We could have been thinking the same thing, I must admit, but he was the first to utter it.

'Bloody hell,' he said, 'I wish they'd dropped the bomb a bit nearer the railway station.'

You can't remain over sensitive forever, life goes on.

Across the small Shimabara Peninsula I came to the Amakusa Islands, a ferry hop and a short bridge span linking the two separate landfalls of Shimoshima and Kamishima, and it was here that I found the one distinctly major aspect of Japan that had so far eluded me. The steep conical hills, huddled together like frozen sea waves, were adorned with the blossom of citrus trees and terraced in a splayed-out fashion, not quite in the horizontal style seen in China, but sloping to all angles and directions like a pack of cards that had been thrown down. The variety of crops and farm buildings served to give the scene a greater depth and you could imagine the surrounds as a woodcut landscape, only here it was real life. Of my highest expectations of Japan before my arrival, there were no longer any to be met.

On my way over to climb the Aso Volcano back on Kyushu, I had stopped off at a lonely Shinto temple to do 20 minutes of early morning meditation, which had been a passing

513

phase of mine then. I was irritated by some loud music playing in the agricultural workshop next door, which made it difficult for me to settle and I eventually gave in to the noise. Going over to the perimeter fence to see what it was all about I was met with a memorable scene, which made the stop far more worthwhile than a vain 20 minutes of attempted transcendence, as there in the yard were about 15 mechanical workers, standing in regimented lines while listening to a school ma'mish voice, calling over the sound of an upright piano. With no need for translation, it was clear that those present were being guided through a series of mild exercises along the lines of, ' knees bend, arms stretch, head, nose, touch your toes,' to which everyone slavishly followed. You may feel that such a thing could never become the norm in our part of the world, but there are many strange routines around in site industry now and, if a term of keeping your job was doing the exercise, you'd more than likely suppress the urge for a bit of comedy craic and simply comply. Which is what may have been uppermost in the minds of a few people here I suspect.

The volcano, when finally I did get there, was not a thing of outstanding beauty, but was fascinating in an eerie Gothic sort of way. The walls of the crater were like the slag heap of an old ironworks, with washed out shades of black, grey and oxidised red, while in the lower depths, a lake of sulphuric yellow appeared and then vanished through a cauldron of steam. It smelt like the presence of Satan and was an uncomfortable

514

place to be beyond a short while, which was greater emphasised when it spewed ash and noxious H_2S just a few months after my visit.

Diverted through Shikoku Island on my looping way onto Japan's mainbeam of Honshu, I found the landscape in parts just as sculpted and beautiful as that of the Amakusa Islands, but I was in no mood to delay. I was on my way out to Tokyo now, with a focus much further afield. Back on the main drag of traffic and motorways I came to appreciate all the more my brief sojourn along the country byways, and the noise and whirling lights spoke less of excitement now and more of the vain promise of it. There was still time for one piece of worthwhile involvement though, as I skirted around the edge of Kobe and pulled a short ride into Osaka. The person who picked me up was a young man in a short wheel flat-bed truck; an owner driver who was delivering soft drinks for Canada Dry. He had returned two days previously from Austria, where he had a fiancé and was still full of the travelling spirit. He offered to put me up for the night at his home in nearby Kashiwara and it was an opportunity I was never going to baulk at. To be invited into an everyday home in Japan. Wow! Or two homes as it turned out.

My first impressions of the digs here are quite important, as we went on a massive bender with three of his mates after that and it all became a bit of a blur. The guy's name was Mitsuhiro and he was a very mild natured fellow. He lived in a small apartment with his brother who was a musician and there was scattered paraphernalia around the place in typical musical grasshopper fashion. His brother's girlfriend had moved in, which made it plenty crowded even before I got there. But what struck me most, particularly after stays in economically furnished traditional ryokan and the mind emptying spaciousness of Zen gardens, was how the place was packed with every fashionable home comfort and all the gadgets necessary for a happy life in Japan, i.e., every single one invented that could be bought at a reasonable price and played and fiddled with until the craze ran out. I remember thinking, whatever happened to the famed local minimalism?

Mitsu and his brother were from Okinawa, which cast them slightly as outsiders in Japan. The warm tropical sun on that southern island made them rather more laid back than what was normally accepted here and, like the Brazilian Japanese who had returned to the land of their ancestors, they were looked upon as suspiciously Bohemian. Which is a charge that has come down my own way over the years, and follows me still.

Before going out on the razzle we had a brief watch at the television, which normally wouldn't provide the least attraction to me, but here we had an interesting feature which I had never seen before and never have since. There was a button on the TV remote with which you could switch the language on some programmes from everyday Japanese into an English translation, which gave a fascinating insight into locally held views. The television companies in our country, particularly

516

when there were only a few channels, liked to promote the chauvinistic view that ours was the best TV in the world. Here was the lie to their claim, as the news items on view were commentated on in a far more ethical and articulate manner, with far less evidence of emotive questioning and dumbed down interpretations than anything I'd been used to back home and this even included interviews with passers by in the street. I was quite impressed and, if we had such a thing in our part of the world, I might even start watching it.

If you ask which was the worst thing that Japan ever exported beyond Tojo's Imperial Army, then most people would say Karaoke. But of course, being in a pub in Japan where all your present companions are egging you on and with them knowing that you are only about thirty miles away from being Paul McCartney's next door neighbour, you'd have to have a go. The crowd went wild when I sang Yesterday in a faintly North-West accent and even some romantic smooch from the Carpenters registered high on the clapometer, but when Mitsuhiro and I made a duet attempt at Bridge Over Troubled Water, one of his favourite songs, the taste for it became something acquired, and clearly no 'one had. It was probably down to our pop star inexperience that we failed to adjust to the full octave difference of our voices and while he sang high and I low, which may have worked a bit like Kenny Rodgers and Dolly, we suddenly changed over mid verse in an attempt to harmonise, and then back again until we ended up switching

517

together from high to low, which made it sound like just one bloke trying to do all the variously pitched voices of the Beach Boys. We battled gamely on to the end, where we received not applause, but at least a polite lack of abuse. Yet something told us there, it was time to put the toys away. The only thing I could further remember about the night after that was that those boys could certainly drink.

In the evening of the following day, when I'd just recovered from the previous nights' hangover, we visited Mitsu's sister in Osaka and this time the interior was a bit more traditional. Their flat was small and very light of furniture, as even the residences of quite well off people are in this coastally crowded country, and the thing most highly appreciated here seemed to be the empty space in which to move around. The husband looked like a salary man and ate his evening meal from a table about a foot off the ground, whilst wearing a smart suit. His wife was graceful and calm, smiling occasionally, while he was polite but preoccupied in his attention, as though accustomed to being busy. Sitting upon their tatami matted floor we ate unimposing snacks and, while they engaged largely with Mitsuhiro, I sat with folded knees and worked on my arterial circulation. At last things became a lot less shy and formal as their two small kids appeared from somewhere. They instantly decided I was a magic visitor, like an exotic pet from the zoo or somewhere and they were probably saying, 'Can we keep him

Mum,' or something similar. I thought they were great as well, in fact I thought they all were.

On my second last night in the country I stayed at Suwa, in a fine traditional Ryokan hostel with the full works of shoji paper screens, tatami matted floors, futon beds kept in the cupboard and a therapeutically overheated bath. It was about as locally atmospheric as you could get and would have been a fantastic way to have departed Japan. But as it was, I had to spend my last night here dossing in an airport lounge, awaiting the following days' 9.30 departure. And there was my Japan, at that particular time. One of the most fascinating visits to a country that I've ever enjoyed. I'd been to quite a few places by now where there were plenty of things to amaze me, but the fact I was able to engage myself with so many of them here was largely down to the kindness and courtesy of the Japanese people I met along the way and to all of them, for this unforgettable experience, I must be greatly thankful.

*

Thanks to the phenomenon of the International Date Line, the 7 hour flight eastwards from Tokyo to Honolulu presented you with the unusual experience of reaching your destination on the same date but 12 hours earlier than departure, which created for those onboard, a long 43 hour day. Not much else of phenomenal proportion was to greet my time here however, and it wasn't all Hawaii's fault.

The first thing of note I did in Honolulu resulted from a meeting with a friendly South African fellow in the place I was staying, who kindly loaned me a snorkel mask and directed me towards a marine reserve about ten miles away. This was Hanuama Bay, the crater of an extinct volcano that had collapsed along one crescent wall, which converted it into a kind of steep sided sea inlet. It was an attractive spot even from the passing road, but to glide face down upon its sheltered waters and peer into the wild diversity of its shallow reef was, for me, like a magical entrance into a whole new world. Although I would later travel and dive quite widely in the Western Pacific and South China Seas, my only previous experience of snorkelling had been on freshwater African Lakes where I could see a slightly larger version of the tropical specimens you would find in someone's living room fish-tank, but this was something else altogether and it had me totally mesmerised.

I must have swum there shirtless for more than an hour, oblivious to the fact that an aquatic environment, particularly a saline one, can amplify the harmful effects of UV rays, and the cooling effect of water makes you less aware of the damage being done. I was already red raw as I drip dried out on the beach and that summarised my week in Hawaii; three nights of flame grill agony followed by four more of dry peeling insanity. I had intended to rest anyway but, as per usual, after spending one day doing nothing, the overpowering urge was to go out and gallivant and the restriction was driving me nuts. Still, you can't win 'em all, and things along the journey must have been good if this was my only set-back.

The place I stayed was about two blocks back from Waikiki Beach, which may have seemed a highly desirable spot for some, but for me, with restricted movement, it came to be somewhere you could count the days down to the hours and minutes. When Bob Hope and Bing Crosby used to come here for their holidays in about 1947, to have their photos taken in front of massive upright surf boards with just a handful of beachgoers in the background, this probably would have been a fantastic place to be, but now you could hardly see the beach for a carpet of basking bodies that resembled a seal colony at pupping time and, while the boulevard that separated sand from shopping opportunities deposited its own blanket atmosphere upon those congregated, I could muster only one thought. Why? Why did I arrange a seven day stopover here, instead of only three?

In different circumstances I may have shipped out to one of the other Hawaiian Islands such as Maui or Kauai, where less populated beaches sit below a backdrop of primeval woods and volcanic ribbon peaks, but regardless of the heatstroke issue, there was also the prohibitive cost, as these islands are much further apart than you would normally think. It was sad to know that great places were out there just beyond my reach, but I

521

was stuck within the urban environment for now and was resigned to a disappointingly small radius. The common mood here by which I was enveloped soon became an assault to the senses, with an even mixture of fast forward sociability and plain rudeness, which of course you could find in many a Westernised city (and sometimes without the sociability,) but I felt it more keenly because I'd just come from Japan, where you would rarely encounter either. There was one outlet however that took me back, ironically, to a part of the entwined history of the place I'd just departed and my present location, which brought me face to face with an aspect of Japan's past with which I had surprisingly never engaged on my recent travels. It was Pearl Harbour.

On the morning of December 7th 1941, at a distance roughly 9 miles west of Central Honolulu, there took place one of the most memorable and dramatic events of the 20th Century. Without the prior warning of a war declaration and while peace negotiations were apparently still ongoing, a grand force of 353 various Japanese bomber and fighter planes launched a sustained attack on the US naval facility at Pearl Harbour. By the end of the 90 minute assault, the majority of the US Fleet ships present were either badly damaged or sunk and 2,403 US lives were lost, 1,177 of which were on the USS Arizona. Most of the damaged ships were eventually re-floated and half a dozen of them served on quite successfully throughout the remainder of the conflict, but the Arizona was respectfully left in situ, as a memorial and a war grave. It was a bit strange walking over the SS Arizona on a gangway platform of several adjoining right angles. The main ship-deck surface was only a few feet below the level of clear water that covered it and you found yourself, along with many others I suspect, peering into the depths in trying to identify a coralised bone or even a skull, which gracefully did not appear. Like many such war scenes and memorials around the world it had a moving aspect and made you quite thankful that you'd lived your life in relatively peaceful times, but that wasn't the impression you were allowed to extract or depart with.

On the naval dockside before you reach the Arizona there is a kind of entrance-way cum visitor centre, where you are all invited to watch a 20 minute film on the subject of the attack. The introduction to it by a member of staff was like the chirpy chat from a holiday rep on a tour bus, welcoming you to Sunnylands Camp and not what I'd expected in a place of such gravity. As the film progressed I got the impression that all those who died on the ground were being regarded as heroes, which kind of overstated the point somewhat towards the extent of diminishing it; like suggesting the 40,000 residents of inner London who perished in the Luftwaffe Blitz had perished in the same fashion, despite their lack of influence in the matter. Victims they certainly were, the question of whether they were heroes however has never been raised. I was beginning to get the feeling here that making your own connection with this subject in this particular place was going to be a challenge. Following the

523

film we were off on the very short ferry ride across the harbour to the Arizona itself where, given a little peace and quiet, one may have been able to dwell upon the enormity of past events and the state of a world that brought them about, but no sooner had we cast off than another chirpy voice began to enlighten us with a list of height and breadth statistics that may have lightened up a really dull event, but which merely got in the way of your own thoughts and you were left to depart and ponder the subject from memory elsewhere. On returning to the dockside jetty I felt a deep sense of relief that followed me all the way back to the bus stop and though we weren't quite ready for the B-word yet, I could see we were surely headed that way.

*

The apprehension I felt when hitch hiking out of Los Angeles was something I'd not experienced since beginning my long journey in South America. All the statistics were there to back up my fears, but what I could have done with was a bit more geographical knowledge to ease my way, though the lack of it did broaden my view of the district by an incidental sort of route. Arriving late from Hawaii I had crashed in the airport to avoid wandering around in the dark, and a bright early morning afforded me just the break I needed. With clearer foresight I may have taken a bus from the airport some twenty miles north to begin hitching from there, but Freeway 405 was less than a mile

524

away and the temptation overcame me; which kind of alarmed the fellow who screeched in to give me a lift before I'd even had chance to put my arm out. Beyond a flurry of swearing he told me that, had I been standing at that spot the night before, then someone would certainly have taken a shot at me. He mentioned Watts neighbourhood, of which I had heard due to there being major riots there in the 1960s and upon the edge of which I had been standing, but the name of Inglewood, which has a healthier reputation than most for gang and gun violence, registered with me not at all. We were just entering the age of the crack cocaine epidemic, where turf wars and drive-bys would set the air ringing with random projectiles, but I had two supportive elements here that would see me safely through. An idiot's good luck and the up-for-work morning daylight, that meant most of the crims would be back in bed by now.

Still within the LA suburbs I found myself dropped on the edge of the San Fernando Valley, where people lived a life that was far more comfortable and I began to feel more comfortable along with them. Hitching at the on-ramp, still on 405, a cop car pulled up about thirty yards in front of me and the solitary occupant began to speak into a mouthpiece, to whom I knew not. Suddenly the car loudspeaker came on at full blast,

'*Is that better?*' he blared.

I raised a thumb, realising it was me he was speaking to.

525

'*Get off the fucking freeway,* he said, in a voice polite as his words and, being in no position to contest, I merely complied.

Walking past his parked vehicle to the beginning of the ramp, I noticed he had some kind of buckshot rifle clipped to the dashboard and, as he neither got out of the car, nor even wound down the window, I reckoned this must still be quite a twitchy place for cops and public alike. Once he'd gone, I loitered by the blue sign that stated all the forbidden activities on an interstate freeway and onto which a generation of hitch hikers had scratched their pearls of wisdom. One said, 'Do you know the way to San Jose?' Which was kind of nicely song-evocative and I was probably passing that way soon too, while another quoted a lyric from Gerry Garcia that read, 'When life seems like you're on easy street, there is danger at your door.' Which is just where it hit the spot.

A few miles further on from here I chose a left turning along an adjoining spur that should have taken me towards the famed California Route 1, a journey regarded locally as one of great scenic interest, but remembered abroad as the setting for several John Steinbeck novels. My plans and my peripheral life of this time were an ill fit however, where pure chance was often the better design and so it came about that the journey took its own course and I, in the usual manner, followed. The early part of this new route spanned the Ventura Highway, which struck you not only as a different atmosphere, but another state in a

526

completely different country. Parts of the road had not yet been elevated to freeway status and you found yourself passing through small wooden villages overlooked by dry savannah hills, where the constant scent of lemons and oranges gave the region a strong feel of the Eastern Mediterranean. The people who gave me lifts along the way appreciated the orchard fare I'd collected quite as much as I did.

At Santa Barbara I was planning still to take the coastal route along Highway 1, but a mixture of indifferent and then remarkably good luck had me shelving the idea for that future nevertime. The upgraded freeway here oddly petered out, to begin again just beyond the town, as though awaiting a by-pass or the signing of demolition orders and I hitched at roadside level among a changing bunch of characters and brief chance encounters. Across the way there was a spare plot of land where stood a hugely spreading tree, below which a group of young-ish people had chosen to openly camp. It was like a scene straight out of 1967, when people hit the road with a political attitude, as though striking their own blow for freedom. Not needing to be anywhere, but free. I viewed it, I must admit, a little sentimentally, though at the same time with sadness, sensing that they were locked into some kind of time warp scene from which most others had moved on. I was considering wandering over to share some greetings, but was glad I hadn't when someone later told me that these were no longer the beautiful people of the flower generation, but an assortment of floating transients whose

527

drifting lives may encompass anything within human capability, from hapless victim to serial perpetrator.

An American hitch hiker came by with his happy tale of having enjoyed his youthful days on the road so much that, despite now being in a straight job and family relationship, he would spend his annual 2 weeks holiday hitching the old routes, to keeping the dream alive. Which seems to work well for ageing bikers, though I'm not sure how his partner at home would have felt about it. Beside this were a couple of English blokes, about whom I knew not a great deal, but whose presence would become relevant later on.

Towards sundown here I had an encounter that I found very weird at the time, but which, in later days, I would have undoubtedly dealt with in a better manner. As I stood beyond the traffic lights at which we hitched, a woman in a VW Type 3 saloon pulled around the corner and drove towards me, as though in a slow motion daze. She pulled up right behind me and I opened the door. Through the window I thought she was wearing paint. Not make-up, but something of the household decorating variety. But what she actually wore was a face-pack of cream at least a day old, which had yellowed and hardened a little on the thicker bits, like cheese spread left open too long. To compliment this she wore a contrasting pink lipstick which, in a theatrical setting, may have been designed to draw the eye, or disturb younger members of the audience. Her clothing was just a dirty yellow vest and formerly white shorts that looked as if they'd been involved in some oily mechanical repairs and the car was overloaded to the ceiling, as though she lived in it. I made some enquiry about the road ahead, she nodded and I got in. She appeared close to tears, but when I asked her if she was OK she, without saying a word, implied that she was. Although she could apparently hear me, she either couldn't, or just wouldn't speak and whether she understood everything I said, I was constantly in doubt. She seemed in no hurry to go anywhere immediately until, all of a sudden she pulled out a spirally bound notebook and began to write. I could read the words across her shoulder without having to lean. *I was beaten. My Mother hated me. I didn't get along with anyone in my family.* Further sentences of a similar nature portrayed a life of harrowing persecution, where the person was not encouraged to think well of themselves.

With this being my first day of hitching in the US, I was still a bit spooked by my experiences of departing LA and though not unsympathetic, I didn't really know how to react. Eventually one of the English blokes came along and asked if there was any room for him and his mate and, as there was only one other seat spare, I packed them in and waved them off, wondering for a while and then forgetting to worry about the eventual outcome. Something in the grammar that the woman wrote was odd, yet somehow familiar and I eventually figured that it was some vulnerable Latin American woman going through a huge breakdown while travelling alone; running away from her fears and problems instead of staying in one place to

529

get the problem fixed. But there's the difficulty, maybe there wasn't a settled place, maybe finance was a problem in obtaining the right kind of treatment and perhaps there was no friend or family support. I could see there would be some hard news ahead on the road in America.

I can't recall where I slept that night but it wasn't below the tree of the young hobos. It must have been somewhere dry and secluded though and by dawn next day I was up with the sunrise for an early dart. There was an old fashioned cafe nearby with powder paint writing on the inner glass, which depicted produce and prices and I bought a breakfast burger as big as a plate. The guy there was cheerful and on first name terms with all his customers, including the people of the tree. By mid day however, after 5½ hours at the roadside, the charm provided by the cafe and its friendly gaffer had begun to wear off and I was wishing I'd taken that ride in the VW now, which was going to San Luis Obispo, right at the start of my intended coast route.

Just as I was suspecting the world of conspiring against me however, the roulette ball of fortune dropped right on my even number, with a great 320 mile ride all the way to San Francisco, which by-passed my plan of Highway 1. And how could I possibly turn that one down? The driver was a very engaging fellow who was presently doing a journalistic feature on the Democratic Presidential nomination in California, a process in which the local Governor, Ronald Reagan appeared to be doing quite well. There was a passenger already in the front

530

seat, some other hitch hiker he'd picked up on the edge of LA, who was headed to Seattle to look for work on the trawlers. He had the deadest pair of eyes I'd ever seen on a living creature and whenever he shot a quick glance sideways, it was as though he were looking to see if he'd been nicked for something. About a hundred miles south of Salinas we stopped at some isolated gas station and the hitch hiker got out to use the bath room. As he did so, I noticed the back of his pants were dripping wet and leaning over onto the seat I could see (and smell) that it was running with piss. The guy had just relieved himself there without saying a word. It wasn't like he was shy of asking for something, as moments after we set off again he told, rather than asked the driver to put the radio on as he wanted to listen to some decent music! The driver, poor fellow, just kept a cool head, complied with his record request and pretended not to notice the violation of his vehicle, driving him on up north as earlier arranged. When I got out of the car just south of SF I had to remove my gear from the rear trunk and was able to speak to the driver aside.

'Do you know that guy's just pissed all over your car seat?' I said.

'Yeah, I know,' he said, 'But it's just a chance you take. It's not my car anyway, it's going back off hire tomorrow. Let them clean it up.

Either the fellow was very tolerant indeed or just a little frightened of the bloke, but if someone pissed in a car I was driving he'd be out on his ear as soon as and, if he was lucky, without a sore face. This incident has stuck in my mind for many years, not because of the base nature of it, but because of something that developed as I walked away. The driver had decided to drop us off just beyond San Jose, as he was booked into a hotel not quite in the San Francisco area, but after I'd walked 50 yards on from the car I noticed the Seattle bound fellow was still entrenched in the front passenger seat, apparently in some stubborn conversation. I have often pondered whether I should have done the right manly thing and gone back to persuade the hitch hiker in getting the fuck out of the guy's car and leaving him alone, but that would have left the driver departed and me alone on the pavement with this caveman. Perhaps safe was best. In attempting to make things better it certainly could have got a lot worse.

With the astounding good luck that occasionally accompanied my adventures, I got a quick ride for the short few miles into SF from a young couple who invited me to stay at their place. Tim and Tracy had moved from out East somewhere to live in California and, in San Francisco, they had found just the place for them; even though it did take them a couple of flat moves to find the precise address. Their upstairs apartment in an old 19th Century building had a huge bay window full of light that would have suited an artist to a treat. As it was, it had to make do with a drum kit, which was Bohemian enough. It was great to stay with someone local, because when I usually checked in anywhere I would share the same generalisations with travellers like myself, and here I could impart my impressions among people who might fill in the background. I was invited to stay an extra night so I could have a base from which to look around, which was not only a damn civil gesture, but a very thoughtful one as well, as it was back in Hawaii that I last hiked about without a rucksack on my back. They even gave me a front door key as well , so I could come and go as I pleased.

My preconception of San Francisco was that it was just another big city with some fairly recent history, but I was happy to see my expectations greatly outstripped. The small uptown area of high rise here was surrounded by populated hills that gave the impression you were always in a small neighbourhood, rather than part of an urban sprawl. A place with this kind of individual feel can sometimes transmit itself to the character of its people, and so it seemed here. Up by Haight Street and Ashbury, where the early hippies once used to wander, their shoeless ancestors remained, sitting a-ground and looking suitably spaced; though not much on a weekday, because like many of those who began the trend, they largely only did weekends. Along Fulton and Pearce Streets the surviving houses from the 1906 earthquake were a mixture of every architectural style that ever was, which often appeared within the same solitary building. Their colour shades could vary as much as their construction design and who is to say that mock Tudor must always be black and white? Why not white and yellow? Some traditionalists may question the taste, but SF has a taste of its own and people like it.

The Golden Gate Bridge is an iconic feature here, which has been superseded both in splendour and technical design by others further afield, but its two remarkable surviving features are the photographic archives that plot its construction phase and the story of its safety record over the same period. The photo images illustrate just how hard and dangerous working at heights can be, even up to the present day, with men working off bowsun's chairs made out of planks and walking the open girders while living on their wits. In the expansionist period leading up to this, companies on large bridge and viaduct builds were losing men like straw from a hay wagon and brushing it off as an act of fate, but it was around the inter-war period, particularly in the US, that this awful situation began to be addressed.

The Golden Gate installation lost eleven men overall, which is far too high by present standards, but it represented some improvement on what had gone before. The move in this direction was largely driven by the chief engineer Joseph Strauss, who adopted the now common principle that you don't have to go out and kill people to get a job done. He insisted on the compulsory wearing of the recently developed industrial hard hats to protect from falling rivets and, most importantly, the inclusion of a large moveable safety net at around sixty feet below where most of the height work was taking place. This at significant extra cost. Of the eleven who died, ten were killed in

534

just one incident, where a weakened bolt caused a scaffold platform to collapse, the falling weight of which tore through part of the net. Although ten men didn't survive this incident, nineteen actually did, as they fell upon a part of the net that didn't give way. It was a result on behalf of the new safety culture, which had to be paid for by the client and general public, rather than the men who built it, and signalled the Western trend towards better run projects.

Hitching was initially a great disappointment in the US, but once you got used to the way it was you realised it was the same for nearly everyone. It seemed to be long waits for rides, 5 to 6 hours, or perhaps into the next day and then occasionally a very long ride with which you would make up the expected distance. Actual travel time on the road took me about 2 weeks from SF to New Jersey, via a small part on Ontario. On a roadside sign somewhere in the mid-West I spotted graffiti from a fellow who had taken 15 days to get from LA to Kansas, so I didn't do too badly. The contrast in experiences however was quite extreme, though thankfully not so extreme as to threaten my actual survival.

Hitching out of San Francisco I got a lift towards Sacramento from a young man in a pick-up crew bus, who spoke like someone out of a film. This wasn't uncommon in America and anyone who thinks that the dialogue and acting in popular US films is unrealistic is quite wrong. Whether the films imitate life or vice versa it is hard to tell, but you could often find yourself drifting into a fantasy world and not necessarily one of your own creation. The happy flip side to all this blarney was that when you met good people in America, they were very good people indeed. A similar rolling theme existed with place names, where half the large towns and states that you passed seemed to have had a song written about them, though this wasn't quite so chicken and egg, as I never heard of a town that was named after a song title.

From Sacramento I picked up a hundred mile ride to Reno with a young-ish fellow called Mike, with whom I got on particularly well. Perhaps it was just the nature of the journey, or simply that we appreciated it in the same way, but it was a better example of what I'd experienced departing Argentina into Chile, as we climbed from near coastal countryside, through wheat and orchard fields, across snowy mountain passes and then down into the Nevada Desert. Near every climatic scene within the same half day. At Lake Tahoe, Mike wanted to buy me lunch, but I'd already eaten some corner store stuff by the roadside and so we just shared a beer, which was far more sociable. It seemed by now and would become clearer through the journey ahead, that you needed to be some kind of special person in America to rise above the bullshit and superficiality that surrounded you for 90% of the time and though many Americans would say that California is the world headquarters of such smooth veneer, I would meet these people and their stark opposites, in varying quantities right along the way.

536

At Reno I hitched through the sunset without success and then dossed in the desert, not under twinkling starlight strangely, but a sweep of laser beams that raked the heavens from a far off gambling strip. I don't know what it was with Reno. Was it really predominantly more yahoo than anywhere else, or was it just my own coincidental experience? But on standing there for 5 hours the following morning I received more personal abuse than on several world journeys combined. Eight times I counted where people amused themselves by screaming obscenities out the window, sticking up fingers in rude gestures, pulling over and then driving away (twice) and on one occasion even trying to gob at me out of the passenger side seat, but failing to do so as he couldn't clear his throat in time before I stepped back. I can only put it down to a cultural niche thing, where many would condemn this behaviour, while others might transpose it to a nice toe tapping tune, but it wasn't my scene and I would have had to change my spots to pretend that it was. One guy memorably shouted 'Get a job,' at me out of the driver's side. I'd worked hard enough to get here via the long way round the world and I had a job to return to back home. Fuck me! What did he want me to do, carry a bag of decorating tools with me?

I was descending to a low ebb just here, with five hour waits being a common occurrence and still 2½ thousand miles of unpredictable road ahead, while the impotent rage of being unable to King Kong a couple of cars full of local yobs hadn't helped the mood. As so often did happen in these circumstances however, the luck to which I'd trusted my present life swung around to positive, which would remind me later that, in the overall measure, there was no point in getting too wound up over anything. I'd just been to the gasoline station across the road and with minimally altered timing may have missed this occurrence altogether, but at around one in the afternoon, after half a shift at the roadside, an old blue car pulled in offering me a glorious 1,000 mile ride all the way to Colorado and a well met situation into the bargain.

Chris and Andrew were a couple of Kiwis who had quit their jobs at home and hit the trail, which seems like one giant step for some people, but a clear and obvious one to others. They intended to beat their way round the world for quite some time and America was their first stop. In LA they had bought themselves a 1969 Plymouth Valiant for the princely sum of a hundred bucks and, after a 3 week test-out in SoCal and Nevada they pointed it due east and were now trying to nurse the heavy old banger to New York. It was a handy coincidence that the car body was blue as, with the addition of a couple of cheap spray cans they were able to turn the bonnet into a giant New Zealand flag, which left most people undecided as to whether they were British or Australian. But never mind, they knew the answer. As they continued eastwards the car side panels had gathered ever more graffiti and people would honk as they drove past, usually in an overtaking direction. I may have gone with them all the way to New York, as it was offered, but I wanted to hike a few days in the Rockies, around the city of Boulder and also visit Niagara Falls, so I would get out around Cheyenne/Denver, but it was still taking me nearly half way home.

Fate and coincidence can create a very resounding echo when you are travelling the way I was then, which was memorably illustrated here because, as well as the fluke circumstances of my return to the roadside in time to pick up this lift, it transpired that Andrew's parents had emigrated from my own region 26 years previously, and first port of call for this pair on leaving the US would be Stockport, where some of Andy's relatives still lived. Their arrival in the town would be roughly in time with my own and it would be a strange, though pleasant experience to be back from my travels yet still feel as though I were on the same journey, as I welcomed them to a few Stockport pubs and took them to meet a bunch of my mates.

Moving east from Reno we had departed the Carson Range of California's Sierra, nipped through a corner of Nevada and were soon into the elevated flat lands of Northern Utah. As ribbons of May snow raked the distant mountains we drove through an eerily dead landscape of salt dusted desert. The huge emptiness of such places could create a strangely cosmic atmosphere on early encounters, but after a while you'd have to concede to a degree of boredom. A few Americans I've met could wax lyrical about these huge open wastes where one could, like the Arabian Bedouins, be master of all one surveys. Perhaps it's a grand sense of ownership, or a connection with the history

539

of pioneers, though it was someone else's unwritten history before that. Nevada is entertainment country, while Utah is religion. In Salt Lake City you couldn't buy a drink in most places, but in Nevada drinking, whoring and gambling are all legal and open for business 24 hours a day; which is handy either way if you live near the border. Come to think of it, some of those yahoos who assailed me at the Reno on-ramp could have been week-ending Mormons returning to Utah?

We had halted a night at Wendover, on Nevada's side of the border, where the brightly lit strip of a town looked like a promenade seafront facing not the sea, but Interstate Route 80. In the morning we took advantage of the amazingly cheap casino buffet, which is much easier to do when having your own wheels. The purpose of cheap grub and fairly priced accom here is to lure people into chancing a few bucks on the twinkling apparatus, but we turned out to be true travellers all, as we only availed ourselves of the bargains and fled. There was a fair bit of gaming out on the carpet however, even at 8am, with people slumped over slot machines as though they'd been there all night. I'm not a great expert on this voluminous subject, but it didn't look too good to be honest.

Wyoming came and went in a blaze of colour that rather fascinated me and if there was one part of this road journey where I wished I could have got out and wandered to my heart's content, then this was it. In the bottom left corner of the state there was a Badlands area scattered with wind-blasted red turrets streaked with volcanic grey that evoked images of all kinds of adventures, from geological expeditions to Indian ghost dances. Thanks to the commercialisation of our modern world however the prime image that came to mind was the one of roll your own cig adverts. A cultural image not conjured up by fanciful dreaming was to meet us in a gas station washroom further along the state track at Rawlins, where a scrawled local graffito read, 'Wyoming Cowboys Kill Hippies.' My hair was getting slightly long by now but I didn't feel the danger intended. I merely wondered how easy a trip it would be to be killing peacenik freaks and thought it quite telling how these people would never say, 'We kill all the hardest, baldest people on the planet.' Funny that?

The boys from NZ at last dropped me on Route 25, just north of Denver and I hitched a quick ride into Boulder. The thing that immediately grabbed your attention about Boulder was the 'otherness' of its way of life. Health food shops, vegan restaurants, adverts in cafe windows for meditation classes, acupuncture, herbalist remedies, Hare Krishna groups and est therapy. There was even a health food supermarket here with long isles and trolleys on wheels, which took me a bit by surprise, yet when I mentioned this to a woman from Boulder some years later, she told me there were now *four* health food supermarkets in the town. Boulder never seeks to change its tune, it simply develops on a theme.

I'd stopped here for a wander in the Rockies, but with the kind of journey I was on it couldn't be too great an expedition. I had hiked a few decent hills in Japan, volcanoes and the like, but I travelled more happily with a light load, and a single pair of shoes had done me the whole trip; a pair of Clark's Polyveldt with perfectly smooth soles. I got up to about 8½ thousand feet on some mountains by the edge of town, but I started climbing at around five thousand, which made it an easy ascent. It gave me a feel of the landscape however, which was wind-blasted rock on high, plenty of gully snow and spruce trees that filled the whole world below. I felt that the taller peaks were well within my range had I stayed longer, but I departed still wanting more, which was a good thing, because it really moved something on.

Between the refreshing interlude of higher ground and our departure towards Kansas, there was sandwiched a small incident that I initially thought could have been something to write home about, but it was only someone shooting at us with an air rifle through the youth hostel window. At first we thought it was a real live round, as there was a slap against the pane and a pure clean hole through the glass, but as I and the other two room occupants searched for evidence, we found only a lead slug stuck in the window sash. The manager was informed, cops were called and when the young officer turned up, sagging with the clip-on tools of a tactical assault team, he took one look at the scene, asked who was shot and quickly departed, promising to

542

drop in at the campus accommodation opposite, from where the projectile had obviously been fired. When asked if this was an occurrence previously known to him, the YH Warden said.

'Oh yeah, it's happened before.'

'But from the same people?' I asked

'Yeah, probably.'

It all seemed a bit blasé here, being shot at without being actually killed or injured. A bit like play shooting. Perhaps it was just some student across the way studying the practical side of serial killing? Nothing to worry about there, although we did tend towards the crouch position after that, just in case.

From Boulder eastwards my journey of extremes continued in regard to the landscape, the kind of people I met and in my own personal luck. I'd called in at Denver on the way, on some personal errand and by the end of day had covered only 20 miles, with the last 5 hours at some lonely spot, watching the afternoon sun fade into utter darkness. I got up the next morning and, as if I'd stored all my good fortune in one re-usable place, I received within half an hour, a superb 350 mile ride to Russell, in the state of Kansas. The driver was a cheerful odd job man who carried out warranty maintenance on trailer homes and his patch covered eleven state of the Union. That would have been like doing property repairs across the whole of Western Europe. It's a good job he had a mild on the road temperament, though the traffic was rather lighter in this Mid-Western region. Following Wyoming and the Colorado Rockies, the scenery was

543

getting rather dull around here and with the humdrum noise of the big diesel engine and having to talk to the driver to keep him alert and interested, I was having a job keeping myself awake. I asked the driver if these long rolling hills, about 500 yards up and the same gradual slope down, were the start of the Western Prairie?

'Oh no,' he said, 'This is known as the foothills, (as when one approaches the Rockies.) When you get past Goodland, just into Kansas State, that's the Prairie. Then it becomes really flat and boring.'

Somewhere in the midst of Kansas State I had my second encounter with the US Police, as a wide Black and White pulled up alongside where I was hitching a ride. The lone occupant was less withdrawn this time and called me over to the opened passenger window, to which I approached with some caution, still expecting a verbal third degree. How surprising then to find myself soon perched on the front seat, discussing my travels through Japan and the American West with a quite friendly chap in a lemon squeezer hat, who was sitting behind a dashboard full of assault gear that probably would have been labelled 'hardly used, as new' were it put up for sale. If anything highlighted the stark difference between small town America and the urban sprawl then this was it. I think the guy even told me his first name!

Through Kansas and Missouri I was picked up largely by drunks, the impact of which on my life was thankfully not too resounding. I do recall strongly however a drunk couple with two small kids who took me to Salina, as I rode on the rear cargo bed of their pickup truck. The empty beer cans on the flat deck were quite mesmeric as they levitated in the swirling wind, never quite managing to rise over the tailgate and leave a trail of evidence in the road. I don't know if the cops were really on the ball here, but it was a bit like a wedding car with its retinue of food tins, which said not 'Just Married,' but 'Just Pissed.'

Precisely when I was feeling confident here of my surroundings and with all things under control, I was met with a couple of small encounters that reminded me of my major fears at the outset of this strange North American crossing. Somewhere in mid Kansas State I picked up a ride from a very intense fellow who wore wrap around dark glasses on a heavily clouded day. He told me he was an insurance salesman but didn't say very much else. Feeling slightly uneasy, but without that real specific reason, I kept him talking about any shallow piffle I could set my mind on, much of it concerning nutters I'd met along the road ironically. At the getting out time about sixty miles down the freeway, I pulled the front seat forward to get my luggage out of the back and as I did so, a splay of glossy magazines ran out across the car floor; hard core pornography mags, about sixteen of them. It's a good job I hadn't read any books on psycho-sexual serial killers at the time, as I have read a couple recently and this would have set my mind racing. But perhaps he was really a decent chap having a thoughtful inwardly

545

looking day and he was just carrying this stuff for a friend. At sundown that night, with a bit of rain threatening, I laid out my sleeping bag in the garden shelter of a private burial ground, the entrance board of which said, 'Topeka Cemetery. Where beauty and tradition prevail.' I've never been spooked by echoes and unmoving shadows, as I remembered some words of an undertaker's son, who accidentally disturbed his father at work. 'Don't be afeared o' the dead lad. It's the live 'uns you've got to worry about.'

By the time I got to St Louis I'd had my fourth lift from a partially inebriated person in the space of two days, but from there on things did start to sober up, as they certainly needed to. I'd picked up a lift that was going to Birmingham Alabama, which was some way off my route and here I'd hopped out, right on the hard shoulder of the freeway, at the far side of the Mississippi River. Walking up the on ramp to begin hitching back down, I became aware of a strange urban landscape of part neighbourhood clearance, with some buildings left standing, but little sign of reconstruction going on. An unpainted three story wooden structure caught my eye as some kind of local gathering point, probably a hotel with maybe a night club/dance hall on the ground floor below. It was the kind of place that should have been preserved for posterity, though with the way things were going, I doubt that it was. Not many people were around on this Sunday mid-afternoon and traffic was light, but whenever cars did go past and I stuck out a thumb, I noticed a puzzled

546

expression on most of their occupants faces, as if to say, 'What are you doing? and, Why the fuck are you doing it here?'

I hadn't been aware of any significant difference between downtown St Louis, Missouri, with its unmissable Gateway Arch and East St Louis, across the river in Illinois, but here I suddenly found myself on the edge of an ailing rundown ghetto, where a face like mine obviously didn't fit. I stayed a while longer in what seemed not yet a dangerous, but clearly a wasted exercise, before beating off along the hard shoulder, hoping the cops wouldn't bust me for encroaching upon the freeway. Another turn off was signposted about a mile up the road, but before I got there I noticed a solitary building amid the wasteland to my right, which was easily accessible down the slope of a bank. It was an empty Caltex gasoline station that looked like it had taken a few heavy shots to help it on its way to dereliction. The sun was low on the road ahead and I'd soon need nightime cover, so with this in mind I headed cautiously down. There was no need to search for access, as the front entrance had been blasted wide open by what looked like a ram raid from a stolen car. The reception area was composed of those hollow glass bricks that used to be popular upto the 1950s, with every single one of them now smashed; some still containing the brick fragments that had been used to do so. The back wall was identically the same. In the space between these there was an old brown settee, surrounded by rubble, which had caught a few of the incoming missiles. I tipped it forwards to remove the debris

547

and there tumbled upon the floor enough material to hard core a garden path. I turned the settee around so it wouldn't be facing the open entrance, hid behind it for a while as I rolled out my bedding gear and then climbed in, as though shrouding myself in camouflage. With the sky not yet darkened I lay there in limbo, hoping that those who had trashed the place would not return with further demolition on their mind. It was only after a long period of fading sunlight that the night enveloped me in a pitch darkness, wherein I managed to shut my eyes, but kept my ears ever open.

I slept remarkably well on the soft settee, as it had been a couple of nights on the hard Prairie floor since I'd left Boulder and by first morning light I was packed and fresh away. I walked a mile to the next on ramp and, in the most isolated of lonely spots, received a short ride into open country from the very first vehicle to come past. A life saver. It was a long time later and with better access to browsing facilities when I discovered that, in recent years East St Louis had consistently been rated among America's most dangerous cities, with a murder rate 19 times greater than the national average. Random shootings are common, particularly at the junction where I hitched my departing ride and sometimes cars are actually fired at on the passing freeway. Often it is better not to know these things when present in such a location, especially when you've had little choice in being there in the first place.

I'd made just 38 miles by seven that evening when, with by now consistent contrariness, I picked up an amazing 500-odd mile truck ride across Illinois and Indiana, to Detroit, Michigan. Driving on through the night, things didn't get too interesting until daylight arrived, but as was common on this journey of extremes, it didn't stay dull for long. First of all we got the trailer back wheels stuck squarely in a ditch, as the driver, on missing his way, attempted a 3-point turn in the road. I'd offered to guide him around, but he being a bit headstrong, ignored me, which eventually cost him 200 bucks for a couple of wrecker trucks to haul him out. That's where I found myself standing in the centre of a foggy road with a lighted distress flare in my hand, guiding passing vehicles on a wide diversion around. One of those to pause for enquiry was a sliding door work-van with a load of characters in the back wearing bib and brace overalls, wide straw hats and sporting Abe Lincoln beards. A puzzle to me at the time, but something that would become clear on a broader scale quite soon. We'd had to drop some steel bar off at a factory near Fort Wayne, Indiana and on the way there drove through a village of old buildings from the frontier period, with walking boards outside and horse hitching posts that were still in full use. A woman in a black cape and Pilgrim bonnet rode by in a spindly horse drawn buggy and men strolled about, bearded in the aforementioned Abe Lincoln style. The name of the village was probably Grabil and these were the Amish people, a Puritan religious group of Swiss German origin who still held to the old

549

ways of life, rejecting automobiles, phones, television and much else of modern technology. Though it was kind of weird to see them straight off, living their everyday lives, on learning more I came to respect their course of strong individuality. Eventually what interested me most about this subject however was the realisation that, between the millionaire houses and the mean streets, there were many other communities within rural America holding fast to their own histories, though perhaps not quite so religiously, nor with anything like the same profile.

In the City of Detroit I was getting a similar vibe to the one I'd been getting in East St Louis and was through there pretty quickly on a weekday afternoon. It wasn't until much later I discovered that both had closely contested the title of America's most dangerous city over recent years. My one outstanding memory is of an elderly Polish fellow I met at a suburban bus stop, who jabbered in nervous tones and hung onto me for dear life as we boarded a crowded, stand only bus. That's usually the result of being visited by recently traumatic events. From the Central Bus Station I took a 10 cent subsidised service under a river that joined two of the Great Lakes and I was in Canada.

*

Arriving in Windsor Ontario created such a release from the erratic strains of being on the road in the US that it felt

550

like walking out into Springtime once again. Gone was the unpredictability between human warmth, hostility and danger, while in Ontario I had the advantage that the culture was personally more recognisable, with its most agreeable feature being obvious straight away. You never felt the threat of those few rogues among the population being able to turn you over without you offering a show of resistance. It was America without the guns.

I remained in Windsor an extra day, not because of any special attraction, but simply road tiredness, and that overnight in a truck from St Louis took some getting over. But the following day I was on my way. I'd had half a mind to visit Niagara Falls on my way across North America and that last ride to Detroit was the dream lift in that respect. So suddenly there I was, 250 miles down the road, in the small town named after the famous natural wonder. On a short range basis the hitching in Canada seemed a lot easier than the US and a bit more trusting I guess, although I hadn't really sampled the larger urban environments. A glimmer of this latter was revealed to me as I picked up a lift near Hamilton from a brisk talking young fellow who had a pair of handcuffs clipped around his rear view mirror, as you might hang an air freshener or a pair of fluffy dice. Sighting some elephantine subject I attempted a crass joke about what they might be for, which came back as flat as it went out, as he sternly replied,

'No, they're not for that. As a matter of fact I'm a member of a Guardian Angels citizens patrol in Toronto.'

This, it appeared, was an urban vigilante group that dressed like a troop of Boy Scouts but rather set out to kick some ass. I recall many years ago diving headlong into situations where two sides were engaged in some heavy kind of public dispute and it's not a good place to be, believe me. I wished him good luck with that.

The last short ride into the town of Niagara was from a very well met fellow named Rick, who not only gave me a place to stay, but also put on a BBQ in the garden as a welcome greeting. The fine May weather was just about right here for me and though I wasn't yet home, I was made to feel as though I was. Rick had recently parted from his wife and had a three-bedroom house all to himself, which was presently on the market. People often mope in these situations, with all the hassle of division and maudlin memories, but he had a right positive attitude and seemed as happy as Larry in his new circumstances. Sometimes you just have to realise it's all for the best. Although it was warm here in late Spring, Rick described the cold winters where it could freeze your bones. He had worked away from home a lot in quite distant parts and described one time of returning to find his water bed frozen into a solid block, which had swollen and bust open the seams. He had to break it up with a lump hammer and throw it outside.

The Falls at Niagara in the late afternoon sun were an awesome spectacle, worthy of diverting your route from even the longest of journeys. There are water features around the world of far more intricate beauty and some even within our own country, but as a show of raw natural power, little could equal this spot. The 800 yard width of a snowmelt swollen river dropping 190 feet off a glacial cliff, created an enveloping crash and spray that nearly had you in there. The distant view was of a flat grey wall of limestone-tainted water thundering into a cloud, while close up you could see that, as the river left its upper rapids it would sieve over the jagged shelf and become combed into a veil of mesmeric ribbons running side by side. A welcome feature of the public arrangements here was that, although the attraction was a very commercial one, none of the businesses had been allowed to encroach upon the waterfall area, which allowed you to make your own personal connection with this rare and breathtaking scene.

Back at Rick's house I was invited to stay another day as I'd mentioned having to sort out a bit of airline business and he kindly made his house phone available for a brief call. I'd hoped to pick up a cheap flight home from Toronto, but a one way ticket from here was about £200 more than the recently emerging competition down in New Jersey and so, after becoming rather comfortable in Ontario, it would be back to the US, which was something of a worry. I had counted my blessings on thumbing across much of America and though not regretful of the experience, was certainly glad that I'd quit while ahead. Now it was down again, into a part of the country that I'd always viewed as being the most threatening, which apart from a tiny little bit at the end, didn't turn out that way at all. So next day it was along the road to Kingston, where Lake Ontario narrows into the St Lawrence River and a right turn took us down on Highway 81, through New York State.

*

For someone who'd always associated this eastern region with traffic jammed streets and urban mayhem, the rural lands of Upstate New York and Northern Pennsylvania were a revelation. Common in many a country are these escape route areas where you wouldn't believe you were within thirty miles of some of the world's most densely populated districts. A fellow who gave me a lift along the way pulled into a popular rest stop called the Delaware Water Gap, a geological feature where a broad river cuts through a ridge of the Appalachian Mountains. Here was the entrance to a national recreation centre for those in pursuit of clean fresh air, where people hiked, climbed, water-rafted and as I saw, paddled along in Native American canoes. Though not yet the wild frontier, it was that most inspiring of places for many a city dweller, the very beginning of the great outdoors.

On my last night out alone on American roads I made myself scarce under a warm sky and the following morning picked up a ride for the last couple hundred or so, from Syracuse down to Newark Airport. A young Italian-American, who lived in New Brunswick went well out of his way to drop me at the North Terminal. Driving into the heavy suburbs there appeared a blonde haired young woman, hitching alone in the opposite direction to where we were headed. She was lightly dressed and had no luggage. I couldn't for certain say exactly what she was doing, but she was taking a huge risk in doing it.

From the New Jersey Turnpike (and there's another song reminder), you could plainly see the stacked skyline of New York City across the water. It was a view that only faintly tempted me, knowing that you'd need a few days of spirited involvement and a good preparation to do the place real justice. I no longer carried much of either and passed by with few regrets. Back along the way I recalled a message that some rider had scratched on the rear of a traffic sign, it read,

If I had a quarter for every car that's passed,
I'd have enough money to buy a pound of grass.

I'd have had enough to buy a new car by now and probably a first class ticket home. As it was, it was to be the most threadbare of budget flight carriers, the legendary People Express Airlines.

Right at the start of when entrepreneuring spirits were trying to shake up the cartels that existed in the airline industry, there was Freddie Laker, a real cat among the pigeons. Then

555

came People Express, with the same, and by modern times, accepted model of a low cost/no frills package, where you bought your ticket close to flight time and purchased whatever refreshments you required on the plane. It is a style easily recognisable in the Europe of today in the workings of EasyJet/Ryanair and in the US, at Continental and United Airlines; who successively by the way, bought out People Express. This way of travel was obviously harder work than your standard, and the quality of service could most politely be described as inconvenient, but I minded not one bit, as it provided just what was required. A flight across that wide expanse of ocean, at a price I could well afford.

At Newark you could register your ticket on the spot and simply await the next plane which, if you were there before mid morning, may possibly be the same evenings' 7.30pm departure to Gatwick. I was marginally too late for this and found myself on the stand-by list, which closely failed to get me on the next flight, so I was stuck there all night in an airport geared towards keeping people uncomfortably awake. I asked around over the possibility of going into town to mooch for a hotel after dark, but was broadly advised against this on safety grounds. Which is how I ended up, for the sake of peace, on a quiet circuit road by the runway fence, where I parked my old sleeping bag behind a low privet hedge and forcibly slept; thanking my stars for this port in a storm, the latter of which there was happily none.

556

The following day I knew I'd be on the flight, so the pressure was eased somewhat, but I still found it an exacting business to check onto the plane, with people jostling, throwing fits and pretending they'd been slighted, but really just trying to shove in. It was the poor bloke on the desk I really felt for, who looked about ready to cave in with all the mock angry people waving ticket receipts at him and demanding priority. The reason I have enlarged upon this mundane subject of boarding a cheap flight is because it brought home to me for the first time what budget deals often mean, not only to punters, but for people who actually work for the organisation. Soon after the plane took off you were invited to purchase a light meal that wasn't included in the fare price and large bowls were offered around, containing a mixture of cold packaged goods. I was surprised to see that, among the small crew of cabin staff, was the stressed out man who had earlier taken a buffeting on the check out desk and, noting him disappear occasionally into the front of the aircraft, was mightily relieved that, though I was ever watchful, he never once emerged with a pilot's hat on.

Chapter 10

Everywhere Else

By now it was becoming clear that I couldn't continue much longer in this footloose manner. The travelling spell was still much upon me, but the places I now would visit were all further afield and journeys to there increasingly complex. The finance I required would be much harder to raise and I had a fairly unspectacular job. I'd always flown close to the wind where accommodation was concerned and work opportunities weren't laid on a plate, so with only a marginal adjustment in events, I may have ended up descending from the highs of travel adventure into homelessness and penniless unemployment. Further to this, my fitness was not great. I was just past thirty and, as people do when they reach an age with a zero in it, I was thinking, My God, I'm so old! I needed a lot more things than I then realised, but at least I understood that a bit of boring stability would help my cause and so I took a steady job and a flat, and set about the mysterious business of normal life.

I had been impressed with the calmness of people in Japan and when told that all children in secondary schools there must do some choice of martial art in their PE lesson, I drew on this connection. I took up a Japanese karate style, which turned out to be not calm at all in the aggressive world of urban Britain and got hooked on the violence of it for a while. But it started to get me fit at an age where I could have stayed in the last chance

558

saloon and just carried on drinking. I made moves towards a full driving licence, as cars had never previously fitted my off-stream lifestyle. And then, in the random fashion that most things happened to me around this time, I received a huge slice of luck.

One fine day, still minus a full driving licence, I was hitching up to Cumbria to climb some big hill, probably Skidaw or Scafell Pike, when I got a lift from a bloke who was working on a utility construction project over Shap Top. I'd somehow mentioned to him my desire to change employment and he asked me why I didn't try the job he was in, which was a place on the inspection team of a new gas pipeline.

'Best number I've ever had,' he said, 'Well paid and out in the countryside all day.'

I quickly gathered that the courses relating to this kind of work were short and very intense, with as much home revision time as required before taking the exams. There were various levels ranging from industrial coatings, through to the more complex subjects of ultrasonics and radiography, and you could study your way through many of these while you worked at the job, provided you got that first start. I wasn't immediately sold on the idea, as I hadn't come from a mechanical background and I explained to him my varied painting experience.

'Not to worry,' he said, 'They also do paint inspection courses.'

It has been pointed out to me recently that good fortune comes largely to those who were looking for that one opportunity

559

in the first place and that's right where it found me. I was hooked on the idea from that moment and before long was booked onto a course for industrial paint technology, down to my last grand and paying £700 for course fees. When things are that tight you make damn sure you pass the bugger.

It was a long road through all the various subjects up to Senior Pipeline Inspector and none of it was easily given out, but on comparing myself to my preceding generation, who acquired trades at an early age and were forced to continue in them for life, it felt amazing to be learning and progressing in a lucrative new profession, from beyond the age of thirty. In the course of time I would be working on offshore installations, power plants, gas/oil terminals and mostly cross country pipelines, which I must say got right into my blood. It was a perfect fit for someone who loved the outdoors, was happy with changing scenery and preferred to cram work into 7 or 8 months of the year, with the rest of the time free to do their thing. The financial side was also a big change as, rather than scrimping like before, I simply always had dough in the bank, even when returning from far distant journeys. Several things conspired to aid my fortunes at this time, not least of which was a serious attempt at improving my fitness and I did benefit from a time out from my former nomadic life. I can also credit my own hard efforts, as almost anyone can, but the one thing that saved my whole future from being gambled away upon youthful impulses was that brief